D0088955

A Prayer a Day: 366 Days in the Presence of God

Published by New Seasons Press in the United States of America.

ISBN 13: 978-0-9772409-7-5
ISBN 10: 0-9772409-7-5

Cover Design: Christoper Thomas of Chris Thomas Graphics
Interior Design: Brandi K. Etheredge
Copy Editor: Yvette R. Blair-Lavallais

A

A DAY

366 DAYS IN THE PRESENCE OF GOD

WILLIAM D. WATLEY

DEDICATION

To My Grandchildren
Madison, Max, Skylar, Alexandra, Juwan, Tujuana, N'daja,
You have been given a legacy of faith and prayer that extends back to many generations and that you have seen practiced in the lives of your great grandparents, grandparentsand your parents. My prayer is that the legacy of faith and prayer that have been passed down to you may live, nourish, flourish and prosper in your lives as well as the generations that you will produce and foster.

We all love you more than you will ever know.
Thank you for all the joy you bring to my life as well as the other elders of our family. We all pray for you daily and without ceasing.

Pop-Pop

ACKNOWLEDGEMENTS

The journey from reflection to composition to editing to fine tuning to bringing a completed work to the broader market place is always an interesting journey. This book is no exception and I have been blessed to have some very competent and committed co-laborers and traveling companions on this journey. I continue to be grateful to Mrs. Muriel Watley, Rev. Jennifer Maxell Watley, Rev. Charles Maxell and Mrs. Carolyn Scavella for their editing assistance. Also, Rev. Russell St. Bernard for his valuable leadership in facilitating the production of this publication. I am especially grateful to my Executive Assistant, sister in Christ and friend, Ms. Felicia Kennedy, for her diligence, caring, and loyalty, which those of us who know her have come to expect and respect as integral to her character and definitive to who she is as a person.

Let me also express my heartfelt appreciation to the team which she assembled: Ms. Chaunetta Jones, Ms. Janice Armstrong, Ms. L'Tarra Moore, Mrs. Schandra Jones-Gaines, Mrs. Beverly Griffin, Ms. Tanesha Griffin, and Mr. John Griffin, III. Without their combined efforts, faithful work and willing spirits this work would not have been published on schedule. I pray that whatever blessings this book brings to those who read it will in some measure be returned to their lives.

To the Glory of God...nothing more, nothing less, and nothing else. In the name of the Lord Jesus Christ! Hallelujah! Amen!

INTRODUCTION

The title of this prayer journal and meditation book is derived from the old adage, "an apple a day keeps the doctor away." While extensive research has the health benefits derived from eating apples, common experience has also shown that the apple is no health panacea or preventive measure against all possible diseases. Eating an apple a day does not eliminate the need for doctors or other medical professionals in our lives. However, apples contain valuable disease fighting nutrients for our bodies. Consequently eating an apple a day contributes to the overall health and wellbeing of our bodies, which in turn can lessen our visits to the doctor for those ailments that can be addressed by a healthy and balanced diet.

In the same way a prayer a day, or a lifestyle of daily prayer does not keep the devil, that is the biblical paradigm for the realities of sin and evil, away from our lives. As a matter of fact, the devil will attack us in our prayer time and on our praying ground. Even as we attempt to focus on God and settle in for a time of prayer, evil thoughts can enter our mind, negative feelings can infiltrate our spirits. Sometimes the presence of evil and the negative can be so near and so real that we have to mentally and forcefully persevere in our efforts to come into the presence of God.

People who pray not only experience the assault of the Evil One as we pray, praying people also experience evil attacks in our lives. Praying people also have the same problems as infidels who mock God and prayer. People praying also get sick. Praying people also lose loved ones who are suddenly snatched by tragic and unexpected death. Praying people also experience career and financial crises. Prayer does not keep the devil or all trouble away, any more than apples keep all doctors and all possible diseases away.

Like apples, however, prayer infuses various nutrients such as adoration and assurance; confession and conviction; thanksgiving and tenacity; salvation and supplication; and healing and hope into our lives that fortify our spiritual, mental, emotional and even physical well-being. The experience of infusion and fortification, despite the attack of evil, was one that Paul testified to when he wrote to the Church at Corinth:

"I know a person in Christ who fourteen years ago was caught up to the third heaven — whether in the body or out of the body I do not know; God knows And I know that such a person — whether in the body or out of the body I do not know; God knows — was caught up into Paradise and heard things that are not to be told, that no mortal is permitted to repeat....Therefore, to keep me from being too elated, a thorn was given me in the flesh, a messenger of Satan to torment me, to keep me from being too elated. Three times I appealed to the Lord about this, that it would leave me, but he said to me, 'My grace is sufficient for you, for power is made perfect in weakness.' So I will boast all the more gladly of my weaknesses, so that the power of Christ may dwell in me. Therefore, I am content with weaknesses, insults, hardships, persecutions, and calamities for the sake of Christ; for whenever I am weak, then I am strong."[1]

As you pray as you read, and read as you pray the prayers in this book, my sincere hope and prayer is that you will have transforming experiences with Almighty God, our Heavenly Parent; in the person of our Lord Jesus Christ, and the presence of the Holy Spirit. I pray that you will be empowered daily to live in newer, higher and greater dimensions because you have spent quality time in prayer.

The testimony that William H. Walford gave in 1845 concerning the delights of prayer is my prayer of expectation for you:

Sweet hour of prayer! Sweet hour of prayer!
That calls me from a world of care,
And bids me at my Father's throne
Make all my wants and wishes known.
In seasons of distress and grief,
My soul has often found relief,
And oft escaped the tempter's snare,
By thy return, sweet hour of prayer!

Sweet hour of prayer! Sweet hour of prayer!
The joys I feel, the bliss I share,
Of those who anxious spirits burn
With strong desires for thy return!
With such I hasten to the place
Where God my Savior shows His face,
And gladly take my station there,
And wait for thee, sweet hour of prayer!

Sweet hour of prayer! Sweet hour of prayer!
Thy wings shall my petition bear
To Him whose truth and faithfulness
Engage the waiting soul to bless.

---

[1]II Corinthians 12: 2-4, 7b-10

And since He bids me seek His face,
Believe His Word and trust His grace
I'll cast on Him my every care,
And wait for thee, sweet hour of prayer!

Sweet hour of prayer! Sweet hour of prayer!
May I thy consolation share,
Till, from Mount Pisgah's lofty height,
I view my home and take my flight.
This robe of flesh I'll drop and rise
To seize the everlasting prize,
And shout, while passing through the air,
"Farewell, farewell, sweet hour of prayer!"

William D. Watley,
January, 2016

– DAY 1 –

RUTH 2: 8-9; 21-23

Gracious God, we praise You for the Bible, Your word, God, represents a whole harvest of blessing for us. Every day You wake us and invite us to stay in Your field. Whatever we need is right in Your field. If we need direction and guidance, there is something in the field for us. David declared, "Your word is a lamp to my feet and a light to my path."

If we need some good news to meet and overcome the bad news that we receive every day, there is something in the field for us. John declared, "God so loved the world that He gave His only begotten Son that whosoever believes in Him should not perish but have everlasting life." If we are feeling guilty, there is something in the field for us. One New Testament writer declared, "If you confess your sins, He [Jesus] is faithful and just to forgive and cleanse you from all unrighteousness."

If we desire a foundation for financial freedom, breakthrough and prosperity, there is something in the field for us. You have declared through Your prophet Malachi, "Bring the full tithes [and offerings] into the storehouse so that there will be meat in my house, and thus put me to the test says the Lord of hosts; see if I will not open the windows of heaven for You and pour down for You an overflowing blessing."

If we need to be delivered from something that has had us bound, the Lord Jesus has declared, "He [or she] whom the Son sets free is free indeed." If we are wondering if we can have a different life, a more glorious life and life on another level from anything we have known in the past, there is something in the field for us. Paul declared, "If anyone is in Christ there is a new creation; everything old has passed away; see, everything has become new."

We confess Gracious God that we have made some poor and some wrong choices. Even though Your field holds harvest, we have allowed the devil to take us away from the field that has been a blessing to everyone who has stayed in it. We recognize however, that if this New Year is to bring as much as we hope, we must start making some different choices. We know You, Lord Jesus Christ, are the smart choice and the right choice. Thank You for choosing us before we chose You. In Your name do we offer this prayer of thanksgiving and commitment, Amen.

– DAY 2 –

GENESIS 6: 5-22

As Noah of old obeyed everything he was commanded, we are grateful for the detailed work of redemption that You accomplished among us. The miracles You performed, the lives You touched, the things You did and said were the details of who You are as Savior and Lord over life and death. When You walked on water and calmed the raging sea, that action detailed You as Lord over nature. When You fed five thousand with two fish and five barley loaves, that action detailed You as Lord of provision. When You cast out demons, that action detailed You as Lord over the devil. When You healed the sick, that action detailed You as Lord over disease. When You cleansed lepers, that action detailed You as Lord of the untouchables. When You raised the dead, that action detailed You as Lord of the impossible.

When You told Nicodemus that he had to be born again, that action detailed You as Lord of new beginnings, no matter what age or stage of life. When You told a woman who had been caught in sin to go in peace and sin no more, that action detailed You as the Lord of forgiveness. When You gave living water to a Samaritan woman who was a divorcee at Jacob's well, that action detailed You as Lord of new beginnings. When You ate at the house of the despised Zacchaeus, that action detailed You as Lord of forgiveness.

When You prayed in Gethsemane and surrendered to Your Father's will, that action detailed You as obedient servant and Son of God the Father. When You granted access to a dying thief on a cross, that action detailed You as Lord of access to glory. When You were hung high and stretched wide on Calvary, that action detailed You as the Savior of the world. When You rose early Sunday morning, that action detailed You as the key holder to death, hell and the grave. When You ascended on high, that action detailed You as conquering King. Now that You reign on high, that action details You as our preparer for our home in glory. One of these days when You will come back again, that action will detail You as the King of Kings and Lord of Lords who reigns forever.

Lord Jesus, we pray for commitment to be as detailed in our service to You as You were in Your life among us as our Redeemer. In Your name Lord Jesus do we offer this prayer, Amen.

DAY 2

– DAY 3 –

ACTS 28: 30-31

O Lord, our Lord, we pray we will live each moment to the fullest and take advantage of every opportunity for growth and use every gift you have bestowed upon our lives. We seek Your forgiveness for the times we have taken Your blessings for granted and for the opportunities we have wasted. We seek Your forgiveness for the potential You have placed within us that we have allowed to go unrealized. We seek Your forgiveness for the gifts of the Holy Spirit You have anointed us with that we have failed to use for Your glory.

Now Lord, we pray we will be ever mindful and ever grateful for every day and the rich potential each day holds. We pray we will be more vigilant regarding the gifts You have placed within us. We rebuke, in Your name, the spirit of jealousy and the demon of insecurity that makes us resent others for their success and makes us feel less than others. We pray we will always remember You have given us everything we need for success, for victory and for happiness. Help us to realize we have no need to be resentful and jealous or feel less than others when we do not use everything You have given to us.

Give us discipline to match Your vision for our lives. Give us discipline to work and help us to balance our spiritual quest with the practicalities of life. We pray we will never be accused of being so heavenly minded that we are no earthly good. We pray we will have the courage to ask ourselves the hard questions that provide the groundwork for growth.

We pray for a welcoming spirit that helps us to be open to change and what is different. We pray for a holy dissatisfaction that prevents us from becoming so comfortable we fail to grow with the new challenges life is always throwing our way.

In all things and at all times, we pray we will live so our lives will be a constant witness to Your saving grace, Your keeping power and Your abiding love. Help us in deed as well as with words to proclaim the good news of the kingdom of God and to teach about the Lord Jesus Christ, who came to save us and who lives to intercede for us and who is coming back for us. In his name do we pray, Amen.

– DAY 4 –

PSALM 56: 13

O God, thank You for Your delivering power experienced in days gone by. You have delivered our souls from death and our feet from stumbling. You have turned our hell bent minds around and melted hearts of stone and turned them into hearts of flesh. When we became stubborn and rejected Your word, Your hand and the counsel of those who You sent to help us and we stumbled and fell, You did not forsake us. Through grace and in mercy You rescued us. Great is Your faithfulness, mighty is Your patience, infinite is Your love and unerring are Your ways.

We praise You on this day not simply because of what You have done but we are mindful of why You have rescued and redeemed us---that we might walk before You gracious God in service and sanctification, in worship and work, with praise and power, in prayer and peace, with joy and justice all the days of our lives.

You did not redeem us O God to repeat old patterns in the past. You did not redeem us O God to gloat in our own self-righteousness. You did not redeem us O God for us to do our own thing and pursue our own agenda. You did not redeem us O God for us to look down on others who are still in darkness and who have made and are making terrible mistakes with their lives. You have redeemed us to walk before You and others in humility and holiness, as examples of excellence so You will get the glory from our lives.

O God, we pray not only will our talk but our walk will honor You and we will be a blessing to others. Thank you for delivering our souls from death and our feet from stumbling. Now help us Lord; give us a mind and willing spirits, creative hands as well as determined hearts to go and do likewise to others. In Jesus name we pray, Amen.

– DAY 5 –

ACTS 28: 11-14

In shady green pastures, so rich and so sweet,
God leads His dear children along;
Where the water's cool flow bathes the weary one's feet,
God leads His dear children along.

Some thru the water, some thru the flood,
Some thru the fire, but all thru the blood;
Some thru great sorrow, but God gives a song,
In the night season and all the day long.
(George A. Young, "God Leads Us Along")

Gracious God, we are grateful You lead us along. When storms rise You lead us to safety. When our weaknesses cause us to stumble, You pick us up and lead us back to Your loving embrace. When temptations attack, You show us a way out. When demons threaten, You lead us to Your word. When weights and sin so easily beset us, You lead us to a rock higher than we are. When burdens oppress us, You lead us to strength made perfect in weakness. When we feel downcast and discouraged, You lead us into Your presence where there is fullness of joy. When trials come, You lead us into a testimony of Your goodness. When we make mistakes and fail in our trying, You lead us to a second chance. When we are running on empty, You lead us to the Holy Spirit, our Comforter, Guide, Energizing Fire and Empowerer. When we are lost, You lead us to Jesus, the way, the truth and the life.

O God, will you lead us to the places you have envisioned for us? Will You be patient with our rebellion and stubbornness in doing things our way and not Yours? Will You continue to shape us according to Your will, word and likeness? Will You lead us from sin to salvation and from shame to sainthood? Will You lead us from whining to worship and from pettiness to praise? Will You lead us from greed to generosity and from shallowness to substance?

O God, we love You for giving us vision beyond where we are and goals we have to reach and strain for. O God, please walk with us, talk with us and carry us when necessary as we press our way through the storms of life to the prize of Your upward call. We thank You even now for all You will do and for all we will accomplish through You. In Jesus name do we pray, Amen.

– DAY 6 –

JOHN 1: 43-46

Lord Jesus, we praise You because You have set before us a noble example of servanthood and what it means to be a servant leader. We confess O Lord that rather than following Your example, we have often chosen to engage in the endless pursuit of status seeking. O Lord, we do not have a strong sense of self-worth, so we spend our lives looking for stuff or people to add status or importance or prominence to our weak or broken self-esteem.

Many of us are miserable to be around and impossible to live with because of our propensity and inclination to seek status. Many of us are resentful of others who have done nothing to us and who often have less than we have, because in our perception they have something or someone we desire that would feed into our perception of greater status. Many of us are about to drown in debt because we have purchased what we cannot afford and often do not need and sometimes do not really care for because we are trying to boost our status or how we look in the eyes of others.

Many of us are working ourselves or worrying ourselves into early graves because of a never-ending pursuit to reach some elusive goal of having status. Many of us are in bondage to weak self-esteem because we feel we need more and more status to make us feel worthwhile. We confess Lord Jesus that we have forgotten that self-worth can never be purchased or received from someone else. We have forgotten that self-worth can never be acquired by laying on our backs or by compromising our convictions or sacrificing our standards or morals to be acceptable to someone else. Some of us choose churches, neighborhoods, automobiles and certain clothing, no matter how ridiculous we look in them, because we believe that they will give us status.

Lord Jesus, we pray that like Your servant St. Philip, we will find fulfillment in following You because You and You alone have a vision for our lives that is greater than any vision we can have for ourselves or that others can have for us. Give us passion and courage to follow You even when servant hood leads to a cross on a hill called Calvary. Help us to remember that You can elevate us in a way that our own status seeking can never do. You did it for Philip. You are living proof of elevation beyond status seeking when we serve You. Thank You Lord Jesus. Lead on and we will follow, as did Philip. In Your name do we offer this prayer and that with thanksgiving, Amen.

– DAY 7 –

JOHN 14: 8-9

Lord Jesus, we worship You, glorify You, honor You and love You for who You are. We confess that sometimes like Philip we stumble over the true meaning and understanding of who You are. When such failure of understanding occurs we know that You have the right to ask us like You asked Philip of old, "Have I been with you so long Philip, (or Phyllis or Patricia or Patrick, or Williams or Wanda, or Mary or Michael, or Donald or Darlene, Carolyn or Charles, Linda or Larry, John or Joan) and you still don't know me?"

"Have I been with you so long Doctor, Lawyer, Professor, Teacher, Social Worker, Preacher, Mother, Father, Grandmother, Grandfather, Husband, Wife, Student, Caregiver, Homemaker, Provider, Laborer, Foster Child, Widow or Widower and You still don't know me?"

"Have I been walking with you, keeping you, blessing you, making a way for you all this time and you still don't know me? Didn't I help you raise your children and you still don't know me? Didn't I help you get through school and you don't know me? Have I been with you through seven troubles, and did not forsake you in the eighth, and you still don't know me? Didn't I save you from dangers seen and unseen, and kept you sane when you thought you were going to lose your mind and everyone else expected you to, and you still don't know me?

Didn't I deliver you from a habit or an addiction that had you in bondage so long that you didn't think you would ever be free? Have I been with you from the rocking of your cradle and kept you by power divine up to this present moment and still you don't know me? Have I done all I have for you and you still don't know me? By now you should know that I am the Lord God, Almighty who works miracles and brings my children out as more than conquerors."

In the midst of life's changing scenes and circumstances we pray that we put all You have done for us are signs and samples of who You are as Savior and Lord of the world. We give ourselves to You anew as our Savior and Lord. In Your name do we offer this prayer, Lord Jesus, Savior Almighty and our Redeemer, Amen.

– DAY 8 –

RUTH 1: 6-8

Gracious God when like Your servant Naomi of old, we pray that we will never forget that there is life beyond Moab. She went to Moab for peace and problems assaulted her; for security and sorrow overtook her. However, rather than surrendering to a Moab attitude and spirit she had a vision for recovery and for life.

Save us O God from a Moab attitude and spirit when trouble comes into our life as a flood. A Moab attitude and spirit is one that has become comfortable in being miserable and is afraid to be happy because something just might go wrong. A Moab attitude and spirit is one that is always suspicious and always expecting the worst. In life you generally find what you are looking for.

A Moab attitude and spirit is one that always looks for the downside in everything and everyone. A Moab attitude and spirit is one that spends more time worrying about what might go wrong, instead of working to make sure that things go right. Save us from such an attitude and spirit we pray.

Like Naomi, we pray we will never forget that the tragic and heart-rending experiences we encounter in Moab do not constitute the end of the world. That divorce is not the end of the world. That breakup is not the end of the world. That bankruptcy is not the end of the world. That the loss of a job is not the end of the world. That public embarrassment and scandal are not the end of the world.

We pray that we never forget that rejection by a certain group or a certain person is not the end of the world. That the death of a dream is not the end of the world, the death of that person is not the end of the world. That report from the doctor is not the end of the world or that foreclosure is not the end of the world.

We pray we will never forget that there is life beyond Moab. That was the testimony of Job who could declare in the midst of his troubles, "God knows the way that I take, and when he has tested me, I shall come out like gold." That was the testimony of the Psalmist, "May those who sow in tears reap with shouts of joy. Those who go out weeping bearing seeds for sowing shall come home with shouts of joy, carrying their sheaves."

We offer this prayer in the name of the Lord Jesus, Amen.

– DAY 9 –

RUTH 1: 7-1

Gracious God, we pray for the spirit of Naomi in the scriptures. Even thought she was financially broke, she was not broken. We pray that like her we will also understand that even though we are burdened, we are not beaten. Even though we have cried, we are not conquered. Even though we are down, we are not defeated.

Even though we are disappointed, we can still be determined. Even though we are forlorn, we can still fight. Even though we are in grief, we still do not give up. Even though we are hurt, we can still be hopeful. Even though we have experienced loss, we can still be lovely.

Even though we are in pain, we can keep pushing. Even though we are penniless, we can still be powerful. Even though we are suffering, we can still strive for excellence. Even though we are tired, we can still keep trying. Even though we are in the valley, we can still have vision. Even though we are weary, we can still keep working.

We praise You for the assurance that also like Naomi, we pray that we will always remember that we are worth far more than the money in our pockets. We are worth far more than the stocks and bonds in our portfolios. We are worth far more than the amount on our insurance policies. We are worth far more than the jewelry around our neck and on our finger. We are worth far more than the designer name on our clothes.

We are worth far more than the car we drive. We are worth far more than the house address where we live. We are worth far more than the title behind our name. We are worth far more than the fraternity, sorority, club or lodge we belong to. Even though we may be broke, we are not broken.

We praise You, Gracious God, for the value You see in us and for the value You place upon us. We praise You because You have valued us so much that You became flesh in the person of the Lord Jesus who died on a cross and rose forever more so that we may see ourselves as You see us. Forgive us when we undervalue ourselves and help us to live according to the value You have placed on us. In Your name, Lord Jesus, do we offer this prayer, Amen.

DAY 9

– DAY 10 –

RUTH 1: 19

Gracious God, we confess that we have been damaged. However, we are grateful that damaged does not mean that we are damned. Damaged does not mean that we are destroyed. Damaged does not mean that we have to remain scarred or broken or leaking for the rest of our life. Damaged does not mean that we are useless. We are grateful for the Gospel that asserts that we can be damaged and still functional. We can be damaged and still be repaired. Thank You, Lord!

We further confess, O Lord, that there are times we are afraid to face people because of the guilt, shame and fear we carry because we have been damaged and are in recovery. However, we pray that You will give us courage and a vision for recovery that is so strong that we do not allow pride or fear or guilt to stand in the way of the new future You desire and will for us. If Naomi had allowed pride, guilt and fear to stand in her way, she would not have found her way out of Moab, and the new possibilities that her home in Bethlehem held for her.

If the Prodigal Son had allowed pride or fear or shame to stand in his way, he would have died in the hog pen. If the Samaritan woman had allowed pride or fear or shame to stand in her way, she never would have been able to bring the same townspeople who had considered her damaged goods to the Lord to receive the Gospel. If Zacchaeus had allowed pride or shame or fear to stand in his way, he never would have climbed the sycamore tree and the Lord would not have seen him and saved him.

If the woman with the issue of blood had allowed pride or fear or shame to stand in her way, she never would have reached through the crowd to touch the hem of the Master's garment and been healed. If Peter had allowed pride or fear or shame to stand in his way, he never would have recovered from the damage he received when he denied the Lord. If Saul of Tarsus, who became the Apostle Paul, had allowed pride or fear or shame to stand in his way, he never would have been able to preach the same Gospel and the same Christ he once persecuted.

O Lord, do with and in our damaged lives what You have done with others. Restore, heal and deliver we pray, in Your own name Lord Jesus, Amen.

– DAY 11 –

RUTH 1: 19-20 AND 3: 1

Gracious God, we give You praise not only for Your past provision, but also Your care and keeping. You are still in the blessing business. You are still in the door opening business. You are still in the way making and miracle working business. You are still in the unmerited favor granting business. You are still in the Boaz making business. Even though each season and chapter of our lives is different, You can still bless and open doors and opportunities to match each new chapter.

God, You can have a door for us to walk through at 50 like You had a door for us to walk through when we were 10. God, You can have a door for us to walk through at 60 like You had a door for us to walk through when we were 20. God, You can have a door for us to walk through at 70 like You had a door for us to walk through when we were 30. God, You can have a door for us to walk through at 80 like You had a door for us to walk through when we were 40. God, You can have a door for us to walk through at 90 like You had a door for us to walk through when we were 50. What You did for Abraham and Sarah and what You did for Noah, You can do for us.

Gracious God, You can have a door for us to walk through as a single person just like You can open a door for us to walk through if we are married. You can open a door for us to walk through as a widow or a divorcee just like You had a door for us to walk through before death or divorce. You can have a door for us to walk through after bankruptcy just like You had doors for us to walk through before bankruptcy.

You can have a door for us to walk through after addiction just like You had a door for us before addiction. You can have a door for us to walk through after incarceration just like You had a door for us before we went to jail. You can have an open door for us after we lost that last job just like You opened the door for us with that last job. You can open a door for us after sickness just like You opened the door for us before sickness. You can open the door for us after retirement just like You opened doors for us before retirement.

The Lord Jesus declared, "Look, I have set before You an open door, which no one is able to shut." And in his name we offer this prayer, Amen.

– DAY 12 –

RUTH 1: 19-22

God, we praise You for times of infilling and harvest, because like Naomi we remember the times of emptiness. There is no doubt in our minds as to how we became filled, and we know that we did not bring the harvest. We remember the state we were in when we left Moab and came to Bethlehem. We remember how lost and confused we were. We remember the sleepless nights we spent worrying about how we were going to make it.

We remember now the tears we shed in secret so that we could smile and be strong in public. We remember the times that death felt like a viable option. We remember lying down to sleep at night and not caring if we woke up in the morning and when morning came we had to force ourselves to get up out of bed. We remember the times we thought we were going to lose our minds.

We remember the times when people looked the other way when they saw us. We remember when they spoke, they kept looking around or down and could barely look at us in the face, as if they were uncomfortable, embarrassed or ashamed to do so. We remember the phone calls that were never returned. We remember the times when we were down, people buried us in their minds and concluded that we would never be full again.

Lord, we remember the times that we secretly wondered and questioned if they were right. We remember the times we were so depressed and confused that we could hardly pray. We remember the times we felt like our prayers were bouncing up, hitting the ceiling and falling back in our face, mocking us.

We remember the times life contradicted everything we believed, and we began to wonder if You, O God, had forsaken us or even existed. We remember the times we felt we had all we could handle and that we could not take another thing, and then another thing happened and knocked us even lower than we were.

We give You praise that even when we felt distant from You that You did not withdraw Your hand from us. Your hand held us, strengthened us and guided us. Now as we prepare for the harvest season, we pray that we will always remember You, O God, filled us, and that we will always live to honor and glorify You. In the name of the Lord Jesus we do offer this prayer, Amen.

– DAY 13 –

RUTH 2: 1-7

Gracious God, we are grateful that when we like Ruth and Naomi of the scriptures, make one step away from the places of our pain, You not only walk with us but You also go ahead of us to work things out for our good. We praise You with the wisdom of our elders who declared that if we make one step, You would make two.

If we make one step in asking, we believe You will make two in answering and anointing. If we make one step in belief, we believe You will make two in blessings and breakthrough. If we make one step in commitment, we believe You will make two in caring and cleansing. If we make one step in faith, we believe You will make two in forgiveness and fruitfulness.

If we make one step in prayer, we believe You will make two in peace and power. If we make one step in repentance, we believe You will make two in redemption and restoration. If we make one step in surrender, we believe You will make two in salvation and strength. If we make one step with a tithe, we believe You will make two in triumph and transformation. If we make one step in virtue, we believe You will make two in vision and victory.

Our prayer, Gracious God, is that You will give us courage to make that one step towards freedom from the generational curses that have been in our family for years. Help us to make that one step towards being free from the sin, the weaknesses and the bondage that have been holding us down. Help us to make that one step which is blocking our breakthrough and keeping us in bondage to the devil and threatening us with an eternity in hell. Help us to make that one step towards a peace that passes understanding.

One step stopped the rich young ruler from having eternal life. One step stopped Pilate from being remembered as the man who freed Jesus rather than the man who sentenced him to death. One step stood between Judas as the trusted disciple and Judas the disciple who betrayed the Lord.

Help us we pray, to make that one necessary step so that You can work Your sovereign will in our lives. We offer this prayer in the name of the Lord Jesus, Amen.

DAY 13

– DAY 14 –

RUTH 2: 17-23

Gracious God, as Ruth gleaned in the right fields and received such overflow of harvest that she was able to share with her mother-in-law Naomi; we confess that at times we have gleaned in the wrong fields. If all we have is money and possessions, then we have been working in a field whose value will end at the grave and will not produce any harvest in the judgment.

If we still have low self-esteem, then we have been working in a field that is filled with unresolved issues from the past. If all we have to show is consumer debt and financial bondage, then we have been working in a field of weak discipline. If we still have the need to please and be popular, and must keep up with the Joneses, we are working a field with no long-term vision or goals.

Lord Jesus lead us to the right fields, Your fields of harvest and overflow. Persons who are able to withstand and fight back the assaults of the enemy upon themselves, their bodies, their homes and their loved ones, have been working in the field of prayer. Persons who have been knocked down but keep getting backed up, have been working in the field of determination and endurance.

Persons who are able to say something positive and encouraging, no matter the tough time they may be going through themselves, have been working in the field of praise. Persons who can look through the darkest of nights and claim that there is a bright side somewhere, have been working in the field of worship.

Persons who are able to be a blessing to others, have been working in the field service. Persons who are living free from the guilt of the past and shame from any mistakes, have been working in the field of salvation. Persons who are able to love, have been working in a field of love.

Persons who are about growth, and not merely standing still longing for the good old days, have been working in a field of vision. Persons who are financially free and have abundance, have been working in a field of tithing, living within their means, discipline and long-range goals.

Lord Jesus lead us into Your fields so our lives will always glorify You. Lord Jesus, lead us into Your fields so we may be able to bless others. In Your name, Lord Jesus, do we offer this prayer, Amen.

DAY 14

– DAY 15 –

RUTH 2: 17-23

Gracious God, we are grateful that not only are You our blesser, You are also our protector. We are grateful for the witness of scripture that teaches us about Your faithfulness in both blessing and protecting. We thank you for the witness of Shadrach, Meshach and Abednego who were thrown into a fiery furnace, but looked up and saw a fourth person in the furnace with them who covered them with so much protection they did not even have the smell of smoke on them.

The Israelites were witnesses of God's power to protect when You made a way out of no way through the Red Sea, and then drowned Pharaoh's horses and chariots when they pursued them. Daniel was thrown in the lion's den and stayed all night long and the next morning testified that Your angel stopped the mouth of the lion. The Syrian army surrounded the prophet of Elisha's house when he was in Dothan but the prophet looked and saw that the mountains were filled with horses and chariots of fire from glory that had assembled to watch over him.

The disciple Peter was put into jail and chained between two guards but that night Your angel loosed his chains and opened the prison door and set him free. Paul and Silas were thrown into prison. However, they were praying and singing hymns at midnight when all of a sudden the earth quaked, their dungeons shook and their chains fell off. John the Revelator was put on the island of Patmos but while there he had a vision of the exalted and reigning Christ who opened the windows of glory and gave him a sneak preview of the ultimate victory. We praise You Lord because You can open doors that no man or demon in hell can shut and shut doors that no man or demon in hell can open.

We are grateful that even when we do not experience miraculous deliverance in the way we desire, You have more than one season of harvest. As we live to experience other seasons of harvest, we are able to testify that all things work together for good to them who love the Lord, to those who are called according to his purpose.

Gracious God, we pray this prayer of thanksgiving and faith as we abide in Your blessings and protection during all of our seasons of harvest. We offer this prayer in Jesus name, Amen!

– DAY 16 –

RUTH 3: 1-5

Gracious God, we pray for a spirit of obedience, even as Your daughter and servant Ruth had in days of old. We recognize the power of obedience to open up doors of blessing and breakthrough and cause overflow to come into our lives. We acknowledge, O God we will not get to the next level of blessing and breakthrough, of power and prosperity, of anointing and abundance and of seeing our vision become reality until we reach a new level of obedience.

We pray for a spirit of obedience, not just prayer, because we can pray and still be in disobedience to Your word, will and vision. We pray for a spirit of obedience not just Bible Study because we can read Your word and know Your word by heart and still be in disobedience to the very word we read so much and know so well. We acknowledge, O God that we will not reach the place You see for us until our obedience lines up with the prayers we offer, the worship and praise we give and the Bible we love to read and quote. So we pray for a spirit of obedience.

We acknowledge, O God that the foundation of prosperity and financial freedom and independence You envision for us is our obedience to the word of God regarding tithes and offerings. The key to the devil getting out of our homes and our relationship is our obedience to Your word regarding some things we are doing in our relationships and some things that are going on in our homes. The key to success in our careers and business is found in our obedience to Your word regarding some things we are doing in our careers and in our business.

Long ago the prophet Samuel told a rebellious King Saul, "Surely, to obey is better than sacrifice and to heed better than the fat of rams (1 Samuel 15:22)." Long ago, the Lord admonished us to not only be hearers of the word but doers as well. Therefore on this day, we pray for a spirit of obedience to Your word, Your will, Your voice and Your vision. In the name of the Lord Jesus who was obedient even to death on a cross that opened to him a new dimension of living and authority, do we offer this prayer, Amen.

DAY 16

– DAY 17 –

RUTH 3: 1-6

Gracious God, we will believe what You tell us, we will follow where You tell us and we will do what You tell us to do even if obedience leads us to the threshing floors of life. We will follow You because You have a track record for helping Your children recover from whatever we have been through. We are grateful we are not the first life You have helped to recover.

We are not the first divorcee or heartbroken person You have helped recover. We are not the first abused or misused person You have helped to recover. We are not the first alcoholics, addicts or ex-cons You have help to recover. We are not the first person who has lost a job or who has faced a setback in a career You have helped to recover. We are not the first person who has been lied on and gossiped about You have helped to recover. We are not the first person who has gotten pregnant out of wedlock You have helped to recover.

We are not the first person who has had a nervous breakdown You have helped to recover. We are not the first person with all kinds of generational curses attached to them You have helped to recover. We are not the first in debt or bankrupt person You have helped to recover. We are not the first lonely and depressed person You have helped to recover. We are not the first person weighed down with guilt or shame, we are not the first person others have written off as a failure and damaged goods You have helped to recover.

God if You send us to the threshing floor, we believe the reason is You know we have what it takes to stand. We believe You know we have potential to make it and be successful on the threshing floor. Therefore, if You send us to the threshing floor we can trust Your judgment. You know just how much we can bear and You know we can find success on the threshing floor.

Therefore speak Gracious God, we Your servants are listening. Command Lord, we Your servants will obey. Lead Holy Spirit, we Your servants will follow. In Your name, Father, Son, Holy Spirit, do we offer this prayer, Amen.

DAY 17

– DAY 18 –

RUTH 3: 1-15

As Ruth went to the threshing floor of Boaz, we are grateful Lord Jesus You have established the church as our threshing floor. We are grateful the church is not about beating us up but church is the place where some things can be beaten out, so our virtue and our honor can come forth. We are grateful that the purpose of the word of God is not to beat us up but to beat out chaff so character can come forth. The word of God beats out sin so salvation can come forth.

The word of God beats out wickedness so wheat can come forth. The word of God beats out brokenness so the wheat can come forth. The word of God beats out greed so the grain can come fourth. The word of God beats out grief so goodness can come forth. The word of God beats out weakness so Your worth can come forth. We praise You for Your word Lord Jesus.

As Ruth met Boaz on the threshing floor, we are grateful when we come to church to worship we can meet You Lord Jesus. When we meet You, You do not embarrass us or parade our weaknesses and faults before others. You don't condemn us and You don't reject us. Rather You welcome us and You appreciate our turning to You instead of choosing the devil. You throw Your arms around us to cover us and to comfort us, to protect us and to bless us. Thank You, Lord Jesus.

If we spend time with You, You will not leave us depleted and empty but You will fill our life with peace and power, joy and confidence we can carry away with us. No one who has spent time with You has left empty handed. Nicodemus spent time with You and received a new birth. A five-time divorcee spent time with You and received living water. Zacchaeus spent time with You and received deliverance from bondage to money and greed. A woman caught in sin that others wanted to stone spent time with You and received compassion, forgiveness and another chance. A dying thief on a cross spent time with You and received Paradise.

We come now to You and we pray Lord Jesus do it again. Save and redeem again. Forgive and set free again. Grant peace and power, purpose and Your presence again. Bring joy out of sorrow and victory out of defeat for Your glory and honor. In the name of Jesus do we offer this prayer, Amen.

– DAY 19 –

RUTH 3: 18

Gracious God, we praise You for Your call and claim upon our lives. You have called us to be more anointed than the abuse we have received. You have called us to be bigger than the betrayals we have experienced. You have called us to be better than the bitterness we have felt. You have called us to be more compassionate than the cruelty we have endured and to be more Christian than the cursing we have encountered. You have called us to be more excellent than our embarrassment.

You have called us to be greater than our grief. You have called us to be healed from our hurt. You have called us to be more loving than the littleness of others. You have called us to be mightier than the meanness of enemies and so-called friends. You have called us to be nicer than the nastiness shown to us. You have called us to be more pleasant than pettiness and more powerful than our pain. We pray, O God, we would hear Your call and obey it now.

Some two thousand years ago, the Lord Jesus Christ came from heaven to earth to show us how much he cared for us and how much he was willing to go through so we could walk into another dimension. Today he offers us the same power that he used to face whatever comes at us and still be victorious over it. We pray for wisdom to receive that power today and do it now. He offers forgiveness of sins and mistakes. We pray for faith to receive that forgiveness today and do it now.

The Lord Jesus offers us the authority of his name that overcomes every demon and stronghold. We pray for courage to receive the authority of his name today and receive it now. He gives peace that passes understanding and joy that is everlasting and full of glory. We pray for grace to receive that peace and that joy today and do it now. He offers grace from guilt, salvation from sin, deliverance from demons, a future for our failures and miracles for our mess. We pray for humility to receive his grace, his salvation, his deliverance, his future, and his miracles.

We pray we would not be guilty of procrastination. We receive You, we obey Your word and call and we submit ourselves to You. We do it today and we do it now. In Your precious name do we offer this prayer, Amen.

DAY 19

– DAY 20 –

RUTH 4: 1-6

We praise You Lord Jesus because You are more than meets the eye. Herod thought he could destroy You when You were still a helpless baby but he could not because You were more than met the eye. Angels telegraphed every move ahead to Your parents before Herod made it. The devil thought he could turn You around in the waste howling wilderness but he could not because You were more than met the eye. You had the word of God hidden in Your heart and You knew how to call upon that word and stand on that word in Your times of testing. Your family who did not believe in You and Your disciples who did not understand You could not turn You around because Your faith was focused on the will of God.

The hostile mobs, the self-serving religious leadership and the Roman authorities could not turn You around because You kept Your mind focused on the power of God. The crucifixion could not turn You around because You had prayed determination into Your spirit. Death could not hold You because the same God to whom You had devoted Yourself to completely and thoroughly, raised You to stoop no more with all power in Your hands.

We praise You Lord Jesus because You are prepared to give that same persevering and resurrecting power to anyone who commits his or her life to You. Whatever we are facing or recovering from, You want us to know that as You were more than meets the eye, so are we. With You as our Lord and Savior, we are the salt of the earth. With You as our Lord and Savior, we are the light of the world. With You as our Lord and Savior, we are members of a holy nation and a royal priesthood. We are God's own people. We are more than Blacks or Hispanics or Whites or Asians or Native Americans or other ethnicities. We are more than male, female or gay. We are more than persons with physical challenges. We are more than poor people, cons or addicts. We are more than persons who have failed or made mistakes in the past.

We are more than divorcees or unwed mothers or fathers. We are more than persons with hidden issues. We are the children of God who have been redeemed from our past and empowered to live triumphantly in the present so we can lay claim on a future only God can see. Whatever mountains we face, with You in our life Lord Jesus we can climb them. Whatever foes stand in our way, with You Lord Jesus in our life we can defeat them.

Whatever obstacles or hurdles block our path, with You Lord Jesus in our life we can overcome them. Whatever issues in our past, with You Lord Jesus in our life we can live them down and let them remain where they belong, in the past. Whatever we need to overcome, with You Lord Jesus in our life You can do it. We can do it. We can do it. We can do it because in You we are more than meets the eye. In Your name, Lord Jesus, do we offer this prayer, Amen.

DAY 20

– DAY 21 –

RUTH 4: 1-10C

Gracious God, we pray in the midst of our spiritual warfare we might always remember that our enemy, the devil has never been concerned about stuff around us; he has always been after us. He uses stuff around us, to capture us. The devil has never been after our automobiles, he has been after our anointing. The devil has never been after our careers, he has been after our character. The devil has never been after our families, he has been after our faith. The devil has never been after our houses, he has been after our holiness. The devil has never been after our jobs, he has been after our joy. The devil has never been after our money, he has been after our minds.

The devil has never been after our possessions, he has been after our potential. Lord, help us to remember that the greater our potential, the greater will be the attack of the enemy against us. Some of us are under attack because the devil sees more in us than we probably see in ourselves. However, whenever the devil comes after us, we pray for faith to stand upon the promise of I John 4: 4, "Little children You are from God and have conquered them; for the one who is in You is greater than the one who is in the world." The devil has never been after our stuff, he has been after our souls.

As Boaz purchased all the land so he might gain Ruth, help us to believe and guard our self-worth and all You went through so we could keep it. Therefore above all, help us to guard our sense of self-worth. As we love our families and stand up for our beliefs and principles, help us to guard our sense of self-worth. As we pay attention to our money and save and invest for our future, help us to guard our sense of self-worth. As we work honorably on our jobs and give a fair days work for the compensation we receive, help us above all guard our sense of self-worth. As we are loyal to our friends and those who have been loyal to us, help us above all guard our sense of self-worth.

As we have pity upon those who are in need and as we lift the fallen, help us above all guard our sense of self-worth. No matter what lies the devil tells or rumors he spreads or attacks he mounts or weapons he forms, help us above all guard our sense of self-worth. A number of us, who are serving You O Lord, do not have a healthy sense of self-worth because we have paid too much attention to the words and works of the devil. Restore to us the sense of self-worth You have called us to have. In Your name, Lord Jesus, do we offer this prayer, Amen.

– DAY 22 –

RUTH 4: 13-18B

Gracious God, we praise You because You were able to use Naomi's and Ruth's vision of recovery in such a way that it produced ripples that flowed into the life of David, Israel's greatest king and even the lineage of the Lord Jesus Christ. We confess O God, that rather than creating ripples that blessed the lives of others, we have produced undercurrents that brought others under. Forgive us O God and give us a rippling producing rather than an undercurrent generating life.

We recognize O God anticipation produces ripples but apathy produces undercurrent. Anointing produces ripples but arrogance produces undercurrent. Belief produces ripples but belittling produces undercurrent. Building produces ripples but backbiting produces undercurrent. Compassion produces ripples but cheapness produces undercurrent. Commitment produces ripples but carelessness produces undercurrent. Discipline produces ripples but debt produces undercurrent. Determination produces ripples but the devil produces undercurrent. Delight produces ripples but discouragement produces undercurrent.

Encouragement produces ripples but envy produces undercurrent. Faithfulness produces ripples but fear produces undercurrent. Friendliness produces ripples but meanness undercurrent. Generosity produces ripples but greed produces undercurrent. Gratitude produces ripples but grabbing produces undercurrent. Godliness produces ripples but getting-over produces undercurrent. Good news produces ripples but gossip produces undercurrent. Helping one another produces ripples but hindering one another produces undercurrent. Joy produces ripples but jealousy produces undercurrent. Kindness produces ripples but kicking produces undercurrent.

Lifting produces ripples but lying produces undercurrent. Love produces ripples but lust produces undercurrent. Morals produce ripples but mess produces undercurrent. Perspective produces ripples but pettiness produces undercurrent. Praise produces ripples but put-downs produce undercurrent. Principles produce ripples but politics produce undercurrent. Prosperity produces ripples but poverty produces undercurrent. Salvation produces ripples but sin produces undercurrent.

We give praise for salvation through our Lord Jesus Christ who is able to produce ripples from our lives even now. In his name do we offer this prayer, Amen.

– DAY 23 –

1 SAMUEL 17: 30

Gracious Lord when Your servant David was rebuffed and rejected by his brother Eliab, he had the wisdom to turn to another. We pray for wisdom to turn to another when we are assaulted by the negative voices of life. Some of us will never come into our season of love or breakthrough or overflow or success or prosperity or abundance or happiness or holiness or fulfillment as long as we listen to Eliab in our lives. It's time we turn to another.

It's time we stop talking to Eliab every day, allowing him or her to depresses us, hurt us, discourage us and pour rain on our parade. It's time we stop listening to Eliab tell us we will never recoup what we have lost or we will never be anything. It's time we stop listening to Eliab tell us we can't make it without them. It's time we stop taking the verbal or emotional or physical abuse of Eliab. It's time we turn to another.

It's time we stop giving money to Eliab and allowing Eliab to take advantage of our goodness, our love, our kindness or even our religion. It's time we stop being content with the crumbs that fall from Eliab's table. We have shed enough tears because of what Eliab continues to say or do. Eliab has hurt us enough, betrayed us enough, lied to us enough and made us cry enough. It's time we turned to another.

Lord Jesus, we are grateful that when the Eliabs' in our life have buffeted us and when we are surrounded by voices of negativity we can turn to You for fulfillment, happiness and peace of mind. If we need someone for restoration, forgiveness, another chance, deliverance and encouragement, we can turn to You. You can build up what the Eliabs' has torn down and prevent the destruction the Goliaths' want to bring.

Lord Jesus, You have the words of eternal life and You are the living word of eternal life. You loved us enough to give Your life on Calvary to die for our sins and to give us another chance. You have such power and authority not even death could keep You down and the grave could not hold You. You will come again to take us to Yourself where the Eliabs' cease from troubling and the weary are at rest.

Lord Jesus, we turn to You. Thank You for receiving us. We offer this prayer in Your name, Amen.

– DAY 24 –

GENESIS 22: 1-14

Gracious God when we must pass a trust test help us to call upon everything and bring to remembrance everything we know about You. You are faithful. You are loving. You are forgiving. You are trustworthy. You are all powerful. You keep promises. You can and You will do everything You say. When we are struggling to remain faithful to the tithe during inflationary times; when gas and food prices are soaring beyond anything we have ever seen before. When we are striving to be faithful to the tithe; when we are barely making it now and are not sure how we are going to make it in the future. Help us to call upon everything and bring to remembrance everything we know about You. You are faithful. You are loving. You are forgiving. You are trustworthy. You are all powerful. You keep promises. You can and You will do everything You say.

When it seems as if the harder we work, the worse things get and all of our praying, believing, and trying to do the right things are not doing any good, help us to call upon everything and bring to remembrance everything we know about You. You are faithful. You are loving. You are forgiving. You are trustworthy. You are all powerful. You keep promises. You can and You will do everything You say. When we feel lonely, misunderstood and forsaken or when the enemy has us under attack and doubters and scoffers are standing around with their cynical false accusations and their taunting questions about where is our God, help us to call upon everything and bring to remembrance everything we know about You. You are faithful. You are loving. You are forgiving. You are trustworthy. You are all powerful. You keep promises. You can and You will do everything You say.

When we have become tired, weary, almost burned out and we don't feel as if we can hold out any longer, when we earnestly call on the Lord and heaven answers with a stony silence, help us to call upon everything and bring to remembrance everything we know about You. You are faithful. You are loving. You are forgiving. You are trustworthy. You are all powerful. You keep promises. You can and You will do everything You say.

On Calvary, the Lord Jesus gave himself as a sacrificial Lamb for our sins. We pray we will have faith to follow his example of loving faithfulness and trusting obedience. In Your name Lord Jesus, Lamb of God, do we offer this prayer, Amen.

– DAY 25 –

MATTHEW 4: 1-4

Lord Jesus as You were tested and tried by the enemy, we know that as we follow You and walk in the vision You have for our lives, we know we also will be subjected to various tests. We pray You will prepare us for those seasons of testing no matter how the enemy comes after us. We recognize that the devil comes after us with tests that don't seem to be tests and with weapons that are not particularly evil in and of themselves. Often he comes after us with traps and tests that look like treats.

Sometimes the devil comes not as an accuser but as an adviser, not with an attack but with attraction, not with animosity but with affection. Sometimes the devil does not come as beast but as beauty, not with bondage but bounty, not with a curse but with a compliment, not with coldness but with caring, not with complications but with conveniences, not with a cross but a crown. Sometimes the devil does not come as a demon but as delight, not with enmity but with ease, not as foe but as friend, not with a frown but with favor, not with fight but with fun.

Sometimes the devil does not come with grief but with generosity, not with hindrances but with help, not with a hit but with a hug, not with hurt but with hypocritical holiness, not with instigation but inspiration, not with jealousy but with jewelry, not with a kick but with kindness, not with loneliness but with a lift. Sometimes the devil does not come with meanness but with money, not with nastiness but with niceties, not with obstacles but with opportunities, not with problems but with promotions, not with putdowns but with politeness, not with persecutions but with presents, not with peril but with prosperity.

Sometimes the devil does not come with rejection but with rewards, not with strongholds but with a smile, not with a slap but with a suggestion, not with trash but with treasure, not with undermining but with understanding and not with warfare but with worship.

Lord Jesus, we pray that however and whenever he comes he will have the faith to fight and the assurance of victory that helps us to declare that the place of our testing is not the place of our defeat or our demise. We may be Joseph who was sold into slavery by jealous brothers and then imprisoned by a lie but slavery and prison are not going to be the places where we die.

Or we may be Naomi reeling from the deaths of loved ones but bitterness and bereavement and sorrow are not going to be the places where we die. We praise You for the victory we have in You and in Your name we offer this prayer, Amen.

DAY 25

– DAY 26 –

MATTHEW 4: 5-6

Lord Jesus, we are so grateful that when the tempter came to You in the wilderness and challenged You to jump from the pinnacle of the temple so You could have a ministry of sensationalism rather than substance, You didn't jump. If You had jumped, there would have been no Christmas to celebrate because Your birth would have no special meaning. If You had jumped, there would be no Easter because resurrection from the dead was reward and celebration for Your not jumping.

If You had jumped, there would be no Day of Pentecost and outpouring of the Holy Spirit upon believers who were gathered in the upper room in the name of their resurrected and ascended Lord who did not jump. If You had jumped, there would be no salvation in Your name and no blood to cleanse us from all our sins. If You had jumped, there would be no victory over demons, disease and death. If You had jumped, there would be no New Testament – No Gospels, no Acts of the Apostles, no Pauline or Pastoral Epistles and no Book of Revelation.

If You had jumped, there would have been no Hallelujah Chorus for Handel to write about – No declaration that "He is King of Kings and Lord of Lords and that He shall reign forever and ever, Hallelujah! Amen!" If You had jumped, there would have been no "Amazing Grace" for John Newton to testify of and no "Beams of Heaven" to guide the feet of Charles Albert Tindley. If You had jumped, there would have been no reason for Julia Ward Howe to declare "Mine Eyes Have Seen the Glory of the Coming of the Lord" or for Fannie Crosby to say, "I Am Thine O Lord".

If You had jumped, there would have been no "Precious Lord" for Thomas Dorsey to call upon in his hour of need and no reason for James Cleveland to assert that "Jesus is the Best Thing That Ever Happened to Me". If You had jumped, there would be no reason for our ancestors to sing about a "Balm in Gilead" to heal the sin sick soul and make the wounded whole or for them to say, "I Want Jesus to Walk With Me".

We praise You for not jumping Lord Jesus. We pray Your presence in our lives will be so strong and our relationship with You will be so close that when the tempter tells us to jump, we will remember Your example, rely upon Your power in us and claim the victory that comes to those who trust in Your name and not jump either. We offer this prayer to You in Your name, Lord Jesus, Amen.

– DAY 27 –

MATTHEW 4: 5-7B

Lord Jesus, we confess that many times when the tempter comes to us in the lonely moments of our lives, we jump too quickly. We jump because we want to. We jump because we are curious. We jump because we are stupid. We jump because it is easier to yield to the pressure of the moment than remain steadfast. We jump because we lose sight of our long-range vision and goals. We jump because we do not heed the word God has put in our Heart to answer the enemy. We jump because we are greedy.

We jump because we feel the need to prove certain things to certain people even if we have to do things that work against our own best interests. We jump to get attention. We jump because we want immediate gratification. We jump because we do not invoke Your name, Lord Jesus. We jump because everybody else around us is jumping. We jump to be accepted by and acceptable to a certain crowd. We jump because we are envious of what others have. We jump because jumpers seem to get ahead faster than those who stand on Your word that has been put in our heart and the vision You have placed within our head.

We jump because we are fearful that if we don't jump, we may miss out on the future, the relationships and the life we have always dreamed of. We jump because we are desperate. We jump because we are needy. We jump because we are envious of what others have. We jump because we are insecure. We jump because we really don't know if we can believe the promises of God. We jump because we are tired and frustrated at the moment. We jump because somebody told us we were cute and special. We jump because somebody told us we were strange and weird for not jumping.

We jump because somebody told us we are the exception to the rule and that the tragedies and troubles which have happened to other jumpers would not happen to us. We jump because we think we are smarter and slicker than anybody else. We jump because we are young and want to have a good time. We jump because we are trying to capture youth we no longer have. We jump because we are in a mid-life crisis. We jump because we have low self-esteem.

Forgive us Lord Jesus for obeying the voice of an inferior power, one You have put under our feet. Forgive us for jumping when we should be standing and walking in the authority we have in You and through You. In Your name, Lord Jesus, do we offer this prayer, Amen.

– DAY 28 –

MATTHEW 4: 8-11B

Lord Jesus, we praise You because You are a mother for the motherless, a father for the fatherless, a sister for the sister-less, a brother-less, and a friend for the friendless. We are grateful that no one need ever feel lonely or forgotten or forsaken, if they know You personally as Lord and Savior. You turned Your back on the riches of this world just so You could demonstrate how much we are loved and how much we are treasured by You. You bore a cross up to Calvary to show us how much of a treasure we are. You went to heaven to prepare a place for us because You look upon us as treasure even when we act like trash.

Even now, You watch over us and are prepared to receive our repentance and grant us forgiveness, a new life and a new future because of the treasure and wealth You see in us. You will never leave us or forsake us and You will be with us every step of the way in whatever we face because of the treasure and wealth You see in us. When we fall, You pick us up and then You take us into Your arms and love us as if we have never sinned. When others give up on us, You continue to believe in us. Why? Because of the treasure You see in us. One of these old days You are coming back again to take us home to be with You forever, because of the treasure and the wealth You see in us.

When some have the need to validate their rights and affirm their self-worth, they turn to the admirable words of the Declaration of Independence: "We hold these truths to be self-evident that all men are created equal, they endowed by their Creator with certain inalienable rights that among these are life, liberty and the pursuit of happiness." However, we are grateful we can turn to Your word, Lord Jesus, which teach us and remind us of the treasures we are: "For God so loved the world that he gave his only begotten Son that whosoever believes in him should not perish but have everlasting life (John 3:16)."

Forgive us O Lord when we live far beneath our potential and our privilege. Forgive us O Lord when we listen to the devil and the voices of negativity so much we forget that You saw so much treasure and wealth in us You turned down the riches of the world for our redemption. Forgive us when our lives, our thoughts, our words and our actions mock the treasure You see in us. Lord Jesus, we pray You will continue to reach into the depths of our hearts and souls and bring out the treasure and hidden wealth You see that may even be hidden from our own eyes. In Your name, Lord Jesus, do we offer this prayer, Amen.

– DAY 29 –

LUKE 4: 13

Lord Jesus, in our warfare against the devil, we pray that we will never forget he always comes back. As he came back to You, he will come back to us. Sometimes he comes back with the same things and sometimes he comes back with new things but he comes back. Sometimes he comes back immediately and sometimes he comes back after a long interval but he comes back. Sometimes he comes back with attacks that are obvious and sometimes he comes back with anguish that is subtle; sometimes he comes back through a burden and sometimes he comes back through a blessing but he comes back.

Sometimes he comes back through our career and sometimes he comes back through our church; sometimes he comes back with a command and sometimes he comes back with compromise; sometimes he comes back through criticism and sometimes he comes back with a compliment but he comes back. Sometimes he comes back to destroy and sometimes he comes back to discourage; sometimes he comes back with a demand and sometimes he comes back with a deal but he comes back. Sometimes he comes back through our family and sometimes he comes back through a friend; sometimes he comes back through fear and sometimes he comes back through frustration but he comes back. Sometimes he comes back with a game and sometimes he comes back with a gift; sometimes he comes back as a helper and sometimes he comes back as a hindrance but he comes back.

Sometimes he comes back with an issue and sometimes he comes back as intimacy; sometimes he comes back with joy and sometimes he comes back with junk but he comes back. Sometimes he comes back through a kick and sometimes he comes back through a kiss but he comes back. Sometimes he comes back with love and sometimes he comes back with loneliness but he comes back. Sometimes he comes back through money and sometimes he comes back through mess; sometimes he comes back through an obstacle and sometimes he comes back through an opportunity but he comes back. Sometimes he comes back through pain and sometimes he comes back through pleasure; sometimes he comes back with a problem and sometimes he comes back with a promise but he comes back.

As You were persevering, we pray for the same perseverance so the enemy does not get an easy victory because we have grown weary of fighting him. We praise You for Your example that teaches us how to be victorious. In Your name, Lord Jesus, do we offer this prayer, Amen.

– DAY 30 –

I CORINTHIANS 10: 13

Gracious God, we praise You for the promise and assurance of Your word that tells us, "No testing has overtaken us that is not common to everyone. God is faithful and he will not let You be tested beyond Your strength but with the testing He will also provide the way out so that You may be able to endure it."

Therefore, when like Cain, we are confronted by jealousy and resentment over our brothers and sisters favor, when like Noah we find ourselves backslidden on the eve of our breakthrough or when like Abraham we are confronted by failing faith and a delayed promise, we pray we remember the promises of Your word. When, like Jacob, the mistakes of our shady past threaten the new steps we are trying to make in the present, when like Elijah, we are confronted by the Jezebels that put fear in our heart in spite of our victories of faith. We pray we may remember the promises of Your word. When like David, we are confronted by our Bathshebas on the roof; we need to remember the words of our text. When like Esther, selfishness grips our spirit, when like Naomi, bitterness tries to consume us because of our losses or when like Job, we are so burdened we want to curse the day we were born, we pray that we remember the promises of Your word. When like Solomon, we find ourselves distant from God or when like Jeremiah, the weight of our burdens is about to drain us of the joy of service, we pray we remember the promises of Your word.

When like the Prodigal Son, we have misspent and misused what has been entrusted to us or when like John the Baptist, we are so confused and fearful we don't know what to believe or when like Peter, we discover we don't have the faith to stand up under the weight our words, we pray we remember the promises of Your word. When like Mary Magdalene, we are falsely accused because of our loyalty to the Lord or when like Legion we have so much troubling us and haunting us, we hardly know who we are anymore; we pray we remember the promises of Your word. When like Martha and Mary, we sought the Lord with our whole hearts and death still claimed our loved ones or when like Judas, we have so disgraced ourselves that death seems a viable option, we pray we remember the promises of Your word.

When like the Lord Jesus in the Garden of Gethsemane, we may have to drink from some cups we desperately want to pass from us; we pray we remember the promises of Your word. We offer this prayer to You now in the name of the Lord Jesus, the original Promise Keeper, Amen.

DAY 30

– DAY 31 –

I CORINTHIANS 10: 13B

Lord Christ, You are the eternal word of God by whom, through whom and with whom all things were created and in whom all things have their being. Lord Christ, You are God wrapped up in human flesh and as such You are the way, the truth and the life.

We worship You, we praise You, we love and adore and we follow You because of who You are. You are the way out and the way through every test of life we must face. If the way we would choose as the way out is the way we can honestly say You would choose, Lord Jesus, then that is God's way out. If the way we would choose as the way out is something we would not mind You catching us doing if You should return at that very moment, then that way is God's way out. If the way we would choose is something that we can defend when we stand before Your judgment seat, Lord Christ, then that is God's way out.

If the way we choose is something that honors Your sacrifice on Calvary when You gave Your life, Your best and Your all for our redemption, if it's something that demonstrates that You did not die in vain, and that Your faith, sacrifice and love for us were not in vain, then that is God's way out. If the way we choose shows the devil that in Your name, Lord Jesus, we have the victory, then that is God's way out.

Your name Lord Jesus is God's way out of every test we face. Therefore, when demons attack us, we can call on the name of Jesus who set Legion free from the multitude of demons that held him in bondage. When we are tested by the yearnings of the flesh, we can call on the name of Jesus who told a woman caught in sin to go in peace and sin no more.

We praise You for the power and authority we have when we call and use Your name. Now we pray for presence of mind and to remember You are God's way out when we are tested. In Your name, Lord Jesus, do we now offer this prayer, Amen.

DAY 31

– DAY 32 –

MARK 1: 9-13

Gracious God, we praise You for Your wisdom that drives us to the wilderness, into the grips of the enemy because there are some things only the wilderness can teach us. No one chooses the wilderness of sickness but that is how we learn that either You will heal us or that Your grace is sufficient for us and Your strength really is made perfect in our weakness. No one chooses the wilderness of forsakenness and betrayal but that is how we learn the meaning of Your faithfulness. No one chooses failure and mistakes but that is how we learn that You will give us a second chance.

No one chooses to be broke and without what we need, but that is how we learn that You will make a way out of no way. No one chooses to be lost but that is how we find that You will find us where we are, pick us up and establish us and put us on a street called straight. No one chooses crosses of shame but that's how we learn about crowns of glory and resurrection from death.

We praise You, O God, for the wilderness that takes us to a new level of our faith walk and relationship with You. The Jordan River gives us a new baptism but the wilderness experience gives us new breakthroughs. The Jordan River gave us new caring but the wilderness gave us new courage. The Jordan River gave us new delights but the wilderness gave us new determination. The Jordan River made us glad but the wilderness experience made us grateful. The Jordan River made us holy but the wilderness experience made us humble.

The Jordan River gave us new joy but the wilderness gave us new justification. The Jordan River gave us new opportunity but the wilderness gave us new obedience. The Jordan River gives us new praise but the wilderness gives us new power. The Jordan River gave us new revelation but the wilderness experience gave us a new redemption. The Jordan River put a new song in our life but the wilderness experience put new life in our song. The Jordan River gave us a new shout but the wilderness experience gave us new strength.

We left the Jordan drinking milk but we left the wilderness eating solid food. At the Jordan, we were baptized with water but in the wilderness, we were baptized by fire. We offer this prayer in the name of the Lord Jesus Christ who is our example for conquering every wilderness that we will face, Amen.

DAY 32

– DAY 33 –

LUKE 4: 1-3

Lord Jesus, we praise You because You know about every wound we have received as we have worked through private conflict. You know about an Abraham wound when we are wrestling to hold on to a promise that is long in coming to pass. You know about a Joseph wound when we have been trying to do right and things still go from bad to worse. You know about a Job wound that comes because we are under attack, can't figure out why and are being falsely accused. You know about an Elijah wound when in spite of our victories of faith, certain enemies have struck fear into our hearts and put us on the run. You know about a John the Baptist wound when we are beginning to doubt what we once were so sure of. You know about a Paul wound when people will not let You forget past mistakes.

You know about wounds that inflict the heart when family does not understand. You know about wounds that burden the spirit when those closest to us deny, betray and desert us. You know about Gethsemane wounds that cause agony when God is telling us to make a sacrifice that is the most painful thing we have ever been asked to do. You know about crucifixion wounds that can cause us to feel distant from God when enemies get the upper hand. You know about burial wounds when people have written us off and considered us gone for good.

Even when we are too burdened, too confused, too depressed and too angry to pray, You know about those battles too. Because You have had the same private battles as we have, You know just how we feel and You will do what is best for us. When we feel You are applying pressure in certain places in our life, since You have fought the same battles as we have, we are grateful for confidence You know what You are doing. When prayers are answered in certain ways, You know what You are doing. When certain situations work out in ways we may not understand, because You have been where we are, we are confident You know what You are doing. We praise You, Lord Jesus.

As Your private battles did not prevent You from doing anything You came to do, we know that even if we have to fight some battles again and again and again, as long as we do not yield to the encroachments and the attacks of the enemy upon our soul and our mind, we can still be everything You desire us to be. We praise You Lord Jesus for the victory we have in You and we offer this prayer in Your name, Amen.

– DAY 34 –

JOHN 20: 1

Gracious God, we are so grateful that dark season and times do not stop You from working. We are grateful You can still work miracles, answer prayers, make ways out of no ways and accomplish Your will and vision for our life even in times of darkness. As You raised the Lord Jesus while it was still dark, You can do the same for us.

Forgive us, O God, for those time when our own perceptions and images caused us to doubt Your never failing power and presence that was at work even in the dark. We confess, O God, there may have even been times when we rejected Your resurrection for us because we did not seek Your direction but leaned on our own understanding. Because our resurrection did not look like we thought it would – they were shorter than we thought, they were fatter or skinnier than we thought, they may not have been making as much money as we wanted them to make at the time and so we sent them away. They may have been older or younger or a different race than we wanted them to be or they may have come from a different background than we wanted or their educational level may have been different than we pictured and so we sent them away.

You may have sent our resurrection from that last job or Calvary career experience but because it wasn't what we had pictured – it was in a different location than we wanted, the starting pay may not have been what we wanted; it was something different than we thought it would be, we may have rejected our own resurrection. Forgive us, O Lord, we pray.

We now fall on our faces and pray as did our ancestors: "Father I stretch my hands to Thee, No other help I know, If Thou withdraw Thyself from me, Ah, whither shall I go."

Give us faith to trust You even when we can't trace You, to believe in Your faithfulness and claim Your promises even when we may not understand all You may be doing at any given moment in our lives. O Faithful Father, You who raised Jesus while it was still dark move in all lives as You see fit because we know that You doeth all things well. In the name of our Lord Jesus Christ, the light of the world and the light of our lives do we offer this prayer, Amen.

DAY 34

– DAY 35 –

MATTHEW 4: 8

Lord Jesus, we praise You for Your victory over the money test that You passed in the waster howling wilderness. A number of us have had to take and are taking this same test right now. Anyone who has known poverty or anyone who has grown up poor would have to wrestle with the test. Anyone who has ever had trouble sleeping at night because they were hungry or awakened with hunger pangs gnawing at their insides would have to wrestle with this test. Anyone who has had to spend sleepless nights wondering how they were going to make ends meet, how they were going to keep a roof over their heads, how they were going to keep food on the table or how they were going to take care of their family, would have to wrestle with this test.

Any parent, who has ever had to say no the request of a child when everything in them wanted to say yes, would have to wrestle with this test. Any parent who has ever had to work overtime to help their child not feel inferior or less than some other child because of the financial lack in their family would have to wrestle with this test. Any parent who has not been able to send their child to the school they knew would be a blessing to that child's education and future would have to wrestle with this test. Any husband or wife or lover who has ever seen something in the store or on television or catalogue that they desperately wanted to give their loved one, they could see how they would look in it but could not because of a lack of money, would have to wrestle with this test.

Anyone who has ever had to fight with feelings of inferiority or not being as good as someone else because they did not have the money to do what others were able to do would have to wrestle with this test. Anyone who has ever been poor but is now doing well but is afraid that they may one day fall back into the poverty they have worked so hard trying to get out of would have to wrestle with this test. Anyone who has ever found themselves with broken and diminished health because they are working themselves into an early grave because of the financial pressures of the times would have to wrestle with this test. Any couple or family that is constantly arguing about and fighting over money issues would have to wrestle with this test.

We pray that You will give us Your mind, Lord Jesus, so when we are faced with the money test or any other kind of test, we will face it not in our strength but in Yours. We pray in Your very own name, Lord Jesus, Amen.

– DAY 36 –

LUKE 4: 1-13

Lord Jesus, we are grateful that You rejected Satan because turning around lives was more important than turning stones to bread. Justice was more important to You than jumping from the pinnacle to the temple. Redemption was more important to You than the riches of the world. Your anointing was more important than the appeals of Satan. Your commitment to God was more important than the conveniences of Satan.

You rejected Satan because deliverance was more important than the delusion of Satan. Eternity was more important than the enticements of Satan. Freedom was more important than the fame of Satan. The Gospel was more important than the greed of Satan. Your integrity was more important than the instigation of Satan. Liberation was more important than the lies of Satan. Obedience was more important than the promotion of Satan.

When an insanely mad and enraged Satan comes back for a rematch with us, we pray we will know that those reasons are still important enough to persist in fighting him. Being able to sleep at night is still a sufficient reason to keep fighting Satan. Commitment to people we love is still a sufficient reason to keep fighting Satan. Not disappointing people, who believe in You and who trust You, is still a sufficient reason to keep fighting Satan. Being free from what has bound us in the past is still a sufficient reason to keep fighting Satan.

Being cleansed of sin is still a sufficient reason to keep fighting Satan. A new future and another chance are still sufficient reasons to keep fighting Satan. Following God's vision for your life that is greater than any vision we can have for ourselves or that others can have for us, is still a sufficient reason to keep fighting Satan. Hearing God say "Well done good and faithful servant. You have been faithful over a few things; come on up and I'll make You ruler over many. Enter the joy of Your Lord (Matthew 25:21)" is still a sufficient reason to keep fighting Satan. We offer this prayer in Your eternal name, Lord Jesus, Amen.

– DAY 37 –

ACTS 8: 26-40

God of grace and God of glory, You who gave Your servant Philip victory and success when he ministered in ancient Samaria, we pray for his faith and his trust when You speak to us and call us to leave the comfortable Samarias' of our lives and follow Your word and vision to the desert roads in the wilderness that lead to Gaza. We confess O God many of us are now living in the tension between good Samaria, comfortable Samaria, blessed Samaria, successful Samaria, and the bleak, barren, unknown, risky, desert road that leads towards Gaza in the wilderness.

When we have nothing why not tithe, We don't have anything to begin with? The tithe is so small that it's not going to make that much difference in our financial situation anyway. But when we hit or approach six or seven figures and we are making more that we have ever made, ten percent looks different. When we are on fixed income and gas and food prices, rent and mortgages, taxes and living expenses are shooting through the roof, ten percent looks different. When we are drowning in debt, a tithe looks different. In those circumstances, a tithe looks like the desert road in the wilderness that leads to Gaza.

When we are overweight but happy, a diet looks like a desert road in the wilderness that leads to Gaza. When we are in sin but basically content, obedience looks like a desert road in the wilderness that leads to Gaza. When we are secure in a job that pays the bills, a promotion that unsettles us or a new business opportunity looks like a desert road in the wilderness that leads to Gaza.

When we are content attending church with no responsibility, joining church or becoming more active in church that cuts down on time we could spend on ourselves, looks like a desert road in the wilderness that leads to Gaza. When we are living less than our potential but are content, growth and change look like a desert road in the wilderness that leads to Gaza. When we are in bondage but content with temporary escapist highs we have always known, discipline and determination can look like the desert road in the wilderness that leads to Gaza.

In those circumstances, give us faith that trusts You for the outcome, knowing that You who have begun a great work in us will bring it to completion. In the name of the Lord Jesus do we offer this prayer, Amen.

DAY 37

– DAY 38 –

ACTS 12: 1-17

Lord Jesus, as the early church had to face the challenge of Peter's arrest and possible death, immediately after the martyrdom of the disciple James; there are times when we are also hit by the double whammy. There are times when life seems to slam us against the wall and knocks us to the mat. Then while we are reeling and rocking from that blow, before we can fully recover and get back up on our feet, we are hit with something else that slams us to the wall again or sends us staggering or that knocks us back down again.

The double whammy – before we can get over the death of a loved one, another loved one dies. The double whammy – not one child but both children start acting up or come under attack. When such occurs, we find ourselves asking You, "What is happening with or to our family?" The double whammy – before we can pay off the furnace bill, the transmission in the car goes. Before we can finish repairing the roof, the pipes burst.

The double whammy – before we can finish helping one close friend or relative with their problem, another one calls with a crisis in their lives. The double whammy – before we can get over one operation or illness, another health challenge sends us back to the doctor. The double whammy – before we can get over the crisis in our career, we have to face a crisis in our relationship or in our marriage. The double whammy – before we can get over the betrayal from a friend or spouse or trusted colleague at work, we have to deal with disappointment in the pastor or the church people or the teacher or doctor or lawyer or someone else we trusted and looked up to.

The double whammy occurs when it seems as if everywhere we turn we run into trouble and everybody we meet or talk with or are close to seems to be going through a season of stress and we begin to feel as if life is either closing in upon us or collapsing under us. We wonder where we can find some peace or comfort or laughter. The double whammy is what makes us raise our hands to You, Lord Jesus and ask, "Where are You? What's going on? What's next?"

In such times, we pray we will remember Your faithfulness. When we are caught between a rock and a hard place, when we are reeling and rocking from the double whammy that has hit us on both sides, help us to remember Your faithfulness and that You will keep us from falling and present us faultless before the presence of Your unblemished glory with great joy. In Your name faithful Christ do we offer this prayer, Amen.

DAY 38

– DAY 39 –

LUKE 9: 1-2

Lord Jesus, we are grateful that when the word of God says You gave Your disciples authority over all demons, You meant just that – **all** demons. As Your followers, we have authority over **all** demons; **All demons** – including financial demons; **All demons** – including debt demons; **All demons** – including shopping and spending demons; **All demons** – including alcohol demons; **All demons** – including drug demons; **All demons** – including pornography demons and sex demons; **All demons** – including overeating and self-indulgence demons; **All demons** – including heartbreak and loneliness demons.

We, your followers have authority over **all demons** – including bitterness and resentment demons; **All demons** – including anger and mean-tempered demons; **All demons** – including gossiping and lying demons; **All demons** – including shame and guilt demons; **All demons** – including jealousy and insecurity demons; **All demons** – including family and home demons; **All demons** – including generational and abuse demons; All demons – including church and corporate, and business and busybody demons.

We, your followers have authority over **all demons** – including workaholic and other escapist demons; **All demons** – including self-righteousness and judgmental demons; **All demons** – including narrow-mindedness and pettiness demons; **All demons** – including whining and low self-esteem demons; **All demons** – including curse maintaining; non-tithing demons; **All demons** – including sickness and disease demons. Lord Jesus you have given us authority over **all** demons.

Forgive us Lord Jesus when our lack of faith and our failure to be anchored in prayer, Your word and the spiritual disciplines have caused us to be defeated by demons, opponents and enemies You have already given us the victory over. Whenever we forget that **all** demons mean just that – **all** demons, we pray the Holy Spirit would bring to our remembrance the rich promises and power of Your word. In Your name, Lord Jesus, do we offer this prayer, Amen.

DAY 39

– DAY 40 –

LUKE 24: 45-47, ACTS 1: 6

Lord Jesus, You have a vision for our lives that is greater than any vision we can have for ourselves or that others can have for us. However, we confess that sometimes we often choose to remain small because we don't know where Your vision will lead us. Therefore, we opt for the smallness we know rather than the newness we don't know.

We choose the agony we know over the anointing we have not experienced. We choose the bondage we know over the breakthrough we have not experienced. We choose the crisis we know over the Christ we have not experienced. We choose the crowd we know over the church we have not experiences. We choose the devil we know over the deliverance we have not experienced. We choose the enemy we know over the excellence we have not experienced. We choose the fears we know over the faith we have not experience. We choose the hell we know over the heaven we have not experienced. We choose the kicks we know over the kindness we have not yet experienced. We choose the loneliness we know over the love we have not experienced.

We choose the mess we know over the miracles we have not experienced. We choose the nastiness we know over the newness we have not experienced. We choose the opposition we know over the opportunities we have not experience. We choose the problems we know over the power we have not experienced. We choose the rejection we know over the revelation we have not experienced. We choose the sin we know over the salvation we have not experienced. We choose the trouble we know over the testimony we have not experienced. We choose the valleys we know over the vision we have not experienced. We choose the whining we know over the worth we have not experienced.

As You have saved us from our sins, save us from our small thinking O Lord and empower us to walk in Your newness and Your largeness. In Your name, Lord Jesus, we pray, Amen.

DAY 40

– DAY 41 –

I CORINTHIANS 3: 11

O Christ of God, Solid Rock we praise You for being the faithful, unfailing, never flinching, sure and steady, unmovable, all sufficient, foundation of our lives. We are grateful we do not have to face life and all of its challenges or the devil and all of his terrors and temptations depending upon our strength and energy, wit and wisdom alone. We praise You we do not have to face our future dependent upon our own skill and knowledge alone. Even when we must lay down and press a dying pillow we are grateful You will be there even then to be the bridge across death's divide and carry us to a land that is fairer than day.

We pray now for faith to stand upon You, O Rock of our Salvation, when we are being tested and tried. We pray for faith to stand upon You, O Rock of our Salvation, when we are being talked about and criticized. We pray for faith to stand upon You, O Rock of our Salvation, when our finances are under attack. We pray for faith to stand upon You, O Rock of our Salvation, when our families, our relationships, our homes and careers are under attack. We pray for faith to stand upon You, O Rock of our Salvation, when our faith and all we believe is being challenged by the machinations of the Adversary. We pray for faith to stand upon You, O Rock of our Salvation, when our bodies and our health are under attack. You are faithful. We pray for faith to trust and to stand, to endure and excel, to withstand and to worship, to pray and to give You praise when we are under attack.

Thank You for hearing us O Rock of our Salvation. Thank You for answering us and renewing us even as we call upon You, O Rock of our Salvation. We will stand upon You when we are under attack. We will remain faithful even when life contradicts what we believe. We will trust You even when things happen we do not understand. We will affirm Your will even when You say no to our prayers because we have either asked amiss or because You willed something better for us. We will cleave to You O Rock of our Salvation until this fleeting and meandering journey called life is over. We will love You until travelling days are done and then in a new and brighter day we will love You throughout all of eternity. We offer this prayer in the name of the Rock of our Salvation, Jesus Christ our Lord, Amen.

– DAY 42 –

I CORINTHIANS 4: 1-2

Gracious God, we are grateful that You trust us. You are faithful and trustworthy. In so many ways and at so many times we have fallen far short of Your track record of faithfulness. Yet You still trust us to be stewards of Your mysteries. Thank You Lord. We are privileged to be caretakers of the mysteries of prayer. Thank You Lord. We are privileged to be caretakers of the mysteries of Your word. Thank You Lord. We are privileged to be caretakers of the precious name of Jesus. Thank You Lord.

Thank You Lord for Your trust. We marvel at Your trust of us. We fail You and sin against You and others every day by thought, by word and by deed, and still You trust us. We break our promises and forget our vows and still You trust us. We offend Your holiness and Your righteousness and still You trust us. We grieve Your Spirit and wound Your heart and still You trust us. We even fail to give You the full tithe and offerings that belong to You and still You trust us. Great is Your faithfulness and Your trust in us.

Thank You Lord for seeing potential and trustworthiness in us, even when we do not see it in ourselves. Thank You for imprinting Your image so deeply upon us that You can deem us trustworthy no matter how much sin has marred our countenance. Thank You for looking beyond our faults and seeing what can be salvaged and saved, sanctified and strengthened. Thank You for bringing us close to You and revealing Yourself to us.

We praise You for being so trustworthy Yourself that You can see trustworthiness in us. Now O God of love who dares to trust us, we affirm again our trust and belief in You. You alone are deserving of our highest praise and our total devotion. You alone are worthy. You alone are worthy. And in this moment of consecration and mediation we give ourselves anew to You, because You alone are trustworthy. In the name of our trustworthy Savior, Jesus Christ our Lord, do we pray, Amen.

DAY 42

– DAY 43 –

I CORINTHIANS 4: 6

Gracious God, we praise You for Your written word. We praise You for its timelessness. Even though it was written centuries ago to an ancient people, its truths are eternal. It still speaks to our current affairs and everyday circumstances. It still comforts the old, offers guidance to the young and empowers the middle aged to continue their journey toward wholeness, completeness and excellence. Old laws shed new light upon us. Old commandments inspire new commitments. Old stories speak to new situations. Old truths birth new testimonies. Old prophecies give new power.

We praise You for the right now message of Your ancient word. When our hearts are open and when we seek the guidance of the Holy Spirit, we can hear You speak through Your word, right now. Your word can fill us right now. Your word can increase our faith right now. Your word cheers us right now. Your word is a right now weapon against the enemy. Lord will You send a fresh word right now?

We praise You for the comprehensive and all-inclusive character of Your word. Your word has direction and deliverance, guidance and grace, power and perseverance, truth and triumph, salvation and strength, prosperity and power, finance and faithfulness for each of us no matter our circumstances.

Gracious God, we praise You for being who You are, the keeper and guarantor of every promise found in Your word. We praise You for Your holiness that sanctifies Your word. We praise You for Your perfection that completes Your word. We praise You for Jesus Christ the living embodiment of Your word. We praise You for the Holy Spirit who breathes Your word into us.

Grant us faith, we pray, to abide in Your word until we see You face to face. In Jesus name, do we offer this prayer, Amen.

– DAY 44 –

I CORINTHIANS 4: 7

Gracious God, we praise Your for loving kindness' and tender mercies that are so abundantly bestowed upon us far beyond our deserving. We praise You for mercy that is granted when we seek it and even when we fail to ask for it. We praise You for Your amazing grace. We praise You for the unsought and unmerited favor You pour into our lives.

Forgive us when we fail to appreciate all You do simply because You love us. Forgive us when we become inflated with pride and false self-righteousness because of the abundance of Your blessings. Forgive us when we allow the enemy to trick us into believing that we could ever deserve or that we could ever merit all of the rich benefits You pour into our lives.

We pray for a thankful heart and a contrite spirit that always seek to give You the glory. We pray for a generous spirit that seeks to bless others even as You have blessed us. We pray for bigness of spirit that does not begrudge Your favor that falls upon others. We pray for largeness of heart that is able to rejoice in the blessings of others. In Your name, we come against any spirit of littleness that seeks in any way to compare our blessing with others. We pray for discernment and right judgment to know whatever You have for us is for us, and whatever You have for others it is for them. We pray we will always remember that You have abundance we cannot even conceive and there is no competition for Your blessings. You have abundance for all of those who love You, who seek You and who strive to do Your will.

We thank You for grace heaped upon grace and mercies heaped upon mercies. We praise You for the grace of the Lord Jesus Christ who though he was rich he became poor so we through his poverty might become rich. We praise You for salvation that comes not by works but by grace through faith. We give You praise now for Your grace and in a nobler sweeter day beyond this life we anticipate praising You eternally.

When we've been there ten thousand years, Bright shining as the sun
We've no less days to sing Your praise than when we first begun.

(Amazing Grace, John Newton)

In Jesus name do we pray, Amen.

DAY 44

– DAY 45 –

I CORINTHIANS 4: 20

Gracious God, we praise You for power. We are grateful we do not have to live in fear of any demon because we have power. We are grateful we do not have to be bound by any limitations others may seek to impose upon us because we have power. We are grateful we do not have to stay down because we have been knocked down because we have power. We are grateful we can overcome whatever shame, mistakes or deficiencies there may be in our past because we have power.

We are grateful that our power does not originate in us and You are the source of our power. You, O God, who wakes the sun every morning and commands the stars to twinkle and the moon to glow in the midnight sky are the source of our power. You, O God, who has created the heavens and the earth and everything that is, are the source of our power. You, O God, who did not allow Your Son Jesus to remain in the tomb are the source of our power. You, O God, who are eternal, are the source of our power. You, O God, who has loved us with a perfect love, You, O God, who alone is worthy of all worship and adoration, You O God who is faithful beyond measure and human imagination are the source of our power.

Since, You are the source of our power, we can endure any midnight until joy comes in the morning. We can live through any season of trial until our change comes. We can wrestle with any stronghold until our breakthrough comes. Since, You are the source of our power we can withstand any criticism until the day of our vindication comes. We can face any demon knowing they may rise but they cannot prevail without our participation and consent.

We praise You God for Your creating power overshadows us. We praise You Jesus for Your redeeming power that abides with us. We praise You Holy Spirit for Your sustaining power that lives within us. Help us O Lord to live as the people of power You have created, called and consecrated us to be. In the name of the Lord Jesus, do lift this prayer, Amen.

– DAY 46 –

I CORINTHIANS 5: 6

Gracious God, we are grateful for Your redeeming power that helps us to overcome the weaknesses in our lives. We pray we will always remember we do not have to live in bondage to the weaknesses and the sins that still arise in our lives. We pray that we will always remember the damaging power of a little dab of sin. We pray that we will never be content with imperfection. We pray we will never be content with the journey over which we have come. We pray we will always remember we can go farther with You.

As Your redeemed and blood bought children, we pray we will always remember we represent You. In our conversations and in our concerns, we represent You. In our sorrow and with our smiles, we represent You. In our sickness and in our strength, we represent You. In our troubles and with our testimonies, we represent You. On our jobs and in our joy, we represent You. In our families and in our friendships, we represent You.

We pray we will represent You well as lights of the world, as salt of the earth and as a city that is set upon the hill that cannot be hidden. We pray we will represent You well as "a chosen race, a royal priesthood, a holy nation, God's own people, in order that (we) may proclaim the mighty acts of Him who (has called us) of out of the darkness and into his marvelous light." We pray we will represent You well as ambassadors and as messengers of Your saving truth.

Forgive us O God when we fail to represent You well. Forgive us O God when we start representing ourselves and our own self-serving agendas. Forgive us O God when we forget who we are and whose we are. Forgive us O God when we start acting as if our own hand delivered us and our own strength has brought us.

On this day, we again surrender ourselves to You and pray You will have Your way. Wherever we are, whether at home or at work, at church or at play, we surrender ourselves to You and pray You will be able to use us anywhere and at any time. Lord our heart's desire is to represent You well. And so we say to You, have Your way. To You be the glory for great things You have done. In the name of our redeemer, Jesus Christ our Lord, do we pray, Amen.

DAY 46

– DAY 47 –

I CORINTHIANS 5: 9-11

Gracious God, we confess that often Your word catches us and strips us naked of all self-righteousness, pretension and hypocrisy. We confess the weaknesses and failures that grieve Your spirit and cause us to fall short of Your glory. We confess, O God, the weaknesses and failings that cause us to live beneath our potential and beneath the vision You have for our lives. We repent of the times we should have said no when we said yes and those times when we should have said yes and said no. Forgive us for our foolishness and shortsightedness O God. Forgive us for failing to use the weapons of our warfare, which would have given us the victory in our times of testing.

However, we praise You O God for the compassion of Your word when our thoughts, words and deeds would condemn us. We praise You O God for the renewal as well as the reprimand that comes from Your word. When Your word exposes our problems, it also embraces us with a prescription, Jesus Christ our Lord. When Your word exposes our disobedience, it also embraces us with deliverance. When Your word exposes our rebellion, it also embraces us with redemption. When Your word exposes our mess, it also embraces us with mercy. When Your word exposes our hypocrisy, it also embraces us with help. When Your word exposes our sins, it also embraces us with salvation. When Your word exposes our weaknesses, it also embraces with a welcome. When Your word exposes our addictions, it also embraces us with affection. When Your word exposes our failures, it also embraces us with faith. When Your word exposes our guilt, it also embraces us with grace. When Your word exposes our habits, it also embraces us with healing. When Your word exposes our pettiness, it also embraces us with power. When Your word exposes our jealousies, it also embraces us with Jesus.

We praise You for love that is broad enough to hold all of us. We praise You for blood that covers all of us. We praise You for ears that hear all of us. We praise You for eyes of pity that look upon all of us. We praise You for Jesus who saves all of us. In his name do we pray, Amen.

DAY 47

– DAY 48 –

I CORINTHIANS 9: 1-2

Gracious God, we are grateful for an anyhow faith. We are grateful that You love us anyhow. When we are at our worst, You love us anyhow. When our sins grieve Your very heart, You love us anyhow. When we do not love ourselves, You still love us anyhow. When we break our vows and forget our promises to You, You still love us anyhow. When we fail to tithe in obedience to Your word, in thanksgiving for all Your blessings and in faith for Your continued provision, You still love us anyhow. When we give the devil more play and credit than we should, You still love us anyhow. When we take You for granted and act as if we have delivered ourselves by our own hands, You still love us anyhow. When we fail to say thank You and when we fail to give You the praise and when we fail to live for Your glory, You still love us anyhow.

We praise You for the anyhow love of the Lord Jesus, who we rejected and crucified and yet he died for our sins anyhow. We did not believe in his promise of resurrection and yet he rose anyhow. And now even though many of us have forgotten about the promise of his second coming, our Lord who never breaks a promise is coming back for us anyhow, whether we are ready to receive him or not.

Since You, Lord God, have set an example of an anyhow faith, we are grateful we can have such a spirit and attitude. Even though like the apostle Paul, there are others who may not like us, with You we can succeed anyhow. We have received power to be triumphant anyhow. No matter how long we have been in bondage or what we are in bondage to, through the Lord Jesus we can be free anyhow. We can be cleansed anyhow. We are saved and redeemed anyhow. We can become new creatures anyhow. We can have peace that passes understanding no matter what storms in life arise, anyhow. We have the victory anyhow; no matter how hard the enemy works to stop us.

We are so grateful for an anyhow faith, spirit and attitude. Now that we have been set free, help us to live as those who are truly free in Christ Jesus. And when it's all over Lord receive us to Yourself into the domain of eternity, anyhow. This we ask in the name of the Lord Jesus Christ, Amen.

DAY 48

– DAY 49 –

I CORINTHIANS 9: 19-22

We praise You Heavenly Father because You are not a one size fits all God. When we call upon Your name, You send a specific answer with our name on it to meet our specific problem. You have tailor made solutions for our difficulties and tailor made blessings for our situation. You have tailor made words for our dilemmas. You have a tailor made miracles for our circumstances.

Your salvation is tailor made for our sin. Your healing is tailor made for our sickness. Your power is tailor made for our need. Your mercy is tailor made for our mistakes. You have tailor made second chances for our failures. You have tailor made victories for our defeats. Your joy is tailor made for our sorrows. And when it's all over the Lord Jesus has prepared a place in heaven where we will abide in Your presence forever.

O God, in our witnessing to others and in our service to You, we pray we will be as flexible as You are. We pray we will bend without breaking and we will know when and how to compromise our methods without sacrificing our principles. We pray like the Apostle Paul we will become all things to all persons so we might gain some for Christ. We want to do Your will God not ours. We want to glorify You not ourselves. We desire to testify to Your goodness and not to any of our accomplishments.

Help us at all times to keep egos in place and the correct priorities in focus. We pray we will abide in You and You in us. We pray that we will not only be blessed but we will be a blessing to others. Even as the Lord Jesus gave his life as a ransom for many and even as Dr. Martin Luther King, Jr. lived and died to save others, we pray we too will live a life of service rather than selfishness and one of giving and not simply getting. For as Your servant St. Francis of Assisi has reminded us, "It is in giving that we receive and it is in dying that we are born again unto eternal life."

If we can help somebody as we pass along,
If we can cheer somebody with a word or song,
If we can show somebody where they are going wrong
Then our living will not be in vain.

(If I Can Help Somebody, Mahalia Jackson)

This we pray in Jesus name, Amen.

– DAY 50 –

I CORINTHIANS 9: 24

Gracious God, You have allowed us opportunities for victory. We do not have to live in fear or in bondage to our demons and our weaknesses. We do not have to live with shame or guilt. We do not have to live in fear or in failure. We can win. We can win in the race for freedom and deliverance. We can win in the race for integrity and intelligence. We can win in the race for morality and truth. We can win in the race for salvation against sin.

In the name of Jesus, we have the victory. In the indwelling presence of the Holy Spirit, we can win. Through Your rich and powerful word, we can win. Through Your sufficient grace and Your strength that is perfected in our weakness, we can win. Through the blood of Jesus, we can win. Through Your love and Your forgiveness we can win.

We can win over sickness and we can win over sorrow. We can win over depression of the mind and we can win over death of the spirit. We can win over our economic yokes and we can win over the mistakes that have kept us in strongholds of timidity. We can win over the strongest demons in hell; we can even win over the devil himself.

We pray we will run to win. Not simply run to finish but run to win. Not simply to place but run to win. No matter the opposition or the number of roadblocks, we pray we will always run to win. Even if we fall down, we pray we will get back up and run to win. We pray for correct prioritizing so we can run to win. We pray for proper preparation so we can run to win. We pray for power so we will run to win. We pray for perseverance so we will run to win. We pray for determination, dedication and daring so we will run to win.

We pray most of all that we will run looking to You Lord Jesus the author and perfecter of our faith who for the joy that was set before You, despised the cross, endured the shame and is now living Lord of our lives. Give us a vision of You as we travel our Damascus Roads, as Paul had, so we will run to win. Give us a vision of You as Stephen had in his dying hour, so we too will run to win. Give us a vision of You that John on Patmos had when he was in the Spirit on the Lord's Day, so we too will run to win. In Your own name do we pray, Amen.

DAY 50

– DAY 51 –

I CORINTHIANS 10: 16

Lord Jesus, You have bought us with a price; we are not our own. We live to glorify You. Lord Jesus, we know we were not redeemed with corruptible things like silver and gold but with Your own precious blood. Lord Jesus, we are grateful that if we confess our sins You are faithful and just to forgive and to cleanse us from all unrighteousness. Lord Jesus, You save to the utmost and Your blood cleanses us from all our sins. Lord Jesus, You came into the world to save sinners. We are witnesses of that truth because You have saved us.

Lord Jesus, we praise You for Your grace and Your willingness to exchange Your riches for poverty so we who were poor might become rich through Your poverty. Lord Jesus, Christ of God, the eternal creative word in the bosom of the Father who became flesh and dwelt among us, we adore You and whenever we bow at the communion table we remember how great a price was paid for our salvation.

Thank You for Your spilled blood and broken body, which testify to the stripes wherein we are made whole. Thank You for the cup of blessing which unites us with all You are. You are love and when we lift that cup we are united with that love. You are healing and when we lift that cup we are united with that healing. You are faithful and when we lift that cup we are united with that faithfulness. You are power and when we lift that cup we are united with that power. You have the victory over hell and the grave and when we lift that cup we who are believers are united with You and recipients of that victory. You are sufficiency and when we as believers lift that cup we are united with that sufficiency.

Thank You for the cup of blessing, the cup of cleansing and the cup of reminder. Thank You for the cup of thanksgiving and the cup of praise. "Your precious blood shall never lose its power till all the ransomed church of God be saved to sin no more." We love the Lord Jesus and we partake of the cup and the broken body with humility, with gratitude and with unending praise. In Your name do we pray, Amen.

DAY 51

– DAY 52 –

I CORINTHIANS 11: 20-22

Lord Jesus, we are grateful You do not discriminate. Your heart is large enough to love everyone one of us. Your arms are open wide enough to receive all of us. Your grace is sufficient for all of us. Your blood is able to cleanse each one of us. Your name is powerful enough to still the demons in each of our lives. Your presence is far reaching enough to be with each one of us. Your word is strong enough to support and to guide each of us.

We give honor and praise to the Holy Spirit whose fruit can blossom in the lives of all of us, whose comfort is available to all of us, whose gifts are bestowed upon each of us and whose power can equip all of us. We are grateful that the anointing, the empowering presence of the God, can fall upon each of us.

We are grateful Your plan of salvation has a nondiscriminatory clause that says, "Whosoever will, let him or her come." Whosoever needs forgiveness let him or her come. Whosoever needs another chance let him or her come. Whosoever needs a rock in a weary land and a shelter in a time of storm let him or her come. Whosoever needs renewal and new lease on life let him or her come. Whosoever has been stained by sin and assaulted by the devil let him or her come. Whosoever is broken and need healing let him or her come. Whosoever has been talked about, lied on and falsely accused let him or her come. Whosoever has been discouraged and needs strength to keep pressing their way to victory let him or her come.

> Just as we are without one plea but that Your blood was shed for us
> And that You bid us come to You, O Lamb of God we come, we come.
>
> Just as we are You will receive, will welcome pardon, cleanse, relieve
> Because Your promise we believe O Lamb of God we come, we come.
>
> (Just as I am, Without One Plea, Charlotte Elliot)

We come to You Jesus, lover of our souls, take us as we are and make and mold us into what You would have us to be and we shall give You the praise both this day and forevermore. In Your name do we offer this prayer, Amen.

– DAY 53 –

I CORINTHIANS 11: 19

Gracious God, we are grateful You work through the difficult situations in our lives to teach us who our friends are, to teach us something about ourselves and to teach us new things about You as well as to confirm the promises You have made. We are grateful like the stars at night, we see You most clearly and trust You most intimately in the darkness.

We taste of You in the daylight but we come to trust You in the darkness. We behold Your majesty in the daylight but we behold Your miracles in the darkness. We see Your righteousness in the daylight but we see Your redemption in the darkness. We see Your law in the daylight but we feel Your love in the darkness. We see Your holiness in the daylight but we see Your help in the darkness. We see Your command in the daylight but we feel Your caring in the darkness. We see Your fairness in the daylight but we see Your faithfulness in the darkness. We see Your strength in the daylight but we see Your salvation in the darkness. We see Your tenderness in the daylight but we see Your triumphs in the darkness.

We praise You even for those difficult situation from which our testimonies have come. Because we have been sick we can testify that You heal. Because we have fallen we can testify that You lift. Because we have been lonely we can testify that You are a company keeper. Because we have sinned we can testify that You forgive. Because we have made mistakes we can testify that You give second chances. Because we have been in need we can testify to Your sufficiency. Because we have been lost we can testify that You rescue and You restore. Because we have been worn down we can testify that You renew and revive. Because we have been confused we can testify that You guide. Because our way has been blocked we can testify that You make a way out of no way. Because we have had problems we can testify that You are a problem solver. Because we have been burdened we can testify that You are a burden bearer. Because we have carried heavy loads we can testify that You are a heavy load lifter.

We pray, O God, that You would speak to us anew and reveal Yourself afresh in the situations and circumstances in which we find ourselves and we will give You the glory. In Your name do we pray, Amen.

– DAY 54 –

I CORINTHIANS 11: 23-26

Gracious God, we are grateful for Your generous favor. When You bless us we do not feel burdened with guilt. You love us without lecturing us about our shortcomings. You lift us without berating us. You befriend us without belittling us. You forgive us without parading our failures in front of us. Like the disciples who sat at the table with You, You know all about our future desertions, denials and betrayals, and yet You invite us to Your church, Your kingdom and Your communion table.

No matter who we are, You welcome us to Your kingdom, Your church and Your communion table. No matter how we are dressed or how we look You welcome us to Your kingdom, Your church and Your communion table. No matter what we have done, You welcome us to Your kingdom, Your church and Your communion table. No matter what our race or gender or sexual preference, You welcome us to Your church, Your kingdom and Your communion table. No matter our background or who our parents are, no matter what kind of life we have lived or the kind of life we are living now, if we are willing to receive You, Lord Jesus, as our own personal Savior and Lord, You invite us to Your kingdom, Your church and Your communion table.

Thank You for Your gracious invitation to come and dine and come and live. If we need a Wonderful Counselor, a Mighty God, an Everlasting Father and a Prince of Peace, You have graciously invited us to come and dine and come and live. If we need a Sanctifying Savior, a Righteous Redeemer, a Faithful Friend and a Soul Satisfier, You have invited us to come and dine and come and live.

We came to You as we were,
Weary worn and sad,
We found in You a resting place
And You have made us glad.

(I Heard the Voice of Jesus Say, Horatius Bonar)

Thank You Gracious Lord for accepting, receiving and loving us. We now give ourselves anew to You, Lord Jesus and we pray during this season our lives will glorify You in new ways. In Your name do we pray, Amen.

DAY 54

– DAY 55 –

I CORINTHIANS 12: 14-15

We are grateful gracious Lord that we belong to You and You hold us fast. When we rebel against You, You still hold us in the hollow of Your hand. When we are engaged in self-destructive behavior, You still hold us in the hollow of Your hand. Until we give ourselves over totally to deprivation and to the devil, You still hold us in the hollow of Your hand. And even when we have gone completely astray, You still keep an eye upon us and are willing and ready to receive us back. We are grateful for the connection we have with You O Lord God, our Creator, Redeemer, Sustainer and Friend.

O Lord, we confess at times we break our connection with You. We recognize we are connected to You and to Your church as the foot and the other organs of our body are connected to each other. We are graven upon Your hand and are kept as the apple of Your eye. And so gracious Lord if in any way we have broken our connection with You, we come now to get reconnected again.

If like the Prodigal Son, we have strayed, we come now to get reconnected to You. If like Zacchaeus, we have allowed other people to block our view of You, we come now to get reconnected to You. If like Legion, we are haunted by demons by day and anxieties at night that cause sleep to flee, we come now in this moment to get reconnected to You. If like the Samaritan woman, we have or have had relationship problems that have separated us from You, we come now to get reconnected to You. If like Peter, our mistakes have brought us shame, we come now to get reconnected to You. If like Judas, we have betrayed our vows, our principles and our home training, we come now to get reconnected to You. If like the disciples, we have failed You in any way, we come now to get reconnected to You.

Or if like Nicodemus, we are feeling unfulfilled and are searching for a new depth in You, we come now to get reconnected to You. Receive us as we are O loving Lord and bring fresh fire to our spirits, new power to our witness and new joy to our service as we give ourselves anew to You even at this very moment. In the name of our Lord and Savior Jesus Christ do we pray, Amen.

DAY 55

– DAY 56 –

I CORINTHIANS 12: 18

Gracious God, we are grateful we have a space and a place in life. We have a space and a place because we have a function to fulfill. We have a space and a place because we are in Your will. We have a space and a place because we are Your work. As the hands and arms and feet have a place and a space in the body, we also have a place and a space in Your kingdom, Your church and in life.

No matter how others perceive us or classify us, we are grateful Your own hands have given us gifts and ensured we have space and a place. We are not a spare part, because You have assigned us a place and a space. We are not junk, You don't make junk; You make jewels. As Your gems, we have the red of the ruby because the blood of the Lord Jesus has covered us. As Your gems, we have the purple of the amethyst because we are royalty. As Your gems, we have the turquoise of the aquamarine because our horizons are as unlimited as the blue sky. As Your gems, we have the deep blue and black of the sapphire because we are they who have come over a way that with tears has been watered and our struggles have made us strong and beautiful. As Your gems, we have the clarity of the diamonds because our desire is to be so transparent that the beauty of the Lord Jesus can be seen in us.

Thank You Lord for creating us in Your own image, shaping us with Your own hands and gifting us with the same dexterity that causes the rain to show up as red in the rose, purple in the violet and yellow in the daffodil. Now gracious Lord, we seek Your forgiveness if in any way we have become disconnected from You and from Your body. We come now to claim our space and our place in You for those who the Son has set free are free indeed. We come now to claim our space and our place in You for greater is the one who lives in us than he who lives in the world. We come now to claim our space and our place in You because if anyone is in Christ they are a new creation, old things are passed away and all things have become new. In his name do we offer this prayer, Amen.

DAY 56

– DAY 57 –

I CORINTHIANS 15: 12

O risen, living, reigning and triumphant Christ, we pray for faith to believe in resurrection. No matter how devastating and demoralizing our crucifixion Fridays may have been, we pray for faith to affirm and to remember there is life beyond them. There is life beyond anxiety and anguish. There is life beyond bankruptcy and brokenness. There is life beyond defeat and divorce. There is life beyond fear and failure. There is life beyond our problems and our pain. There is life beyond loneliness and lostness. There is life beyond sin and shame. There is life beyond trials and tribulations.

O risen, living, reigning and triumphant Christ save us from a crucified mind that cannot move past the pain of Good Friday so the healing of Resurrection Sunday can rise with victory in its wings. Forgive us when we find it easier to believe in crucifixion than resurrection and in the finality of death more than life beyond it. Forgive us when we doubt Your resurrection and consequently our own.

O risen, living, reigning and triumphant Christ, we praise You for Your power to see signs of life when others, when even we ourselves, can only see death. Where others only see a mess You see a miracle. Where others only see an addict You see the anointing. Where others see only a habit You see healing. Where others only see a derelict You see deliverance. Where others only see problems You see potential. Where others only see gayness You see greatness. Where others only see weakness You see willpower. Where others only see a victim You see a victor. Where others only see helplessness You see hope. Where others only see a reject You see redemption. Where others only see a criminal You see one of Your children.

O risen, living, reigning and triumphant Christ,
Because You live we can face tomorrow,
Because You live all fear is gone.
Because we know that You hold the future,
And life is worth the living, just because You live.

(Because He Lives, William and Gloria Gaither)

In Your name do we pray, Amen.

– DAY 58 –

I CORINTHIANS 15: 3-5

Lord Jesus, we are grateful we do not have to live with shame anymore; we are grateful not only is Your love for us greater than our mistakes but Your vision for our lives is greater than our vices and Your victories are greater than our valleys. In spite of how we feel about ourselves and some of the things we have done or have been done to us, You still have a vision for our lives.

No matter what our past, You still have plans for us. No matter what our troubles You still have triumphs for us. No matter what our failures, You still have a future for us. No matter what our mistakes, You still have miracles to be birthed through us and from us. No matter what our problems, You still see potential in us. No matter what our history, You still have hope for us. No matter what our guilt, You still see greatness for us. No matter what our shame, You still have strength for us. No matter what our embarrassment, You still see excellence in us.

We are grateful we are still somebodies in Your sight. The world may look upon us as nobodies and mess-ups but the world does not see what You see. No matter what the verdict of others may be – no matter what the conclusions of our families, our friends, our spouses, our significant others, our coworkers, our schoolmates, even church people may be, You still see what they cannot see. No matter what the devil sees, You see what the devil does not see. While others look at the outward appearance, You look at our heart. Praise You Lord Jesus.

Thank You Lord for saving us not only from sin but also from shame, not only from enmity but also from embarrassment and not only from greed but from guilt. Even now, You are calling us from shame to self-acceptance, from guilt to growth and from embarrassment to eternity. As You appeared to Your disciple Peter in days past and gone, we pray we too will receive a new vision of You and the new life You are now calling us to lead and to live as we follow You, Your word and Your vision for our lives. In Your name Lord Jesus, do we offer this prayer, Amen.

– DAY 59 –

I CORINTHIANS 15: 3-5B

Lord Jesus, we are so grateful we do not have to live in fear anymore. We do not have to fear others. We do not have to fear the enemy because greater is the one who lives within us than the enemy who is in the world. We do not have to fear failure because You are a forgiving Lord who grants second chances. We do not have to fear sin because if we confess our sins, You are faithful and just to forgive and to cleanse us from all unrighteousness. We do not have to fear financial obligations and bills because You have promised to supply all our needs according to Your riches in glory. We do not have to fear the future because the earth is Yours and the fullness thereof, the world and they that dwell therein. We do not have to fear temptation because no temptation or testing has come to us that are not common to others. You are faithful and You do not allow us to be tested beyond our strength and with every test You provide a way out.

No matter how devastating our Calvary's may be, we do not have to fear them because You live. Because You live, Calvary does not have the last word. Because You live, humans and their judgments, their conclusions and their schemes do not have the last word. Because You live, our enemies, foes and opponents do not have the last word. Because You live, death does not have the last word. Because You live, lies do not have the last word. Because You live, the devil does not have the last word. Because You live, failure does not have the last word. Because You live, sin and shame do not have the last words. Because You live, fear does not have the last word. Because You live, hell does not have the last word.

You live to lift and You live to love. You live to forgive and You live to fight our battles. You live to inspire and You live to intercede. You live to protect and You live to preserve. You live to bless and You live to break strongholds. You live to reign and live to return.

> Because You live we can face tomorrow,
> Because You live all fear is gone,
> Because we know You hold the future,
> And life is worth the living, just because You live.
>
> (Because He Lives, William and Gloria Gaither)

In Your name Lord Jesus, do we offer this prayer, Amen.

– DAY 60 –

I CORINTHIANS 15: 6

Lord Jesus, we are grateful that before You stepped on a cloud and ascended back to Your heavenly Father, You took the time to appear to more than five hundred believers who had nothing to commend them except the fact they were believers. In that appearance, You showed us we have worth and value to You. Our prayers and our praise have worth and value to You. Our lives and our love have worth and value to You. Our tears and our testimonies have worth and value to You. Our souls and our service have worth and value to You. Our desires and our deliverance have worth and value to You.

We are grateful You appreciate faithfulness. We are grateful You appreciate those who belong to You even though we may not be considered important in the eyes of the outside world or even superstars in the eyes of the church. We do not have to be exceptional achievers to be loved by You. We do not have to be extraordinary to be loved by You. You love and honor those who are considered less talented as much as those who are considered more talented. You appreciate great followers as well as great leaders. You appreciate lesser lights as much as You do so-called greater lights. You appreciate the background as much as You do the foreground. You appreciate the second string on a team as much as the starting lineup.

When we would be tempted to put ourselves down, we pray we would remember how much You value us and how much worth You place upon us. We are worth so much to You, You left heaven's glory to be born among us, to live among us, to die for us. We are worth so much to You, You got up from the grave and went back to glory so You could continue to intercede for us as we wage war with the devil. You love us so much one day You are coming back for us to take us to a land fairer than day, to a home You have prepared for us, so we can abide with You forever.

Thank You for loving us and valuing us as You do. We pray we will love as persons who have been bought with the price of Your precious blood. We pray we will remember we are called to be a chosen race, a royal priesthood, a holy nation and Your own people so we might declare Your wondrous works Lord Jesus. Thank You for calling us out of darkness and into Your own marvelous light. In Your name do we offer this prayer, Amen.

– DAY 61 –

I CORINTHIANS 15: 7

O God, we praise You for dreams and visions. We pray You will continue to give us dreams and visions even when others do not understand and even when others think we are crazy. After all a number of Your servants as well as others who were used to advance humanity were considered to be crazy.

The great astronomer Galileo was called crazy. Great African Americans such as John H. Johnson, Harriet Tubman, Booker T. Washington, George Washington Carver and Dr. Martin Luther King, Jr. were all called crazy. Believers such as Noah, Moses, Esther, Shadrach, Meshach and Abednego were all called crazy. Philip, John the Baptist, Mary Magdalene, the women who were witnesses of our Lord's resurrection were all called crazy. The apostle Paul was called crazy and even our Lord and Savior Jesus Christ was called crazy.

O God, give us faith to walk to the beat of a different drummer. Give us boldness to follow where You lead even when others do not understand. Give us a discerning spirit so we can recognize You when the Holy Spirit speaks. Give us obedience so we will pursue what You show to us no matter what the cost.

And if along the way, we miss and mess up our opportunities, we pray for the knowledge that because our Lord lives we are forgiven for our mistakes and are given other chances. We pray we will not spend present time and energy speculating on what we might have done or what could have happened if we had taken advantage of opportunities that we may have missed. Give us boldness O Lord to live each day to the fullest for You.

We are grateful You are not finished with us yet and every new day testifies that we still have a charge to keep, a God to glorify and never dying souls to save and fit them for the sky. Help us to serve the present age, our calling to fulfill. We pray all of our powers will be engaged to do our Master's will. Now Lord of new opportunities help us to redeem the present so we can lay hold on our futures as we continue to live for Your glory and honor. In the name of our Lord, Jesus Christ do we offer this prayer, Amen.

DAY 61

– DAY 62 –

I CORINTHIANS 15: 7B

O eternal, reigning Christ, Your appearance to the apostles indicated their failures in the past were forgiven. Your appearance to the apostles indicated whatever failures they had were not fatal. Your appearance to the apostles indicated You are alive and well. We are grateful we are forgiven and even though failures frustrate, they do not have to be fatal. We are especially grateful that You are alive and well.

Because You are alive and well, we are never alone. In our ups and in our downs, when our backs are up against the wall and we do not know how we are going to make it, because You are alive and well, we are never alone. When we are so burdened we don't know where to begin with our prayer, because You are alive and well, we are never alone. When we are so strung out we feel we are going to pop or explode at any moment, because You are alive and well, we are never alone.

When everywhere we turn there is stress and trouble and tensions and demands, because You are alive and well, we are never alone. When those closes to us are doing the best they can and the mountain is still there, because You are alive and well, we are never alone. When loved ones have gone to glory, when family does not understand and friends have failed us, because You are alive and well, we are never alone.

When we are being laughed at like Noah, frustrated like Moses, attacked like Job and bereft like Naomi, because You are alive and well, we are never alone. When we feel challenged like Samson, when we are facing persecution like Daniel, even then we are never alone. When we are not welcomed like Elijah or when we are weeping like Jeremiah or have to watch our backs like Nehemiah, even then we are never alone.

When our hearts are breaking like Mary Magdalene, when we are desperate like the woman with the issue of blood, when we have sacrificed our all like the widow with two mites, even then we are not alone. When like You, Lord Jesus, we are rejected by our own, betrayed, misunderstood, mocked, deserted, falsely accused, crucified and buried, even then we are not alone. For You, O Lord, are alive and well. Praise to Your glorious and eternal name. It is in Your name, Lord Jesus that we offer this prayer and that with thanksgiving, Amen.

– DAY 63 –

I CORINTHIANS 15: 8-10

Gracious God, we are grateful for Your grace that is so freely and so fully given. We are grateful You not only bless us far beyond our deserving but You also bless us even without our asking. We are grateful for Your grace and Your goodness that cancels out our past. Because You love us, we do not have to feel intimidated by anyone anymore. Because You have cleansed, forgiven and set us free, we do not have to feel intimidated by anyone anymore. Because You have blessed us with talent and because You have blessed us in ways that are specific to our situation, we do not have to be intimidated by anyone anymore. Because whatever You have for us, it is for us, we do not have to be intimidated by anyone anymore.

Gracious Lord, we pray Your grace will not be extended to us in vain. When we hear, we pray we will heed. When we are burned, we pray we will learn. When we have been set free, we pray we will not again submit ourselves to yokes of bondage and strongholds of oppression. When we have been granted another chance, we pray we will not presume upon Your grace and mercy. When we fall and when we fail, we pray we will not be bound by guilt and by fear.

Now we have been loved and lifted, saved and strengthened, redeemed and restored, forgiven and freed, we pray we will bear fruit for the kingdom. Lord our desire is to be productive for You. We want to honor You with everything we have and everything we are in such a way that the lives of others will be blessed. O Lord, thank You for Your grace towards us. We recognize we are what we are and we have achieved whatever we have achieved by Your grace. Not by our goodness but by Your grace. Not by our contacts or our politics but by Your grace. Not by our wisdom but by Your grace. Not by our strength but by Your grace. Not by our righteousness but by Your grace. Not even by our efforts but by Your grace.

Help us, we pray, to live a life of grace towards others. Freely we have received, help us to freely give. Your word has told us those to whom much is given much is required. Help us to give to others not because it is required but because we are able to love with the same love with which we have been loved. In the name of Jesus do we offer this prayer, Amen.

– DAY 64 –

I CORINTHIANS 15: 31

Gracious God, we are so grateful for Your willingness and readiness to lift us up when we fall, to forgive us when we sin, to correct us when we stray and to love us when we are unlovely. We are grateful for Your voice which ever calls to us and Your hand that is always extended to us to save and to hold. We are grateful for the grace of the Lord Jesus Christ who though He was rich, He became poor so we who are poor might become right through His poverty.

We come on this day to make a new surrender to You. On this day, we die again to our sin so we can rise to Your salvation. We die again to our vices so we can rise again to Your vision. We die again to our vision so we can rise again to Your victories. We die again to self so we can rise again to Your strength. We die again to guilt so we can rise again to Your grace. We die again to Satan so we can rise again to our Savior, Christ. We die again to our ways so we can rise again to Your will. We die again to our rejection so we can rise again to Your redemption. We die again to our wants so we can rise again to Your wisdom.

We die again to our plans so we can rise again to Your providence. We die to our pettiness so we can rise again to Your pardon. We die again to our jealousies so we can rise again to Your joy. We die again to our greed so we can rise again to Your growth. We die again to our pride so we can rise again to Your purpose. We die again to our failures so we can rise again to Your faithfulness. We die again to our feelings so we can rise again to Your fullness. We die again to our flesh so we can rise again to Your forgiveness. We die again to this earth so we can rise again to eternity.

As we commit ourselves anew to You this day, we pray for staying power. When the adversary attacks, when opponents appear, when impatience builds, when unexpected difficulties come, we pray for staying power. When we are discouraged and frustrated, when we are troubled on every side and tempest tossed and storm driven, we pray for staying power. As You have been faithful to us, we pray we will remain faithful to You. In the name of our Lord Jesus Christ, do we offer this prayer, Amen.

DAY 64

– DAY 65 –

I CORINTHIANS 16: 8-9

We praise You for the opportunities You, gracious God, bring to our lives. We recognize opportunities also bring challenges and they come with opposition. We pray for faith to stay focused on opportunities rather than dwelling on the challenges and the opposition they bring.

We praise You because the door of opportunity to salvation and deliverance is wide open. We praise You because the door to healing and wholeness is wide open. We praise You because the door to freedom and fulfillment is wide open. We praise You because the door to prosperity and abundance is wide open. We praise You because the door to excellence and to eternity is wide open.

We praise You O Triune God, who in Your fullness has opened the door from death to life. We praise You Heavenly Father for grace that opens the door. We praise You Lord Jesus for being the door that leads to life. We praise You Lord Jesus for opening doors that no one can shut and for shutting doors on our past, our failures and our mistakes that no one can open. And because You have gone to prepare a place for us and because You are coming again to takes us with You to a land that is fairer than day, where we will be with You forever, we praise You for the door in heaven that is wide open to us. We praise You Holy Spirit for guiding us to the door. We praise You Holy Spirit for opening the door to Your fruits and to gifts You anoint for service. We are grateful for the word of God that opens Your promises to us.

We praise You for the door of the church that stands wide open and leads from sin to sainthood, from grace to glory and from dependence to deliverance. No matter what we have done, the door is opened wide enough to receive us. No matter who we are the door is now opened wide open to receive us. No matter how we look the door is now opened wide enough to receive us.

Now Lord, we pray we might live boldly as heirs of the promises who have been given power over all opposition that would hold us back from anything You will for us. O Lord help us to live humbly as those who are recipients of Your grace and mercy. This we ask in the name of the Lord Jesus, Amen.

DAY 65

– DAY 66 –

I CORINTHIANS 1: 1-11

Gracious God, we praise You for the redeeming, sanctifying, demon breaking, devil defeating, miracle working, transforming Lordship of Jesus Christ in the world and in our lives. We praise You because we have been sanctified and called to be saints. We praise You for the fellowship of believers in the Lord Jesus Christ. We praise You for the fullness of Your abundant unmerited and unsought grace. We praise You for Your peace, which the world cannot give and the world cannot take away without our consent and cooperation. We praise You for whatever gifts that have been bestowed by Your gracious hand and which enable us to be useful in Your service and a blessing to others. Most of all, we praise You for Your faithfulness.

O God, we pray for faith to live in confidence even when we are attacked and demeaned, criticized and denigrated by those who would do us harm. We praise You even now in accordance with Your word and promise, no weapon formed against us shall prosper, and every word that rises against us, You shall confute. We praise You for Your gifts that cannot be taken away by viciousness or destroyed by littleness and jealousy. We pray we will always be humble before the cross so You can rescue us in times of trouble and use us at all times and in all places.

We give You glory and honor for Your righteousness and holiness. We exalt Your name for Your might and majesty. We worship You and love You for who You are. We love You and adore You for Your faithfulness and Your forgiveness, Your power and Your patience; Your love and Your life. We pray at this season of our life, Your glory will be manifested in us. We pray we will bring forth-new life as the spring, blossom as the summer, reach maturity as in the fall and remain strong in the blast of winter. Thank You Lord even now for victories yet to be experienced, tests yet to be passed, mountains yet to be climbed, lessons yet to be learned, new levels yet to be reached and new glories yet to be encountered so You will get new glory from our lives. In Jesus name do we pray, Amen.

DAY 66

– DAY 67 –

I CORINTHIANS 2: 2

At the cross, at the cross where I first saw the light
And the burden of my heart rolled away,
It was there by faith I received my sight,
And now I am happy all the day.
(Alas, and Did My Savor Bleed, Isaac Watts)

Lord Jesus, we praise You for the cross, which is the eternal reminder of how much, You love us. Lord Jesus, we praise You for the cross which is the eternal reminder of how far You are willing to go for us. Lord Jesus, we praise You for the cross which is the eternal reminder of the great price by which our salvation was attained. Lord Jesus, we praise You for the cross which is the eternal reminder of Your obedience and submission to the will of God the Father. Lord Jesus, we praise You for the cross which is the eternal reminder of victory. Lord Jesus, we praise You for the cross which is the eternal reminder that the devil is defeated and he has no more authority over us and no hold upon us that has not already been broken.

We pray for the anointing of the Holy Spirit who empowers us to live up to our potential as those who have been redeemed by the cross. We pray for the guidance of the Holy Spirit who will instruct us how to stay free from the sin and the lifestyles that once held us in captivity. We pray for the presence of the Holy Spirit who comforts us as we continue to be harassed by a defeated devil. We pray for the power of the Holy Spirit who strengthens us in our weakness and give us courage to continue to look toward the cross as our emblem of hope.

As You have been obedient to death on the cross, we pray for an obedient spirit to Your word and will. As You have loved us with a perfect love, we pray our love will reflect Your faithfulness to us. As You have gone all the way for us, we pray we will not put our hands to the plow and look back. We pray we will go all of the way with You and for You. As You have completed the plan of salvation through the cross, we pray we will finish our course as we fight the good fight and keep the faith. As You have attained victory, we pray we will lay hold on the victory that has already been won for us. Jesus Christ, You who are Calvary's conqueror and Lord over the grave we offer this prayer in Your name, Amen.

– DAY 68 –

I CORINTHIANS 3: 1-4

Gracious God, we praise You for the journey over which You have brought us. We praise You for the growth we have experienced in You. Our desire O God is to reach the next level of our maturity as believers and followers of the Lord Jesus Christ. We want to grow from sin to salvation and then from salvation to sanctification and then from sanctification to strength and then from strength to service. We want to grow from endurance to excellence and then from excellence to eternity.

We want to move from guilt to grace and then from grace to giving and then from giving to generosity. We want to move from hurt to hope and then hope to healing and then from healing to helping and then from helping to heaven. We want to move from problems to prayer and then from prayer to power and then from power to praise. We want to move from fear to faith and then from faith to freedom.

O Lord, show us how to be victorious over the weights and sins in our lives that grieve You and prevent us from moving to the next level. Show us how to handle the people in our lives, our families and our friends as well as our foes, who may prevent us from moving to the next level. Help us to overcome our own laziness and comfort zones, our traditions and our habits that prevent us from moving to next level.

O God, prepare us now to go to the next level. We pray for faith to launch out into the deep. We pray for vision to see greater things. We pray for an obedient spirit to follow where You lead. We pray for willingness to sacrifice whatever hinders us. We pray for determination that does not give up and for perseverance and endurance that presses its way until higher heights are achieved.

Speak Lord, we Your servants are listening. Touch Lord, we Your servants are ready to start moving. Reveal Yourself O Lord, we Your servants are ready to see. Give us opportunities O Lord, we Your servants are ready to respond. In Jesus name, Amen.

DAY 68

– DAY 69 –

ACTS 1: 4-5

O God, we praise You for Your vision for our lives that is greater than any vision that we have for ourselves. Now God help us to discern what Your vision for our lives is and give to us the faith and the boldness to live in it, to walk in it, to anticipate it even before it happens. And when we are tempted to become involved in small and petty things, help us to remember You have a great vision for our lives. And when we are tempted to stoop to things that are beneath us, help us to remember You have a great vision for our lives.

O God, we pray You will prepare our hearts and our lives to receive all You have for us this very day. Help us to be obedient to Your word, Your Spirit and the leadership You have sent to us so we might receive the fullness You have for our lives. Help us to trust You in all things, to trust Your love and to know whatever You will for us is good and right and best, so we can be prepared to receive the fullness You have for our lives. Help us to be available and open to however You choose to bless us so we can receive the fullness You have for our lives. Help us to remember growth begins right now from where we are so we can receive the fullness You have for our lives.

And in our efforts to become bigger and better persons, in our efforts to become more prayerful and more attentive to Your word and Your will, in our efforts to live a more God glorifying life, help us to remember when we stumble and fall we do not have to stay down. Because we belong to You and because You are a loving, patient and forgiving God and Savior, we can dare to get back up. We can call upon Your name and You have promised to hear us and give us another chance. We praise You O God for Your faithfulness. We praise You Jesus for Your redeeming love and Your cleansing blood. We praise You O Holy Spirit for Your renewing power. Help us to know You O Holy Spirit as the abiding presence of God who never leaves us and help us to rely upon You in the midst of our warfare and in our efforts to grow to Your glory.

Now that we have spent this time with You, help us to know we are prepared for whatever we will face this day and this night and that greater is the power that is within us than any power that is in the world or in the very pit of hell. We go forth in Your name and we claim victory in the power of the Holy Spirit. We offer this prayer through our Lord Christ and through the intercession of the Holy Spirit who teaches us how to pray and what to pray for, Amen.

– DAY 70 –

ACTS 2: 1-4

We praise You Holy Spirit for Your presence among us. We praise You Holy Spirit for Your anointing upon us. We praise You for Your instruction and guidance of us. We praise You Holy Spirit for Your ministry of comfort to us. We praise You Holy Spirit for empowering us for service and for struggle. We praise You Holy Spirit because You abide with us forever. We pray You will help us to grow in our knowledge and in our relationship with You. We pray we will not only know You as fire or as force and simply as a spirit or ghost but as a person who loves and who lifts, who informs and who inspires and who enlightens and who encourages.

We praise You Holy Spirit for Your presence in the life of the church. For when You came, You came to the church. Individuals were privileged to receive You and to grow in You because they were gathered with Your church. Grow us through Your church to Your glory and honor we pray. When we start believing we can reach our maximum without the instruction and accountability of Your church; if arrogance of spirit ever draws close to our hearts and minds, O Holy Spirit will You gently humble us and lead us back into communion and fellowship with Your church. We love You Holy Spirit for who You are in and of Yourself. Forgive us for those times we grieve You or quench Your presence. Forgive us and help us to surrender and overcome those things in our lives, which hinder Your work of growth in our lives.

Holy Spirit help us to discover our gifts and to use them to edify You and strengthen Your church. We pray for Your fruit Holy Spirit to be manifested in our lives. We pray for love, joy, peace, patience, kindness, generosity, faithfulness, gentleness and self-control. Now, Holy Spirit encourage our hearts when we feel like giving up, renew us when we are drained and give us peace when we are stressed. Help us live so when life's uneven journey is complete we will be able to praise You throughout ceaseless ages. In Your precious name do we pray through Christ Jesus our Lord, Amen.

DAY 70

– DAY 71 –

ACTS 3: 1-6

Gracious God, we come to You grateful that in the name of Jesus we can walk away from all of those things that have held us bound, have held our spirits and our minds captive and have placed our souls in jeopardy. We are grateful we do not have to remain where we are and the way we are, in the name of Jesus we can stand up and walk away from what is demeaning, belittling and unlike You; and from what is beneath us as children of the Heavenly King. We praise You Jesus for another chance. We praise You O Holy Spirit for power to walk away. We praise You gracious God for Your keeping power.

We pray, dear Jesus, we will never be content with handouts when You are offering us hope, we will never be content with begging when You are offering us bounty and we will never be content with sin when You are offering us salvation. We praise You Jesus for the power of Your name. Your name gives victory over disease and drugs, depression and dependency and over death and damnation. We pray as we live every day of our lives we will take the name of Jesus with us as a shield from every snare and when temptations around us gather, we pray for faith to breathe that holy name in prayer. "Precious name, oh how sweet, hope of earth and joy of heaven; Precious name oh how sweet, hope of earth and joy of heaven." (Precious Name, Lydia O. Baxter)

Now dear Lord, we pray that our lives will glorify You this day for all You have done in us and for us and for all You continue to do through us and with us. We pray our lives will be one continuous anthem of praise and glory to You. And if we are ever tempted to think negative about ourselves and doubt our capability to overcome anything that comes our way, we pray for faith to remember Your name has given us power not only to walk away from some things but to walk in power, in faith and in the confidence Your word has promised that no weapon formed against us shall prosper and that greater is the power that is within us than any power that is in the world or under the world. We praise You Jesus, we love You and we glorify You for who You are and we thank You for all ou have done and for walking in power . In Your precious name do we offer this prayer, Amen.

– DAY 72 –

ACTS 4: 13-14

O God of grace and glory, we praise the opportunities You send every day to keep growing to Your glory. We recognize O Lord if we seek to grow to the vision You have for our lives we will not only have supporters we will also face some opposition. We pray no matter what the opposition we face, no matter where it comes from, no matter how many barriers are in our way or how high the mountains or how deep the valleys, we pray for faith to stay focused on You who will give us the victory. As our Lord Jesus steadfastly set his face to go to Jerusalem, we pray for the same persevering spirit to keep our eyes on the prize of the upward call and to stay fixed on growth.

So grow us Lord we pray. Grow us beyond doubters and skeptics. Grow us Lord. Grow us beyond racism, prejudice, sexism and any of the other "isms" in life that limit growth. Grow us Lord. Grow us beyond procrastination, excuse making and the "I Can't Spirit." Grow us Lord. Grow us beyond being overly concerned about the limited perspectives, opinions and judgments of others. Grow us Lord. Grow us beyond mean spirited competiveness and small-minded jealousy and statue reducing pettiness. Grow us Lord. Grow us beyond fear and into faith. Grow us beyond guilt and into grace. Grow us beyond sin and into salvation. Grow us beyond weakness and into wisdom. Grow us beyond poverty and into prosperity. Grow us beyond messes and into miracles. Grow us so the life we live will speak for us. Grow us so the work we do will speak for us. Grow us so the service we give will speak for us. Grow us so the victories we achieve through You will speak for us. We pray what You do in us and with us and through us will answer whatever opposition to our growth that we encounter in our lives.

We pray that our words, our works, our worth and our worship will be living testimonies to the truth we have been with You and You have done extraordinary things with our ordinary lives. We pray this very day, yes even in this moment, our lives will begin to grow fruit to Your glory. In the name of Jesus do we pray, Amen.

DAY 72

– DAY 73 –

ACTS 5: 1-11

Gracious God, we praise You for Your power and we thank You for the ministry of Your Holy Spirit which gives us the victory even in situations of discouragement and difficulty. We confess O Lord there are times when we feel like giving up because we have met persons who have disappointed us in the church and elsewhere. We confess O God we sometimes become very angry and cynical when we discover that some persons are not what they seem. But when we would be too harsh in our assessments and judgment of others would You gently remind us O Lord we are not perfect either and we also fall short of Your glory.

Therefore we pray for patience when we meet persons with an Ananias and Sapphira spirit, persons who are manipulative and who have the façade of sincerity and generosity and caring but not the substance. Help us Lord to be real in what we do and say. We come against self-seeking vainglories in our own spirit and life. Help us to keep our own egos in check. We pray for a spirit that keeps us humble before the cross so You can get the full glory out of our lives.

We are grateful You are Lord of the church. And when we would take ourselves, our power, and our roles too seriously, O Lord we pray for Your guidance in turning our focus towards You. Not ourselves but You O Lord. Not our will but Yours O Lord. Not the faults or failings of others but You O Lord. You alone bring healing for our diseases and You alone save to the utmost. You alone will bring us through the difficulties of life and You alone can bring the growth to our lives and our faith that we need. You alone hold a vision for our lives that is greater than anything we can imagine. So God, we pray for faith to make new commitments to You even in our discouragement and even when we have been hurt or disappointed by others because You alone can bring us through our valleys and into new victories. We pray this prayer in the name of Jesus, Amen.

DAY 73

– DAY 74 –

ACTS 5: 12-21

We praise You Gracious God for the Holy Spirit who fills our lives. We praise You for the Holy Spirit who anoints and equips our lives. We praise You for the Holy Spirit who bestows gifts upon and brings forth fruit from our lives. We praise You for the Holy Spirit who directs our footsteps. We praise You for the Holy Spirit who enlightens our minds. We praise You for the Holy Spirit who inspires our hearts and who puts fire into our souls. We praise You for the Holy Spirit who flows through us.

We seek a right understanding of the Holy Spirit. Help us O Spirit of truth to understand that You come into our lives not only to bless us but also to flow through us into the lives of others. We pray we will be fit and worthy vessels for the in pouring and the outpouring of Your Holy Spirit into the lives of others. We pray for a spirit of giving and a spirit of generosity. We pray we will not covet or hoard Your gifts or Your blessings. We pray we will always remember we are blessed to be a blessing and we receive in order to give to others so You O God will be glorified. We come against a spirit of selfishness, arrogance or greed regarding the blessings You so abundantly pour into our lives.

Thank You for whatever You have given to us, now Gracious God help us to give back not grudgingly or of necessity but joyfully, prayerfully and with thanksgiving. For as we give, You continue to give back so much more to us. We praise You Lord for the continuing generosity You pour into our lives. And if we ever come under attack because of the gifts You pour into our lives, we pray for faith to remember You will deliver when the enemy seeks to steal our joy if we would put our trust in You.

So here we are Lord Your servants. We commit our lives, our money, our possessions, our families, our loved ones, our careers, our faith and our church to You. In our darkness, we trust You for the light. In our valley, we trust You for the victory. In our struggles, we trust You for Your salvation. In our trials, we trust You for our triumphs. When we are burdened, we trust You for our breakthroughs. In our loneliness, we trust You for Your love. In our depression, we trust You for Your deliverance. In our sickness, we trust You for healing and for grace that is sufficient and for strength that is perfected in our weakness. In the name of Jesus do we pray, Amen.

DAY 74

– DAY 75 –

ACTS 5: 27-32

O God, we praise You for Your word because Your word is true and eternal. We praise You for Your holiness because You are altogether lovely and right and we cannot err when we follow You. We praise You for Your mercy that is available to all generations. We praise You for Your salvation that redeems the lowest from their sins to the highest from themselves and their pride. We praise You for Your love that is unconditional and reaches farther than the farthest star in the heavens. We praise You for Your presence that is closer than breathing and nearer than hands and feet and that never leaves us or forsakes us.

Because of who You are and all You are we will follow You rather than human authorities. You have the last word over our destinies and our lives. You have the last word over our sicknesses and diseases. You have the last word about our salvation. We pray for sense to follow You no matter where You lead us. We pray for courage to follow You no matter where You lead us. We pray for love and faith to follow You no matter where You lead us. If You lead us to Calvary, we know that resurrection is the last word. If You lead us to the very valley and shadow of death, even there Your rod of power and Your staff of love shall comfort us. If You lead us into affliction and sickness we know Your grace will be sufficient and Your strength perfected in our weakness.

When the voices of this world and the tempter speak loudly in our ears, trying to pull us away from You, we pray for presence of mind as well as, the will to call upon the name of Jesus and we will continue to walk in paths of righteousness. Therefore speak Lord, we Your servants are listening. We will follow You because we have learned not only from Your word but from our own experience, that all things work together for good to them who love You; to those who are called according to Your purpose. In the name of Jesus do we pray, Amen.

DAY 75

– DAY 76 –

MATTHEW 21: 1-17

Gracious Lord, we pray when we experience our Palm Sundays of glory, we will have Your focus and not allow our heads to be turned or to swell from shouts of glad Hosannas from an adoring but fickle crowd. We pray for faith that keeps us grounded, for conviction that keep us stable, gratitude that keeps us humble, worship that keeps us thankful and an eye that is single to Your glory.

We pray we will remember even in moments of glory, we will need the same things that helped us to get where we are. We cannot face forward and watch our back at the same time. When we are facing forward, we will need people to help watch our back. And when we are looking backwards, we will need someone to help guide us forward.

The same praise and prayer that helped us get to certain places is needed to keep us there. The same discipline and hard work that helped us get to certain places is needed to keep us there. The same commitment and devotion that helped us get to certain places is needed to keep us there. The same determination and perseverance that helped us get to certain places is needed to keep us there. The same kindness and smile that helped us get to certain places is needed to keep us there. The same Holy Spirit and holiness that helped us get to certain places is needed to keep us there.

Therefore, if our name is Abraham, we pray we will keep believing. If our name is Joseph, we pray we will keep dreaming. If our name is Moses, we pray we will keep leading. If our name is Job, we pray we will keep trusting no matter what. If our name is Deborah, we pray we will keep fighting. If our name is Daniel, help us to keep praying. If our name is Malachi, we pray we will keep tithing.

If our name is John the Baptist, help us to keep preaching. If our name is Jesus, help us to keep forgiving. If our name is Paul, help us to keep writing. If our name is Barnabas, help us to keep encouraging. If our name is Mary Magdalene, help us to keep giving and making sacrifices. If our name is Dorcas, help us to keep serving.

You have empowered us to live through difficult times. Now give us presence of mind and focus of faith to triumph over the seduction of success that can overcome us in a Palm Sunday moment. We offer this prayer in Your name, Lord Jesus, Amen.

DAY 76

– DAY 77 –

ACTS 5: 33-39

We come to the garden alone, while the dew is still on the roses
And the voice we hear calling on our ear, The Son of God discloses
You walk with us; You talk with us; You tell us that we are Your very own,
The joy we share as we tarry there, none other has ever known.
(In the Garden, Charles Miles)

O God, we praise You for the abiding presence of the Lord Jesus Christ. His presence in our lives means we cannot be stopped. Sickness cannot stop us because his grace is sufficient for us. Trials can't stop us because He is a conquering king. Persecution can't stop us because greater is His presence with us than anything that we will face in the world. Sin can't stop us because He saves to the utmost. Our weaknesses can't stop us because He is our strength. Demons can't stop us because His name causes devils to flee. Not even death can stop us because He is the resurrection and the life.

We pray dear Lord we will always be centered in Your will and Your plan because when we abide in You and You abide in us not only do we find our highest and greatest joy, we also find our truest strength and the source of real power. We pray for a faith that will stand the test of time and for faithfulness that will press its way until our victory is consummated and complete. We love You Lord for who You are and for providing everything we need in Your word, in the name of Jesus and in the ministry of the Holy Spirit to live saved and sanctified in this life that these mortal bodies might be glorified in the life to come.

Now Lord, while we remain in this life please continue to glorify us to Your glory so the beauty of the Lord Jesus might be seen in us to the end that Your erring children might be inspired to seek You and to know You for themselves. We marvel Lord when we look back and see from where You have brought us. Now take us to new and more vibrant places in You. We pray we will continue to grow to Your glory for as long as we live. Speak to us Lord, we Your servants are listening. In Jesus name do we pray, Amen.

DAY 77

– DAY 78 –

ACTS 6: 1-7

O God, there are so many distractions to turn our attention away from You and the vision You have for our lives. There are so many temptations to focus on things other than that which leads to growth. And we confess O Lord there have been too many times we have taken our eyes off of the prize and been carried away with the fleeting pleasure of sin. We confess that we have often comprised our faithfulness because of our own fears and we have not walked in the way of salvation because of our own shortsightedness. We confess O Lord that too often we have listened to the voice of discouragement rather than the small prompting and nudging of the Holy Spirit and too often we have followed the counsel of others instead of the promises of Your word. There have even been times when we have allowed our personal feelings and our perceptions of slights done to us in the household of faith to take our eyes off of You the giver of every good and perfect gift.

Forgive us O God for the times we have allowed small things to turn us aside from high purposes. We now make new commitments to stay in Your word and to develop a prayer life. When we keep our focus on You and when we are guided by Your word, stuff and circumstances that arise to irritate us and distract us will not define our priorities, diffuse our fire, defeat our vision, destroy our focus or drive our life. So Holy Spirit, we pray You will speak to our lives afresh this day. Word of God living, incarnate and now reigning and interceding, O Lord Christ will You show us again Your salvation when we are tempted to live lower than we should. O God our Father will You hold us close when tempests rage and storm clouds rise. We pray the vision You have for our lives will arise before us when the devil attacks so we might stay on course and stay in You.

Our desire is to stay focused on You in spite of the stuff that arises to turn us around. Even as we labor with stuff in our lives and even before new stuff comes, we thank You and praise You even now for our victory. In Jesus name do we pray, Amen.

– DAY 79 –

ACTS 6: 8-15

Gracious God, we praise You because no matter the categories where others have placed us and have tried to keep us, we can grow beyond them. When others try to convince us that because we are women or men or young or old or black or white or Hispanic that we can only expect to rise but so high, we praise You that we can outgrow the expectations of others and even ourselves. When others try to convince us that because of our backgrounds or past mistakes we can only expect to go so far and do so much in life, we praise You for Jesus our Savior and Lord who helps us to grow beyond the expectations and categories of others. We praise You for the Holy Spirit whose anointing makes our rising possible. We praise You for the promises of Your word, which makes our rising possible. We praise You for each new day, which call us to rise and outgrow the accomplishments of yesterday.

We praise You that those whom the Son has set free are free in deed. We are free from guilt and from fear. We are free from the limits imposed upon us by others. We are free from the eternal hold of death and sin and the devil. We praise You when we abide in You we never stop growing and there is always some place new to go and to grow in You. Like Your servant Stephen of old, give us an anointing that allows us to grow beyond the categories of people. Like Your servant Stephen of old, implant Your word in our hearts and minds so we will not stray but will grow beyond the categories of people. Like Your servant Stephen of old, give us a heart for You so that we can grow beyond the categories of people. Like Your servant Stephen of old, give us boldness and power in our witness. Like Your servant Stephen of old, give us grace in our growth so we will not become arrogant and filled with conceit as we grow beyond the categories of people.

And like Your servant Stephen of old, grow us so much we will be privileged to see You face to face and hear Your hearty "Well done" when life's uneven journey is over. This we ask in Jesus name, Amen.

DAY 79

– DAY 80 –

PSALM 94: 14

O God on this day, we praise You and celebrate You for Your faithfulness. You have not forsaken us. When we would not obey Your law, You sent prophets and when we would not listen to them, You sent Your only Son Jesus whom You have appointed joint heir of all things.

We praise You for the obedience of Jesus Christ and the length, breadth and depth he went for our redemption. We praise You for his incarnation. We praise You for his 33 year sojourn among us during which time the sick were healed, demons were cast out, the dead were raised and the poor had the good news preached to them. We praise You for his example of caring and his paradigm of obedience. We praise You for his call to fickle disciples such as we are to demonstrate our possibilities in him. We praise You for his prayer life as well as his passion, suffering and even the death by which we have been redeemed. We praise You for the institution of the Lord's Supper as a perpetual reminder of the faithfulness of a promise keeping God who did not withhold his only Son for our redemption but freely gave him up for us. We praise You for his example of humility in foot washing and his new commandment that we should love one another. We praise You for his resurrection which established him as Lord indeed of life and history. We praise You for his ascension, exaltation, ministry of intercession and promise of return.

God over and over again You have shown You will not forsake Your people and You will not abandon Your heritage, Your redeemed, Your believing remnant, Your church — those who are faithful to You. Our continuing prayer is we will be as faithful to You as You have been to us, as loving of You as You have been to us, as zealous for You as You have been for our salvation and as earnest about You as You have been about us. In Jesus name do we pray, Amen.

DAY 80

– DAY 81 –

ACTS 8: 14-17

Holy Spirit, we greet You with joy and thanksgiving. We seek to come to a closer knowledge of You as a person. We seek to understand more fully how You live within us and how Your gifts operate in our lives. Our desire is not only to know You casually but intimately. Our desire is not simply for You to dwell within us but to experience Your full baptism and release of the power and the presence that is within us. Those of us who have received Your baptism desire a new in filling. Holy Spirit even as we pause in prayer will You be released in us in new ways right now? Holy Spirit, will You refresh us and restore us and build up the torn down and worn down places in our lives and spirits right now? Holy Spirit, will You bring forth Your gifts for Your glory and the edification and strengthening of the church? And Holy Spirit will You teach us how to walk in those gifts and when and where and how they are to be used? Holy Spirit will You plant and bring forth Your fruit of love, joy, peace, patience, kindness, generosity, faithfulness, gentleness and self-control.

We praise You for Your presence that enables us to confess Jesus Christ as Lord. We praise You for Your faithfulness in that You abide with us forever. We praise You for the comfort, the fire, the energy, the growth, the boldness, the prayer power and the victories that You bring. We pray You will continue to have Your way in our lives. Our desire is for self to be crucified so our Lord Christ will be glorified. Our desire is to be more and more like Jesus every day. Our desire is to grow from strength to strength and from glory to glory. So have Your way Holy Spirit. In our worship and praise have Your way. In our witness and work have Your way. In our giving and in our living have Your way. We love You Holy Spirit for all that You continue to do through us and sometimes in spite of us. Teach us the way we should go, lead us into the path wherein we should walk and then give us the love, the courage and the discipline and diligence to walk where You lead. In the name of Jesus do we pray, Amen.

DAY 81

– DAY 82 –

ACTS 8: 14-17 AND 25

We praise You gracious God for the power of the Holy Spirit that breaks generational bondage. We are grateful that no matter what our background, our heritage and our history we can become new persons in Christ Jesus. We praise You for the power of the Holy Spirit that overcomes all weaknesses and all history. We are grateful that Jesus did not respect long-standing traditions of prejudice and division that existed between his people and the Samaritans. We are grateful that the Holy Spirit fell upon the Samaritans even though they were not in the number on the Day of Pentecost. We praise You for the non-discriminatory policy of heaven that says whoever confesses Jesus with their lips as Savior and believes in their hearts that he has been raised from the dead, can be saved. We praise You for the non-discriminatory policy of the Holy Spirit who is poured out upon all flesh, whether male or female, or rich or poor, or black or white.

Now Gracious God, we pray we might have the courage and the boldness to walk in the freedom and the liberty we have been given in Christ Jesus and by the Holy Spirit. We praise You that no weapon formed against us will prosper. Now help us to battle the demonic forces that seek to divide Your people and Your kingdom. We pray we will always walk in the reality that we can outgrow our generational bondage. When others try to impose ceilings on our dreams and aspirations, Your vision for us and Your gifts bestowed upon us, we pray we will always remember greater is Your power and presence that lives within us than any challenge we will face in this life. What matters in Your sight is not where we came from but where we are going and in Christ Jesus and through the power of the Holy Spirit, we are going upward and forward, not looking back except as a point of reference and not looking down. Holy Spirit, please renew us now and if we have allowed ourselves to become bound again, touch us again and fall upon us afresh we pray, in the precious name of Jesus, Amen.

DAY 82

– DAY 83 –

RUTH 4: 13-17

Lord Jesus, we are grateful that today You not only have a vision for our recovery, You have a vision for our resurrection. Recovery is about getting over something that has happened but resurrection is about newness You cannot even conceive coming to You. Recovery is about getting over bitterness but resurrection is about new birth. Recovery is about getting over disappointment but resurrection is about deliverance. Recovery is about getting over emptiness but resurrection is about the coming of excellence.

Recovery is about getting over frustration but resurrection is about fulfillment. Recovery is about getting out of hell but resurrection is about happiness. Recovery is about getting over loss but resurrection is about new life coming to You. Recovery is about making it but resurrection is about a make-over. Recovery is about moving beyond pain but resurrection is about the coming of power. Recovery is about survival but resurrection is about salvation. Recovery is about getting over nightmares but resurrection is about new dreams.

That is the reason the story of Naomi and Ruth is a good example of no matter what we have been through, no matter how old or how young we are and no matter how many of our dreams have not come true, "It's all right to dream again." The resurrection of Jesus says to each of us, "It's all right to dream again."

Even though some things have not turned out as we had hoped and even though things look darker and more uncertain than they have ever looked before, still, "It's all right to dream again." No matter what we have been through and no matter what the devil, life, enemies or our own shortsightedness and foolishness have done to our dreams in the past, "It's all right to dream again." No matter what other folk say or think, a living and loving Jesus who went to the cross and overcame it so we could have forgiveness for sins and another chance at life wants us to know, "It's all right to dream again."

O Living and Resurrected Lord, we praise You for the privilege to dream again. We are grateful that You still have a vision that is greater than any vision we can have for ourselves or that others can have for us. Now we pray that our dreams would be aligned with Your vision and You would give us courage and faith to follow only You as You lead us to vistas of living that far exceed our expectations. In Your name, Lord Jesus, do we offer this prayer and that with thanksgiving, Amen.

– DAY 84 –

ACTS 9: 1-9

We praise You O God for grace and mercy that interrupted our lives and put us on a new course. We give praise for Jesus who interrupted our lives when we were headed in the wrong direction and put our feet on a street called straight. We give praise for the Holy Spirit who gives new programming for our lives. O God when You are speaking and we are too stubborn and self-centered to hear, we seek Your forgiveness. When You are trying to grow us and we are so set upon our own agenda, we refuse to move to another level, we seek Your forgiveness. When are so blinded by short term thrills and pleasures we jeopardize and sacrifice long term gains, please O Lord forgive us. Save us from ourselves O Lord according to Your steadfast love.

When we would walk in our own willful ways and follow our own minds, interrupt us with Your word of correction and truth. When we would be led astray by the wiles of the devil and the fleeting pleasures of sin, interrupt us O God with Your hand of might and grace. When we become so confused and we listen to the wrong voices and follow the wrong counsel, interrupt us O God with love and forgiveness. When we allow disappointment and discouragement to turn our heads from You and Your will, interrupt our rebellion lest we lose the joy of our salvation.

We are grateful for the gospel that interrupts depression with hope. We are grateful for the blood of Jesus that interrupts bondage with deliverance. We are grateful for the Holy Spirit that interrupts weakness with power. We are grateful for Your grace that interrupts self-pity with blessings that are unsought and unearned. We are grateful for the church and for the saints that interrupts loneliness with fellowship of like-minded believers. We are grateful for Your word that interrupts error with the truth.

O Lord grow us beyond our original programming. And when we receive Your word of truth, salvation and grace we pray we will have the courage to change channels so Your program of redemption and transformation, of salvation and new opportunities and a new creation will be played in our lives. This we ask in Jesus name, Amen.

DAY 84

– DAY 85 –

ACTS 9: 10-18

O God, You have such a great vision for our lives. Help us to grow beyond our reservations and hesitations. Forgive us O God when we are our own worst enemies. Forgive us O God when we stand in the way of our own blessings and breakthroughs. Forgive us O God when we give in to our fears rather than trusting in Your vision for us. Forgive us O God when we allow our comfort zones to stand in the way of new thresholds You desire to bring us to. Forgive us O God when we allow our traditions to straight jacket us and limit our flexibility to the new things You desire to do in our lives.

O God, we know there is another level You desire to take us to-another level of living and loving, another level of giving and service, another level of blessing and being a blessing, another level of worship and work, another level of power and peace, another level of virtue and victory. Like Your servant Ananias of old, we pray for faith to follow where You speak. We pray for discernment to recognize Your voice when You speak. We pray for a prayer life that allows time for You to speak to us. We pray for boldness to follow Your instructions when You speak. We pray for the anointing to do what You ask us to do when You speak. We pray for an obedient spirit that follows You when You speak even when what You ask is difficult or not something that is in our will or mind to do.

Speak Lord Your servant is listening. Speak Lord and we will follow. Speak Lord because we have a heart for You. Speak Lord for our delight is to do Your will. Speak Lord because we are open and available to You. We love You Lord so grow us just a little taller and take us a little deeper into Your will and word this day and move us from beyond our hesitations and our helplessness, our reservations and our reservations. For it is only in our yielding we receive the fullness of life. In Jesus name do we pray, Amen.

DAY 85

– DAY 86 –

ACTS 10: 1-8

O God, we pray for faith to follow You even when we can only see one step at a time. We confess O God our desires to want to know more than we should and to see farther than we ought. We confess while we recognize we walk by faith and not by sight; so many times our desire is to walk by sight. We confess O Lord our desire for a roadmap rather than guidance by Your unseen hand and by the Holy Spirit.

We pray for the measure of faith that is content to trust You to work out the details of the visions You show to us. We pray for a discerning spirit that recognizes Your will and Your voice in our lives. We pray for boldness and courage to follow You even when You call us to walk in paths where we have never gone before. We pray for openness of mind and spirit that calls us to grow to levels where we have never even thought about going before. We pray for openness of mind and spirit that is not afraid of the new, the different, the untested, the untried and the non-traditional.

We praise You for Your omnipotent power. You are able to accomplish what You desire for us when we yield ourselves to You. We praise You for Your watchful eye. You not only see all we do but You see how others may plan to block Your vision for our lives. We praise You for Your care and compassion. You love us enough not only to watch over us but also to protect us when we yield ourselves to You.

So speak Lord and we will follow, as we trust You to work out the details of Your plan for us. Thank You even now for leading us from the valley and the shadows of death into eternal green pastures of rest and renewal. Thank You even now for leading through Calvary to the glory and victory of the resurrection experience. We praise You because all things still work together for good to them who love You, to those who are called according to Your purpose. In Jesus name do we pray, Amen.

– DAY 87 –

GENESIS 11: 1-9; ACTS 2: 1-12

Gracious God, we praise You for the privilege of prayer. We seek discernment so we will know when You are speaking to us and directing us and when we are speaking and directing ourselves. Your word has instructed us that if in all our ways we acknowledge You then You will direct our paths. O God when we come to You there are times when we are assaulted by so many conflicting voices from within and without. We pray You will speak clearly, move clearly and reveal Yourself clearly so we will know beyond a shadow of a doubt it is You.

Forgive us O God when we have run ahead of You. Forgive us O God when we have been so caught up in our own agenda we failed to consult You and then failed to heed You when Your Spirit tried to direct us. Forgive us O God when we have relied on our own strength. Forgive us O God when we tried to get the glory for self. Forgive us O God when we listened to Satan when we should have listened to You. Forgive us O God when we doubted You even though You have never failed to keep one promise You have made.

We pray we will not be like the people who attempted to build the tower of Babel who sought to make plans without Your direction and who sought to build for self-glory. We pray we might be like Your church that was gathered on the Day of Pentecost that You blessed as they waited in prayer on You. We pray we will have their endurance when we encounter obstacles and we will have their peace and their power when we face the enemies of vision and the foes of righteousness. Bring us through as You brought them through. Bring us through even as You raised Your Son Jesus from the dead to stoop no more.

We give You glory even now for all You will yet do in our lives and we praise You for completing whatever You have begun in us. In the name of Jesus do we pray, Amen.

– DAY 88 –

ACTS 11: 1-3

O God, we praise You for the opportunity to keep growing beyond our sometimes narrow, self-limiting, miracle denying perceptions of ourselves and our possibilities. Sometimes O God because we are accustomed to seeing death and lack instead of abundance, we are inclined to be narrow and self-limiting in the goals we set for ourselves and even in our expectations of You. We confess O God often we are content with a half of a cup when You have an overflowing cup waiting for us. We confess O God often we feel jealous of the blessings of others and sometimes we feel overly possessive and insecure regarding what You have given to us. We confess O God sometimes we act as if another person's blessings and gifts will take something from us.

O God, we pray for a vision and an understanding of Your abundance and Your sufficiency. Help us to remember our sufficiency is in You and You are able to supply our needs according to Your riches in glory. Help us to remember what another person has does not affect our blessings and whatever You have for us it is for us. You have blessings galore with our individual names on them. You have miracles which have our addresses attached to them. You have answers that are tailor made to fit our own individual needs. You have salvation and deliverance to meet the particularities of our bondage. You have healing for our specific illnesses and afflictions. And You have love for the loneliness of our lives.

We praise You for Your abundance O God. Now grow us beyond our narrowness so we might have broadness of vision and faith to match the abundance You have for our lives. We pray our vision will be broad enough to do great things for You and to see the needs of others. We pray our vision will be long enough to stretch all of the way into eternity where we might receive the rewards given to those who have a heart for You and who press their way from selfishness to service, from jealousy to joy, from mediocrity to excellence and from bondage to breakthroughs. This we ask in Jesus name, Amen.

DAY 88

– DAY 89 –

ACTS 12: 1-3

O God, we praise You for Your keeping power when we come under attack. O Jesus, Christ of God, our Savior and Redeemer, we praise You for the victory we have in You when we come under attack. O Holy Spirit, our Comforter and Guide, we praise You for Your living presence within us, we praise You for the gifts with which we are equipped to stand and withstand when we come under attack. We praise You O Eternal God in all of Your fullness that we do not have to fear any of the wiles of the Adversary because You have already given us everything we need when we come under attack.

In our moments of loneliness, we praise You for the friends and the advocates You will raise for us when we come under attack. When disease attacks our bodies, we praise You for the healing that overcomes all sickness and for Your sufficient grace and strength that is perfected in weakness when thorns remain. We praise You for the Gospel that inspires and feeds the depressed spirit when Satan shoots us with arrows of discouragement. We praise You for being Jehovah nissi, God our banner, when hurting words assault our reputation and war against our character. We praise You for the standard of righteousness and the truth You will raise up for us when we feel defenseless against the work of rumormongers. We praise You for Your promises upon which we can stand and to which we can cling when we come under attack. We are grateful for the blood of Jesus, which sanctifies us for battle and for the name of Jesus, which is our battle cry when we come under attack.

O God when King Herod of our experience assault us and attempt to break our faith, as Peter was arrested and imprisoned in the Book of Acts, we trust You to rescue us and redeem us, to defend and deliver us. We praise You for the certitude of victory that comes to those who put their trust in You. O God give to us the measure of faith that will allow us to pray with expectation of deliverance. Give us patience to wait and to work and to work and to wait under Your guidance when the battles of life rage hot and heated. We pray for the peace of Christ, which passes understanding and which keep us steady when the storms of life are raging.

– DAY 90 –

ACTS 13: 44-49

O God, we are grateful even when we are rejected by others, we are received by You. Even when others put us down, You lift us. Even when others do not believe in us, You do. Even when others misunderstand us, we are understood by You. Thank You God for loving us as we are. We praise You Jesus for making us better than we could ever have been on our own. We praise You Holy Spirit because as we abide in You and You in us, it still does not yet appear all that we can be.

Now we have changed from death to life and from weakness to strength, we pray You will equip us with the patience to reach out to those whom we love with the gospel, the good news of change and a second chance through our Lord Jesus. Save us from self-righteousness and arrogance of spirit as we reach out to those who are our first love. Give us the right words to say and the right spirit with which to witness. Help us to walk our talk before an on looking world that needs examples of truth and honesty, and of character and integrity.

When some of those whom we desire to reach do not receive our witness, we pray for determination to keep growing, for presence of mind to move beyond self-blame and guilt and for the tenacity to look for others already prepared by You who are waiting to receive our witness. Help us to grow beyond our pain to power. Help us to grow beyond our hurt to healing. Help us to grow beyond our rejection to redemption. Help us to keep growing even as Jesus did. He came to his own and his own received him not but as many as receive him he gave power to become children of God.

We are witnesses that he ever searches to save. We are grateful that one day we heard his voice calling our names. Now Lord equip us with such gifts and graces this day that we might ever be a blessing to others even as You have blessed us. In the name of Jesus do we pray, Amen.

– DAY 91 –

ACTS 14: 8-10

Gracious God, we praise You for Your continuing availability to us. Whenever we need You Lord to hear us and to heal us, to redeem us and to renew us, to deliver us and to bless us, You are always available to us. No matter how late or how early we call upon You, You are available to us. No matter what our burdens are, Your bounty is always available to us. No matter what our sins are, Your salvation in Jesus Christ is always available to us. When we are lonely and afraid, Your presence is always available to us.

Now Lord, we pray for faith to be healed. Your availability is only one part of the formula for our deliverance. We must have faith to be healed. We must be willing to listen and then heed Your word. We must have a desire for change that is so strong we do not let our past dictate what we can or cannot do. We must believe so strong we do not allow the devil or other humans to tell us what we cannot do. We must believe so strongly no matter how many mistakes we have made in the past or how many times we have failed in the past, we can still walk in newness of life.

So Lord, we pray for faith to be healed — healed from all bitterness and brokers, healed from all guilt and grief, healed from all hurt and helplessness, healed from all anger and anxiety, healed from all depression and co-dependent relationships, healed from all pettiness and jealousy, healed from all sin and sickness. We pray for faith to know our healing is not a distant hope but a present reality.

We pray for faith to hear Your word that calls us to growth right now, that calls us to seize the new opportunities that are all around us even now. We pray for faith that challenges us to rise from where we have been and follow You to where You desire us to be. O God like the lame man in Acts 14: 8-10, we pray this day for faith to be healed. Like the lame man in Acts 14: 8-10, we pray for boldness in Your name and under the authority of Your word to do what we have never done before. Like the lame man in Acts 14: 8-10, we pray for faith to obey without hesitation because we believe and trust Your word. In Jesus name do we say, Amen.

DAY 91

– DAY 92 –

ACTS 14: 19-20

Gracious God whose mercies cannot be numbered, we come to You on this day to praise You for Your faithfulness to us. Sometimes like the townspeople in the scripture, we have such short memories. Sometimes we forget too quickly the promises we have made to You, to others and to ourselves. Sometimes we forget Your goodness to us and give way to the doubts planted in our spirits by the enemy. Sometimes we even forget to say thank You for the many blessings You bestow upon us because we begin to take them and You for granted. Sometimes we forget who we are and how we are to live as Your redeemed, blood bought children. Sometimes in our forgetting, we return to old ways of thinking and living and conversation.

Forgive us O God when we too quickly forget what we should always remember. We pray we will always remember the kindnesses of others, when we start feeling no one cares for us. We pray we will always remember Your goodness in days past and gone when we start feeling forsaken by You because things in our present are at a standstill. We pray we will always remember the promises we made to You when we were in trouble or when we gave our lives to You. We pray we will always remember to put You first in our tithes and offerings. We pray we will always remember to give You the praise when we would take pride in our own accomplishments. We pray we will always remember to say thank You when You bless us beyond our deserving. We pray we will always remember to carry ourselves as the redeemed. We pray we will always remember that no matter what happens from day to day and time to time, all things work together for good to them who love You, to those who are called according to Your purpose. We pray we will always remember we do not live by bread or material things alone but by Your written, revealed and triumphant word.

O God, You have been so faithful and good to us, we pray we will be as faithful to You. Help us O Holy Spirit to live this prayer and not just to say it. This we ask in Jesus name, Amen.

DAY 92

– DAY 93 –

ACTS 14: 19-20

Gracious God, we are thankful for all You have brought us through. We are thankful for strength You have provided that has proven to be sufficient to the tasks. We are grateful for a reasonable portion of health that only comes from You. We are grateful for being clothed in right minds that You have given us. We are grateful for the privilege and for Your helping us to pray when we did not know what or how to pray or when we did not feel like praying. We are grateful for the measure of faith with which we have been blessed that helped us to keep fighting when it would have been easier to give up.

We are grateful for the rain that has taught us to appreciate the sunshine and has helped us to grow. We are grateful for the sunshine that has brought pleasure and warmth to our lives. We are grateful for the knowledge of Your word and the laws and promises contained therein that have helped us to order footsteps that would have surely gone astray. We are grateful for Jesus Christ our Lord who saves us. We are grateful for the Holy Spirit, Your presence living in us, who abides with us forever. We are grateful for Your grace that is always more than sufficient and for strength that has been perfected in our weaknesses.

We are grateful that through it all we have survived and You have given us everything we need to survive. Help us O God in our moments of reflection never to become so caught up in thinking about what we have gone through we fail to remember we did survive. Somehow and in some way You helped us to make. We praise You O God for our journey.

But more than that, we are grateful we are not only survivors but also we are conquerors. We have not simply come through but we have come through richer, stronger and more blessed. We have not only come through the firer, we have come through refined. We have not simply come through the flood, we have come through more convicted, determined and assured about the truths we believe. We have not simply come through burdens we have come through blessed.

Thank You for the privilege of living as conquerors in Christ Jesus our Lord. Help us to always remember no matter what we face — we have conquered in the past, we are conquering even now and we will conquer in the future, through Christ Jesus our Lord, Amen.

– DAY 94 –

ACTS 15: 10-11

Gracious God, we pray for wisdom and understanding so we will always keep the main thing, the main thing. You are our first love and our tithe is our first commitment. During the Christmas season, we will always remember that Jesus is the reason for the season. During Thanksgiving, we pray we will always remember gratitude to You and not our dinner, our appetite and our plans is the main thing. During Easter, we pray we will always remember the resurrection is the main thing. At the beginning of a new year, we pray we will keep Your will, have new commitments to follow, to love and to trust in You.

As we grow older, we pray we will continue to keep You, O Lord, as the first love of our lives. Save us from the error of Your servant King Solomon who in his later years allowed his heart to be turned away from You. Save us from self-pity O Lord. Save us from selfishness and the tendency to stay focused on our problems, our needs, our wants, our frustrations and our hurts. And if loneliness ever holds us in its grip and depression settles upon our spirits, we pray for the presence of mind to remember Calvary's cross which is the eternal reminder of Your love for us. We are grateful Jesus kept us as the main thing even when humans denied, betrayed, deserted, mocked and crucified him. We are grateful he kept our redemption and salvation as the main thing when the masses wanted to make him an earthly king. We are grateful Jesus kept our deliverance as the main thing when the devil assaulted him. We are grateful Jesus kept our healing and our wholeness as the main things when he could have called ten thousand angels to set him free. Now O God, we pray for faith to keep him as the main thing in our lives.

Save us from petty jealous, draining feuds and narrow politics. Save us from turf guarding dispositions and unfounded distrust of others. Help us always to stay focused on what You will have us to do and to be. We love You O God. We love You O God. We love You O God. We love You O God. You are the center of our joy and the foundation of our being. And we give ourselves anew to You. In Jesus mighty name do we pray, Amen.

DAY 94

– DAY 95 –

ACTS 16: 6-10

Oh God, we pray we will always trust Your vision for our lives even when You say no to some of our plans. O God, we pray for guidance of the Holy Spirit and the discernment to always know what Your vision and Your will for our life. We pray for passion to do and to follow Your will. We pray for judgment to know Your will is always best for us. Thank You for willing the best for us O Lord.

We confess often we do not know what is best for us. We confess O God even when Your word tells us what is best for us, at times we fail to follow the best way, the right way, the morally upright way. We confess at times, we follow what we have already decided. We confess at times we do what we want to do no matter what Your word says. We confess sometimes we are resistant and even rebellious toward Your will and vision. We confess sometimes we do what is most comfortable and familiar. We confess O Lord we sometimes listen to others and that we sometimes care more about what others may think than we should. We confess O Lord sometimes we allow the Adversary to plant doubts in our minds and spirit. We confess O Lord sometimes we have more fear than faith.

We praise You for Your patience and Your loving kindness and tender mercies. We praise You for Your understanding of our fickleness and for Your loving us even when we disappoint You and hurt You. We are grateful You are still calling our names. You are still calling our names with new opportunities for service, greatness and growth. You call our names every day with another opportunity to get it right. You are still calling our names for salvation. You are still calling our names as objects of Your love and affection. You are still calling our names as Your very own children. You are still calling our names with new visions.

Thank You for loving us as You do the way You do as only You can do. We return our love to You and we joyfully yield to the Macedonian calls that come to us from You. In Your name do we pray, Amen.

DAY 95

– DAY 96 –

ACTS 17: 6-7

Gracious God, we praise You for Your vision for our lives. We pray for faith to follow and the willingness to be completely open and available to You. We yield ourselves to our Lord Jesus to give us a new viewpoint of life, of our abilities and ourselves and of You. We yield ourselves to be made anew and transformed by the Holy Spirit. We pray we will not fear Your will for our lives even if that will is something far different and far larger than anything we have envisioned for ourselves. Even if Your will cause us to change our career plans or relationship hopes, we yield ourselves to You. Even if Your will leads us by way of Calvary, we yield ourselves to You. Even if those closest to us do not understand our actions, we yield ourselves to You.

We love You Lord Jesus and honor You as our conquering and reigning King. We pray for an understanding of the freedom and the joy that comes when You are King of our life. We pray for the courage to do new things with confidence and the new self-image that comes to us when we really accept Your reign and will as king of our life. We are grateful to have You as our King. You never break promises. Your kingdom and Your reign last forever. You have all the power. Your desire is to give Your best to those who follow You. You always give back more than You require. You have even sacrificed Yourself for our redemption. We are so grateful to have You as our King.

Ride on King Jesus! Ride on Emmanuel! You reign forever! You reign forever! You reign forever! All hail our conquering King! Your name is above every other name. Even now You are interceding for us in the heavenlies as we engage earthly embodiments of the principalities and the powers. Even now, You are preparing a place for us in glory to be with You forever. O King Jesus, we are so grateful to have You as our King. In Your name do we pray, Amen.

DAY 96

– DAY 97 –

ACTS 17: 10-15

Gracious God, we praise You for Your word that instructs us on who You really are and which teaches us about Your love. We praise You for the lives of others in which we can see the truths of Your word being fulfilled and made manifest. We praise You for the lives of others, which exemplify Your love and Your saving and delivering power. We praise You for the witness of our own lives. We praise You for our own story. We praise You for saving us, hearing us when we call and drawing near to us even when we fail to reach out to You. We praise You for the many ways You use us and receive glory from our lives. We praise You for the anointing of the Holy Spirit that others see and we feel that resounds to Your glory and Your honor.

Our desire O Lord is to be more like You every day. Our desire is to be true men and women, boys and girls who love to live for You and who live to love You. Create within us O Lord a clean heart and renew within us a right spirit so we can love You and live for You, as You desire. We pray we will catch a vision of You desire for us O Lord Jesus. As a deer pants for the bubbling brook, so our souls long and reach out for You. As spring manifests resurrection, as summer represents maturing, as fall represents harvest time and as winter represents transition so grow us, refine us, make us abundant and change us according to Your image and likeness.

Teach us how to pray and then help us O Lord to live our prayer. And when the enemy assaults us in our efforts to live for You, we pray for the guidance of the Holy Spirits and the presence of the mind to always examine the evidence of Your grace, Your will and Your power. O God, You are an ever present help in a time of trouble. O Holy Spirit, You abide with us forever. May Your beauty and Your glory be manifested in us in new ways this day and all the days of our life. We love You O Lord Jesus for who You are and who we can become in You. In Your precious name do we pray, Amen.

– DAY 98 –

ACTS 18: 5-6

Gracious God, we praise You for another opportunity to come into Your presence. At this time of the year, we praise You for Your love that will not let us go. When others are confronted with the limitations of their love, we praise You for Your love that knows no limits and which lasts throughout eternity. When others face difficulties in expressing their love, we praise Your for Your love that continues to express itself in new ways. O Lord, You are good all of the time. We praise You for Jesus Christ the highest expression of Your love. We praise You for the Holy Spirit who is the ongoing and abiding expression of Your love. We praise You for Your word that teaches us about Your love. We praise Your for You daily blessings, which are the ongoing benefits of Your love. We praise You for Your forgiveness and mercy that are expressions of Your love bestowed upon us when we are most unworthy.

O Christ, You are the Alpha and Omega of love; You are the beginning and the end of love and everything in between. All we do and all we give are only response to Your loving us first. O Christ You are the good shepherd who loved us so much You gave Your life for us. O Christ, You are the door and the gate through which we walk to find love that is eternal. O Christ, You are the way to love in its fullest expression, You are the loving truth that never deceives and You are the love that gives life. O Christ, You resurrect the cold embers of the love when we have allowed the troubles and disappointments of life to blow our flames out. O Christ, Your love flows like waters for the thirsty spirit and Your love is bread for the hungry heart. We worship You as Savior, we follow You as Lord and we love You as the one altogether loving and lovely.

O Holy Spirit, we are grateful for the love You have placed within our hearts. O Holy Spirit teach us how to love in ways that honor You as well as bless those who are the human subjects of our love. O Holy Spirit increase our capacity and patience to love. Give us the kind of thankful heart that makes loving easy. O Holy Spirit give us a love that shines like stars in the midnight sky and brightens and warms like the noonday sun. O Holy Spirit, we pray for love that blossoms like a flower and bears fruit in its season.

O God, Father, Son and Holy Spirit, we pray You will receive this song of love as we strive to live in such a way that the beauty, joy, power and presence of Your love will be reflected in our lives as well as in the lives of others. In Your own precious name do we pray, Amen.

– DAY 99 –

ACTS 18: 24-28

Gracious God, we are so grateful You desire growth for us. Even when we would stay in our comfort zones, You still desire growth for us. Even when we resist Your leading, Your discipline and Your word, You still want growth for us. Even when the enemy attacks and we become more focused on our problems than You the Problem Solver, You still desire growth for us.

We are grateful You can grow us in all circumstances and in all places. Whether sick or health, whether faithful or failing, whether at work or in worship, whether on the mountain of ecstasy or in the valley or shadow of death, You can grow us to Your good pleasure. We are grateful You can turn things the enemy meant for our destruction to our salvation and to our growth.

So grow us Lord according to Your vision for our lives. As You grow us, we pray for a spirit like You servant Apollos in the scriptures. We pray for openness of mind and new spirit to new teaching and instruction. We pray we will not be too proud to admit there are things in our lives and gaps in our education from which we need to grow. We pray we will not be so wedded to any tradition or be so loyal to any person or be so devoted to any belief, idea or doctrine we will resist the more accurate teaching that comes from Your word.

O Holy Spirit lead us into a more accurate knowledge of the Way of the Lord. Lead us into a more accurate walk in the Way of the Lord. And when to the right or the left we would stray, O God, we pray in that moment You would renew Your vision of growth in our consciousness so we might remain fixed and focused on Your purpose and will for us. O Lord help us to live new and improved lives as we serve You in new and improved ways that reflect the growth that You will for us. In Jesus name do we pray, Amen.

DAY 99

– DAY 100 –

ACTS 19: 1-10

O Lord, our Lord, how excellent is Your name and Your ways in all the earth. We come to You to praise You for the ways in which You grow us and the time You take to grow us. We praise You for loving us enough to envision the very best for us. We praise Your for Your faithfulness to us when we settle for less than You envision for us. We praise You for Your forgiveness when we listen to the vain promises of the enemy instead of the truth of Your word and the witness of the Holy Spirit.

O God help us to remember Your timetable may not be ours but Your timing is always best and always perfect. Forgive us O Lord when our short-sightedness and our impatience and impetuousness cause us to run ahead of You. Forgive us O God when our headstrong ways slow down the consummation of Your will for our lives. Forgive us O Lord when our impatience thwart the good things You have planned for us. Save us O Lord from ourselves.

Your servant Paul labored in Ephesus until Your church was established on a firm foundation and until persons everywhere heard the good news of Jesus Christ. Therefore, we pray for strength to labor in love and patience in the places where we are, until Your will for that place becomes reality, until strongholds are broken and until Your children who do not know You are saved. Help us to march to the drumbeat of the Holy Spirit. We pray our steps will be in with Your word and Your will. We pray we will patiently follow Jesus the author and perfecter of our faith. And when we would grow weary in well doing we pray we will remember Your word that promises that we shall reap, if we do not faint.

O Lord, we surrender ourselves anew to You this day. Have Your way with us. We pray for persevering power to work with patience, to pray with patience, to live in patience, to love in patience, to prepared with patience knowing in the fullness of time the harvest will come and Your will, will be done on earth as it is in Heaven. In the name of Jesus, our patient and timely Lord, do we pray, Amen.

DAY 100

– DAY 101 –

ACTS 19: 11-20

O God, You have created us in Your very own image and You have given to each of us our own distinctive personality and style. Each of us is unique in Your sight and none of us is a carbon copy of the other. You have loved us and blessed us individually. You have heard our individual prayers, You see our individual tears, You hear our individual groans and You minister to our individual hurts. You have equipped each of us with our own individual gifts and talents. You have numbered the hairs on our heads and You know each of us better than we know ourselves. This very day you have prepared individual blessings with our names on them. We praise You O God for seeing and treating us as individuals.

We praise You for the individual stories and testimonies we have about Your care and Your love, Your grace and Your mercy. We praise You for our individual stories and testimonies we have about how You answer prayer and how You have intercede in our lives to save us from the adversary, from others and even from ourselves. Now God as You have made us unique, we pray we will not copy anyone else's style of praise or anyone else's way of singing or witnessing or serving You. We pray we will be real with You and we will praise You as Your Holy Spirit moves upon our spirit and burns on the main alters of our hearts. We praise You for direction and guidance we receive from Your church and Your word. We know even as Your Spirit moves upon us to praise You with our unique personality, Your Spirit will never create either confusion or rebellion when Your Spirit is moving in the life and in worship in Your church.

Help us to be humble in our praise. We pray that any spirit of self-seeking vainglory or showmanship will be bound. We pray for discernment so we will know what is true from what is not about You. We pray that our spirit of worship and praise will always blend in and never detract from Your Spirit or Your word or Your glory. We pray the words of our hearts will always be acceptable in Your sight. We pray our deportment in worship and our behavior, as we praise You, will always bring honor and glory to You. In Jesus name do we pray, Amen.

– DAY 102 –

ACTS 20: 7-12

We praise You Gracious God for Your mercy and grace that intercedes for us when we fall. We praise You for Your power that is able to lift us after we fall. We praise You for the Holy Spirit who fills us after we have been restored from a fall. We praise You for Your word which ministers to us when we fall. We praise Your for Your church that instructs and encourages us after we have been restored from a fall. We praise You for our testimony and our personal knowledge that there is life after a fall.

Now O God we pray for a caring heart and a compassionate spirit toward those who have fallen. We pray we will always remember but for Your grace and mercy there go we all. We pray we will always remember the admonition of Your word "if any among us is overtaken in a fault, then we who are spiritual should restore such a person with a spirit of meekness and gentleness" (Galations 6:1). O God save us from hard heartedness and self-righteousness. Help us to always remember the judgment we give will also be the judgment we receive.

On this day O Lord we pray for grace and power to live as Your beloved and redeemed children. Thank You for keeping us graven upon Your hands and for loving us and believing in us when we were not at our loveliest. Thank You for recognizing worth and potential we did not see in ourselves. We pray for power to say no to the tempter whenever he strikes and wherever and however he would attempt to lead us back to where we once were. We pray for wisdom and presence of mind to rely on You and to call on the saving name of Jesus and not just on our good intentions and our own strength.

Forgive us when we neglect to pray and to stay in touch with You as we should. We pray this day we might order our footsteps in new ways according to Your word and will. On this day, we pray we will take more time to be holy and to speak more often with You. Speak O Lord, we Your servants are listening. In Jesus name do we pray, Amen.

DAY 102

– DAY 103 –

ACTS 21: 1-7

O God, we praise You for the company of the saints and the fellowship of the household of faith. Sometimes in our efforts to live for You and do Your will we feel lonely, misunderstood and afraid. Sometimes we get weary in the way if not weary of the way. In such times O God, we praise You for the company of believers. We praise You for persons with whom we can share the greatest bond – saving knowledge of the Lord Jesus Christ.

We are grateful for other believers who can pray us through. We are grateful for other believers who also stand upon Your word and claim Your promises. We praise You for other believers whose lives have also been bought with a price and ransomed from above. We praise You for other believers who are also being transformed from grace to glory. We praise You for the other believers with whom our bonding, death cannot even shatter. We praise You for other believers who also share the perfect love—Your love generously poured out and given in the Lord Jesus Christ.

As believers, we pray we are positive in our outlook and encouraging in our spirits. As believers, we pray we will also be lifters of the hopes and heads of others. As believers, we pray the beauty of the Lord Jesus may be seen in our lives so You will be glorified. As believers, we pray we will follow You wherever You lead us. As believers, we pray we will always have a heart for You and compassion for others. As believers, we pray we will always be useful and worthy servants.

Now O God, we pray as believers You will live in us. Live in us as fire dwells in the sun and light dwells in the stars. Live in us as songs live in the birds of the air and movement lives in the wind. Live in us as colors dwell in the rainbow and as wetness dwells in water. We love You O God for the privilege of being believers. Now live in us even as Your presence abides in the heavens—forever more. In Jesus name do we pray, Amen.

– DAY 104 –

ACTS 21: 37-40

Gracious God, we praise You for the reality of salvation and for opportunities to serve You. Now Gracious God, we pray for faith to stand and strength to endure. When like Your servant Paul, we find ourselves under attach, we pray for faith to stand and strength to endure. When like Your servant Paul, we are falsely accused and misrepresented, we pray for Faith to stand and for strength to endure. When like Your servant Paul we have done our best and our best does not seem good enough, we pray for faith to stand and for strength to endure. When like Your servant Paul, we have prayed for healing and release and thorns remain and no breakthroughs come, we pray for faith to stand and strength to endure.

When we have sought Your face and Your face seems hidden from us, we pray for faith to stand and for strength to endure. When the vision tarries and we seem to be making no progress towards our goals, we pray for faith to stand and strength to endure. When we must exercise the discipline of patience as Your will slowly unfold in our lives and as Your purposes ripen according to Your timetable, we pray for faith to stand and strength to endure. When we have more questions than answers and when there is so much we do not understand, we pray for faith to stand and strength to endure. When we are tempted to break our vows and lay aside the promises we have made to You, we pray for faith to stand and strength to endure.

When we must enter into our own private Gethsemanes and undergo seasons of prayer and agony, we pray for faith to stand and strength to endure. When we encounter treachery among our friends and weakness in those we thought were strong, we pray for faith to stand and for strength to endure. When we feel burdened by the crosses we bear and the Enemy tries to break our spirit, we pray for faith to stand and strength to endure. When we have our Calvary moments and our seasons when all seems for naught, we pray for faith to stand and strength to endure.

We pray for faith to stand and strength to endure until joy comes in the morning, until our strength is renewed and we mount up with wings like eagles. We pray for faith to stand and strength to endure until Crucifixion Fridays become Resurrection Sundays. We pray for faith to stand

and strength to endure until Your perfect will is consummated in our lives. And then when we are enjoying the heights of success, we pray for faith to stand and strength to endure. Help us to stay humble with our minds focused on You, lest we start relying upon our own strength and lose our faith and fail in our endurance.

Gracious God, we are so grateful for the reality of salvation and the joy of service. We pray for faith to stand and strength to endure until you come again for us. We pray on that day, we will hear your hearty and joyous, "Well done good and faithful servant. You have been faithful over a few things, come on up and I will make you ruler over many. (Matthew 25:21)" Until that time, we pray for faith to stand and strength to endure. This we ask in Jesus name, Amen.

– DAY 105 –

ACTS 22: 6-16

O resurrected and living Lord Jesus Christ, we come to You with thanksgiving and praise for Your victory over sin and evil, over the devil and the forces of darkness and over death and the grave. Lewdness could not defeat Your love. Violence could not defeat Your virtue. Hatred could not defeat Your holiness. Rejection could not defeat Your redemption. Desertions could not defeat Your devotion. Cruelty could not defeat Your compassion. Mocking could not defeat Your mercy. Crucifixion could not defeat Your commitment. We praise You O victorious Savior.

You were gracious enough to extend Yourself to a persecutor of the church like Saul of Tarsus. You were loving enough to give him another chance. You were mighty enough to turn his life around and give him a new reason for living. What You did for him, we know You can and will do for us if we yield ourselves to You. We come, Lord Jesus, to make a new surrender to You.

We pray Your peace, O living loving, reigning and interceding Christ, will settle upon our spirits. We pray Your will, O forgiving, faithful and returning Christ, will be revealed to us and we will have the commitment and the courage to follow where You lead and as You lead. We pray Your love, O sacrificial, serving and sanctifying Christ, will flow through our hearts. We pray Your power, O mighty and magnificent Christ, will make us into a new creation.

Walk with us now in the secret places of our lives. Walk with us now in ways we can understand. Abide with us now as we seek to do Your will. Breathe upon us now Your spirit of joy and gladness. Work with us now even when we are resistant to change. Love us now as only You can. Strengthen us now as we face our ongoing battles with the Adversary. Resurrect us now from despair and from our mistakes and failures. Appear to us now even as You appeared to Saul on the Damascus Road. Live in us now so we may live with You always. In Your own name do we pray, Amen.

DAY 105

– DAY 106 –

ACTS 23: 11

Gracious God, we praise You for all we have in You even when so much is against us. We praise You for Your promise of deliverance and for Your assurance of victory. We stand even now on Your promise that no weapon formed against us shall prosper. We stand on Your promise to answer our prayers and hear our every groan. We stand on Your promise to supply our every need according to Your riches in glory. We stand on Your promise to grant the overflow if we faithfully tithe and give offerings to You.

We praise You for the preparation You have given to us. No matter what we face, we know You have already equipped us with everything we need to be victorious in the end. O Lord, we pray for revelation and discernment of the spiritual gifts You have placed within us to stand. We pray for wisdom to put on Your whole armor and then knowledge of how to use the weapons of our warfare. We praise You for every tear and every trial that has prepared us for the seasons of testing we must endure.

We praise You for Your presence that never leaves us. Even when we rebel against You, even when our sins grieve Your heart, we praise You for holding us in the hollow of Your hand lest we destroy ourselves with our own foolishness and impetuousness. We pray for sense to hold on to Your unchanging hand. We pray for awareness of Your presence when the devil tries to persuade us that we are by ourselves. Abide with us O Lord God. Walk with us dear Lord Jesus. Grant us Your peace Holy Spirit.

We praise You for Your power O God. As Your power wakes the sun, thank You for waking us each and every morning. As Your power brings out the stars at night, please bring forth our best qualities during tough times. As You bring forth the rainbow after the storm, we pray we will discover new beauty in You, in ourselves, in life and in others when seasons of stress are over.

We praise You O God for Your promise, Your preparation, Your presence and Your power. Help us to walk in what You have given to us even when so much may be against us. This we ask in Jesus name, Amen.

– DAY 107 –

ACTS 24: 24-27

We praise You O God for the many opportunities You give to us to correct the mistakes we have made in the past. Every new day is another opportunity to overcome our past errors. Every new day You demonstrate Your patience and faithfulness to us. We pray Lord that we will not live in regret and guilt but live each day to the fullest as we build upon the foundation of our past.

Now O God, we pray for courage to accept Your word as it comes to us to correct and instruct us. We pray for courage to walk by Your word no matter what lifestyle changes may be involved. We pray for faith to stand upon Your word no matter how uncertain things may appear at any given moment. We pray for faith to walk in Your word as we surrender our wills to Yours. We pray for discipline to live by Your word even when we are tempted to take matters into our own hands. We pray for such a love for Your word we meditate upon it day and night. We pray for such a love for Your word we allow it to order our footsteps. We pray for wisdom to understand Your word and discernment to comprehend the deep things of Your word.

We rebuke the spirit of procrastination that would delay Your blessings to flow into our lives because we have not yielded ourselves to Your word. Forgive us for thoughts, words and deeds that prevent Your word from being fulfilled in our lives.

Come Lord Jesus even now and speak to us Your word of peace. Come Lord Jesus even now and speak to us Your word of empowerment. Come Lord Jesus even now and speak to us Your word of deliverance. Come Holy Spirit even now and give to us the comfort of Your presence. Come Holy Spirit even now and give to us Your direction and Your teaching. Come Holy Spirit even now and give to us Your anointing and Your fire.

We receive You O God, Father, Son and Holy Spirit in all of Your fullness. We receive Your word and we yield ourselves to obedience and to discipleship in new ways as we seek to grow in new ways and strive for another level and deeper depth in You. In Your name do we offer this prayer, Amen.

DAY 107

– DAY 108 –

ACTS 25: 6-12

Gracious God, we are grateful we can appeal to You. When others have judged us unfairly and treated us harshly, we are grateful we can appeal to You. When our mistakes and misdeeds would condemn us to a lifetime of sin and shame, we are grateful we can appeal to You for mercy and another chance. When we are weighed down with guilt, we are grateful we can appeal to You for grace. When we are beset by fears, we are grateful we can appeal to You for faith. When we are lonely, we are grateful we can appeal to You for love.

We are grateful for the access we have to Your throne. We are grateful for the blood of Jesus that allows us to have bold access to Your very presence. We do not need to rely upon other saints or angels to intercede for us, because of the blood of Jesus we have access to You ourselves. We have access to the power that lights the sun and places the moon in the nighttime sky. We have access to the power that raised our Lord from the dead and has conquered death. We are grateful when we are sick, lonely or afraid we have access to You Heavenly Comforter and Mother to the motherless, Father to the fatherless, faithful friend and abiding companion. We are grateful for our access to You because in Your presence there is fullness of joy and at Your right hand there are pleasures forevermore.

Gracious God, since we have the right of appeal and access to You, we also have anticipation. We are grateful when we pray we can anticipate an answer and when we call we can anticipate a response. No matter how old we are or what we have or have not done, no matter what promises we have made or vows to You we have forgotten, because of the blood of Jesus and because of Your faithfulness to us, we can still anticipate You treating us fairly and justly and with love and mercy. We pray we will so live in You and abide in You when life's uneven journey is over, we can anticipate being with You forever more where the wicked cease from troubling and the weary are at rest and all the saints and the angels will gather at Your feet and blessed. We offer this prayer in the strong name of Jesus Christ, our Savior and Lord, Amen.

DAY 108

– DAY 109 –

ACTS 26: 12-20

O Light from haven shine upon us. O Power from heaven flow through us. O Word from heaven speak to us. O Truth from heaven correct our erring footsteps. O Salvation from heaven save and deliver us. O Spirit from heaven anoint and revive us. O Joy from Heaven fill us. O Peace from heaven possess us. O Vision from heaven inspire us. O Glory from heaven enrapture us. O God of grace and glory, truth and light; O Christ of salvation and power; O anointing and joyful Holy Spirit, we come before You to seek Your vision for our lives. We are grateful no matter who we are, how old we are or how much time we have left, You still have a vision for our lives.

On this day, we seek new breakthroughs. Break through our stubbornness with Your love. Break through our sin with Your salvation. Break through our fear with Your promises. Break through our loneliness with Your presence. Break through our being lost with Your word. Break through our anxiety with Your peace. Break through our weakness with Your strength. And grow us to Your glory. Grow us beyond ourselves. Grow us beyond our self-imposed limitations. Grow us beyond our doubt. Grow us beyond our past. Grow us beyond death. Grow us to Your glory.

Grow us through the blood of Christ, which cleanses us. Grow us through Your grace that is always sufficient. Grow us through worship and praise. Grow us through Your church. Grow us through Your word that is written, revealed and proclaimed. Grow us through Your work that is incarnate, living, resurrected, reigning and interceding in Christ Jesus. Grow us through the indwelling presence and power of Your Holy Spirit. Grow us to Your glory.

O God give us faith so we will not be disobedient to the heavenly vision You have for us. Help us to walk in new boldness in places where we have been fearful. Help us to always remember what You show to us, no matter how great or impossible it may seem, You are able to bring it to pass. For the battle is not ours it's Yours. O Awesome Visionary God grow us in new ways to Your glory and we shall praise You and serve You in new ways. Show us this day something new for our lives and for Your church that we have never seen before. And like Your servant Paul, whose life You turned around on the Damascus Road one day, we will not be disobedient to the heavenly vision. We pray this prayer in the strong name of Jesus, Amen.

DAY 109

– DAY 110 –

ACTS 26: 24-26

O God, we praise You for Your passion. You have such passion for our salvation You came in human flesh in Jesus Christ. We are grateful for the passion of Jesus Christ. We are grateful for His passion that moved Him to tears at the death of His good friend Lazarus. We are grateful for his passion that cleansed the temple when dishonest business dealings were polluting holy ground. He loved with holy passion and He burned with holy zeal.

Now Lord, our desire is to love You with passion as You have loved us. We pray we will never be so callous as to take Your goodness for granted. We pray we will never take Your sacrifice on Calvary and all You went through on our behalf for granted. We pray we will passionately claim Your promises, passionately believe Your word and passionately live out Your will for our lives.

We pray we will pray with passion like Hannah pleading for a child or like Jesus seeking Your will in Gethsemane. We pray we will praise and worship You with passion as David did when he danced before the Ark of the Covenant when it was brought in to Jerusalem. We pray we will preach and sing with passion as Paul and Silas did when they were in the Philippian jail. We pray we will witness with passion as the Samaritan woman did when she left the well after our Lord gave her living water. We pray we will love You with passion even as our Savior did when He went to the cross.

We pray we will have a passion akin to the apostle Paul who was on such fire he used every opportunity he had to tell anybody who would listen about Jesus Christ. O God, we pray for a passion for lost souls. We pray for a passion for growth. We pray for a passion for righteousness. We pray for a passion for truth. We pray for a passion for justice with peace and peace with justice. We pray You will turn our passions of the flesh to passions of faith.

Now God, we give ourselves wholly and completely to You, body, mind, spirit and soul. Consecrate us now completely and totally to Your service. In Jesus name do we pray, Amen.

– DAY 111 –

ACTS 27: 21-26

O God, You are a great promise Keeper and Provider for all of those who put their trust in You; we praise You for the inviolability of Your word. We praise You for the honesty and truthfulness of Your word. We praise You for the foundation Your word provides for our living and our dying, our serving and our giving. We praise You for Your righteousness that backs up Your word with untainted and undefiled integrity.

We praise You for the assurance with which we can face life that whatever You have spoken, written or revealed will turn out just as we have been told. No matter what storms we face and no matter what the devil does to try to defeat Your vision for our lives, things will turn out just as we have been told. If we trust in You, if we abide and depend upon You, if we obey You, if we love You with our whole heart, things will turn out just as we have been told. Thank You Lord. We can depend upon You and that is why You are worthy of all praise, glory and honor.

Now Lord, we pray You will speak words of assurance and assistance to us as we go through the storms of live. We pray you will speak words of hope and help to us as we go through the storm of life. We pray you will speak words of ennoblement and encouragement to us as we go through the storms of life. We pray You will speak words of comfort and compassion to us as we go through the storms of life. We pray You will speak words of faithfulness and forgiveness if we falter as we go through the storms of life. We pray You will speak words of peace and power to us as we go through the storms of life. We pray You will speak words of revelation and redemption to us as we go through the storms of life. We pray you will speak words of strength and salvation to us as we go through the storms of life.

Speak Lord, we Your servants are listening. Speak Lord, we Your servants are ready to act in accordance with Your word. Gracious God, You never forget any vision You have for us. We pray we will never forget Your vision for our lives, even when we go through storms. This we ask in the name of Jesus who stills all storms, Amen.

DAY 111

– DAY 112 –

ACTS 27: 21-26

O God, we praise You for Your power that keeps us when the storms of life are raging. We praise You for the covering of Your word that hangs over us when the storms of life are raging. We praise You for the covering of the anointing of the Holy Spirit that hangs over us when life storms rage. We praise You that we are covered by the blood of Jesus when storms rage.

We praise You for grace and mercy that covers our loved ones. We praise You for the privilege of intercessory prayer. We praise You for hearing us even as You have heard and continue to hear others who call on our behalf. We pray Lord that You will grant grace and mercy, provision and protection, until those for whom we intercede come to themselves and turn to You. We pray we will not grow weary in well doing and in praying but we will have the faith to pray through until we can see our prayers answered and until Your perfect will is done in the lives of our loved ones.

We praise You that even though we may be damaged by storms we will not be destroyed in storms. We praise You for the testimony of Your servant Paul who declared, "We are afflicted in every way but not crushed; perplexed but not driven to despair persecuted but not forsaken; struck down but not destroyed" (2 Corinthians 4: 8-9). Even though we may sustain some losses, if we trust in You, if we abide in You, our gains far outnumber our losses and our good days far outweigh our bad days. Thank You Lord. Thank You for the testimonies we have because of our storms. Thank You for the strength and revelations we received because of our storms. Thank You for the humility and the gratitude we have because of our storms. Thank You for the new friendships and persons who came into our lives as we lived through our storms.

Great is Your faithfulness. Great is Your truth. Great is Your love. Great is Your righteousness. Great is Your word. Great is Your power. All of which we learned to trust in new ways as we came through the storms of life. Now O Lord, as we stand in the place where we have landed. We will serve You, love You, trust You and give to You in new ways. O mighty God, You still move in mysterious ways, Your wonders to perform. You plant Your footsteps in the sea and You ride on every storm. In Jesus name our ever-present companion in all storms, do we pray, Amen.

– DAY 113 –

JOHN 12: 42-43

Gracious God, we are grateful for those who You send into our lives to affirm and encourage us in the midst of life's struggles and the devil's attacks. We pray for faith to focus on You for our ultimate approval. Save us O God from approval addiction, which causes us to live in bondage to the approval of others.

Help us to remember O God approval is a good servant of one's spirit but a bad master. Approval is affection but approval addiction is affliction. Approval is beautiful but approval addiction is bondage. Approval is complimentary but approval addiction is crippling. Approval is encouragement but approval addiction is encroachment.

Approval is good but approval addiction is grief. Approval is helpful but approval addiction is hindrance. Approval is inspiration but approval addiction is inferiority. Approval is nice but approval addiction is needy. Approval is praise but approval addiction is problematic. Approval is strengthening but approval addiction is a stronghold.

We are grateful O God no matter what others say or think, You always have the last word. When people say "can't," You, O God, can say "Can" and You always have the last word. When people say "won't," You can say "will" and You, O God, will always have the last word. When people say "impossible," You, O God, can say "To be continued" and You will always have the last word.

When people say "failure," You, O God, can say "Another Chance" and You will always have the last word. When people say "addict," You, O God, can say "Anointed" and You will always have the last word. When people say "convict," You, O God, can say "Changed" and You will always have the last word.

Gracious God, we pray at the end of our earthly journey, we will hear a final word of approval from our Lord Jesus Christ. In his name do we offer this prayer, Amen.

DAY 113

– DAY 114 –

JOHN 3: 1-8

Gracious God, we are grateful we can not only grow beyond our conditioning, through the Lord Christ and the power of the Holy Spirit, we can actually be born again. We pray for faith to trust You as You birth new life in us and from us. After all, Lord God, if You knew enough to make us, then You know what to do with us. If You knew enough to design us, then You know what's best for us. You alone are our maker and designer and we can trust You.

When we are broken, we can trust You, our maker and designer, to know how to fix us. When we are confused, we can trust You, our maker and designer, to know how to clean us up. When we are dirty, we can trust You, our maker and designer, to know how to clean us up. When we are sad and are in sorrow, we can trust You, our maker and designer, to know how to strengthen us.

When our way gets blocked, we can trust You, our maker and designer, to know how to make ways out of no ways for us. When we have needs, we can trust You, our maker and designer, to know how to supply our needs. After all You know the plans You have for us, plans for our good and not for our harm to give us a future with hope.

Now Lord, You have brought us through all we have come to and are at the point of bringing forth the life You have planted within us. We pray for faith to push past birth pains and weariness to new life. Help us to push with the anointing and push with assurance. Help us to push with conviction and push with Christ. Help us to push with faithfulness and push with fortitude. Help us to push with holiness and push with humility.

Help us to push with life and push with love. Help us to push with praise and push with perseverance. Help us to push with power. Help us to push with the revelation and push with redemption. Help us to push with salvation and push with strength. Help us to push with a tithe and push with a testimony. Help us to push with vision and push with virtue. Help us to push with worship and push with work.

We push in the name of the Father. We push in the name of the Son. We push in the name of the Holy Spirit. We offer this prayer in the fullness of Your Name, Amen.

– DAY 115 –

II TIMOTHY 4: 6-18

Lord Jesus, we are grateful we have the assurance according to Your word and promise, You will rescue us from every evil attack and save us for Your heavenly kingdom. That's why we are going to be faithful even when we don't feel like it.

Because of this assurance, we anticipate making the same kind of declaration that the apostle Paul made in II Timothy 4:6-8, when he said, "As for me, I am already being poured out as a libation, and the time of my departure has come. I have fought the good fight, I have finished the race, I have kept the faith. From now on there is reserved for me the crown of righteousness, which the Lord, the righteous judge, will give to me on that day, and not only to me but also to all who have longed for his appearing."

We are so grateful Lord Jesus that when we are faithful to the end even when we don't feel like it, there is a "from now on" of breakthroughs and victorious living You allow us to experience. We will go from strength to strength and from grace to glory. The King James Version simply says, "Henceforth" from now on or henceforth, we shall come forth like gold. From now on or henceforth, those who have gone out weeping bearing the seed for sowing shall come home with shouts of joy carrying their sheaves. From now on or henceforth, those who have wept through the night will find joy coming in the morning.

From now on or henceforth, those who have been faithful in few things will be made rulers over many. From now on or henceforth, those who bore the image of the earthly will bear the image of the heavenly. From now on or henceforth, the wicked will cease from troubling the weary will be at rest. From now on or henceforth, those who mourn shall be comforted. From now on or henceforth, the pure in heart shall see God. From now on or henceforth, You are the salt of the earth. From now on or henceforth, You are the light of the world.

From now on or henceforth, "the Lord will rescue [us] from every evil attack and save [us] for his heavenly kingdom. To him be the glory for ever and ever, Amen." We praise You Lord Jesus for the "from now on" and the "henceforth" of our faith. In Your name do we offer this prayer, Amen.

– DAY 116 –

JOHN 21: 15-18 AND MATTHEW 13: 45

Lord Jesus, You are the pearl of great price. You alone saves to the utmost. Your name has power over every demon. Your blood can make the foulest clean. Your word is never broken and your promises are always kept. Your presence never leaves. You are the best heaven can give for our soul's salvation. You are the best we can acquire for our soul's satisfaction. You alone can journey with us from the cradle to the grave and transport us on a calm tide across deaths tempestuous and chilly seas to the grave and land that's fairer than day. We praise You Lord Jesus.

Today You are asking each of us the same question You asked Simon Peter many years ago on the shore of the Sea of Tiberias, "Do You love me more than these? Do You love me more than anything? Do You love me more than pearls?" We pray for faith to let go of our pearls so we might gain You the true pearl of great value. Whatever inhibitions we have, we pray for faith to let go. Whatever anger or bitterness we have, we pray for faith to let go. Whatever pain or hurt we have, we pray for faith to let go.

Whatever disappointments we have, we pray for faith to let to. Whatever guilt or shame we have, we pray for faith to let go. Whatever fears we have, we pray for faith to let go. Whatever concerns we have about what other people say and what they think, we pray for faith to let go. Whatever concerns we have about looking foolish, we pray for faith to let go. Whatever worries we have about failing, we pray for faith to let go. Whatever concerns we have about not being good enough, we pray for faith to let go.

Whatever questions we have about our backgrounds or qualifications, we pray for faith to let go. Whatever issues we have about our age or our looks, we pray for faith to let go. Whatever concerns we have about how we dress or how much money we have, we pray for faith to let go. Whatever feelings we have about family, we pray for faith to let go. Whatever feelings we have about church people or preachers or organized religion, we pray for faith to let go.

We have heard Your call Lord Jesus to give up our pearls so we can possess You, the pearl of great price or value, and new life. We now let go and surrender ourselves to You. Have Your way in and with our lives Lord Jesus. In Your name do we offer this prayer, Amen.

– DAY 117 –

JOHN 9: 34-35

Gracious Lord, we are so grateful You are a Savior who seeks us out. Some of us can testify we are here not simply because we sought You but because you sought us out. Sometimes we were so burdened, confused, lost and angry, we couldn't pray but You still sought us out with the blessings we needed, the strength we needed, the help we needed to endure those who wanted us to be kept out.

Sometimes we felt so buffeted and the ups and downs of life had shaken our faith so much, we had more doubt than belief but You still sought us out. Sometimes our weaknesses, mistakes and failures left us so filled with shame and guilt, we are too embarrassed to call on You, O Lord but You still sought us out with a word of forgiveness, grace and mercy. Sometimes we were so bound, we did not know how to reach You but You still sough us out. You do more than just sit high and look low, You seek us out.

Like a good shepherd who leaves the ninety-nine sheep in the wilderness and goes after the one who has gone astray, You seek us out. Sometimes like the man born blind, we have been in darkness bondage when You find us. Sometimes like the man born blind, we have been delivered and still find ourselves on the outside by those who resent us when You find us.

Sometimes like Peter, we have fished all night long and caught nothing, we have tried our best and have little or nothing to show for ourselves when You find us. Sometimes like the Saul of Tarsus, we are traveling the wrong way fast down on Damascus Roads when You seek us out. Sometimes like John on the isle of Patmos, we find ourselves exiled and excluded because we have dared to speak up for the Lord, when You seek us out.

We praise Your Lord Jesus because You are still seeking us right now. You are seeking with cleansing. You are seeking with restoration. You are seeking with new life and a new future. You are seeking with forgiveness. You are seeking with healing for our hurts, joy for our sorrow and deliverance for our bondage.

Like the man born blind, we worship You O seeking Savior and we commit our lives to You. In Your name Lord Jesus do we offer this prayer, Amen.

DAY 117

– DAY 118 –

JOHN 20: 19 AND ACTS 2: 1-13

Gracious God in times like these when there is so much glitter that is not gold and when there is so much that passes for the real thing and is not, we are grateful You are real and true. When we read about the transformation that took place with the disciples between John 20:19 when our risen Christ first appeared to them and the boldness that characterized their praise and transformed them forever on the Day of Pentecost in Acts 2, we know Your power to be real.

Only a real God, with a real word; only a real Spirit as the manifest presence of Almighty God with real power to make true and lasting change could have changed the disciples from the anxious to the aggressive, from the bashful to the bold and from the bereaved to the brave. Only a real God, with a real word; only a real Spirit as the manifest presence of Almighty God with real power to make true and lasting change could have changed the disciples from the cowardly to the courageous and from the complainers to conquerors.

Only a real God, with a real word; only a real Spirit as the manifest presence of Almighty God with the real power to make a true and lasting change could have changed the disciples from the defensive to the daring and from the fearful to the faithful. Only a real God, with real God, with a real word; only a real Spirit as the manifest presence of Almighty God with real power to make true and lasting change could have changed the disciples from the helpless to the hopeful and from the intimidated to the inspiring.

Only a real God, with a real word; only a real Spirit as the manifest presence of Almighty God with real power to make true and lasting change could have changed the disciples from the pitiful to the powerful, from the sorrowful to the strong and from the timid to the tremendous. Only a real God, with a real word; only a real Holy Spirit as the manifest presence of Almighty God with real power to make true and lasting change could have changed the disciples from whiners to winners and from wimps to warriors.

Only a real God who speaks a real and true word, whose Son's blood gives real cleansing and whose Holy Spirit gives real anointing can so transformed us; we who have borne the image of the earthly will one day bear the image of the heavenly. In the name of the Father, Son and Holy Spirit do we pray, Amen.

– DAY 119 –

JOHN 20: 19-20(B)

Gracious God, we pray we will be disciples indeed who are faithful through good times and bad, and not simply customers who walk away when things do not go their way. Help us to understand even when difficulties are hatched in the laboratory of the enemy to destroy us, You can use them as part of the plan to bring us to the perfect end and the greater revelation of Your power and glory You desire us to have and to experience.

The lies and attack others have us under to break us can become part of Your plan to keep us focused and leaning on You. The walk through the valley and shadow of death can become the plan to help us overcome fear and build faith. The temporary victory of the enemy can become the plan to show us how far You can bring us back, how much of a miracle You can work in our life and how powerless enemies are when You begin to move. The long time it seems to be taking is part of the plan to teach us patience and endurance so we can handle the stuff we will have to put up with once You come out on top.

Being on top means, we are better targets for more people to shoot at. However because of all we have been through to get to where we are, we can handle being shot at without panic or a breakdown. We praise You Lord Jesus because what others mean for our destruction, You can turn around for our deliverance. We praise You Lord Jesus because what others mean for our rejection, You can turn around for our redemption. We praise You Lord Jesus because what others mean for our burial, You can turn around for our breakthrough.

We pray for the diligence of the disciples that gathered at the appointed time and place even when their hearts were broken and their minds confused. We are grateful that at such times You show up and speak peace, breathe renewal into us and reveal a vision for our future that is greater than any vision we can have for ourselves or that others can have for us.

Here we are Lord, Your imperfect, failing and sometimes selfish disciples. Forgive us for our failures and give us a new revelation of Your never failing power and presence that turns situations of defeat into bright life transforming experience of victory. In Your name Lord Jesus do we offer this prayer, Amen.

– DAY 120 –

JOHN 20: 19-20

Gracious Lord, as You speak to us in the midst of our fears, we pray You will replace our heart of fear with a heart of faith. You want to demonstrate Your provision and power in our lives in new ways. However for that to happen, we will have to trust You in new ways. We pray You will replace our heart of fear with a heart of faith.

You are telling some of us to start our own business. You are telling some of us to try out for a new position or to put our name in the mix for a promotion. We pray You will replace our heart of fear with a heart of faith. You are telling some of us to leave a certain relationship we have become too co-dependent upon and You are telling others of us to open our heart to new love and not to keep it closed and guarded because of past hurt and rejection. We pray You will replace our heart of fear with a heart of faith.

You are telling some of us to stay where we are and fight and not run away and You are telling others of us to move to another job, or another location or another church but we have become comfortable and are afraid of new and unfamiliar territory. We pray You will replace our heart of fear with a heart of faith.

You are telling some of us it is time to tithe or to give beyond the tithe but we continue to worry about how our bills are going to be paid. You are telling some of us that it's time to go beyond where anyone in our family or neighborhood or among our friends or associates has gone but we are afraid some people may not like us. We pray You will replace our heart of fear with a heart of faith.

You are telling some of us who are members of the church it is time we get more involved in the life of the church but we are afraid of some of the church people we see. You are telling some of us it's time we turn our life over to You, Lord Jesus. We pray You will replace our heart of fear with a heart of faith and we will follow You wherever You lead us with a glad and willing heart and with an open and contrite spirit. In Your own name Lord do we offer this prayer, Amen.

– DAY 121 –

MATTHEW 16: 17-19

Gracious Lord, we are grateful for the promise You have given us that we as people of God can take over whatever territory the devil has claimed for himself. Not even the gates that the devil has erected to protect and keep out the people of God when we decided to go after it.

We are grateful for the keys of the heaven You have given us which we can open up hells gates. Prayer is a key heaven uses to open the gates of hell. Faith is a key heaven uses to open the gates of hell. Worship and praise are the keys heaven uses to open the gates of hell. The name of Jesus is the key heaven uses to open the gates of hell. Surrender to Jesus Christ as Savior and Lord is a key that heaven uses to open the gates of hell.

Obedience to the word of God is a key heaven uses to open the gates of hell. Tithes and offerings are keys heaven uses to open the gates of hell. Faithfulness is a key heaven uses to open the gates of hell. Steadfastness is the key heaven uses to open the gates of hell. Love is the key heaven uses to open the gates of hell. Forgiveness is a key heaven uses to open the gates of hell. Gracious Lord, we pray for courage and vision to use the keys You have given us.

You have not only given us keys to open the gates of hell, You have also given us power to bind and release. In Your name, we can bind addiction and release the anointing that has been held captive by addiction. We can bind backbiting and release breakthroughs. We can bind demons and release deliverance. We can bind debt and release wealth. We can bind disease and release healing.

We can bind excuses and release excellence. We can bind fear and release freedom. We can bind lies and release life. We can bind obstacles and release opportunity. We can bind poverty and release prosperity. We can bind put downs and release potential. We can bind rejection and release recovery. We can bind Satan himself and release salvation.

We pray we will use wisely and effectively all You have given us to Your glory and Your honor. In the name of the Lord Jesus do we offer this prayer, Amen

DAY 121

– DAY 122 –

LUKE 24: 32

Oh living Lord, You put fire in the hearts of burned out disciples whom you walked with and communed with as they journeyed from Jerusalem to Emmaus. You also gave fire to a much married and divorced Samaritan woman to carry Your message to people who once looked down on her. You gave fire to a woman caught in sin to sin no more. You gave fire to Nicodemus for a second birth. You gave fire to a demoniac to live without his demons. You gave fire to Zaccheus to stop exploiting his own people and become a blessing to others. You gave fire to a man who had been born blind not to back down on his testimony about what You had done for him, no matter what others thought. Lord Jesus our prayer is we too will catch Your fire.

You gave fire to a man who had been bound to his bed for 38 years to take up his bed and walk. You gave fire to a dying thief to enter Paradise. You gave fire to a group of believers gathered in an upper room on the Day of Pentecost to turn the world upside down. You gave fire to Peter to be bold for the Lord. You gave fire to Saul of Tarsus to become a new creature in Christ. You gave fire to Paul and Silas to worship and praise You until their dungeons shook and their chains fell off. You gave fire to John the Revelator for a new heaven and a new earth. Lord Jesus our prayer is we too will catch Your fire.

Your fire is the only fire that will last from the cradle to the grave and then bear our souls over on a calm tide across death's chilly waters to a land that is fairer than day. Your fire is the only fire that saves. Your fire is the only fire that will light up a sick room and give us light as we walk through the valley of sorrow and bereavement.

Your fire burns away dross. Your fire burns away anger and bitterness. Your fire burns away shame and hurt we have been carrying for too long. Your fire cleanses. Your fire purifies. Your fire transforms. Your fire gives hope. Your fire revives and revitalizes. Your fire makes brand new. Your fire burns throughout the darkest nights. Your fire warms the coldest of hearts.

Lord you are risen indeed and you are still lighting torches in the hearts of those who need something the world cannot give. We pray for your fire. In your name do we offer this prayer, Amen.

– DAY 123 –

MATTHEW 25: 31-46

Lord Jesus, we confess while you have called us to be sheep, there have been times when we have chosen to believe we were goats. Because some of us were called goats, we start believing we were goats and so we started thinking, acting and talking like goats. We adopted goat attitudes and have goat anxieties. We fed on goat food and had goat fears. We adopted goat habits and had goat hopelessness. We adopted goat jealousies and reveled in goat junk. We adopted goat lifestyles and have goat laziness. We adopted goat morals and made goat messes.

We adopted goat sin and lived in goat strongholds. We adopted goat values and goat vision. We adopted goat ways and had goat weaknesses. Or because we lived around goats, we started believing a goat existence was all we could expect from life. Some of us know what it is to have people look at our age, our race, our gender, our mistakes and our background and conclude we are goats.

However, we praise You for the testimony, You looked beyond what others saw and what we believed about ourselves and came up with another assessment of who we are. When others would have written us off as goats and when we would have done the same thing, You reached out to us Lord Jesus and said we are Your sheep and we belong to You.

We praise You Lord Jesus because You have guided us, fed us, cared for us and protected us as a Good Shepherd. You have kept Your eyes and hands upon us even when we strayed away from your word and from your will. As our Shepherd, You laid down Your life to save us from the satanic world that sought to destroy us.

Now Lord, we have been transformed into your sheep, we pray we will give in accordance with Your word and will not worry how much we are giving or how our sacrifices will be perceived. Your word has promised You are not unmindful of our giving and you will reward. If we do not grow weary in well doing, You will reward.

Give us a spirit of giving Lord Jesus even as we have received so much from others and even as You have given so much to us. We offer this prayer in the name of the Lord Jesus, Amen.

DAY 123

– DAY 124 –

II CORINTHIANS 5: 17-18

We praise You, Lord Jesus, for Your strength. You are so strong You are not only able to destroy the generational baggage that we know about, You are able to destroy even the stuff that we don't know about but You see holding us back and holding us down. Through You we can become new. Not new and revised but new not new and improved but new not new and updated but new.

We praise You, Lord Jesus, for strength. You are so strong that nothing the devil throws at us can stop us because all the devil can do is throw stuff Dash old lies, old sin, old weaknesses, old hurts, old fears, old bondage. However, old stuff does not even faze the new person we can become in You.

We are grateful Lord Jesus that the testimony of the apostle Paul has become our story two, "if anyone is in Christ, there is a new creation; everything old has passed away; see, everything has become new." Through Jesus Christ we can be new, not rebuilt because some things we don't need rebuilt, we need them destroyed and torn down altogether. Through You Lord Jesus we can be new, no reconstituted, because some things we don't need re-reconstitute it, we need to be reassured of now, henceforth and forever.

Through You Lord Jesus we can be new, not revised because some things don't need a revised, we need them wiped out and thrown away. Through You and in You Lord Jesus, we can be new, not simply revived. Some things we don't need revived we need them banished and burned up. Through You and in You Lord Jesus, we can be new not strengthen and fortified, because there are some things we don't need strengthened and fortified again. We need them to be burned and cast down into the sea of operation where there will not rise to hot in this life nor Ross up in condemn us at the judgment bar.

Lord Jesus we are ready for newness. Not simply new habits and a new routine, our desire is to be new person. Not simply new relationships, our first desire is to be new persons. Not simply a new job first desire is to be new Parsons. Not simply new prosperity, our first desire is to be new persons. Not simply an emotional moment or an inspirational and up lifting service, our first desire is to be new persons make us new persons Lord Jesus, even as we offer this prayer in Your name, Amen.

– DAY 125 –

I CORINTHIANS 15: 7

Lord Jesus, we confess like James, Your own brother, who did not follow You very much while You lived, we confess we too have passed up opportunities for service, for witnessing and even for victory over the devil. However, as the ladder of forgiveness and another chance was extended to him so he could reach from sin to salvation; we also praise You because the same ladder is still here for us.

The ladder from poverty to prosperity is still here. The ladder from addiction to freedom is still here. The ladder from sickness to health and wholeness is still here. The ladder from damnation to deliverance, from hell to heaven and from earth to glory, is still here. The ladder from frustration to fulfillment and from emptiness toe excellence is still here. The ladder from courage to faith and from strength to weakness is still here. The ladder from being negative and cynical to being positive and hopeful is still here. The ladder to happiness and accomplishment is still here.

For us, the ladder is in the form and shape of the cross at the top of which stands Lord Jesus. Even now You are reaching out to us saying, "If you just give me your hand, I'll pull you up. If you give me Your hurt and your pain, your sin and your shame, your broken heart and your issues, I'll pull you up." We praise You Lord Jesus.

Since the ladder is still here when we wake up, instead of singing the blues about all the opportunities we have missed perhaps we can sing the words of Psalm 118: 24, "This is the day that the Lord has made; let us rejoice and be glad in it." We confess we made some mistakes in the past but this is a new day with new opportunities and we shall rejoice. We let some opportunities go by we should have jumped on but You have given us a new day with new opportunities and we shall rejoice.

No matter what yesterday or last week or last year was like, You have given us a new day with new opportunities: we shall rejoice and be glad in it. We don't have time to shed tears over spilled milk and water gone under the bridge; we are too busy rejoicing because this is a new day with new opportunities. We shall pick up the pieces of our life and continue to press on. We shall live each moment to the fullest. We shall rejoice and be glad in it.

In Your name Lord Jesus we offer this prayer of thanksgiving, Amen.

– DAY 126 –

II CORINTHIANS 12: 8-10

Gracious God, we pray for faith that stays with You even when we are disappointed with You and even when the thorns that pierce us remain. What did Moses do when You told him that he could not go into the Promised Land? He still stayed with You because nobody but You brought him as far as he had gone in his life. What did Joseph do when he was sold into slavery by those he had trusted and when he was unjustly imprisoned? He still stayed with You because only You could sustain him in the places where human vindictiveness had placed him.

What did Jeremiah do when he was frustrated because he saw the wicked prospering and scoundrels enjoying peace? He still stayed with You because You were in his life like fire shut up in his bones. What did Job do when he was under attack and You were silent? He still stayed with You because he knew his Redeemer lived and He would stand at the latter day upon the earth and though the skin worms destroyed his body, yet in his flesh he would see You and his eyes would behold You and not another. He still stayed with You because his witness was in heaven and his record was on high.

What did David do when he was denied his dream of building the temple? He still stayed with You because if it had not been for You on his side, he never would have been king. What did Jesus do when You did not remove the bitter cup of Calvary from his lips.? He still stayed with You through all of the persecution, the beatings and the pain, through all of the lies and through all of the mocking, desertion and betrayals because he knew the thorns that pierced would not have the last word.

What did Paul do when after three times of being disappointed in prayer, the thorn remained? He stayed with You and brought his thorn to You again. You spoke to Paul and said, "My grace is sufficient for you, for power is made perfect in weakness." We are so grateful, Lord Jesus that when a thorn remains You will still be more that the thorn. The thorn will not wipe out your blessings. The thorn will not wipe out Your favor. The thorn will not stop Your love. The thorn will not prevent Your breakthroughs. The thorn will not cancel Your miracles.

We pray You will continue to get the glory out of our lives, even when thorns remain. We offer this prayer in Your name Lord Jesus, Amen.

– DAY 127 –

ACTS 1: 6-11

Lord Jesus as we come into Your presence to worship You in the fullness of who You are, we pray You will save us from the paralysis of fear that leads to inaction because we are still grieving over the various losses we have encountered in our lives. When we would become stuck in the pain, anger, brokenness, guilt and regret of loss, we pray we would remember we still have a job to do.

Your vision God for our lives is still operative. The anointing and the calling You have placed upon our lives, the responsibility You have placed within our hands, the word You have placed within our hearts have not been revoked simply because we have sustained a loss. The field of labor is all around us and the job is ahead of us waiting for us to get started.

We confess, O God, sometimes we are so focused on looking behind us and crying over what is gone, we do not see what is around us and what is ahead of us. There are opportunities all around us waiting to be discovered, there are needs all around us waiting to be met and there are people all around us waiting to be noticed---yes, even in the place where we now work or live or go to church or socialize but we cannot see them because we are still looking back mourning over what or who we lost.

Help us to remember O Lord, we still have a life. We may be hurt but we must move beyond our pain because You have still blessed us to have a life. We may be angry but we must move beyond our anger because You have still blessed us to have a life. We may be lonely but we must move beyond our loneliness because You have still blessed us to have a life. We may not be able to do what we used to do but we can't spend the rest of our days wishing for health and vitality, we do not have. You have still blessed us to have a life.

Save us, O Lord, from becoming so attached to anything or anyone that we forget we still have a life even without them or it. Save us, O Lord, from becoming so attached to anything or anyone we can't imagine our being able to survive without them or it. Holy Spirit, we pray You will so saturate us with Your presence and Your fire that the pain of loss will cease blocking us from our breakthroughs. In your name Father, Son and Holy Spirit do we offer this prayer, Amen.

DAY 127

– DAY 128 –

MARK 9: 14-28

Gracious Lord, we pray for faith to learn how to stay focused on You no matter what is happening in our lives. No matter what demons are doing, no matter how much confusion the enemy is causing, we can remain calm when we keep our eyes focused on You, Lord Jesus.

When the tormenting spirit convulsed the epileptic boy, You spoke to the father to strengthen his faith. In essence You were saying to him "Don't worry about the demon, look at me. Don't worry about the disease---look at me. Don't worry about what the enemy is doing or what the enemy may be planning to do---look at me. Don't worry about what people may be saying or trying to do to you—look at me. Don't' worry about what you lack---look at me."

We now hear You speaking to us as we face the challenges of our own lives. We hear Your voice through the Holy Spirit also speaking to us and saying, : Don't worry about the Red Sea in front of you, the high mountains on either side of you and Pharaoh's army in back of you---look at me. Don't' worry about the giant Goliath or the gallows Haman has erected to destroy you----look at me. Don't worry about the lions in the den surrounding you---look at me."

"Don't worry about the fiery furnace---look at me. Don't' worry about the false prophets of Ahab and Jezebel who have you hopelessly outnumbered---look at me. Don't worry about this host that has come out against you, because the battle is not yours but mine---look at me. Don't worry about the weapons that have formed against because if you look at me they won't prosper and every word of judgment that has risen against you, I will help you to confute."

"Don't even worry about Calvary, just look at me. They hung me high, they stretched me wide but I kept looking to the Father and early Sunday morning, He raised Me to stoop no more. Beloved in this world you will have tribulations but be of good cheer and look at me, I have overcome the world. Because I live, if you keep looking at me, you can and you will live also and the enemy that has tormented you and those under your covering will be defeated." We look to You, Lord Jesus and praise You even now for victory. In your name do we pray, Amen.

– DAY 129 –

ACTS 16: 16-18

Lord Jesus, we pray You will move us from revelation to relationship because like the girl in Acts 16: 16-18, we recognize we can have the right revelation but still be in bondage to the wrong masters. We can have the right revelation and still be in bondage to fear, anger and bitterness. We can have the right revelation and still be in bondage to drugs, alcohol, a mean temper and the flesh.

We can have the right revelation and still be in bondage to guilt and shame, feelings of insecurity and low self-esteem. We can have the right revelation and still be broken and bleeding. We can have the right revelation and still be under a non-tithing curse. We can have the right revelation and still be petty and small minded, stubborn, resistant to change and stuck on stupid and stuck in our own comfort zones and traditions.

However, we know the power we need for change in our lives and newness and in victory depend not simply on our revelation but also on our relationship with You, Lord Jesus. Power to live differently, power to overcome fear, anger and bitterness depends not just on our revelation but also upon our relationship with You, Lord Jesus. Power to face demons and handle temptation without yielding depends not only on our revelation but also on our relationship with You, Lord Jesus. Power to overcome guilt and shame of the past as well as any generational curses still lingering around, depends not only on our revelation but also on our relationship with You, Lord Jesus.

When we have a relationship with You as Lord, we have no problem tithing because everything we have and everything we are belongs to You. We can defeat any foe or challenge that rises to block God's vision in our lives from being fulfilled when You are Lord because we understand greater is the one who lives within us than anything that comes upon us or against us in the world. We do not live in fear of other people, of the future or anything else when You are Lord, because we know our lives and our futures are in Your hands. Lord Jesus, we surrender ourselves to You. Reign as Lord over us, we pray. In your name do we offer this prayer, Amen.

DAY 129

– DAY 130 –

MARK 8: 34 37

Gracious God, we desire to live with You in new dimensions and to experience breakthrough living. We know such dimensions and breakthroughs come by sacrifice on our part even as our salvation came through the sacrifice of our Lord and Savior Jesus Christ. God, You are exalted in praise, however You elevate sacrifice. You inhabit praise; however You are inspired by sacrifice. You are manifested in praise but miracles come by sacrifice. You are manifested in praise but miracles come by sacrifice. You receive praise but you reward sacrifice. Praise is an acceptable offering to You but sacrifice brings an awesome overflow.

If we are willing to make a sacrifice to You, then it does not yet appear what we can still be. Across the ages we still hear Jesus saying, "If any person would come after me, let him or her deny themselves and take up the cross and follow me. For those who want to save their life will lose it and those who what to lose their life for the sake of the gospel, will find it. (Matthew 16: 24-25)"

Lord Jesus, we hear Your voice saying to us, "Follow me, not some quick and easy, sugar coated name it and claim it Gospel that makes promises it can't keep and leaves you frustrated and bitter. Follow Me, not your own mind and wishes. Follow Me, not some crowd that is looking for a good show and delightful entertainment. Follow me, not some crowd that is looking for a religious high that still leaves you living in the lowland valley. Follow Me, not some preacher whose main agenda is for you to sow into his or her own kingdom and not the kingdom of God. Follow Me, not some preacher or some church afraid to speak truth to power. Follow Me and see what I can do with you and where I can take you. Give up your anger and I will give you my anointing. Give up your bitterness and I will give you my best. Give up your hatred and I will give you my holiness. Give up your pain and I will give you My power. Give up your sin and I will give you my salivation."

Lord Jesus, we pray for courage to make whatever sacrifices we must make so we can walk in the fullness of the vision You see for us and our lives. We will give you resounding and eternal glory. In the name of the Lord Jesus do we offer this prayer, Amen.

– DAY 131 –

LUKE 5: 4-11 AND ACTS 2: 37-41

Gracious God, we recognize that our situation is like Simon Peter's. Sometimes there is a great gap between the promise and reality and between vision and fulfillment. However, we are grateful You give us power to keep on believing and keep on trying, no matter what. The only explanation for our surviving a heartrending divorce or the death of our loved one was the fact You gave us power and supplied all our needs. The only explanation for our making it through a period in which we had no job or when our debts became so deep we had to declare bankruptcy was You gave us power and supplied all our needs.

The only explanation for our victory when doors were closed in our faces and the devil blocked our path was You gave us power and supplied all our needs. When those we thought would be with us were nowhere to be found, You gave us power and supplied all our needs. When we were under attack from without and fears and anxieties were working overtime from within, You gave us power and supplied all our needs. So God, we praise You no matter what.

We praise You for what You have already done and the faithfulness You have already shown. We praise You no matter what others say or think or how the situation at hand may look. We praise You for Jesus Christ incarnate, crucified, resurrected, ascended, exalted, reigning, interceding and soon coming back. We praise You for the Holy Spirit because the Holy Spirit gives us power to pull in our catch.

When Peter praised You on the day of Pentecost, his catch was brought to the place of his praise and Your Spirit gave him power to pull in the catch You promised him.

In Your name Lord Jesus, do we offer this prayer, Amen.

DAY 131

– DAY 132 –

LUKE 15: 25-32

Gracious God, our Holy Divine Parent, we are grateful like the father of the Prodigal Son, You regularly extend an invitation to a worship and praise party that says, "O come let us worship and bow down, let us kneel before the Lord, our Maker! (Psalm 95:6)"

We are grateful that every week there are those of us who accept your gracious invitation and experience Your presence because You inhabit the praises of Your people. We are grateful when we accept Your gracious invitation, we find release from bondage because where the Spirit of the Lord is, there is liberty. When we accept Your gracious invitation, we are saved and delivered, healed and made whole.

Every week, we who accept your gracious invitation are transformed as we receive an anointed word from God and as we receive a new vision for our lives from You that is greater than any vision we can have for ourselves or others can have for us. Every week, we who accept Your gracious invitation to worship and praise are renewed in the midst of our struggles and strengthened for the journey ahead. Every week, there are those who accept God's gracious invitation to His worship and praise party and give tithes and offerings and experience overflow in their lives as their giving lines up with the word of God.

Every week, we who accept your gracious invitation and line up with the vision of Your house see the spillover of what happens in Your house, in our own lives in miraculous ways. Every week, we who accept Your gracious invitation receive Pentecost power that helps us rout the demons in our own lives and we walk away for addictions and habits that have held us in bondage. Every week, we who accept Your gracious invitation are given the assurance that generational bondage and curses that have been in our families for much too long can be broken.

Every week, we who accept Your gracious invitation to Your worship and praise party are given the assurances that no matter what the culture and society say, we can live financially free and we can strive for and attain excellence. Receive our worship and praise even as we accept Your gracious invitation. We pray in Jesus name, Amen.

DAY 132

– DAY 133 –

I JOHN 1: 1

Lord Jesus, we pray for the kind of faith that was simplified and lived out by the early Christians. They were able to stand firm, face raging lions, all kinds of persecution and ridicule not because they had seen with their own eyes what it could and would do. Your work, Your power and Your spirit hit touchdown lives. Their own lives were living testimonies of the truth that You our Savior, and that You are God in the flesh because nobody but Jesus Christ could have done what had been done in their lives. Some things we believe by faith and somethings we hear we accept by faith.

We pray for the same kind of faith and witness, Lord Christ we may not know about the miracles of the Bible but we pray that we will always remember who we are — we are walking miracles. We were not supposed to finish school. We were not supposed to bounce back from that setback. We were not supposed to get up off that sick bed. We were not supposed to ever be free or clean or sober or happy. We were not supposed to be where we are and have what we have. However we are here against all odds because we call on Your name Lord Jesus and that name makes the difference.

Therefore no matter what we heard or read, we pray for strength to stand on what we personally know about You. We know You save to the upmost. We know that You forgive sin because You have forgiven us. We know that the Lord loves us with a perfect love. We know that if it had not been for You we would not be alive today. We know Lord that You healed us. We know Lord that only You can deliver us. We know You called us. We know You will make a way somehow. We know You are merciful. We know You will hear a sinners prayer. We know Lord that You restored double and triple what the devil has taken away. We know You keep promises. We know You are faithful. We know You will walk in when others walk out. We know You will help pay bills. We know You will help raise children and hold families together. We know Lord You will help us finish school. We know who brought us.

When others tell us that we are just lucky or what has happened to us it's coincidence or by chance, we know that we called on You and we can testify that You are Jesus Christ the living word of God. We only ask Lord Christ that You receive this prayer of thanksgiving and petition, which we offer in Your name, Amen.

– DAY 134 –

II CHRONICLES 33: 12-13

Gracious God, we praise You that when we fall we can get back up again. Even if our name is Manasseh, and we have messed up big time, we can still get back up again. Even if our name is David and we have done the unthinkable, we can still get back up again. Even if our name is Naomi and we feel as if life has dealt You a cruel blow, we can get back up again. Even if our name is Job and we are going through a season of suffering that is greater than anything we ever imagined, we can still get back up again. Even if our name is Elijah and fear has overtaken our faith, we can get back up again. Even if our name is Jeremiah and we find ourselves always on the verge of tears, we can get back up again.

Even if we are the Samaritan woman at the well and try as best we might, we can't seem to make a relationship work, we can get back up again. Even if our name is Simon Peter and Satan has shown us to be weak where we thought we were strong, we can get back up again. Even if our name is Legion and demons are on the verge of ruining our life, we can get back up again. Even is our name is Paul and Silas and our standing for the right thing has landed us in trouble, we can get back up again. Even if our name is John the Revelator and we are trying to get a word from the Lord in a difficult place, we can get back up again. Even is our name is Jesus of Nazareth and enemies have gotten such a victory over us that a comeback seems impossible, we can get back up again.

Even when the pressures of life have gotten the best of us, we can still get back up again. Even when we are about ready to give up and walk away or if somebody has given up on us and walked away from us, we can get back up again. When it seem that every time we get close to our breakthrough and every time we take one step, something snatches us two steps back, we can still get back up again. "For a saint is just a sinner who fell down, and got up!"

Hear us Gracious God when we call, come to our rescue and grant us victory to Your glory and Your honor. You did it for Manasseh and You have done it for others. Now Lord, do it for us. In the name of the Lord Jesus Christ do we offer this prayer, Amen.

DAY 134

– DAY 135 –

PROVERBS 18: 21

Lord Jesus, we are grateful that even though the power of life and death are in the tongue we don't have to receive words of negativity and death that are spoken into our lives, our careers, our families or our future. We can return them to the sender. We can return negative words back to the sender. We can return words of death back to the sender. We can return gossip and pettiness back to the sender. We can return words of discouragement back to the sender.

Lord Jesus not only are we able to reject words of negativity and death, we are also able to receive Your word of life for us. You have a word for us that says,

We are loved.
We are forgiven.
We are cleansed.
We are free.
We are saved and delivered.
We have value.
We can become a new person.
We have a bright future.

I have a vision for your life that is greater than any vision you can have for yourself or that others can have for you.

Jesus still has a word of life for us that says,

Blessed are the poor in spirit, for theirs is the kingdom of heaven.
Blessed are those who mourn, for they will be comforted.
Blessed are the meek, for they will inherit the earth.
Blessed are those who hunger and thirst for righteousness, for they will be filled.
Blessed are the merciful for they will receive mercy.
Blessed are the pure in heart, for they will see God.
Blessed are the peacemakers for they will be called the children of God.
Blessed are those who are persecuted for righteousness' sake, for theirs is the kingdom of heaven.
We are the salt of the earth…
We are the light of the world…

Lord Jesus we receive You as Savior and Lord and Your words of life for us so that we will not only speak life to ourselves but life to others. In Your own name Lord Jesus do we offer this prayer, Amen.

DAY 135

– DAY 136 –

GENESIS 9: 8-17

Lord Jesus, we are grateful for Your long term vision. We are grateful that You are more interested in long-term rainbows than simply effecting quick fix rescues. You work on long-term building while we are working on short-term battles. You work on a long-term design while we are only interested in short-term deliverance. You work on long-term growth while we are only interested in a short-term get-a-way. You work on winning long-term wars while we are only interested in short-term work.

Because You work on long-term vision You place rainbows of favor over our heads as Your sign and pledge that some things are behind us forever and that we will not have to face certain storms again. As the rainbow signified that the flood was behind Noah never to be encountered again, we praise You for the cross of Calvary that testifies to the truth that the guilt and the shame we once carried have been removed from our life, and we don't have to carry it anymore.

The poverty mindset, the low self-esteem and the limited vision that once characterized us has been removed, and we don't have to be bound by it anymore. The sentence of death and the judgment we once carried before we came to Christ has been removed, and we don't have to live under divine wrath anymore. And when people who knew us when try to remind us of what we used to be and the mistakes we used to make we can tell them that the yoke has been broken, the debt has been paid, the sentence has been cancelled and we are now free and new creatures in Christ Jesus. We have a rainbow of Jesus redeeming blood over our heads that reminds us that past life is G-F-G: GONE FOR GOOD!

We are grateful Lord Jesus for the rainbow of forgiveness, the rainbow of a new future and new possibilities and the rainbow of a new attitude that we ought to have now that it has been placed over our heads. We pray for forgiveness when we would put ourselves back under a cloud or when we allow others to put as under a cloud. Now Lord Jesus we give ourselves anew to You and pray for new fire, new vision, new growth, and new determination. In Your own name do we offer this prayer, Amen.

DAY 136

– DAY 137 –

GENESIS 22:1-19

Gracious God, JEHOVAH-JIREH, we praise You. Almighty God, JEHOVAH-JIREH, we worship You. Ever living and Ever reigning God, JEHOVAH-JIREH, we love You. We are grateful that You are JEHOVAH-JIREH, the God who provides. We may not know how, when, where or through whom or by what configuration, arrangement, or reengineering of circumstance, to fit Your vision, heaven's agenda for our good. But, this much we know, You are JEHOVAH-JIREH, the God who provides.

We make plans for our future as well as the future of our loved ones because we believe in You, JEHOVAH-JIREH, the God who provides. Many of us have set out to do great things with no other reason then to believe that we could do them because we serve You, JEHOVAH-JIREH, the God that provides. And many of us have testimonies that our faith has been justified because You have lived up to being, JEHOVAH-JIREH, the God that provides.

We know how our bills are going to be paid if we tithe. You are JEHOVAH-JIREH! We know how we are going to make it if we lose our job. You are JEHOVAH-JIREH! We know how we are going to make it if we lose the support or love or friendship of those who have been with us thus far. You are JEHOVAH-JIREH! We know how we are going to make it now that our loved one has gone home to be with You. You are JEHOVAH-JIREH! We know how we are going to school or follow the vision that You have for our life of starting our own business or branching out in some new area that is totally new to us. You are JEHOVAH-JIREH!

We know how we are going to make it now that our heart is broken because of the relationship that did not work out though we gave it our all. You are JEHOVAH-JIREH! We know how we will get the strength to keep on keeping on when we feel tired, drained and battle weary. You are JEHOVAH-JIREH! We know how we are going to succeed when so many forces are against us and so much undermining is going on behind our backs. You are JEHOVAH-JIREH!

We worship You JEHOVAH-JIREH and we offer this prayer in the name of our Lord Christ, provider of salvation and access to the very throne of God, Amen.

DAY 137

– DAY 138 –

DEUTERONOMY 15: 6 AND PHILIPPIANS 4: 13

Gracious God, we praise You for Your gracious promise that we can become lenders and never borrow again and that we can be rulers rather than those who are ruled. We praise You that in Christ Jesus we can fulfill the vision You have for our lives.

In our moments of doubt we pray for the faith of Paul that we can do all things through Christ who strengthens us. We can get out of debt, live financially free, and experience such overflow that we becomes lenders and never borrow again, through Christ who strengthens us. We can overcome addictions that have held us in bondage and generational curses that have plagued our families, through Christ who strengthens us.

We praise You O God that we can overcome the shame and mistakes of our past and hold our heads up and claim a new future through Christ who strengthens us. We can overcome heartache and anger, embarrassment and fear through Christ who strengthens us. We can be happily married and we can be single and fulfilled through Christ who strengthens us. We can overcome the lust and weakness of the flesh through Christ who strengthens us.

Thank You Lord Jesus. We can go back to school, we can own and operate our own business, we can be successful in places that others told us we would fail, through Christ who strengthens us. We can have a productive life even though others say we are too old, or too young or too sick, through Christ who strengthens us. We can some back from surgery, come back from bankruptcy, come back from divorce, come back from abuse, come back from being talked about and written off as over and done with, through Christ who strengthens us.

We can do all things — dreams that other laughed at us for having, sacrifices other told us we were foolish for making, promises that the devil told us we would never keep, goals that even some of our closest friends and supporters told us we would never reach, mountains that people said we would never climb — we can do all things through Christ who strengthens us.

Therefore when You speak Lord we obey because You have never left us, forsaken us, embarrassed us or made a liar out of those who have put their trust in You. In Your name Lord Jesus do we offer this prayer of praise and commitment, Amen.

– DAY 139 –

GENESIS 41: 37-44 AND JOB 42: 10-12

Gracious God, we pray for faith akin to that of Your servants Joseph and Job, and like Your servant Nelson Mandela, when we go through seasons of persecution, banishment, stress and trail. We pray for perseverance to hold on even when we get tired of holding on. Give us faith to hold on even when it seems that the happiness that has come to others keep passing You by. We pray for the faith to hold on anyhow.

If we can't hold on with our hands, we pray for faith to hold on with our fingers. If we can't hold on with our fingers, we pray for faith to hold on with a prayer. If we can't hold on with prayer, we pray for faith to hold on with scripture. If we can't hold on with scripture, we pray for faith to hold on with a song. If we can't hold on with a song, we pray for faith to hold on to a saint who knows the worth of prayer. If we can't hold on to a saint we pray for faith to hold on to a dream You gave us a long time ago. If we can't hold on to a dream, we pray for faith to hold on to a memory of something that You have done in our lives that we know nobody but You Gracious God, did.

As You were faithful then, as You kept us from falling then, and when we fell, if You picked us up then, Gracious God we know You have not forgotten us now. If You heard us when we called You then, if You delivered us and made a way out of no way then, we know that You are still on the throne now and Your still have the last word over our lives. If You helped us pay our bills then, if You kept us in our right mind then, if You silenced Your enemies then, we know we are still Your child who has been kept as the apple of Your eye.

God we believe You have not just brought us this far simply to repay us for what we lost. We believe You have brought us this far to bless us double for our trouble and to give us breakthroughs far beyond our serving. Nelson Mandela's latter days after prison were greater that his past. Joseph's latter days after prison were greater than his past. Job's latter days were greater than his past. We believe O God that what You did for them, You can and You will do the same for us. Our latter days can be better than our past. Thank You Lord. In Jesus name do we offer this prayer, Amen.

DAY 139

– DAY 140 –

DEUTERONOMY 15: 6 AND JOHN 8: 36

Gracious God, we are grateful for Your promise that we can become lenders and not borrowers and that we can be free indeed, no matter what our past has been or how certain things have been in our families. We give You praise that in the name of Jesus, all generational curses in our background are broken, demolished, destroyed and cast away from us forever. They have no hold upon us anymore.

We give You praise that in the name of Jesus we are free to pursue the vision You have for us, that is greater than any vision we can have for ourselves or that others can have for us. We give You praise that in the name of Jesus we are free to become the lawyer, doctor, teacher, preacher, engineer, businessperson or the astronaut, we've have always thought about becoming.

We give You praise that in the name of Jesus we are free to go back to school and finish school like we have always wanted to do. We give You praise that in the name of Jesus we are free to own property, including apartments and be the developer we have always wanted to become. We give You praise that in the name of Jesus we are free to run for political office, yes even the highest one that we have thought about aspiring to.

We give You praise that in the name of Jesus we are free to become the wife and mother, the husband and father, in a God ordained marriage that we have always wanted. We give You praise that in the name of Jesus we are free not to marry but to live saved, sanctified and satisfied, if that is our desire. We give You praise that in the name of Jesus we are free to marry again, if love comes our way a second time or a real first time , no matter if the last marriage ended by either divorce or death. In the name of Jesus.

We give You the praise that in the name of Jesus we are free to join a church that feeds our spirit, that speaks to our soul, that ministers to where we are right now, no matter what legacy has been handed to us. We give You praise that in the name of Jesus we are free to live without debt and borrowing, and we are free to prosper without guilt no matter how long poverty has been in our background.

Now that we have received Your word and Your promise, we pray for faith, courage and commitment to live according to what Your will and vision is for our lives. We offer this prayer in Your name Lord Jesus Christ, Amen.

– DAY 141 –

PSALM 58

O God, save us from a vengeful and vindictive spirit. Save us from mean thoughts which reduce us. Save us from unkind words which inflame and injure rather than heal and reconcile. Save us from unkind deeds which inflict the same pain upon others we have received. Save us from a spirit that desires the destruction and the pain of those who have hurt us. Help us at all times to remember the admonition of Your word, "Beloved, never avenge yourselves but leave room for the wrath of God; for it is written, 'Vengeance is mine, I will repay, say the Lord'..... Do not be overcome by evil but overcome evil with good." (Romans 12: 18 & 21)

O God, help us to have the desire to forgive. We confess O God that when hurt and pain are deep and when those whom we love have received an injustice; we don't even have the desire for forgiveness, less known the power to forgive. We confess we even have trouble praying for a forgiving spirit. Help us O Lord to desire what is right, which is best for ourselves as well as for others and what pleases You. How should one pray about someone who has raped, robbed and abused us or those whom we love? How does one pray about slave masters or those who continue to perpetuate racism and violence on Your people? How do we seek justice without hatred and bitterness? Give us passion O God without poison.

Give us patience when the wheels of justice are grinding exceedingly slow even as they grind exceedingly fine. Give us patience when it seems, from our limited perspective, like you are not moving fast enough. Give us faith when your people are suffering violence at the hands of unrighteousness. If we can't have understanding, give us endurance until Your perfect will is consummated. O God, save us from cynicism and pessimism. Help us to love others even as You have loved us. And guide us, O God, in our dealings with our enemies or those who have hurt us or those whom we really don't like. In Jesus name do we pray, Amen.

DAY 141

– DAY 142 –

ACTS 28: 30-31

Gracious God, we come to you this day to make a new surrender to Your vision for our lives. We confess, O Lord, there have been times when we have held back from totally surrendering ourselves to You. We have held onto weights and sins that so easily have beset us. We have held on to things that gave us the illusion of pleasure and happiness. We now realize You, O Lord, are the source of all joy and happiness. We have held on to money because of the illusion of security it provides. We now confess, O God, You are the only real security in this life. We now surrender our tithes and our offerings to you. We confess O Lord, we have allowed our concern about what others may say or think prevent our total surrender to you. We now realize You are the giver of every good and perfect gift and what You give no one can take from us without our permission and cooperation. We now realize you, Jesus, lover and Savior of our souls are the friend that sticks closer than anyone else.

Our desire is to please You. Our desire is to return love to You. Our desire is to do Your will. Our desire is to give to You. Our desire is to hold nothing back from You. Our desire is to follow Your vision for our lives. And so, we say yes Lord, use us to continue the ongoing work of the kingdom even as you used Paul, Peter and the other believers of the Book of Acts. Use us as instruments of Your Holy Spirit even as You used the believers in the Book of Acts.

Thank you Lord, for how You have used us in days past and gone. We stand on tiptoe in expectation as we live each day and as we anticipate the future to see how You are going to use us in new ways to glorify You. We pray the words of our mouths, the meditations of our hearts, the work of our hands and the service of our lives will be acceptable in your sight O Lord our strength and our redeemer. This we ask in in Jesus name, Amen.

– DAY 143 –

ACTS 28: 1-10

O God, we are grateful that whether on land or sea or in the air, your power holds us, keeps us, protects us and provides for us. O God, we are grateful that no matter what forms the enemy takes when he attacks, the anointing, the covering over our lives still holds. O God, we are grateful that no matter where we are, the promises of Your word are still good. We are grateful that no weapon formed against us shall prosper and every word that rises in judgment against us, You shall refute. We are grateful that they who delight themselves in You and wait upon You can ask and receive; seek and find; knock and doors are opened to them. We are grateful for Your power and promises that hold through it all and despite all.

O God, we pray we will always remember who we are as Your servants so when things happen, when storms rage, when vipers attack, we will remember we are in Your hand and You will get the victory for us. We pray for faith to shake the vipers that attack in the fire, as Your servant Paul did in Acts 28. We give You glory for Your faithfulness, we pray for faithfulness to Your will and purpose. We give You glory for Your love and forgiveness, we pray for a love for You that lasts through storms and trials, and for forgiveness that knows when and how to let go of that which impedes our growth. We praise You for the glory that is revealed around us every day. We pray our lives will reflect and refract Your glory.

O God, You have made ways for us in the past. We pray for faith that anticipates You doing even greater things in our life. Because You live and because You are a miracle working God, we know Your best for us is still yet to be. We are grateful for all that You have brought us through and how You have blessed us in days past and gone. However, we stand on the tiptoes of faith looking forward to other blessings You will for us and other ways we can serve You. We pray for growth that allows us to live for You in new ways. Even so, Maranatha! Come Lord Jesus! In his name do we pray, Amen.

DAY 143

– DAY 144 –

PSALM 63: 1-5

O God, we come into Your presence to just praise You. So many times we come with burdens but today we just want to praise You. We've come to feast on the joy of Your presence. We've come to feast on the peace that time spent with You gives. We've come to feast on the strength we receive whenever we draw near to You. We've come to feast on the salvation we have in Jesus Christ and the victory which is ours to claim in Him in all situations, in all places at all times.

Like the Psalmist, we say to You, O God, You are my God, I seek You, my soul thirsts for You; my flesh faints for You, as in a dry and weary land where there is no water. So I have looked upon You in the sanctuary beholding Your power and glory. Because Your steadfast love is better than life, my lips will praise You. So I will bless You as long as I live. I will lift my hands and call on Your name. My soul is satisfied as with a rich feast and my mouth praises You with joyful lips.

We love You Lord. When we think about how far You have brought us and how You continue to keep us day by day and how You forgive us over and over. We just love to praise and serve You because You are good and we are so grateful. Now God, as we shall face whatever we will face when we finish this prayer, we pray that praise will always be upon our lips and You will always be in our view. In Jesus name, Amen.

DAY 144

– DAY 145 –

GENESIS 50: 15-21

Lord Christ, we are grateful for Your love that goes so far beyond human love. When human love gets beside itself, Your love will still go beyond itself. When human love breaks down, Your love, Lord Christ, will build us up. When human love gets confused, Your love will still be comforting. When human love gets deceptive, Your love will still be dependable.

When human love fails, Your love will still be faithful. When human love gets jealous, Your love will still be joyful. When human love gets insecure, Your love will still be inspiring. When human love becomes problematic, Your love, oh Lord Christ, will be a problem solver. When human love stumbles, Your love will still be standing. When human love puts us down, Your love will pick us up.

When the love of family failed and betrayed Joseph and he was sold into slavery, God's love stayed with him and gave him favor in Egypt, in the place of his loneliness in captivity. What they meant for bad You meant for good. What they meant for evil, You meant for excellence. What they meant for slavery, You meant for salvation. What they meant for meanness, You meant for a miracle.

As Joseph forgave his brothers, we pray Lord Christ that we would also have a heart for forgiveness as You continue to forgive us. We confess O Lord that we have sinned and fallen short of Your glory and in our own ways we have hurt You as much as others have hurt us. Yet, You continue to forgive us over and over again. In this we know You love us still. We know You love us in that every day we sin by thought, by word and by deed. Every day we do enough wrong and leave undone enough right to have our footsteps cut short in judgment.

Yet, every day You choose to forgive us of our broken promises and forgotten vows and You wake us up every morning with a finger of love and start us on our way. Every day You keep us from dangers seen and unseen.

We pray that You will never forget how much we have been forgiven so that like Joseph we too can be forgiven. In Your name do we offer this prayer oh forgive me Lord Christ, Amen.

DAY 145

– DAY 146 –

PSALM 55: 22

O God on this day, we cast all of our burdens and cares upon You because You have invited us and also because they are about to get the best of us. Some, we have carried for so long they have become like our shadows---always with us and just waiting for conditions to be right to show themselves. Some are new and we don't' know just what to do with them, about them or how they will impact our lives. We need some breathing room, a breakthrough, a victory, a recess, some recoup or recovery time.

So today, we cast our burdens on You because we are about to slip and lose our grip. Doubt is settling in, frustration is building; the Adversary like a termite is trying to eat away at the foundations of our faith. The Adversary like a flea is making us uncomfortable and causing misery. The Adversary like a mosquito is whirling around our heads buzzing and causing sleep to flee.

O God, we pray for steadfastness so we will not slip or stumble or be moved. We want to be as steadfast as a tree planted by the rivers of waters. We don't have the power to stand by ourselves, so stand with us God even in the midst of our doubts and questions. We don't have the perseverance to run by ourselves, so run with us Lord even in the midst of our sins and failed good intentions.

God thank You for reassuring us of Your presence even as we pour out our hearts to You. Please forgive us when we question You. Please be patient with us. Give us patience and help us to persevere as Your will is worked out in our lives. In Jesus' name, Amen.

– DAY 147 –

PSALM 53: 2

O God, we pray for a heart that truly seeks after You. We pray for the kind of love and devotion that hungers and thirsts for more of Your righteousness and more of Your anointing. We don't simply want a curiosity about You. We don't simply desire head knowledge that would help us to engage in clever conversation or formulate interesting theories about You. We don't simply desire Bible knowledge that allows us to quote scripture. We don't simply desire knowledge of church doctrines that is conversant with history and polity. We don't simply desire familiarity with the great theologians, philosophers and ethicists so we can be skilled in academic discourse.

We pray for a heart that truly seeks after You. We pray for minds that truly seek to know You. We pray for lives that truly seek to glorify You. We recognize some deny You with words and others deny You with works; some deny You with talent and others deny You with tithes; some deny You with debate and others deny You with devotion; some deny You with lies and others deny You with their lives. O God, save us from the foolishness of denial by thought, word and deed. Our sin denies Your authority. Our selfishness denies Your supremacy. Our pride denies Your power. Our rebellion denies Your word. Our egos deny Your reign over us. Our failure to tithe denies Your faithfulness. Our acting on impulses or decisions that are made without first consulting You deny Your will.

O God, we deny You in so many ways. Forgive us we pray and help us to cultivate the seed of faith, love and devotion in our hearts that always seeks after You. As Your servant, St. Augustine has said, "You have made us for Yourself O God and our souls are restless until they find their rest in You." Through Jesus Christ we pray, Amen.

DAY 147

– DAY 148 –

JOB 1: 20

Gracious God, we confess there are times when like Your servant Job of old, we don't understand what You are doing and why You are allowing some things to happen. However, we pray for faith to stay with You and to trust you, even as he did. Even with all we may not understand there are still some things we know about You and can say and stand on without fear of contradiction.

You will never betray us. You will never falsely accuse us. You will never lie to us or lie on us. You will never give us bad counsel or direct us in the wrong way. You will never turn Your heart away from us. You will never bow to any political or any other kind of pressure when it comes to blessing us or being our advocate. You will never take us for granted. You will never turn us over to our enemies to save Yourself.

You will never walk out on us. You will never give up on us. You will never abuse or misuse our love or our trust. You will never leave a prayer unanswered or turn a deaf ear to our cry. You will never leave us without giving us what we need to keep standing until our breakthrough comes. You will never stop believing in us or stop loving us. Even in our troubles, great is Your faithfulness, O God.

We will continue to trust You because no matter what we experience or go through we know there is one word that we will never hear from You and that word is "can't." There is no problem You can't solve. There is no situation You can't turn around. There is no enemy You can't conquer. There is no sickness You can't cure. There is no door You can't open. There is no bill You can't pay.

There is no addiction You can't deliver us from. There is no generational curse You can't destroy. There is no hell-hold You can't enter. There is no devil You can't conquer. There is no yoke You can't break. There is no stronghold You can't bring down. There is no life You can't redeem. There is no soul You can't save. There is no place You can't go.

Therefore we pray for faith to stay with You no matter what happens from day to day or time to time. When things are going well and when our lives have been turned upside down and inside out, we pray for faith to stay with you. We offer this prayer in the name of our Lord Jesus who stays with us no matter what, Amen.

DAY 148

– DAY 149 –

LUKE 9: 28-36

Lord Jesus, teach us how to pray, give us a passion for prayer and help us to pray with such earnestness that our prayer life will also transfigure us, as You were on the mountain. Heaven responded in an unusual way when prayer transfigured You. We recognize O Lord that perhaps heaven is waiting for something to change in us, in our attitude, in our living and in our giving.

Heaven can't do what heaven desires as long as we are under a curse because we will not tithe. Heaven can't do what heaven desires as long as we are letting the devil get the victory over our finances. Heaven can't do what heaven desires as long as we are in rebellion to the spiritual authority the Lord has placed in our lives. Heaven can't do what heaven desires as long as we are abusing and misusing our relationships and friendships. Heaven can't do what heaven desires as long as we keep yielding to our flesh and to our weaknesses.

Heaven can't do what heaven desires as long as we are living in fear. Heaven can't do what heaven desires until our prayer life, our worship life, our Bible study goes to another level in terms of its depth and quality. Heaven can't do what heaven desires as long as we have a negative and petty spirit and a gossiping, rumor spreading and tale bearing tongue.

When something changes in us, we can dare look for Your presence to come into our midst as never before. Teach us O Lord how to reverence Your presence when You show up as never before because anything can happen when we are in Your presence. Answers to prayers we have been offering up can be given right at that moment. Healing can take place right at that moment. Deliverance from every weight and sin that so easily besets us can be given right at that moment. Breakthroughs can come forth, right at that moment. Yokes in our family can be broken right at that moment. Anger and hurt that some of us have lived with for years can leave our hearts right at that moment. Fear that has kept our vision on lock down can leave somebody's spirit right at that moment.

Give us O Lord a transfiguring prayer life and teach us how to reverence Your presence when You show up as never before. We ask this prayer in Your name, Lord Jesus, Amen.

DAY 149

– DAY 150 –

MATTHEW 14: 22-23

Gracious God, as we gather like the disciples in the storm to worship You, we honor You for who You are and we are grateful for the way You have saved us personally. We praise You for our testimonies, "we once were lost but now we are found. We were blind but now we see."

We praise You for all You have done for us that makes our worshipping real. You came to us and You cared for us. You delivered us and You defended us. You empowered us and You exalted us. You filled us and You freed us. You held us and You healed us. You lifted us and You loved us. You gave us mercy and You worked a miracle in our life. You received us and You redeemed us. You saved us and You sanctified us. For all of this and more we give You our heartfelt praise and worship. We declare You and You alone are worthy to be praised.

Forgive us O Lord for the times when we take our eyes off of You, just like Your disciple Peter did many years ago. We recognize that is the reason we can't sleep at night. That is the reason some of us toss and turn every night worrying about problems and what may happen the next day. We have taken our eyes off of You, Lord Jesus. That is the reason some of us are always talking about what we can't do. We have taken our eyes off of You, Lord Jesus. That is the reason some of us stay in bondage to certain habits, sins, addictions and weaknesses. We have taken our eyes off of You, Lord Jesus.

That is the reason some of us believe we cannot live and be happy without certain people in our lives. We have taken our eyes off of You, Lord Jesus. That is the reason that even after we pray and commit certain things to You we still try to work stuff out and deal with it ourselves and only make matters worse. We have taken our eyes off of You, Lord Jesus.

That is the reason some of us are always saying we can't afford to tithe. We have taken our eyes off of You, Lord Jesus. That is the reason some of us have settled for living the rest of our lives in debt rather than being financially free. We have taken our eyes off of You, Lord Jesus.

Forgive us, Gracious Lord, as we recommit ourselves to You in this moment of worship. In Your name Lord Jesus do we offer this prayer, Amen.

– DAY 151 –

GENESIS 13: 2

O God, we pray that like Abraham You would help us build assets as we pursue Your vision for our lives. O God teach us the difference between an asset and a liability. Help us to understand that people, experiences, institutions and situations that add value to our lives, to our walk with You and to the vision You have shown to us, are assets. Those that take away or subtract or detract are liabilities.

Help us to understand that if we feel affirmation then it or they are assets but if we feel burdened, then it or they are liabilities. If we feel caring, then it or they are assets but if we feel coldness, then it or they are liabilities. If we feel defended , then it or they are assets but if we feel defeated, then it or they are liabilities.

If we feel delivered, then it or they are assets but if we feel demeaned, then it or they are liabilities. If we feel delight then it or they are assets but if we feel dread, then it or they are liabilities. If we feel enlightened, then it or they are assets but if we feel empty, then it or they are liabilities. If we feel faith or faithfulness, then it or they are assets but if we feel fickleness, then it or they are liabilities.

If we feel fulfilled, then it or they are assets but if we feel like a fool, then it or they are liabilities. If we feel as if we are growing, then it or they are assets but if we well feel like groaning then it or they are liabilities. If we feel good, then it or they are assets but if we feel guilty, then it or they are liabilities. If we feel hopeful, then it or they are assets but if we feel hopeless, then it or they are liabilities.

If we feel rewarded, then it or they are assets but if we feel revulsion, then it or they are liabilities. If we feel stronger, then it or they are assets but if we feel stifled, then it or they are liabilities. If we feel useful, then it or they are assets but if we feel used then it or they are liabilities. If we feel understanding, then it or they are assets but if we feel undervalued, then it or they are liabilities. If we feel worth, then it or they are assets but if we feel worthless, then it or they are liabilities.

O Christ of God, the hope of glory; O God, Father, Son and Holy Spirit You are our greatest asset and we give You praise. In the name of the Lord Jesus do we offer this prayer, Amen.

– DAY 152 –

NUMBERS 27: 1-7

O Gracious God, like the daughters of Zelophehad, You have made us in such a way we are at variance with the tradition or the law or the way the culture has defined us. You made us with ambition while the culture and tradition have said we are supposed to be lazy and shiftless. You made us to be anointed while the culture and tradition have said we are supposed to be addicted. You made us to be bountiful while the culture and tradition have said we are supposed to be broken. You made us to be bold while the culture and tradition have said we are to be in bondage. You made us to be conquerors while the culture and tradition have said we are supposed to be conquered. You made us with class while the culture and tradition have said we are supposed to be crass. You made us to be creative while the culture and tradition have said we are supposed to be confused.

God, You made us to be financially delivered while the culture and tradition have said we are supposed to be in debt. You made us gifted while the culture and tradition have said we are to be in grief. You made us to be great while the culture and tradition have said we are to be in the ghetto. You made us intelligent while the culture and the tradition have said we are supposed to be ignorant. You made us to be loved while the culture and tradition have said we are supposed to be the least. You made us with laughter while the culture and tradition have said we are supposed to be languishing. You made us with potential while the culture and tradition have said we are supposed to be petty. You made us to be prosperous while the culture and the tradition have said we are supposed to be in poverty. You made us to be redeemed while the culture and tradition have said we are to be rejected.

God, You made us with substance while the culture and tradition have said we are supposed to be shallow. You made us with strength while the culture and tradition have said we are to be in stress. You made us to be saved while the culture and tradition have said we are to be in sin. You made us with self-confidence while the culture and tradition have said we are supposed to have no or little confidence. You made us with virtue while the culture and tradition have said we are supposed to be vulgar. You made us with vision while the culture and tradition have said we are supposed to think like a victim, live like a victim and talk like a victim. You made us to be workers while the culture and tradition have said we are to be on welfare.

You made us with willpower while the culture and tradition have said we are made to be weak. God, You made us to be anointed, creative, intelligent, virtuous and powerful, while the culture and tradition have said such qualities are supposed to belong to others because they have the rights of inheritance and privilege.

Now Gracious God, because You are our true Parent, like the daughters of Zelophehad, we now claim our inheritance. In the name of the Lord Jesus, we claim our inheritance and we offer this prayer in his mighty and matchless name, Amen.

– DAY 153 –

I KINGS 3: 3-15

Gracious God, we praise You for the blessings You continue to pour into our lives that are far beyond or expectations and our deserving. We pray for the wisdom of Solomon who understood there was another way to manage his blessings and thus avoided the waste the Prodigal Son experienced.

Gracious God, we pray we will never forget that being a child of God means we have options and there is another way to live. There is another way beside debt. There is another way beside lashing out in anger and bitterness. There is another way beside the welfare, the poverty, the low self-esteem and low ambitions and expectations, and the mediocrity that has been in our family for generations. Thank You, God, that there is another way.

We give praise to You Lord Jesus for showing us there is another way. You came to a Samaritan woman who was full of shame because of her failed relationships and told her there is another way to live beside being the subject of gossip and the object of men. You came to Zacchaeus and told him there is another way to live beside being a slave to money. You came to Legion and told him there is another way to live beside being a victim to demons.

You told a dying thief on the cross there is another way to live beside getting over on people. You came to Saul of Tarsus on the Damascus Road and told him here is another way to live beside narrowness and hatred. One day You died on a cross and rose again to show us there is another way beside sin and death. One day You stepped on a cloud and went back to glory and one day You shall return again in the same manner You left to take us home to be with You forever because for us there is another way. Whoever we are and whatever our situation, we pray we will never forget there is another way.

Lord Jesus, You are the way, the truth and the light. We pray for wisdom to walk in Your way. We pray for courage to follow Your truth. We pray for passion to follow Your light as we commit ourselves again to You on this day. In Your name Lord Jesus do we offer this prayer, Amen.

DAY 153

– DAY 154 –

I KINGS 11: 1-10

Gracious God, we praise You for Your faithfulness to us, a faithfulness that holds us to death and beyond. We pray for a "till death do us part" faith and walk with You. Hold us O God and keep us so our hearts and affection will not stray from You as did those of Your servant Solomon, whose heart turned from You to other gods in the latter days and waning years of his life. We pray we will stay with You during our ups as well as our downs as You continue to write new chapters to our lives.

As we begin to make changes to get beyond where we presently are, we pray for perseverance to stay with what we have started as long as we live, "till death do us part," because true freedom, true transformation, true prosperity, true deliverance, true salvation and true deliverance, are about permanence and not about patchwork. If we have started growing for Your glory O God, we pray that we will not just grow to a certain point and stop. We pray that we will continue to grow "till death do us part."

If we have started seeking God's face and abiding in Your presence O God, we pray that we will do so until death and that we will never return to only seeking You when we want something from Your blessing hand. If we have started worshipping You on a regular basis or attending church, we pray that we will continue even when things either start going well or bad during certain seasons in our life. If we have started tithing, we pray that we will never stop tithing during those times when our money gets funny or when we begin to prosper so much that ten percent doesn't seem like a whole lot.

If we have started saving and investing, help us to stay with it until death. We pray we don't stop saving and investing once we get a certain amount because it is more than we have ever had. If we have started living within our means and only buying what we can really afford instead of building up credit card debt, help us to continue even to death. We pray we will not stop because we can now have a larger credit line or because we don't have any debt.

O God, You are faithful and You do not break promises. We stand upon Your word and we pray that our commitment to You will be as strong as Your commitment to us as seen in the sacrifice of the Lord Jesus upon the cross. In his name do we offer this prayer, Amen.

– DAY 155 –

II KINGS 4: 1-7

Gracious God, we praise You for Your provision. We are grateful that You are able to take our little and make much of it. When the widow of old came to Your prophet Elisha with her financial need, she told him she had nothing in her house except a jar of oil. We pray, O God, You will help us to understand the importance of whatever little we have to work with.

We pray we will never underestimate the importance of our jar of oil. Help us to understand the importance of our "except." We confess O God that sometimes we say, "I have nothing in the house except prayer. I have nothing in the house except faith. I have nothing in the house except a vision and a dream. I have nothing in the house except one friend or another person who believes in me. I have nothing in the house except determination. I have nothing in the house except a working mind and a committed heart. When we say such things, O God, we sometimes do not understand the importance of what we have in our house or the resources we have left in our hands.

O God, show us the jars of oils and the "excepts" we may be overlooking, which is the right resource for our need. We praise You O God that with nothing except a shepherd's rod, You sent Moses to Egypt to free God's people from over 400 years of Egyptian bondage. With nothing except a march and a shout, Joshua and the people of God brought down the walls of Jericho. With nothing except a slingshot, David brought down Goliath.

With nothing except a little oil in the cruse and a little meal, God kept his prophet Elijah and the widow of Zarephath and her son alive for three years while famine was in the land. With nothing except two fish and five barely loaves, the Lord Jesus fed five thousand. And with nothing except an old rugged cross, he redeemed our souls from a burning hell.

Now, O God, Your power multiplied the resources of the widow who faithfully followed the instructions of the prophet. We pray for her faith and faithfulness so we too will see Your multiplying, miracle working power at work in our situations of debt and other forms of bondage and need. In the name of the Lord Jesus do we offer this prayer, Amen.

– DAY 156 –

II CHRONICLES 25: 5-9

O God, we know within our hearts and minds You have much more for us than anything the enemy offers. However, we also recognize when we choose Your way to prosper and we see others prospering faster, seemingly without our headaches and struggles, there will be times when we feel we are losing or we will not do as well as others who either follow Satan's ways or are following their own devices.

There will be times, O God, when Satan will try to convince us that his way is better than Your way. He will try to convince us that his way of getting things fast is better than Your way of doing things right, even if it takes longer. He will tell us his way of short-term pleasure is better than Your way of long term gain. His way of greed is better than Your way of graciousness. His way of trickery is better than Your way of truth.

His way of politics is better than Your way of principle. His way of compromise is better than Your way of conviction. His way of deceit is better than Your way of devotion. His way of ruthlessness is better than God's way of righteousness. His way of fighting is better than Your way of faithfulness. His way of scheming is better than Your way of salvation. His way of instigation is better than Your way of integrity. His way of plotting is better than Your way of prayer.

His way of backbiting is better than Your way of bridge building. His way of getting is better than Your way of giving. His way of vindictiveness is better than Your way of virtue. His way of undercutting is better than Your way of under girding. His way of meanness is better than Your way of mercy. His way of lying is better than Your way of lifting. His way of tattling is better than Your way of trust. His way of gossip is better than Your way of gratitude. His way of stooping is better than Your way of standing.

O God, when the enemy would tempt us with the lies of his promises, we pray we would remember the truth and faithfulness of Your word as well as the testimony of our own experience. You can and You will give us much more than anything the enemy can offer. In the name of the Lord Jesus do we offer this prayer, Amen.

DAY 156

– DAY 157 –

HAGGAI 1: 2-11

O God of grace and glory, we confess like the people who lived in the day of the prophet Haggai, we have areas of brokenness in our relationship with You. We confess O God that we have broken windows in our lives that are preventing us from going to the next level with God and in life. We have broken windows in our relationship with You O God that are stopping us from pursuing the vision You have for us.

Some of us have an area of life we have not yet yielded to Your word O God. Some of us have habits, pleasures, weights or sins, we have not yielded to You O God. Some of us have unforgiveness or anger that we are holding on to. Some of us are guilty of not speaking to somebody or refusing to work with somebody we worship with every Sunday. There are some of us who have no problem in giving God praise but will not open our mouths to speak to certain people.

Some of us are still holding on to shame, guilt, or mistakes, even though You have forgiven us and the Lord Jesus has cleansed us. Some of us are jealous because we don't look like somebody else, dress like somebody else or because we don't have somebody else's youth, money, mate, education, talents, or gifts. Some of us have gossiping tongues that are too quick to pass on dirt or an anxious ear that is too ready to hear it and a receptive heart that is too quick to believe trash that is brought to us.

Some of us refuse to tithe, or if we tithe, refuse to move beyond the tithe in terms of our giving. Some of us worship tradition and how things used to be in our mind instead of following where the Holy Spirit is taking the church in these latter days.

The prophet Haggai told the people in his day no matter how bad things were for them financially and economically, it was time to start fixing the temple. We recognize the time has come to get our windows fixed. And we are grateful for the gospel that tells us about a broken window specialist and his name is Jesus. Whatever our broken windows are, he is able to fix them.

We bring our broken windows to You Lord, Jesus. Fix us for service and fix us for Your glory. In Your name do we offer this prayer, Amen.

DAY 157

– DAY 158 –

HAGGAI 2: 1-10

God, we praise You first for who You are. We give You glory first for who You are. Then we praise You O God for all You have done and all You are able to do. You alone are able to bring gold out of grime, silver out of slime, miracles out of a mess, testimonies out of trouble, deliverance out of death, life out of lies, salvation out of scheming, strength out of sickness, power out of peril, creation out of chaos, conquest out of Calvary, Resurrection out of rejection and Easter out of envy.

Now, O God, we pray for vision and for faith that prevents us from becoming stuck in former glory. We know You alone, O God, have brought some of us a mighty long way. You have healed us from our diseases. You have answered our prayers. You have worked miracles and made ways out of no way for us. However, everything You have done in our lives is former glory. According to Your word, O God, You have latter glory that far surpasses former glory. With all You have already done for us, Your best is yet to be.

We believe, O God, You have some miracles to perform in our lives that will surpass any we have seen thus far. We believe, O God, You have some worship experiences that will surpass any that we have witnessed thus far. We believe, O God, You have some prosperity to pour into our lives that will surpass any we have seen thus far. We believe, O God, You have anointing and power to pour into our lives that will surpass any that we have seen thus far. We believe O God that You have answers to prayers that will surpass any that we have seen thus far.

We believe Your word, O God, that promises the latter splendor of this house, of this life, of this church, of this vision, shall be greater than the former. We pray for the determined spirit of the writer, who wrote to Your glory:

> I'm pressing on the upward way, New heights I'm gaining every day,
> Still praying as I'm onward bound, Plant my feet on higher ground.
> (I'm Pressing on the Upward Way, Johnson Oatman, Jr.)

> Lord lift me up and let me stand, By faith on heaven's table land,
> A higher plane that I have found, Lord plant my feet on higher ground.

In the name of the Lord Jesus Christ do we offer this prayer, Amen.

– DAY 159 –

HAGGAI 2: 15-19

God You have a tipping point that will bring us into another dimension of living and of service to You. We pray, O God, we will reach our tipping point as others have before us. Abraham reached his when he decided he would do what God told him to do; and was to leave the place where he was as a seventy-five year old man and go where God led him. We pray for faith to do the same.

Moses reached his when he decided to obey the voice of God that spoke to him out of a burning bush and went back to Egypt from where he had run forty years earlier in fear and armed with only a walking stick to tell Pharaoh, the world's mightiest monarch, to let God's people go. We pray for vision to do the same.

Caleb reached his when as an eighty-five year old man, he asked for a mountain that still needed to be conquered. We pray for boldness to do the same. David reached his when he was still a young boy and brought down a giant with only a slingshot. We pray for courage to do the same. Jabez reached his when he prayed, even though his name meant pain, You would still enlarge his territory and the Lord's hand would be with him to keep him from hurt and harm. We pray for insight to do the same.

The widow with the two mites reached hers when she gave her last penny to You believing You would continue to take care of her. We pray for daring to do the same. Mary of Nazareth reached hers when the Holy Spirit came upon her and told her even though others might not understand and falsely accuse her, as a young virgin she would bear a child and call his name Jesus because he would save his people from their sins, and Mary said, "My soul magnifies the Lord…Let it be to me according to Your word." We pray for commitment to do the same.

The Lord Jesus kept reaching his tipping point over and over again because he continued to be obedient to the perfect will of God. He reached it again in Gethsemane after Satan hit him with everything he had and Jesus still prayed to God his Father, "Nevertheless not my will but Your will be done." He reached it when they hung him high and stretched him wide and he kept on dying until Your sins and my sins were all washed away. We pray for love to do the same and in His name do we offer this prayer, Amen.

– DAY 160 –

MATTHEW 25: 19-30

Gracious God, we may not have the same blessings in the same amount, but You have blessed us all beyond our deserving. Someone observed, "If we own just one Bible, we are abundantly blessed; one-third of the entire world does not have access to one. If we woke up this morning with more health than illness, we are more blessed than the million people who will not survive this week. If we have never experienced the danger of battle, the loneliness of imprisonment, the agony of torture or the pangs of starvation, we are ahead of 500 million people in the world."

"If we can attend a church meeting without fear of harassment, arrest, torture or death, we are more blessed than three billion people in the world. If we have food in the refrigerator, clothes on our back, a roof over our head and a place to sleep, we are richer than 75 percent of this world. If we have money in the bank, in our wallet or spare change in a dish somewhere, we are among the top eight percent of the world's wealthy."

"If our parents are still alive and still married, we belong to a very rare group, even in the United States. If we were able to read the Sunday bulletin, we are more blessed than more than two billion people in the world who cannot read at all." Even with our one talent, we have started off with much more than most of the people in the world. Even with all we claim we lack; we are still blessed and highly favored by the Lord.

O God, we do not simply praise You for our blessings, we pray You would awaken in us a passion for helping the hurting and the victimized that do not have what we take for granted. We know suffering is not due to Your will but human greed. We know You desire that all of Your children prosper everywhere and we all live in health.

Teach us what to do O God in the places where we live, work and worship that we might be Your instruments of relief and release, healing and comfort, Your peace and Your presence, for those who are victims of the systemic evil that holds vast populations of Your creation in bondage.

In the name of the Lord Jesus who died, rose and lives that we might be triumphant over the principalities and powers of this world, do we offer this prayer, Amen.

– DAY 161 –

MARK 5: 24-34

We praise You Lord Jesus that the touch of faith that reaches out to You can deliver us from financial barriers, which can prevent us from pursuing the vision You have for our lives. Like the woman in Mark 5:24-34, we refuse to accept our condition as permanent. No matter how long we have been laboring with something or someone, no matter how many times we have tried and failed, we continue to believe there is a touch that will bring life. There is a touch that will bring healing. There is a touch that will set us free from the limitations, anxieties and insecurities that come when we live and bow down before the gold standard. There is a touch that will release us to live in the vision God has for our lives.

There is a touch that will help us stand up straight with confidence rather than slouch with poor self-esteem and stoop with fear. There is a touch that will set us free from what we think is the irresistible pull of the flesh. There is a touch that will set us free from the bondage of habits and the bondage of the past. There is a touch that will bring healing to our hurts and our rejection. We praise You O Lord because where we are is where we happen to be not where we have to be. Our financial and other situations are not fixed; they are fixable, if we have the right touch. Therefore, we reach out to You O Lord.

When we reach out to You something happens between the two of us. Something flows from You and something dries up in us. Acceptance flows from You and anger dries up in us. Bounty flows from You and bitterness dries up in us. Breakthrough flows from You and bondage dries up in us. Delight flows from You and depression dries up in us. Deliverance flows from You and demons dry up in us. Excellence flows from You and excuses dry up in us. Faith flows from You and fear dries up in us. Grace flows from You and guilt dries up in us. Healing flows from You and hurt dries up in us. Love flows from You and loneliness dries up in us. Redemption flows from You and rebellion dries up in us. Salvation flows from You and shame dries up in us. Tenderness flows from You and turmoil dries up in us. Willpower flows from You and weakness dries up in us.

Thank You Lord Jesus for all that takes place between us when we reach out and touch You. In Your name Lord Jesus do we offer this prayer, Amen.

– DAY 162 –

MARK 11: 1-10

Lord Jesus, even as Your coming into Jerusalem was not by accident but by Your forethought and planning, we are grateful for Your power and presence that has kept and guided us even when the plans of the enemy tried to wreck our lives.

We know gracious Lord it's no accident that what was supposed to defeat us didn't. It's no accident that we did not die when we were supposed to. It's no accident we escaped when we should have been caught. It's no accident the money appeared just when we needed it. It's no accident we got up off of that sick bed when people expected to come to our funeral.

It's no accident we walked away from that accident or injury that was not supposed to heal. It's no accident we are still here when others we grew up with or used to hang out with are not. It's no accident when our backs were up against the wall and we did not know what to do, a way appeared out of no way. It's no accident whenever we hear and receive the Gospel, we can make a decision to start living in new ways.

It's no accident the trouble came into our lives when it did because if it had come earlier, we would not have been able to handle it. It's no accident the weapon that was formed against us did not prosper. It's no accident the place where we landed was a better place than the place that was denied us. It's no accident we were able to recover as well as we have after we fell. It's no accident we got a second chance to get it right. It's no accident that we met that person when we did, where we did, the way we did, who has been such a blessing to our lives.

Lord Jesus, we pray You will continue to lead us and guide us according to Your will and vision so our lives will glorify and honor You. In Your name do we offer this prayer, Amen.

DAY 162

– DAY 163 –

LUKE 12: 13-21

Gracious and loving God, we confess that many of us have wrapped our self-worth in the trappings of this world that have left us naked and vulnerable. We have defined ourselves by what we wear, what we drive, where we live and what we do. We have defined ourselves by the negative things our enemies say about us and write about us. We have defined ourselves by the expectations of others and by our professional associations and various social clubs.

We have defined ourselves by our titles and our jobs. We have defined ourselves by our relationships and by our family or our marriage. Some of us have even defined ourselves by some astrological sign of the zodiac. We have defined ourselves by our guilt and our shame. We have defined ourselves by our faults and our failures.

However, all of these definitions have left us naked and exposed to the vicissitudes and humiliation of life. What do we do when like the Samaritan woman, we find ourselves isolated and treated like social pariahs and lepers? What do we do when like the Lord Jesus, we are facing Calvary with all of its pain and suffering and prayer does not take Calvary away? What do we do when like the Lord Jesus we are at Calvary and our enemies are mocking and God seems to have forsaken us?

At such times, we feel weak and exposed, naked and vulnerable to the outside world. With all that we have, with all that we own, in spite of all of those we know, we feel worthless and ashamed as we discover that our self-worth, image and reputations have no clothes on. Our faith has no clothes on. Our significant relationships have no clothes on. Our friendships have no clothes on. Our financial security has no clothes on.

We give You praise for the Gospel, the good news that tells us about Jesus who sees us as we are and draws us to him and covers us with his righteousness, love, forgiveness, cleansing and power and gives us a new understanding of our self-worth. For if anyone is in Christ Jesus, he or she is a new creation, old things are passed away and all things become new (2 Corinthians 5:17). In his name do we offer this prayer, Amen.

DAY 163

– DAY 164 –

LUKE 15: 11-24

Lord Jesus, we praise You for the desire for something more and something better. When like the Prodigal Son, we find ourselves in situations of disgrace and shame, we pray we will never lose our desire for something more and something better. No matter how long we have been where we are or the way we are, no matter how may hogs surround us who have no vision for a better life, no matter how many generations of our family have lived in the pen of low self-esteem and low aim and ambition, we pray we will never lose our desire for something better.

No matter how impossible the odds, no matter how many obstacles, no matter how high the hurdles, no matter how many prophets of doom tell us what we can't do, no matter how difficult the road to recovery and wholeness, we pray we will never lose Your desire for something better.

Lord Jesus of power and authority, we know as long as we have the desire, deliverance is possible. As long as we have the desire, You will help us. As long as we have the desire, miracles can happen. As long as we have the desire, visions can come. As long as we have the desire, the devil cannot defeat us. As long as we have the desire, there is hope for our situation. As long as we have the desire, the hog pen does not have to be our final destiny or ending point.

Lord Jesus when the young man known as the Prodigal Son made a decision to act on his desire for something better with determination, his father welcomed him and gave him a robe, a ring and shoes. O Lord, we are grateful for the robe of anointing, a ring of authority and shoes of acceptance You give to us. We are grateful for the robe of compassion, ring of conquering and shoes of change You give us. We are grateful for the robe of deliverance, a ring of devotion and shoes of dependability You give us.

We are grateful for the robe of excellence, the ring of eternity and shoes of empowerment You give us. We are grateful for the robe of faith, a ring of forgiveness and shoes of fortitude that You give us. We are grateful for the robe of welcome, the ring of well-being and shoes of "Well done" You bestow. In Your own name do we offer this prayer, Amen.

– DAY 165 –

I JOHN 4: 4

We are grateful O God we can take control over the situations that prevent us from achieving the vision You have for our lives. Like the Prodigal Son, we are grateful that as we take control, we can leave the hog pens and other places of bondage behind us. We know the reason, O God, we can take control and it has nothing to do with our own strength and smarts. According to Your word and promise, the one who is in us is greater than the one who is in the world.

We know the reason we can stand and withstand the attacks of the enemy when they come at us from all directions — the one who is in us is greater than the one who is in the world. We know the reason we can hold our heads up when gossip and scandal is printed in the papers, broadcast on the airways, believed by saints and whispered about by so called friends — the one who is in us is greater than the one who is in the world. We know the reason we can believe victory when life contradicts everything we stand for and victory seems a thousand light years away — greater is the one who is in us than the one who is in the world.

We know the reason that no weapon formed against us shall prosper and every word of judgment that rises against us we shall refute — greater is the one who is in us than the one who is in the world. We know the reason we can survive Calvary and emerge as pure gold — greater is the one who is in us, greater is God the Father who is in us, and greater is Christ the son who is in us, greater is the blessed Holy Spirit who is in us, than the one who is in the world.

Greater are You, O God, who kept Joseph from perishing in prison, who opened the way for Moses and the children of Israel at the Red Sea, who spoke to Elijah at Mt. Horeb, who walked with the three Hebrew boys in the fiery furnace, greater is the one who locked the jaws of hungry lions for Daniel — greater are You, O God, who lives in us than the one who is in the world.

Greater are You, O Christ, who walked on water and calmed the raging sea, greater is the Christ who conquered every sickness, withstood every demon and defied every grave, greater is the Christ who rose from the grave himself to stoop no more and who lives and reigns forever — greater are You, O Christ, who is in us than the one who is in the world.

DAY 165

Greater are You Holy Spirit that fell on the church on the Day of Pentecost with fresh wind, fire and new languages, greater is Your power that shook the prison doors open for Paul and Silas as they prayed at midnight — greater are You Holy Spirit who lives in us than the one who is in the world.

When we have whom we have within us, we can look at financial barriers and any other kind of barrier that blocks Your vision for our lives and take control. Thank You and we praise You O God and in Your name do we offer this prayer, Father, Son and Holy Spirit, Amen.

– DAY 166 –

EXODUS 2: 1-4

Gracious God, we are grateful we do not have to accept the death sentences that are pronounced upon us or those whom we love. We pray we will learn how to use whatever You have given us to fight those forces that would hold us back and hold us down. Teach us how to use our brains. Instead of using our brains to come up with excuses and reasons to explain why we can't, teach us how to use our brains to come up with reasons why we can. The same brain that can come up with reasons we cannot do something, can also come up with reasons why we can. Instead of using our eyes to see what we do not have, teach us how to start opening up our eyes to get a new appreciation of what we do have. Instead of using our mouths to complain about what we do not have, teach us how to give thanks for what we do have. The issue is not how much we have but how we use what we have.

When David went up against the giant Goliath, all he had was a slingshot but he knew how to use it. When Gideon went up against the Midianite army, all he had was a small army of three hundred troops but he knew how to use them. When Job lost everything, all he had was faith in God but he knew how to use it. When the Lord Jesus had to feed five thousand in the wilderness, all he had was a little boy's lunch of two fish and five barley loaves but he knew how to use them. When he got ready to redeem the world, all he had was a cross but he knew how to use it. When Peter and James were confronted with a man born blind, all they had was the name of Jesus but they knew how to use it. When Paul and Silas were locked up in prison, all they had were praise and prayer but they knew how to use them. When John was on Patmos, all he had was worship but he knew how to use it.

Back in the 1950's when a group of blacks in Montgomery, Alabama decided they would challenge segregation on the buses, all they had was their churches, their marching feet and a new young pastor by the name of Martin Luther King, Jr. as their leader. However, because they knew how to use what they had, legalized segregation and Jim Crow in the south and the north began to crumble.

Now Lord in the midst of our struggles, teach us how to use what we have in Jesus name, Amen.

– DAY 167 –

EXODUS 3: 7-10

Gracious God, we confess that like Moses a number of us are being held hostage by our past. Like Moses we have done some things in secret that got out and we have been living in shame ever since. Like Moses, a number of us have settled down in Midian because we believe Midian is the best we can expect from life because of our past. When one considers where we were born and the conditions under which we were born the deserts of Midian and the non-descript life we have chosen to live is the best that we can expect.

Like Moses, a number of us started off with so much potential. When we were younger, people expected us to go far in life, however, we made a mistake and we have found ourselves in the desert of Midian. In the desert of Midian, rebounding from one non-fulfilling relationship to another. In the desert of Midian from one job to another never being able to settle down for long in one career or work situation. In the desert of Midian, where we have become addicted, afflicted and anxiety bound. In the desert of Midian, where we just go through the motions day in and day out, week in and week out, year in and year out where life seems to be passing us by. In the desert of Midian, where we have ceased to dream and have visions of a better day.

And like Moses, a number of us have been in the desert of Midian a long time. We come to You with praise and thanksgiving because no matter what our pasts have been, You still have a purpose for our lives. You are still present in our lives. You still see promise and potential in our lives. You can still purge our lives. You still have power to pour into our lives. You still feel positive about our lives. You can still bring praise from our lives. You will still answer the prayers of our lives. You will still provide for our lives. You still have a place prepared for our lives. You still protect and preserve our life. You still see the prince and the princess in our life.

Thank You Lord and in the name of the Lord Jesus do we offer this prayer, Amen.

DAY 167

– DAY 168 –

EXODUS 4: 10

O Lord, like Your servant Moses who had an impediment of speech, a physical stutter that could have impacted his ability to be Your spokesperson and that could have disqualified him from being Your representative, each of us has some kind of stutter that could cause us to stumble and be disqualified to walk in the vision God has for our lives. Some of us stutter with our words and some of us stutter with our ways. Some of us stutter with our tongues and others of us stutter with our temper. Some of us stutter with our pronunciation and some of us stutter with our pettiness. Some of us stutter with our speech and some of us stutter with certain sins.

Some of us have certain habits and inclinations that cause us to stutter. Some of us stutter because of alcohol while others of us stutter because of other kinds of drugs. Some of us stutter because of smoking. Some of us stutter because of sex and others of us stutter because of other inappropriate relationships. Some of us stutter because of deceit and lying. Some of us stutter because of jealousy and pettiness. Some of us stutter because of our insecurities and low self-esteem. Some of us stutter because of our unforgiveness and some of us stutter because of our past. Some of us stutter because of our families, either we feel bound because of the family burdens or responsibilities we carry or we feel guilty because of the unsaved loved ones in our family.

However, Gracious God, like Moses we know You love us in spite of our stutter. Like Moses, You can see something in us besides our stutter. Like Moses, You can use us mightily in spite of our stutter. Like Moses, You can take us from weakness to wholeness, from messes to miracles, from the bottom to the top, from ghettos to greatness, from poverty to power and from sin to sanctification in spite of our stutter. As You did with Moses and You did with the Samaritan woman at the well, as You did with Simon Peter, as You did with Saul of Tarsus, You can work wonders with us in spite of the stutter in our past, our present, our faith or our flesh.

We praise You, O God, for what You can do with stutterers. We praise You, O God, for what You have done with us in spite of our stutter. In the name of the Lord Jesus, who is the Redeemer and Friend of all who stutter, in the name of the Lord Jesus who is our personal Savior, do we offer this prayer, Amen.

DAY 168

– DAY 169 –

EXODUS 4: 10-17

Gracious God, we love You and we are so grateful You called us in spite of the stutters we have in our lives. Others may be more fitted to certain ministries and tasks you have entrusted into our hands by natural talent or by education or financial means or political clout. Others may not have the baggage or the disabilities or handicapping conditions we bring which may impact the effectiveness of the message. Yet in spite of what we lack, You see what we have. You look at our assets and not our liabilities. You look at our potential and not at our problems. You look at our future and not at our past. You look at how high we can rise and not how far we have fallen. Then you find a place for us on Your program even with our various stutters.

Thank You, Lord. We love You for loving us in spite of. We love You for seeing what we sometimes miss and others often overlook. We love You for believing in us even when we sometimes find it hard to believe in ourselves. We love You for equipping us with gifts we sometimes forget. We love You for empowering whatever gifts we have for your glory. We love You for calling us from mediocrity to the miraculous, from fear to faith, from sin to salvation to sanctification and from grief to glory. We love You for not letting us go.

O God, be glorified in us. Be glorified in these lips of clay. Be glorified in our efforts to serve You. Be glorified as we try to live for You. Be glorified in our praise and in our worship. Be glorified in our giving and in our witnessing. Be glorified in our walk and in our work. Be glorified in our conversation and in our commitments. Be glorified in our lives and in our loyalty.

O Lord, be glorified even in our stutters. For as we serve You with our imperfections, You once again demonstrate how You can work with and work through fallible human flesh. You are glorified even in our stutters. You once again show those whom the Son has set free are free indeed. You once again demonstrate that cleansing and transforming love of the blood of your Son Jesus is more powerful than any stutter in our lives the devil tries to enhance and magnify. We love You Lord! Thank You for loving us first. In the name of the Lord Jesus do we offer this prayer, Amen.

– DAY 170 –

I SAMUEL 21: 1-6

Gracious God like David coming to the priest Abimelech, we confess we often come to You in our hours of need. While we ought to be striving for a relationship with you that seeks Your face and loving You for who You are, the reality is a number of us come to know who You really are at the point of need. We come seeking help from Your hand. However, God You are so gracious You meet us at the point when we reach out to You. Although You desire that we seek and love You for who You are and not simply what You will do for us, still if we are at the level of need, God, You meet us at that level.

If we are broken, God, You meet us to build us up. If we are in sin, God You meet us and You save us. If we are lost, God, You meet us and You love us. If we are low, God, You meet us and You lift us. If we are confused, God You meet us at that level and You lift us. If we are in bondage, God, You meet us with breakthroughs.

If we are in pain, God, You meet us with power. If we are sick, God, You meet us with strength that is perfected in weakness. If we are in grief, God, You meet us with grace. If we are children, God, You meet us and care for us. If we are middle aged, God, You meet us and You work miracles for us and in us. And if we are old, God, You meet us and open doors for us. Others may condemn and criticize us because of where we are but God, You meet us where we are and then You begin to bring us up to where we ought to be.

We praise You, O living Christ, for Your living presence in our lives in our hours of deepest need. You have living word for our worries. You have living victories for living victims. You give living hope for living heartbreaks. You offer living salvation for living sin. You deliver us from living hell to a living heaven. We praise Almighty God, Living Christ, Abiding Holy Spirit because You satisfy our hunger and You transform our lives. In Your own name do we offer this prayer, Amen.

DAY 170

– DAY 171 –

I SAMUEL 21: 10-15

There are times Gracious God when our reality contradicts the promises of Your word. There are times when it seems as if the devil and those who oppose us will have the last word. There are times when like Your servant David, we find ourselves in embarrassing circumstances and demeaning situations as we try to survive. There are times O Lord when we wonder if living right and trying to do right really do pay off.

In those times of frustration, discouragement and bewilderment, we pray that You will help us to keep our heads up because You are a present help in times of trouble. In those times, we pray that You will help us to keep fighting because You are faithful. In those times, we pray that You will help us to keep believing because You still fight battles. In those times, we pray we will keep working because You are still in the way making business. In those times, we pray we will keep our morals because You still work miracles. In those times, we pray we will keep our virtue because You still will give the victory. In those times, we pray we will remain positive because You still have all power in Your hands. In those times, we pray we will keep tithing and keep trusting because Your word will triumph at last. In those times, we pray we will keep praying because You still hear and answer prayer, and because the prayers of the righteous, the prayers of Your believing children still avail much. And more things are still wrought through prayer than this world we dream of.

O God like when Your servant David at Gath and Your Son and our Lord Jesus was on the cross, we pray we will remember that life at any given moment does not tell how the story will end. The loss of a battle does not necessarily mean the war is over. Being behind in the race does not necessarily mean the race is over. With You O Lord, it really "ain't over till it is over." O Lord in our times of frustration and discouragement we pray for faith to press our way until the victory is won and until we hear You say, "Well done…" In the name of the Lord Jesus Christ do we offer this prayer, Amen.

DAY 171

– DAY 172 –

I KINGS 18:1

O God, sometimes like the prophet Elijah, You place us in our own personal Zarephaths, our place of resting and preparation for Your next move in our lives. Instead of looking at our Zarephath season as wasted time, we will seek You to discern Your will for our lives. You may have us in this season because like Elijah, we need to learn some patience. We may need to focus more on You O God or our health, because we cannot fully enjoy Your blessing sick. You may be trying to teach us some humility. You may be trying to teach us how to trust You more. You may be trying to teach us how to pray through. You may be trying to teach us that You really are in charge and not us.

God, You may be trying to show us where we have been is not where we should have been. You may be trying to close a chapter in our life and we are still trying to keep it open. You may be trying to turn our life in some new directions. You may be trying to give us a more grateful spirit. You may be trying to teach us how to praise You when things are going our way as well as when things are not.

So if God has sat us down for a season, instead of complaining and whining to God about when You are going to get us out, we are praying, "God help us to see what You are trying to show us during this period of our life. God grow us in the way You want us to grow during this down time in our life. God help us to be open and give us discernment about what You want us to know and understand during this season in our life."

Then God when You speak a word of direction, we pray for faith to follow. No matter if the time is inconvenient from our point of view, we pray for obedience when Your word comes. No matter if the opposition is great, we pray for courage to follow when Your word comes. No matter what the financial picture looks like, O God of all sufficiency, we pray for boldness to follow when Your word calls us out of hiding.

O God You are still able to bring us through to victory and get glory for Yourself when we follow where You lead. Speak Lord we Your servants are listening. In Jesus' name, we will follow and in His name do we offer this prayer, Amen.

DAY 172

– DAY 173 –

ESTHER 4: 12-14

Gracious God, as we face the uncertainty of these times, as Esther in the scriptures called upon her faith tradition to bring her through, we call upon the faith that has brought us thus far as a people. We call upon the tenacity of Sojourner Truth and the courage of Harriet Tubman. We call upon the strength of Frederick Douglass and the boldness of Richard Allen. We call upon the gospel rhythms of Mahalia Jackson and the total praise of Richard Smallwood. We say with James Weldon Johnson, "Lift Every Voice and Sing," we say with Maya Angelou, "Still We Rise," we say with Aretha Franklin, "Give Me Some Respect," and we say with James Cleveland, "Lord Do It Again."

We call upon the historic genius of George Washington Carver. We call upon the fire of Malcolm and the fervor of Shirley Caesar. We call upon the scholarship of W.E.B. Du Bois and we call upon the will of Mary McCloud Bethune. We call upon the economic genius of John H. Johnson and we call upon the building power of Booker T. Washington. We call upon the tough love of Martin Luther King, Jr. We call upon the Pentecostal power of Charles Mason.

But more than these, we call on Jesus, captain of the Lord's hosts, death's conqueror and the grave spoiler. We call upon Jesus, Savior of the world, Lord of history and King of Kings. He is not terrorism, he is not death, he is not fear, he is not violence and he shall reign forever and ever and ever. We do not know what the future holds but we know who holds the future. Jesus Christ is Alpha and Omega, the beginning and the end, the first and the last. And he is the fullness of the God head and will have the last word over our lives, our futures and our destinies. Because he is on our side, we shall overcome… We are not afraid…. We shall live in peace… God will see us through.

In his name, the name of the Lord Jesus, our interceding Savior, do we offer this prayer, Amen.

DAY 173

– DAY 174 –

ACTS 27: 39-44

O mighty miracle working God we praise You. O mighty miracle working God, we give honor and glorify You. O mighty miracle working God, we love and adore You. We are so grateful, O God, for miracles You do not change and whatever You have done in days past and gone, You are still doing it today. You are still working miracles of salvation, deliverance and healing today. You are still working miracles of creation and resurrection today. You are still working miracles of provision and protection today.

You are still bringing Your children out of the lion's den. You are still delivering Your children from fiery furnaces. You are still driving demons for the lives of Your children. You are still holding back Red Seas as You did for Moses and the children of Israel. You are still bringing forth sustenance in difficult places and bringing forth water in dry and arid regions. You are still delivering Your children from storms as You did for Your servant Paul. We are grateful, O God, that all things are still possible to those who believe in You.

We are grateful O God that there are still some things only You can do. In spite of the great technological advances of human beings, there are still some things only You can do. Only You can make a seed grow. Only You can shape a flower. Only You can paint a rainbow. Only You can cause the sun to shine, the stars to twinkle and the moon to glow.

Only You can wake us up in the morning and start us on our way. Only You can keep us safe as we travel daily through mean streets. And only You can bring us back safely to our respective places of abode. You and You alone establish our going out and coming in. O God, only You can take care of our bodies. Only You can deliver us when we are bound. Only You can give us victory in impossible circumstances.

O great miracle working God, we love You for who You are. Would You do a new thing in our lives this day? Our desire is to live for you in new ways. In Jesus name do we pray, Amen.

DAY 174

– DAY 175 –

MATTHEW 14: 28-33

Lord Jesus, we praise You for the opportunities to defy the odds and succeed anyhow. We praise You for Your vision for us that we can go farther than others have ever gone. We praise You for lifting our vision beyond the places where we live and work and worship and see possibilities that would not have crossed our minds. We praise You for the potential You continue to see within us and pull from us.

We pray for faith to listen when You are speaking, to follow where You lead and to be obedient to the Holy Spirit. We pray for faith to stay focused on You. No matter how dark the night or how long the night, we pray for faith to stay focused on You. No matter who tells us what cannot be done, when You call, when You beckon, when You invite, we pray for faith to stay focused on You. No matter how much the wind blows against us or upon us, we pray for faith to stay focused upon You. No matter how many demons rise or fears attack, we pray for faith to stay focused upon You.

And if, O Lord, we begin to lose our bearings, our perspective, our focus and our faith and begin to sin, we pray for presence of mind to call out to You for salvation. We pray we will always remember all is not lost because we fall and all is not hopeless because we stumble. You are still in the prayer hearing and prayer answering business. You are still waiting for us to do great things. You still believe in our possibilities. You still believe in Your vision for us.

If we begin to sink, we pray we will also look up to You, our Higher Power, our Savior, our Redeemer, our Lord, our Friend, You the Master of earth and wind and skies. We pray we will refocus upon You. We pray we will be renewed through You. We pray You will lift us. You have lifted us in days past and gone, and we believe that You will do it again.

We praise You for Your hand that reaches to catch us. We praise You for Your love that will not let us go or give up on us. We praise You for Your faithfulness to those who dare to walk with You. We praise You for Your wonderful miracle working power. You truly are God. In Your own name Lord Jesus do we offer this prayer, Amen.

– DAY 176 –

MATTHEW 26: 20-22

Gracious God, we are grateful we can come before You just as we are with all of our faults and weaknesses. We pray for courage to ask the hard questions of self-examination and introspection. We pray for courage to admit that it is not just our mothers and our fathers, our sisters and our brothers, the strangers or the neighbors but we ourselves who stand in the need of prayer.

We pray for courage to accept whatever responsibilities we may have had for whatever went wrong in the past. If we have done nothing wrong, then we pray for power to let go of spirit consuming anger and soul-destroying bitterness. We pray we will recognize we may not be able to change whatever has happened but we can do something about how we react to what has happened. We pray for courage to accept the things we cannot change, the courage to change the things we can and the wisdom to know the difference.

As we examine ourselves, we pray for balance. We pray we will not think more lowly of ourselves than we should or more highly of ourselves than we ought. Either extreme is damaging and deadly. We are grateful for Your unconditional love. We are grateful that You not only love us, You are able to change us. We are grateful for what You see that we may not be able to see.

We see what we have done wrong; You see our potential for doing right. We see where we have fallen but You see where we can rise. We see our faults but You see our future faith. We see our mistakes but You see the miracles that You can birth from our mistakes. We see our sins but You see our salvation. We see where we have been but You see where we can yet go. We see our problems but You see our power. We see our defect but You see our deliverance. We see our stumbling but You see our strengths.

Lord Jesus, we praise You for the lives that we can yet live when we take a searching and fearless moral inventory of our lives and come up short. We praise You for grace and mercy that cover us and give us another change. We praise You for Your cleansing blood that makes all of us new. We are grateful for the indwelling presence of the Holy Spirit who abides within us to turn our scars into stars, our warts into weapons, our brokenness into battlements and our troubles into testimonies. In Your name Lord Jesus do we offer this prayer, Amen.

– DAY 177 –

MARK 4: 31-35

Gracious God, we come to You to confess that there are issues in our lives we have not yet settled and things that still have us bound. We confess we cannot solve the things or deliver ourselves from our bondage. We confess we still have addictions that we cannot control. We confess we still have addictions to alcohol, drugs, nicotine, caffeine, money and materialism. We confess we are still in recovery from heartbreak and relationships that went sour. We confess we are still in recovery from guilt, fear, shame and deception. We confess that we still blame ourselves for hurtful things that others have done to us. We confess we have problems with forgiving and accepting forgiveness.

We confess, O God, that the storms rage around us and within us are almost out of control. We confess, O God, that we are almost in a state of panic. We confess, O God, that we have tried and tried to control the restlessness and the internal war and we often lose the battle. We call upon You Lord Jesus to rise with power within us. We call upon the presence of the Holy Spirit who abides with us to strengthen and sustain, to empower and to guide. We plead the blood of the Lord Jesus over that which would draw us away from a sacred nearness to You.

We praise You Lord Jesus that amidst the changing circumstances of life You have remained faithful. You have not jumped ship, You are still on board. Our weaknesses have not chased You away. Our failures have not turned You off. Our stubbornness has not disgusted You. Our issues have not caused You to desert us. Our demons have not scared You away. Our enemies have not driven You off. You are still on board.

Our mess has not messed up Your miracle working power. Our lies have not wilted Your love. Our gossip has not cancelled Your goodness. Our rebellion has not abated Your mercy. Misdeeds have not finished Your patience. Our waywardness has not obliterated the power of Your cleansing blood.

Arise O Lord and still the storms and bring peace to our situation. Forgive us for our panic and grant to us Your peace. In Your own name do we pray, Amen.

DAY 177

– DAY 178 –

MARK 9: 24

Gracious Lord, we are so grateful we do not have to have perfect faith for You to work miracles in our lives. You are ready to receive our faith as well as our doubts, our certitude as well as our questions, our convictions as well as our hang-ups. You are ready to receive our belief as well as our unbelief and our liabilities as well as our assets.

Even though our praying is not perfect, Your power is perfect and Your strength is perfected in our weakness. Even though our faith is not perfect, Your faithfulness is perfect. Even though our lives are not perfect, Your love is perfect. Even though our backgrounds are not perfect, Your cleansing blood is perfect. Even though our present circumstances are not perfect, Your provisions are perfect.

We are grateful that the Lord Jesus is an as-we-are Savior. He loves us as we are. He forgives us as we are. He saves us as we are. He accepts us as we are. He will make us over as we are. While others tell us what we ought to be, You Lord Jesus start with us where we are and as we are and You help us to become what we ought to be. While others tell us what we ought to be doing, You Lord Jesus, take us as we are and You help us to live as we ought to live.

Like the father of the son in Mark 9, we come to You Gracious Lord with all of our doubts and imperfect faith and we pray, "We believe, help our unbelief." Forgive us O Lord for the doubts we have. Lord increase our faith. Confirm our hope. Perfect us in love. We pray for faith to be honest with You. And because we have been honest with You; because You are rich in mercy and love, and abundant in patience and understanding, and because we plead the blood of the Lord Jesus, we believe You will work Your sovereign and perfect will in our broken and fragmented lives. Thank You Lord for accepting us as we are. In Your own name do we pray, Amen.

DAY 178

– DAY 179 –

MARK 14: 26-31

Gracious God, we confess at times like the disciple Peter, we become over-confident in our fight against the Adversary. We know how much we love You. We know we have a heart for You. And sometimes we believe the strength of our love and commitment are enough to give to us the victory. And when we rely upon ourselves, like the disciple Peter, we fall and we fail. Save us from the overconfidence O Lord that leads to defeat. Save us from pride that goes before a fall. Save us from the delusion that we can stop doing the things that have given us the victory thus far and remain strong.

We pray for the presence of mind to always look to You for direction and for strength. We pray for discipline to study Your word daily, to seek You in prayer and to remain humble before You. We pray for presence of mind to give You the glory for each and every victory we win over the weights and the sins that so easily beset. And if, O Lord, we stumble and fall, we pray that like the disciple Peter, we will not wander so far and become so mired in either shame or guilt that we will be unable to hear Your invitation to restoration.

We pray like the disciple Peter, we will not allow anything to stand in the way of our restoration and forgiveness. We will not allow any mistake to keep us away from our restoration. We will not allow any misunderstanding in the past or any bad experience to keep us away from our restoration.

As You live forever more, so do Your grace and mercy. As You live forever more, so do Your love and forgiveness. As You live forevermore, so do Your cleansing power and Your sanctifying touch. As You live forevermore, so do Your blessings and Your abundance. It is no secret what You can do, what You have done for others we are grateful that You will do for us. Thank You Jesus! In Your name do we pray, Amen.

DAY 179

– DAY 180 –

LUKE 15: 21-24

Gracious God, thank You for continually deciding to love and forgive us. We confess that every day we fall short of Your glory. Every day we sin by thought, by word and by deed. We continually break our promises to You and often forget our vows. Every day our sins grieve and wound Your heart.

And yet every morning when Your grace and mercy wake us up, You make a decision to love us and forgive us again. Every time You rescue us from our enemies, every time You bring us out more than conquerors, You make a decision to love and forgive us again. Every time You answer our prayers, You make a decision to love us and forgive us again. Every time You send a blessing far beyond our deserving, You make a decision to love us and forgive us again.

Gracious God, we pray for Your love, Your faith, Your forgiveness so we too can make decisions to love and forgive those who have wronged us. Sometimes wounds are so deep and the pain is so severe that forgiveness seems out of the question. Sometimes it is easier to go on hating or to go on being bitter. Sometimes it is easier to go on feeling guilty or feeling sorry for ourselves. Lord as You have made a decision to love and forgive us, help us to make the same decision to love and forgive others.

When we would hold on to the pain of wrongs that have been done to us, we pray for vision to look again at the cross. Whenever we are tempted not to be forgiving and loving, we pray for vision to look at the cross. The cross is our eternal reminder of how much You have loved and forgiven us. If You have loved and forgiven us that much, we pray for decision-making power to love and forgive others.

Because You have loved us so much, we now make a decision to let go of our anger and our bitterness. Because You have loved us so much, we now make a decision to let go of guilt and fear. Because You have loved us so much, we now make a decision to love again, to live again and to forgive again. God we cannot get to the next level when our hearts and spirits are weighed down with so much baggage from our past. We cannot enjoy all of the blessings You bestow upon us when our hearts and spirits are holding so much from our past. We let everything go so we can live again in Your fullness. In Your name Lord Jesus do we offer this prayer, Amen.

– DAY 181 –

JOHN 4: 5-10

O Lord Jesus, we confess like the Samaritan woman at Jacob's well, we have made grievous mistakes that have caused us to be weighed down with guilt, shame and loneliness. We confess there have been times we have allowed gossip and vicious talk from others to get the best of us. O God we confess that we still carry around pain from our past. We confess that we are still holding on to some bitterness and some hurt we should have released. We confess that we have not been able to forgive others as You have forgiven us. We confess that there are some things we have not been able to let go of and there are some things we are not even trying to release. O Lord, we must also confess that we get tired of fighting. We get tired of being angry and uptight. We get tired of being lonely.

O God, You are so good and You are so faithful You continually pour new blessings and new opportunities into our lives. Help us to appreciate them Lord. Forgive us for allowing past pain to block and interfere with present blessings and present opportunities. Forgive us for holding on to things we should release. We desire to begin living differently and feeling differently. We want new attitudes. We want to be healed from old wounds. Lord Jesus give us the desire and give us power to forgive. Lord Jesus give us the desire and give us the power to stop being a victim.

Lord Jesus give us the desire and give us the power to release what we should release so we can start living in new ways, with a new heart, a new spirit and a new attitude, right now. In Your name, Lord Jesus, we rebuke the power of the devil that has our spirits, our mind and our bodies in captivity to the pain from the past. In Your name, we rebuke the pain from past wounds and past wrongs. And in Your name, we declare our freedom and our release. We will be new creations in Christ Jesus and we will give You the glory. In Your name Lord Jesus do we offer this prayer and that with thanksgiving, Amen.

DAY 181

– DAY 182 –

JOHN 5: 6

Lord Jesus, we praise You for the possibility of healing. We are grateful we do not have to stay beside pools of poverty, ignorance, mediocrity, low aim, sin and addiction. We are grateful You can see more for us than we can see for ourselves. We are grateful You believe in us when we do not believe in ourselves. We are grateful You have a word of direction and instruction that leads to healing. We are grateful You bestow grace and gifts upon us that lead to healing.

We are grateful we can rise. No matter how long we have been down, we can still rise. No matter how far we have fallen, we can still rise. No matter how much we have messed up or how many times we have failed in the past, we can still rise. No matter how old we are, we can still rise. No matter how many mistakes we have made, we can still rise. No matter how many people we have disappointed or hurt, we can still rise. No matter who does not believe in us, You believe in us, so we can still rise. No matter what the statistics or the law of averages say, we can still rise. Like dawning after midnight, like a rainbow after the storm, like spring after winter, we can rise. Praise You Jesus, the devil is a liar and we can rise.

We can rise from sin and walk into sainthood. We can rise from loneliness and walk into love. We can rise from excuses and walk into excellence. We can rise from prejudice and walk into power. We can rise from bitterness and walk into breakthroughs. We can rise from addiction and walk into the anointing. We can rise from bad relationships and walk into bold redemption. We can rise from sorrow and walk into strength. We can rise from dependency and walk into deliverance. We can rise from hell and walk into heaven.

We pray for faith to obey when You speak a word of liberation, deliverance and healing. Speak Lord, we Your servants are listening. In Your name do we pray, Amen.

– DAY 183 –

JOHN 19: 38

O God, like Joseph of Arimethea of old, save us from living in fear and being in bondage to what others may think. When we deny who we are and hide our gifts or talents, our education, our creativity or our blessings because we do not want to offend anyone, then we are in bondage to what others think. When we deny what we believe and whom we believe in, support and admire, when we deny our friendships because we do not want to offend others, then we are in bondage to what other people think.

When You, O God, have blessed us and we are afraid to show our blessings, drive our blessings, wear our blessings or invite people to see the blessing where we live, lest they think ill of us, we are in bondage to what others think. When we are always putting ourselves down to make others feel better about who they are or are not, then we are living in bondage to what others think. When we are always concerned about covering our backs lest we offend someone or lest someone blames us for something that went wrong, when we are always trying to shift responsibility and blame to someone else, then we are in bondage to what others think. When we are always trying to please everybody but us, when we have so much of a need to be needed that we are always putting ourselves and our feelings last, then we are in bondage to what others think.

When we allow people to take advantage of us so we can have their so-called friendship, love and approval, then we are in bondage to what others think. When we do not have the confidence to stand on our own two feet but have to call around and get support and approval for the decisions we make, then we are in bondage to what others think. When we are always weighing the social, political and economic implications of every decision we make, then we are in bondage to what others think.

Like Joseph of Arimethea of old, we pray for deliverance from the bondage of what others think. We pray for courage to do the right thing trusting in You to take care of us in the times to come as You have in times past and as You are doing even now in the present. We offer this prayer in Your matchless and mighty name, Lord Jesus, Amen.

DAY 183

– DAY 184 –

PHILIPPIANS 1: 1A

O Lord Christ, we are so grateful to be Your servants. We are so grateful we belong to You. We pray we will always remember we belong to You no matter what the circumstances of our lives may be at any given moment or during any given season.

We do not belong to our sickness. We will not own it or claim it as our own. We belong to You. We do not belong to the money that tries to convince us that more of it will solve all of our problems. We belong to You whose word has assured us that You will supply all of our needs. We do not belong to friends, relatives or others who try to convince us they must approve our actions. We belong to You, the Lord of our salvation. We do not belong to any job that tries to hold us hostage. We belong to You who alone is worthy of our complete loyalty and devotion. We do not belong to any person who tries to make us feel worthless without them. We belong to You who has loved us with a perfect love.

We do not belong to any weakness that has or continues to trip us up in our efforts to live for You. We belong to You whose precious blood has cleansed us from our sins. We do not belong to any devil or demon or enemy or foe who would threaten us or intimidate us. We belong to You O Christ who has put all enemies under our feet, including death. We do not belong to any fear or guilt that may arise to haunt us. We belong to You whose redemption empowers us to live unashamed and unafraid. We do not belong to any need or pain that seeks for immediate relief even if it is a short-term fix that leads to long term regrets. We belong to You in whose name we have the victory.

We belong to You O living and reigning Christ, King of Kings, Lord of Lords, the hope of eternal glory. Thank You for receiving us not only as servants but as sons and daughters. We pray for faith and courage to live as those who belong to You. In Your name do we pray, Amen.

DAY 184

– DAY 185 –

PHILIPPIANS 1: 6

Gracious God, we are grateful we are able to finish what You have begun. So many times, we start things we are not able to finish. Our lives are replete with broken promises and forgotten vows. The road to hell for so many of us has been paved with good intentions. So many times, others have started things in our lives that have fallen by the wayside. Our lives are also full of broken promises and failed intentions of others.

However eternal God, You who have no beginning and no ending, You are able to complete what You have started. O ever living and reigning Christ, the Alpha and Omega, the beginning and the end, the first and the last, You are able to complete what You have started. O creative, life giving Holy Spirit who dwells among us as the eternal Spirit of the eternal Godhead abiding within us, You are able to complete what You have started.

We pray we will do our part so Your part can be done. If we are faithful, You will finish what You started. If we are consistent, You will complete what You have begun. If we praise You, You will perfect our going out and our coming in. If we honor You, You will help us. If we worship You, You will work on our behalf. If we exalt You, You will establish us. If we seek You, You will save us. If we depend upon You, You will deliver us. If we trust You, You will cause us to triumph. If we follow Your vision, You will bring us through to victory.

O God, please start something new in our lives. Start a new work of creation, redemption and anointing within us and upon us. O God birth in us a new heart, a new song, a new witness and a new testimony. O God birth in us new zeal, new joy, new faith and new love. Do it for Your own namesake and glory. O God, we pray we will not only go to the next level in our faith walk with You but we will live and love You in such a way that whatever You have started will be brought to completion by the day of Jesus Christ. This we ask in the name of our Lord Jesus, whose coming in majesty and glory, we anticipate and long for, more than those that wait through the midnight hour for the dawn of a new day, Amen.

DAY 185

– DAY 186 –

PHILIPPIANS 1: 21

Lord Jesus, we love You as Lord of our lives. Lord Jesus, You are our first love. Forgive us when our scheduling and time commitments relegate You to second place. Forgive us when our spending and level of giving relegates You to second place. Forgive us when we allow our feelings for others to relegate You to second place. Forgive us when our commitments to our job and career relegate You to second place. Forgive us when our quest for pleasure that is temporary and fleeting relegates You to second place. Forgive us when our commitments to our own agendas, whether in church or in the world, relegate You to second place. Forgive us when our attachment to the things of this world relegates You to second place.

Help us, O Lord, to realize that putting You first means loving You, serving You and giving to You, even when it is personally inconvenient. And when we would complain about the cost of our love for You, we pray You will humble us with the realization that we are who we are, what we are and where we are, because You have loved us when it was inconvenient for You. Your leaving the celestial heights of glory to sojourn among us in human flesh for thirty-three years was personally inconvenient for You but You came anyway. The whip across Your back, the persecution of the mob, the rejection of the religious leadership of Your day, the crown of thorns, a spear in Your side and nails in Your hands were personally inconvenient for You but You endured them anyway for us. Your death on the cross as the sinless King of Glory was personally inconvenient for You but You died anyway. O Lord, You have proven Your love for us in that while we were yet sinners, You died for us. When it was personally inconvenient for You to love us because we were at our worst and because of the price of our redemption, You were faithful to us.

Now Lord, we simply respond to the love You have given to us. Loving You is not inconvenient. A life of sin and shame is inconvenient. A life of guilt and fear is inconvenient. Eternal damnation and separation from You are inconvenient. On this day, dear Jesus, we commit ourselves to love You, serve You and give to You in new ways. You are not inconvenient O Lord; You are the best person who has ever happened to us. In Your name do we pray, Amen.

DAY 186

– DAY 187 –

PHILIPPIANS 2: 5-11

Gracious God, You will get victory for our lives. Gracious God, Your vision for our lives is that we prosper even as our souls prosper and our bodies enjoy health. We pray for endurance so Your vision for our lives will become a reality. We pray for faithfulness so Your vision for our lives will become a reality. We pray for obedience so Your vision for our lives will become a reality. We pray for humility so Your vision for our lives will become a reality.

Most of all we pray for the same mind that "was in Christ Jesus, who though he was in the form of God, did not regard equality with God as something to be exploited but emptied himself, taking the form of a slave, being born in human likeness. And being found in human form, he humbled himself and became obedient to the point of death — even death on a cross. Therefore, Gracious God, You also highly exalted him and gave him the name that is above every name, so that at the name of Jesus every knee should bend, in heaven and on earth and under the earth, and every tongue should confess that Jesus Christ is Lord, to the glory of God the Father."

Forgive us, Gracious God, when we follow our own minds without first seeking the mind of Christ. Forgive us, Gracious God, when we follow the minds of others who are as finite as we are without seeking the mind of Christ. Forgive us, Gracious God, when we allow the Enemy to intimidate us with fear or with doubt or with guilt or shame without our seeking the mind of Christ. Forgive us, Gracious God, when we fail to follow Your will and word after having received the mind and the word from Christ.

With the mind of Christ comes victory. With the mind of Christ comes peace that passes understanding. With the mind of Christ comes love that bears all things, believes all things, hopes all things and endures all things. With the mind of Christ comes transformation and the gift of the new being. With the mind of Christ comes faith that overcomes the world.

On this day, we seek the mind of Christ. In his name do we pray, Amen.

DAY 187

– DAY 188 –

PHILIPPIANS 4: 11-13

Gracious God, we are grateful we are more and our lives consist of more than where we may be at any given moment of time. We are more than either the mistakes or the successes of the moment. We are more than either the failures or the victories of the moment. We are more than either the joys or the depression of the moment. We are more than either the sickness or health of the moment. We are more than either the poverty or the prosperity of the moment.

Because you have a vision for our lives that is greater than any vision that we can possibly have for ourselves, no moment of time can totally define who we are. Your word defines who we are and your word told us that we are your children. Your will defines who we are and you will that we dwell in high and lofty places. Your creation defines who we are and you have created us in your very own image. Your Son Jesus defines who we are and he has defined us as the redeemed. The Holy Spirit defines who we are and the Holy Spirit has defined us as persons with power.

Gracious God, when the devil tries to seduce us into believing we are failures because we have made a mistake or have failed at something, give us faith and daring to rebuke him in your name and to assert we can abound in any and all circumstances. We can do all things through our Lord Christ who strengthens us. We can conquer demons that rise up against us through Christ who strengthens us. We can conquer those weaknesses that have held us bound in the past through Christ who strengthens us. We praise you for the strengthening power of the Lord Jesus.

Strengthen our prayer life and strengthen our praise. Strengthen our forgiveness and strengthen our faithfulness. Strengthen our feet to walk right, strengthen our hands to do right, strengthen our minds to think right and strengthen our spirits to desire the right thing. Lord Jesus help us to never forget that no matter what we face at any given moment of our lives or in any given circumstances we can do all things through you. Lord Jesus, we thank You even now for your strengthening power and we praise you for your presence and your power, which strengthens, always, even to the close of the age. In your name do we pray, Amen.

– DAY 189 –

LUKE 1: 5-20

Lord Jesus, we are grateful that as the angel appears to Your servant Zechariah, You can still surprise us in worship to speak a word to our lives that lets us know we have not been forgotten, that our prayers have been answered and that You have a word for us no matter who we are or whatever our condition.

If we are old, You have this message for us — we can be born again. If we are young, You have this message for us — suffer the little children to come to me and forbid them not for of such is the kingdom of heaven. If we labor under the strain of generational curses, You have this message for us — he or she who the Son sets free is free indeed. If we are in grief, You have this word for us, "he has sent me to heal the brokenhearted (Luke 4:18)." If we are tired, worn out and burned out, You have this message for us — "Come to me all you who are weary and are carrying heavy burdens and I will give you rest. Take my yoke upon you and learn of me because my yoke is easy and my burden is light (Matthew 11:28)."

If we are in financial bondage, You have this word for us, "Bring the full tithe into the storehouse so that there will be food in my house, thus put me to the test, says the Lord of hosts. See if I will not pour down an overflowing blessing that you will not have room to receive. I will rebuke the devourer for you, so that it will not destroy the produce of your soil and your vine in the field shall not be barren says, the Lord of hosts (Malachi 3:10-11)." If we have made mistakes, You have this word for us, "If you confess your sins he who is faithful will forgive you for your sins and cleanse you of all unrighteousness (1 John 1:9)."

If we are sick, You have this word for us, "My grace is sufficient for you; for my strength is made perfect in weakness (2 Corinthians 12:9)." If we have been betrayed, You have this word for us, "I am a friend that sticks closer than a brother (Proverbs 18:24)." If we are lonely, You have this word for us, "I am with you always, even to the end of the world (Matthew 28:20)." If we are in fear, You have this word for us, "God did not give us a spirit of fear but of power and love and a sound mind (2 TImothy 1:7)." And if we feel unloved, You have this word for us, "For God so loved the world that he gave his only begotten Son that whoever believes in him shall not perish but they shall have everlasting life (John 3:16)."

We pray for faith to receive Your word so we can begin living in new way, beginning right now. In the name of the Lord Jesus do we offer this prayer, Amen.

– DAY 190 –

LUKE 1: 11-18 & GENESIS 18: 14

Gracious God, we confess that there have been times when like Zechariah of old, we have had difficulty in believing Your word for us and to us. We confess we have allowed what seemed to us as interminable delays in answers to our prayers, seasons of disappointment and the obstacles ahead of us, the situations around us, the prophets of doom who speak into our ears and spirit, to cause us to doubt Your word to us and at times even Your love for us. Forgive us O Lord.

When we would doubt Your word to us we pray we may remember the question asked long ago to those who were having trouble receiving the word You had spoken to them: "Is there anything too wonderful for the Lord?" When we think back for a moment about where we started out and look at where we are now, we must ask, "Is there anything too wonderful for the Lord?" When we think about the prayers that have already been answered, the miracles that have already been wrought and the ways out of no ways that have already been made in our life, we must ask, "Is there anything too wonderful for the Lord?"

When we think about the attacks we have been under that we were not supposed to survive and yet we are still here, we must ask, "Is there anything too wonderful for the Lord?" When we lost our loved one, when our career hit rock bottom, when our relationship broke up, when the person we trusted disappointed and hurt us, others expected us to lose our mind and yet through it all we are here clothed in our right mind. We must ask, "Is there anything to wonderful for the Lord?"

When we think about the times we tithed even though we really could not afford to do so and unexpected blessings came in, we must ask, "Is there anything too wonderful for the Lord?" We think about the things people and circumstances said we would never do. They said we would never finish school. They said we would never come back from where they had buried us and where we had fallen. They said we would never be anything. And yet here we are, blessed and favored and doing well. We must ask, "Is there anything too wonderful for the Lord?"

When we think about the Lord Jesus who came to save us, we must ask, "Is there anything too wonderful for the Lord?" Gracious God, we pray that You will receive the praise and thanksgiving of our hearts because You alone are worthy. In the name of the Lord Jesus do we offer this prayer, Amen.

DAY 190

– DAY 191 –

LUKE 1: 5-7

Gracious and loving God, we praise You for Your mercy, love, patience, forgiveness and Your understanding. When we fail to live up to the standards of people, they will jump on us with both feet. When we offend the righteous codes of people ,they will never let us forget it. Whenever they become upset or angry with us, they will throw our error back in our faces.

When we offend the righteous codes of people, our worth is reduced forever in their eyes. They will never look upon us like they did before they discovered we had clay feet, even though they are standing on clay feet themselves. However, when we offend You, O holy and righteousness God, You not only forgive us but You cast our sins in the sea of forgetfulness so they will not rise to haunt us in this life nor condemn us at his judgment bar.

Where would any of us be, O God, without Your forgiveness? Noah was the most righteous of his generation but he had a mean temper when he got drunk. Abraham, father of the faithful, was known to lie and at times waver in the very faith that was supposed to be his strong suit. Jacob became a prince of the faith and father of the twelve tribes that gave the identity of the people of God. But Jacob was one of the biggest crooks in scripture. Moses was his lawgiver but Moses had family issues and a temper that cost him being able to personally lead the children of Israel into the Promised Land.

Ruth and Naomi had a vision for recovery from their troubles but Naomi could be prone to bitterness and Ruth along with her mother in-law could be manipulative. Esther was a great queen but she could also be selfish, looking out for number one until shamed to use her position to help her people. David was the man after God's own heart but he was an adulterer, a murderer and a poor father. Job cursed the day he was born, Jonah was rebellious and Jeremiah whined incessantly.

We would have never heard of that motley group of ne'er do wells the Lord Jesus called to be his twelve apostles and the narrow minded and bigoted Saul of Tarsus who became the apostle Paul. Even Zechariah doubted You and Elizabeth hid herself when Your word and promise began to be fulfilled in their lives.

We praise you O God that since Jesus has come we can declare, Surprise! Surprise! We who have been born in the image of our earthly father will one day bear the image of our heavenly father. And it is in the name of Jesus that we offer this prayer of praise and thanksgiving, Amen.

– DAY 192 –

LUKE 2: 41-51

Lord Jesus, we confess there have been times that like Joseph and Mary, we have lost You. We have followed the wrong assumptions and lost You. We have walked in our own willful and stubborn ways and lost You. We have paid more attention to the crowd we were traveling with and lost You. We have become distracted by the things of the world and lost You. We have become so focused on reaching our destination according to our own schedules and timetables that we have lost.

We confess Lord Jesus, there have even been times we have listened to the devil and have lost You. There have been times when we have listened to our fears rather than our faith and have given more attention to our problems rather than Your presence, Your promise and Your power and have lost You. There have been times when we have paid so much attention to making money instead of making a life and making a career instead of building character that we have lost You.

We seek Your forgiveness and we pray that like Joseph and Mary we would have a turn-around spirit. We pray for courage to retrace our steps to the place where we last say You. We pray we have the courage to retrace our steps to the caring and the commitment, the disciplines and the devotions, the giving and the gratitude, the prayer and the praise, the service and the study, the tithing and the triumphs, the values and the visions, the worship and the work, where we last felt power, fulfillment and joy. Lord Jesus save us from being so headstrong, ego driven and prideful that we continue heading in the direction we are traveling, even when we know that something, that someone, that You are missing.

Give us a persevering spirit to keep searching no matter what. No matter the false starts, no matter the lies the devil whispers in our ears, no matter how may panic attacks we may have to fight off and no matter how many weary and frustrated we become we pray that we keep searching until we find You, O Lord.

When we find You again, we pray as You did with Joseph and Mary, You will receive us and love us as if we had never lost You or left You or failed You. We praise You even now for Your vision for us that abides even when we fall short of the faith and trust You continually put in us. In Your name Lord Jesus do we offer this prayer, Amen.

– DAY 193 –

GENESIS 3: 8-10

Gracious God, we confess that so often we hide from You, from others and even from ourselves. We confess that the gruesome threesome, shame, guilt and fear often hold us in bondage. We are grateful O God that You have called us to do more than clothes ourselves in fig leaves of blame and shame, fear and forsakenness and guilt and grief. You have called us to newness of life because when You created us, when You made us in Your very own image, You created us for great things. You created us to walk in high and lofty places.

O God, not only have You made us with the capacity to sin, You also made us with the capability of being saints. You not only made us with the capacity for failure, You also made us with the capability of being a success. You not only made us with the capacity of falling to temptation, You also made us with the capability to fight temptation. You not only made us with the capacity to make mistakes, You also made us with the capability to overcome and to master our mistakes. You not only made us with the capacity for error, You also made us with capability for excellence. You not only made us with the capacity for shame, You also made us with the capability of being saved. You not only made us with the capacity for guilt, You also made us with the capability for greatness and grace. You not only made us with the capacity for fear, You also made us with the capability for faith. You not only made us with the capacity for hell, You also made us with the capability for heaven.

Forgive us, O God, for living beneath our privilege. We pray for courage to come out of hiding. We know there are consequences for our misdeeds, our mistakes, our sins and our weaknesses. However, we also know You not only have a word of judgment, You also have a word of joy for us. You not only have a word of condemnation, You also have a word of compassion for us. You not only have a command for us, You also have another chance.

We praise You for the second chance and the redemption our Lord Christ Jesus offers to us. We are grateful he saves to the utmost. And it is in his name that we offer this prayer, Amen.

DAY 193

– DAY 194 –

GENESIS 6: 5-8

O God, we pray that like Your servant Noah, we will be different for Your glory. In an era in which humans grieved Your heart, he delighted Your heart. In an era when humans were a burden to Your heart, he blessed Your heart O God. In an era when human beings were a load on Your heart, he lifted Your heart. In an era when humans wore out Your friendship, Noah found favor with God. In an era when humans were rebellious towards You, he lived righteously before You. In an era when human sin smote Your heart, he put a smile in Your heart. In an an era when humans were wicked, Noah was different in that he worshipped You, O God.

We pray we will always remember it is better to be different like he was than to be like those he was different from and in spite of the loneliness, the pain and sometimes the persecution that comes from being different there are times when being different is a good thing. If those who live in poverty or welfare from one generation to another surround us, our being different by working, tithing, living within our means and saving is a good thing, even if, we are called uppity and cheap. If we are surrounded by ignorance and low or no ambition, our being different and getting an education and wanting more out of life is a good thing.

If we are surrounded by those who are shallow and petty and frustrated, our being different and impatience with the mundane, our being different and striving for substance and happiness is a good thing. If those who are always complaining, always criticizing, surround us always talking about people, our being different by being grateful and refusing to participate in the downgrading of others is a good thing. If we are surrounded by those who are always trying to live up to the expectations of others, our being different as we seek the counsel of God is a good thing.

If those with no dreams and visions surround us, our being different by having visions and dreams is a good thing. If those who are lazy surround us, our being different by having initiative is a good thing. O God, help us to think differently, live differently and talk differently for Your glory. In the name of the Lord Jesus do we offer this prayer, Amen.

DAY 194

– DAY 195 –

GENESIS 11: 31-32

O God on this Christian journey, we pray for faith to go all of the way to Canaan instead of stopping at Haran. When we are content with religion instead of a relationship with You, O God, we have settled down at Haran. The purpose of religion is to help us build our relationship with You. Seeking Your face and abiding in Your presence, O God, takes us farther than Haran since the emphasis is on building a relationship with You instead of simply being religious about You, O God.

Having religion is about church membership but having a relationship is about Christian discipleship. Having religion is about fellowship with the saints, having a relationship is about follow ship of You, O Lord. Having religion is about an association but having a relationship is about an anointing. Having religion is about belonging but having a relationship is about believing.

Having religion is about our names being on the church rolls, having a relationship is about having our names in the Lamb's book of life. Having religion is about good feeling, having a relationship is about great faith. Having religion gives respectability, having a relationship produces righteousness. Having religion is about regulations, having a relationship is about regeneration.

Having religion is about a particular way (the Methodist way, the Baptist way, the Pentecostal way) but having a relationship is about You, Lord Jesus, the Way, the Truth and the Life. Having religion is about a denomination, having a relationship is about deliverance. Having religion is about title, having a relationship is about transformation. Having religion is about our power, having a relationship is about Your power.

O Lord Jesus, You could have stopped at Haran on the Mount of Temptation and on the Mount of Transfiguration. You could have stopped at Haran on Palm Sunday and in the agony of Gethsemane. You could have stopped at Haran when they mocked You and called for You to come down from the cross. But You pressed Your way to Canaan and have been given a name higher than any other name. We pray for Your faith, Your obedience and Your love, and Your power so we, like You can press our way to Canaan. In Your own name Lord Jesus do we offer this prayer, Amen.

– DAY 196 –

EXODUS 4: 1-5

Gracious God, You ask us the same question You asked Your servant Moses centuries ago when You spoke to him at the burning bush, "what is that in Your hand?" We are grateful as was the case with Moses, You are prepared to relate to and deal with us just as we are with whatever we bring in our hands and whatever we have in our life. Whatever we being You can handle it. Whatever guilt or shame we being, whatever weakness we bring, whatever habits or addictions or bondage we bring, whatever sin we bring You can handle it. Thank You Lord.

However, when You look into our hands, into our hearts and in our lives, You not only see our liabilities, You also see our assets. You see possibilities, potential and power even at this age and stage in our lives that we do not see. You see greatness, glory and gifts we do not see. You see miracles and ministries we do not see. You see strength and sanctification we do not see. You see cleansing and a new creation we do not see. We praise You Lord and we glorify You because of the worth You see in us.

When Moses told You about the staff in his hand, You commanded him to throw it down and what he threw down became transformed by Your into a instrument of liberation. O God, we pray for the obedience and faith of Moses that we might yield to You what we hold in our hands. We pray for faith to yield to You. If we want to see new uses for old things and ordinary things, we must yield to You.

If we want to see how You can make much out of little, we must lay Your tithes before You. If we want to see how You can work miracles, we must lay our prayers before You. If we want to see how You can give the victory, we must lay our faith before You. If we want to see how much You can do with what we have, we must lay our service before You. If we want to see how You can give strength to go on in spite of, we must lay our worship and our praise before You.

Here we are Lord, we yield ourselves to You. Have Your own way and get the glory from what we bring in our hands and in our hearts. In the name of the Lord Jesus do we offer this prayer, Amen.

– DAY 197 –

EXODUS 14: 13-14

Gracious God, we praise You for Your guiding presence and Your delivering hand, which have brought us from our Egyptian captivity to the place where we stand now. We pray that when we come to our Red Sea moments and seasons when all seems lost, when our way is blocked and we see the armies of our former Pharaoh, we will remember the words of Your servant Moses when he said "Do not be afraid, stand firm [or still] and see the deliverance that the Lord will accomplish for You today; for the Egyptians whom You see today You shall never see again. The Lord will fight for You, and You have only to keep still."

Help us in those trying hours and seasons to be still and know that You are God, You rule over our lives and all Pharaoh and all power is in Your hands. As we stand on the banks of the Red Sea, as mothers and fathers, as guardians and grandparents, we pray we will always remember You have not left us without tools, even in times like these.

We recognize, O Lord, that parenting and motherhood brings new challenges in this new place in the wilderness where we presently are. The challenges at the banks of the Red Sea in a post modern era of increased technology and expanding temptations, of numerous demons and numerous diversions are different than they were in Pharaoh's house. However, life in Egypt was not any picnic either; Life in ante-bellum slavery was no picnic either. Life under Jim Crow and segregation and the suppression of civil, political, economic, educational and human rights was no picnic either.

However, as Moses lifted his rod in the wilderness, our parents also knew how to lift the rod of prayer, the rod of sacrifice, the rod of discipline, the rod of integrity and honesty, the rod of hard work, the rod of clean and righteous living, the rod of love over hate, of hope over despair, and the rod of vision for a better day for their children. As we stand at the banks of the Red Sea, in this day and age, we pray for the courage and faith of mothers and parents to lift those same rods that have wrought wonder and worked miracles in times past and gone because You, O God, who gave power to the rod, are still alive and still on the throne. In the name of our Lord Christ do we pray, Amen.

DAY 197

– DAY 198 –

EXODUS 34: 29-35

O God, we love You. If we have not taken the time to tell You lately how much we love You , O God forgive us. If we have been so busy running here and there and taking care of the daily cares and concerns of this world, that we have not taken the time to be with You as we should, O God, please forgive us. If we have been so busy seeking Your hand for what we need and want we have neglected to seek Your face so we can know You more intimately and love You for Yourself, O God forgive us.

Give us new intimacy with You. Give us, O God, a heart for prayer and a deep and abiding closeness to You. Give us discernment to know Your voice, Your will and Your word. We confess, O God, sometimes we get our will mixed up with Your will and our desires mixed up with Your vision. We confess, O God, there are times when we have trouble drowning out the conflicting voices in our heads so we can hear Your still small voice. We confess, O God, sometimes we become so anxious and so hurried we find it increasingly difficult to be still in Your presence and focus on You.

O God gently teach us and patiently lead us in our walk with You and in our work with others. We pray for such an intimate relationship with You like Moses of old, we will have afterglow that glorifies You and sustains us in the midst of our warfare. O God be merciful so we might have the afterglow that represent more than a momentary experience with You.

Your vision comes as we seek Your face but the victory comes from the afterglow of abiding in Your face. The blessing is in the worship experience but the breakthrough is in the afterglow. Salvation is in the surrender to the Lord Jesus but sanctification that continues the transformation is in the afterglow. Redemption take place with surrender but righteousness take place with afterglow. Peace comes in the worship experience but power comes from the afterglow.

Praise erupts in the midst of worship but perseverance in work is seen in the afterglow. Grace is given without our asking but goodness is developed in the afterglow. Excellence emerges out of the worship experience but eternity is reached in the afterglow. O God give us You, so we might glow afterwards for You. In the name of the Lord Jesus do we offer this prayer, Amen.

DAY 198

– DAY 199 –

EXODUS 34: 29-35

O God, we confess that so often we wear veils and masks to hide and cloak our feelings to the outside world. O Lord, wearing a veil can be bothersome enough when we have to keep our smile and our image, or our pretensions to the outside world of strangers and coworkers. However, some of us come home and still have to wear a veil. Some of us go to bed and still have to wear a veil. Some of us get together with our best friends and still have to wear a veil. Some of us get to family gatherings and still have to wear a veil. Some of us cannot even take the veil off with our parents and children.

Some of us wear our thickest veils around others believers. Some of us wear our thickest veils among other believers with whom we share the strongest bond, salvation in the name and redemption through the blood of Jesus. One would think that the fellowship of saints and other believers would be the place where we would feel free enough to lift the veil but church for a number of us is where the veil is longest and thickest. Some of us may get relaxed enough to lift the veil slightly at home, around a few good friends or even some of our family members. On the job when we are under pressure, we may allow the veil to slip slightly. But heaven forbid we ever allow any one at church to get a glimpse behind the veil.

Consequently, we sit in church pretending we are not moved or touched lest someone suspect something is amiss behind our veils. We sniff back tears and stifle our emotions lest someone suspects there is trouble behind our veils. Or we are the most vocal in crying out "Praise the Lord" and "Amen" so no one will suspect we have trouble behind our veils. We become very judgmental regarding others and holier than thou trying to hide our own weaknesses and inclinations we have behind our veil of piety. Every now and then, we lift our eyes to the heavens and say, "O God, I get so tired of wearing this veil all of the time. I wish I could take off this veil sometimes."

We are grateful for the privilege of seeking Your face, O God, because like Moses of old, when we come into Your presence, we can take off our veils. We praise You Lord Jesus because when You become our Lord and Savior, we can live without veils. In Your name precious Savior, do we offer this prayer, Amen.

– DAY 200 –

I SAMUEL 6: 1-21

Holy, righteous, Majestic, Awesome and Gracious God, unlike the ancient descendants of Jeconiah, we seek Your face and we delight in Your presence. We desire not simply a visitation from You but Your very habitation. We reverence You, O God. We adore You, O God. We glorify You, O God. We honor You, O God. We praise You, O God. We worship You, O God. We love You, O God.

We crave Your nearness and we recognize our need for a closer walk with You, O God. For deliverance from addiction and affliction of mind and spirit, we need a closer walk with You, O God. For deliverance from guilt and grief, we need a closer walk with You, O God. For deliverance from bondage and brokenness, we need a closer walk with You, O God. For deliverance from anger and anxiety, we need a close walk with You, O God.

For deliverance from temptation and temper, we need a closer walk with You, O God. For deliverance from fear and fret, we need a closer walk with You, O God. For deliverance from self-pity and a lack of self-confidence, we need a closer walk with You, O God. For deliverance from worry and weaknesses, we need a closer walk with You, O God. For deliverance from people and procrastination, we need a closer walk with You, O God. For deliverance from sin and shame, we need a closer walk with You, O God. For deliverance from depression and co-dependency, we need a closer walk with You, O God.

We pray to You paraphrasing the words of the old hymn:

Thou [our] everlasting portion, More than friend or life to [us],
All along [our] pilgrim journey, Savior let [us] walk with Thee.
Close to Thee, close to Thee, Close to Thee, close to Thee,
All along [our] pilgrim journey, Savior let [us] walk with Thee.

Lead [us] through the vale of shadows, Bear [us] o'er life's fitful sea;
Then the gates of life eternal, May [we] enter, Lord with Thee.
Close to Thee, close to Thee, Close to Thee, Close to Thee;
Then the gates of life eternal May [we] enter Lord with Thee.

(Thou Everlasting Portion, Fanny Crosby)

In the name of the Lord Jesus do we offer this prayer, Amen.

– DAY 201 –

II SAMUEL 6: 1-11

O God, we confess sometimes like David, we sometimes allow our exuberance to overtake our knowledge of Your word. We confess sometimes in our efforts to do what is right, we are not as grounded in Your word as we should be. We confess, O God, sometimes we handle what belongs to You too tritely and too casually. We treat these bodies that belong to You too tritely and too carelessly. We treat the money You have entrusted us too manage as if it belongs to us. We treat the church that belongs to Your Son and our Savior the Lord Jesus Christ, too tritely and too casually. We treat ministries that Your grace and mercy have allowed us to participate in and to offer leadership in, too lightly and too casually, as if they belonged to us.

We treat the privilege of prayer too lightly and too casually. We treat Your worship too lightly and too casually. We inject self-glorifying spirits into worship that should glorify You. We inject our own traditions and personal preferences in worship that should only glorify You. We burden and grieve Your Holy Spirit, as we try to subject it to rules and regulations in worship experiences that should only glorify You.

Forgive us, O God, for our shortsightedness and our callousness. Forgive us, O God, for taking You and Your blessings for granted. Forgive us, O God, for taking Your grace and mercy that continue to give us chance after chance for granted. Forgive us, O God, for taking the blood of Jesus that cleanses and saves to the utmost for granted.

In our heart of hearts, we really do love You, O God. In our heart of hearts, we really do desire to serve You and please You, O God. We just sometimes get carried away with our own exuberance without being properly anchored in You.

We praise You for Your patience, O God and we pray You will be pleased with our efforts to praise and give glory to Your name. Guide us in our fervor in worship and in our zeal in service. Guide us in our efforts to be bold witnesses for You. We seek Your face because we know without You we would stray. We seek Your face because we know without You we can do nothing. We seek Your face because we love You for who You are. We praise You, Holy Spirit and we thank You even now for the new places You shall lead us. We offer this prayer in the name that Your word gives, the precious name of Jesus, Amen.

– DAY 202 –

II SAMUEL 6: 12-15

O God teach us how to truly worship with our giving. When Your servant slaughtered an ox and fatling with every six paces he demonstrated that giving is integral to worship and worship is integral to giving.

As David danced, he gave his energy to excellence. As David danced, he gave his mind to mercy. As David danced, he gave his voice to victory. As David danced, he gave his heart to holiness. As David danced, he gave his feet to faithfulness. As David danced, he gave his soul to salvation. As David danced, he gave his tongue to thanksgiving. As David danced, he gave everything he had to Your glory, O Lord.

We give You praise, O God, with all we have, because You, Lord God, have the standard. You gave us the best in Jesus Christ. The Lord Jesus gave us his best love on a cross, his best life in the resurrection, his best comfort in the Holy Spirit and when he returns he will give us his best reward.

God You are the greatest lover and You so loved, (the greatest degree) the world (the greatest number) that You gave (the greatest act) Your only begotten Son (the greatest gift) that whosoever (the greatest invitation) believeth (the greatest simplicity) in Him (the greatest person) should not perish (the greatest deliverance) but (the greatest difference) have (the greatest certainty) everlasting life (the greatest possession).

When we think about all You, O Lord, have given, we feel like the writer,

> All to Jesus [we] surrender, all to him [we] freely give,
> [We] will ever love and serve him, In his presence daily live.
>
> [We] surrender all, [We] surrender all;
> All to Thee [our] blessed Savior, [We] surrender all.
>
> (All to Jesus, I Surrender, Judson W. Van De Venter)

Develop within us a spirit of generosity so we may love You as we should and forgive us when we cheapen our worship because we have lessened our giving. In the name of the Lord Jesus do we offer this prayer, Amen.

DAY 202

– DAY 203 –

II SAMUEL 6: 16-23

Gracious God, You have such a vision of bounty for our lives when we seek Your face and when we are in obedience to Your word. O God unlike Michal of old, we pray we will be available to Your and so focused on You that Your vision of bounty will be produced in our lives to Your glory.

The Lord Jesus has said, "I am come that they might have life and have it more abundantly." We pray that his vision of bounty will be brought forth in our lives to You glory. The gospel of John has declared, "In him [in Christ] was life and the life was the light of all people. The light shines in the darkness and the darkness did not overcome it."

The writer of Proverbs has declared, "the sinner's wealth is laid up for the righteous." We will have a barren life that produces nothing beyond itself. Your servant Moses has said to the people of God still assembled in the wilderness, "You will lend to many nations and will not borrow. The Lord will make You the head and not the tail; You shall be only at the top and not at the bottom — if You obey the commandments of the Lord Your God," We pray this vision of bounty will be brought forth in our lives to Your glory.

The Psalmist has said those who delight in the law of the Lord "are like trees planted by the rivers of water, which yield their fruit in their season and their leaves do not wither. In all that they do they prosper." We pray this vision of bounty will be brought forth in our lies to Your glory.

The apostle Peter has said of us, "You are a chosen race, a royal priesthood, a holy nation, God's own people, in order that You may proclaim the mighty acts of him who called You out of darkness into his marvelous light." We pray this vision of bounty will be brought forth in our lives to Your glory.

Now Lord forgive us for the times we have frustrated Your vision for our lives and have thought barrenness and lived barrenness when You desired and saw bounty for us. Have Your way, Your very own way in our lives and we will be careful to give You the praise and to say that the Lord Jesus did it. In his name do we offer this prayer, Amen.

DAY 203

– DAY 204 –

II SAMUEL 23: 13-17

O God, we pray for David's attitude of reverence when his loyal soldiers gave him the gift of water they had secured from the well at Bethlehem at the risk of their lives. He did not take their action lightly. He was humble enough and had enough sense to know he was unworthy to drink water attained through such great sacrifices and by such great risks. And so he poured it on the ground as an offering to You, O God.

As we continue to seek You face, O God, we pray like Your servant David, we too will be moved to honor God with the best and the first. When we realize how underserving we are of the many blessings we have received as we have spent time in Your presence, we pray our hearts will be humbled all the more and we will truly honor the sacrifices of others.

As we stand on the shoulders of others, when we think of all others went through so we could be where we are, such sacrifices deserve only one appropriate response. Like Dave, we ought to pour our lives out as an offering to Your glory, O God. You alone deserve the glory from lives that have been purchased at so great a price.

When we think about all that our mothers and fathers, our grandparents and aunts and uncles went through to get us to this point, we dare not give our lives to the devil or live selfishly as if we owe nobody anything. When we think about how hard our ancestors prayed, how hard they worked, how much they sacrificed so we could enjoy what they never dreamed of, we dare not throw our lives away. Such sacrifice and faith deserves to be honored with lives that are given to You, O God.

When we think about the breadth and depth of Your love for us, how much was risked to reclaim us, sacrificed to restore us, endured to save us and to free us, how can we do anything other than give our lives back in gratitude and devotion, in adoration and service, to the One who loved us so much. Such redemption is too precious to be fully used by us. It can find its fullest and most effective expression in lives that have been given back to You.

We love You, O God, and we pray You will receive all we give back to You because You alone are worthy. In the name of the Lord Jesus do we offer this prayer, Amen.

DAY 204

– DAY 205 –

I CHRONICLES 4: 9-11

God, we are grateful for the vision of new territory and enlarged borders. However, we recognize new territory and enlarged borders come at a price. Sometimes the price is being laughed at for believing what we believe as we follow God's word and do what look like foolishness to others, as was the case with Noah. Sometimes the price is leaving familiar surroundings late in life and striking out for destinations unknown or at least unfamiliar territory, as was the case with Abraham. Sometimes the price is going back to face our past and having to give long and often thankless leadership of those who are still wed to their slave past, as was the case with Moses. Sometimes the price is standing by ourselves against seemingly odds, as was the case with Elijah. Sometimes the price is being persecuted because of what You believe, as was the case with Daniel. Sometimes the price is what seems to be certain career death because one refuses to dance to the political music of others, as was the case with Shadrach, Meshach and Abednego.

Sometimes the price is going beyond predefined roles of race, gender or even profession, as was the case of Mary of Bethany who chose to sit at the Lord's feet and listen to his teaching rather than work in the kitchen as women were expected to do. Sometimes the price is agony in a garden of prayer where the devil throws everything he has at You. Sometimes the price is a cross on a hill called Calvary, as supposed followers forsake You and friends deny You. Sometimes the price is being misunderstood by family, misrepresented by friends and falsely accused by enemies. Sometimes the price involves delight at your down moments and claims the victory over your life and career. The Lord Jesus paid all these prices.

Sometimes the price means making sacrifices again and again for others, as was the case with Harriet Tubman. Sometimes the price is being personally maligned and exposed and even shot down because of the truth You proclaim and stand for, as was the case with Dr. Martin Luther King, Jr.

O God, grant us the faith to pay whatever the price so Your vision for our lives will become reality. We ask this prayer in the name of the Lord Jesus, Amen.

DAY 205

– DAY 206 –

SONG OF SOLOMON 2: 15

O God, we confess we have allowed little foxes to get the best of us. Little foxes are the explanation for our being as negative, cynical and distrusting as we are at times. Little foxes are the explanation for the disappearance of the fire, waning of enthusiasm and the loss of devotion and commitment. Little foxes are what happened to the relationship. Little foxes, explain why we do not have the enthusiasm we once felt about our ministry or doing what we used to be so excited about doing in the church. Little foxes are the reason getting up and going to church or choir rehearsal or club meeting has become such a chore. Little foxes are the reason we cannot look at some people's faces without anger or resentment. Little foxes are sending us home with tears in our eyes and our feelings hurt. Little foxes are making duty that once was a delight, now a heavy load and worship that was once transforming, now a task.

We survived the big things. We dealt with the unexpected deaths or the deaths of those who we dearly loved. We dealt with the fire, the flood and the storm that took away so much of our material possessions and thus made it necessary for us to rebuild our inventory of worldly goods. We dealt with the loss of job, the denial of the promotion or the reversal in our career that could have ruined us. We even dealt with the indiscretion or the disappointment that could have broken our heart or at least caused us to look at the relationship with matured eyes. When You, O Lord, did not answer our prayer the way we thought You should, we even managed to overcome our disappointment with God and still remain faithful.

However, we confess after surviving all we have, the little foxes are about to get the best of us. So we come into Your presence, O God, asking You to put a new song in our life; a song of praise upon our lips, even as You did for Your servant David. When we think about how much You love us, when we reflect upon Your live that was concretized on Calvary, when we think about all the Lord Jesus went through on our behalf, when we think about how invested You are in our salvation and our victory, we will continue to praise You and we will continue to be positive no matter what little foxes try to do to us. In the name of the Lord Jesus do we offer this prayer, Amen.

– DAY 207 –

MICAH 7: 1-7

O God, You have given us decision-making power and what You have bestowed upon us the devil cannot take away. The devil does not have the power over our personal decisions and You have made a decision to respect our personal decisions. The devil cannot overcome our decision making power and You have made a decision not to overcome it. The devil cannot overrule our personal decisions and You will not overrule our personal decisions. You give us opportunities, O God, but we decide whether we will play the hand we are dealt or just take up space at the table.

O God, we pray, we will be ever mindful of the weight and power of our personal decisions. The devil cannot break us until and unless we make a decision to let the devil break us. You, O God, cannot make us into somebody of worth until and unless we make a decision to allow You to make us into somebody of worth. The devil cannot force failure upon us and You, O God, will not force success upon us. The devil cannot force us to stop and You, O God, will not force us to start. The devil cannot force us to stop attending church, praying, studying the bible or giving praise. And God, You will not force these things upon us. The devil cannot stop us from tithing and You will not force the overflow that comes from tithing upon our lives. The devil cannot stop us from joining church and You, O God, will not force us to join. The devil cannot stop us from obeying Your word or from following Your vision for our lives. And You, O God, will not force us to obey Your word to follow Your vision for our lives.

Like Micah of old, we pray, O God, we choose rightly. We pray we will choose to be positive rather than negative. We pray we will choose to be compassionate rather than cynical. We pray we will choose love over hate and faith over fear. We pray we will choose to be victors rather than victims. We pray we will choose life rather than death. We pray we will choose to trust rather than be troubled. Like Micah of old, we pray we too will say, "But as for me, I will look to the Lord, I will wait for the God of my salvation; my God will hear me." In the name of our Lord Jesus do we offer this prayer, Amen.

DAY 207

– DAY 208 –

MATTHEW 2: 1-12

O God, the wise men of yesteryear saw a new star in an old sky. As we seek Your face, we pray like them, we will have eyes to see newness in old skies. We pray for penetrating eyes so we can see possibilities where we have been seeing problems and piercing eyes so we can see through pain and see power. We pray for eyes of faith of that we can see a favorable future rather than the fear and failure we have been observing. We pray for positive eyes so we can see promise in the midst of our perplexities.

We pray for eyes of vision so we can look beyond our valleys and see victories. We pray for eyes of determination so we can look beyond our demons and see deliverance. We pray for eyes of salvation so we can look beyond our sins and see strength. We pray for eyes of hope so we can look through our present hells and see a glimpse of heaven. We pray for eyes of creativity so we can look beyond our crosses and see crowns.

Like the wise men of yesterday, we pray for willingness, even an eagerness to change, to grow, to experience newness and to follow the stars You hang in the skies of our lives. When like the wise men of yesterday we look for the king of glory in the wrong place, when like them, we make a wrong turn and end up in Herod's palace, we are grateful for Your star that continues to shine and to lead us to the place where the king of glory abides.

Like the wise men of yesteryear, we pray for worshipping hearts and giving hearts when we come into Your presence as we seek Your face. Then like the wise men of yesteryear, we pray after seeking You, we will take a different road from the one we have been traveling. Lead us, O Lord, with Your mighty and merciful hand to the road that lead from death to life, from bondage to breakthrough, from shame to salvation and from earth to heaven. And we will give You all the praise Lord Jesus, the eternal Bright and Morning Star, who shines to guide us to a land fairer than day. In Your own name do we offer this prayer, Amen.

DAY 208

– DAY 209 –

MATTHEW 6: 33

O Lord, You have promised if we seek first Your kingdom and its righteousness, then the things those who have the mind and spirit of the world will be given or added unto us. We pray that when we receive Your favor we will still continue to be faithful and we will not start acting foolish. We pray when we receive Your gifts we will still be true and we will not become traitors. We pray when You bless us, we will still serve You like we did when we were struggling.

We pray when God prospers us, we still be prayerful as we were when we were in poverty. We pray when we receive some of our wants we will worship You like we did when we were worried. We pray when we receive some of our desires, we will still delight ourselves in You like we did when we were destitute. We pray when You bless us we will still be bound to You, as we were when we were burdened and we will not start singing "I did it my way."

We pray when we receive Your gifts, we will be grateful, as we were when we were grieved. We pray when we receive forgiveness, we will follow You as we did when we were in fear and we will not become holy overnight and start acting as if You are obligated to hear us and forgive us. We pray when we receive Your love, we will be as loyal as we were when we were lonely. We pray when we receive victory, we will be as virtuous as we were when we were in the valley.

We confess, O God, there have been times when like Noah, we became drunk on the things of this world. Like Jacob before he had an all night long wrestling match with an angel, we started trying to live by our wits instead of by our worship. Like Lot, we became argumentative and selfish. Like Samson, we allowed flesh to get the best of us.

Like David, we started letting our eyes wander where they do not belong. Like Solomon in his old age, we allowed our hearts to be turned away from God. Like the Prodigal Son, we wasted what we have received with and on the wrong people. Like the Rich young ruler, we started believing we are being asked to give too much to God who has given us everything. Like Herod, we failed to give You the glory.

Forgive us O God and we pray for such love for You that we will remain faithful even when we are blessed. We offer this prayer in the name of the Lord Jesus, Amen.

DAY 209

– DAY 210 –

MATTHEW 9: 9-10

Lord Jesus, we pray we will never forget when we are at our worst or at our lowest, that is not who we were created to be. We were not created to be a drunk or an addict. We were not created to be either nicotine or a caffeine addict. We were not created to be a lover of money. We were not created to live in poverty or on welfare. We were not created to be a hustler or a pimp. We were not created to be a low life.

We were not created to be weak and co-dependent. We were not created to be in bondage to our flesh or to anything or to anyone. We were not created to be abused and misused. We were not created to be somebody's love slave and sex toy. We were not created to live in fear and in worry. We were not created to be intimidated because somebody thinks they control our future because they have authority on a particular job. We were not created to be a victim of the political whims and machinations of others. We were not created to be depressed and in tear all of the times. We were not created to always be uptight and always wound as tight as a rubber band. We were not created to be negative, a complainer and a whiner. We were not created to be a gossiper and a busybody. We were not created to be a failure. We were not created to be "broke, busted and disgusted."

O God, we are grateful for Your word that tells us who we can be and what we can do. We were created to be the head and not the tail, at the top and not the bottom. We can do all things through Christ who strengthens us. We are Your children and it does not yet appear what we shall be. But we know that when You Lord Jesus shall appear we shall be like You for we shall see You as You are.

We praise You O God for Your vision of what we can be. We praise You Lord Jesus for opening the way for us to become all we can be. We praise You Holy Spirit for empowering us to be all we can be. And like the apostle Matthew, we pray we too will discover who we really are and we will lead others into the journey of self-discovery through You, Lord Jesus. In Your own name do we offer this prayer, Amen.

DAY 210

– DAY 211 –

MATTHEW 16: 21-23

O Gracious, promise keeping and faithful God, we delight ourselves in You. We are grateful above all and through it all, You are faithful. We are grateful even in spite of us, You are faithful. We are awestruck at the very thought of Your power that causes everything to be that is and sustains everything that is according to Your grace and mercy. We are humbled by Your presence that is everywhere and holds us even when we deserve to be dropped. Your glory reminds us again You alone are worthy to be praised and we worship You for who You are.

But O God, it is Your faithfulness that draws our hearts to You. Because Your love is faithful through all of our foolishness, Your love remains steadfast through all of our lies and broken promises and forgotten vows, Your patience is more powerful than the peril we put ourselves into and Your forgiveness out lasts our fickleness and Your mercy is more enduring than our meanness, we thirst for You as a deer pants for flowing stream. We cling to You because it is in You we move and live and have our being. We worship and adore You and love You with all our hearts that are grateful and with testimonies that know the truth and veracity of Your faithfulness.

Now, O God, in this moment of worship we pray that You would visit us again with power from on high. We ask that again You would do what only You can do — be God in our situation. There is so much we desire and so much we want to see happen in our lives, in the lives of those we love and in the ministries You have entrusted to our care. However in all we would ask and pray for, we pray for this most of all — that You would just be God as only You can be in our situation.

Now, O God, as we prepare for the days ahead, we pray we will always keep the promise of resurrection in view because You alone have the last word over our lives and our destinies. Now, O God, we pray that the words of our mouths and the meditation of our hearts find acceptance in Your sight, O God of faithfulness, our strength and our redeemer. In the strong name of the Lord Jesus do we offer this prayer and that with thanksgiving even now, Amen.

DAY 211

– DAY 212 –

MATTHEW 25: 14-25

Gracious God, we praise and glorify You because You move beyond fairness to bless us. We pray when we begin to feel jealousy toward those who are differently blessed than we are or those who have what we would like to have, we remember You have blessed us beyond abundantly beyond our deserving. When we begin to question why we don't have more, we would remember You have been more than fair with us and You have given us whatever we need to move toward the vision You have for our lives that is greater than any vision we can have for ourselves or that other can have for us.

Gracious God, where would we be if You had just treated us fairly. If You had treated us fairly the Lord Jesus would never have come. You could have looked upon us and said, "I gave them the heavens that declare my glory and they are still determined to live beneath my privilege. I have done my part. I will leave them to their destiny of destruction that awaits them. That's fair." Or You could have said, "I have sent them prophets and preachers to explain the truth to them and they rejected them. I sent Moses with the Ten Commandments. I sent Samuel to walk before them as an example of a true godly man. I sent Elijah with enough prayer power to hold up and release rain in the heavens. I sent Elisha with mighty works. I sent Isaiah with the promise of a messiah. I sent Jeremiah who labored among them with tears. I sent Ezekiel with his visions. I sent Malachi with his teaching about the turnaround in their fortunes if they tithed. I even sent a rascal like Samson to physically rescue them when they got into trouble. I have done my part. I will leave them to the destiny of destruction that awaits them. That's fair."

You could have said all of those things but You didn't. You went beyond fairness and expressed freedom and came Yourself. You gave Yourself a human personality and chose the name of Jesus because it means, 'God [Jehovah] is salvation.'

Because You came, Lord Jesus, we have a song that not even the angels can sing, "Redeemed! Redeemed! We have been redeemed!" Thank You God for moving beyond fairness to take care of us and we now commit ourselves to live anew for Your glory. In Your name, Lord Jesus, we now offer this prayer, Amen.

– DAY 213 –

MARK 15: 25-33

O God, we come before You acknowledging that no matter how arrogant and self-righteous, condescending, independent, stubborn and rebellious we act sometimes, there are some situations we cannot save ourselves in and from. We have to trust You O God to bring us through. Some situations we cannot save ourselves in and from, we have to do things Your way. When we have tithed and the devil has our finances under attack, we cannot save ourselves by holding back what You have said belongs to You. We have to trust You to do what You have said and that is open up the windows of heaven and pour out the overflowing blessing. We are grateful for the witnesses that if we do our part, You will do Your part by blessing in ways we have not even imagined.

When enemies surround us because we have tried to walk in our privilege as Your child, we cannot save ourselves by taking matters into our own hands. We have to trust You to fight our battles and make enemies our footstools just like You said You would. When we have been in bondage and are in need of deliverance and another chance and the enemy knows our weakness, we cannot save ourselves from the penalties of a wasted life. When we have sinned and fallen short of Your glory, there are not enough tears. Tears are not enough promises and good intentions that would merit our being given another chance.

When we have tried to live holy, our righteousness is still but filthy rags in Your pristine presence. O God You are perfectly holy and righteous. We cannot save ourselves from eternal judgment and condemnation. And when death comes creeping into our rooms we cannot save ourselves from its capture and its eternal hold upon us.

We are grateful for the good news that we don't have to save ourselves. We have a Savior and a Lord named Jesus who did not save himself on the cross so he could be raised to save us. We know a man that can save; we know a name that can save and we know blood that can save. We are grateful for the wonder working power of Your presence, the demon chasing power of Your name and the eternally cleansing and freeing power of Your blood. We are grateful that we know You for ourselves as Savior and we are humbled that You have us and have accepted us as children. In the name of the Lord Jesus do we offer this prayer, Amen.

DAY 213

– DAY 214 –

MARK 3: 13-15

O God, we are grateful that You desire to just be with us. We pray for wisdom to take the time to be with You. In Your presence there is fullness of joy and at Your right hand are pleasures forever more. Forgive us for those times O Lord when we worship at the altars of busyness and start believing that the busier we are the more productive we are and the more things we schedule ourselves to do, the more meaningful our lives can become. O God we confess that sometimes our busyness is our excuse from being still and quiet so we can face some things in ourselves and in our lives that are not pleasing to You.

O God would You gently teach us how to slow down and live and how to spend quality quiet time with You. We confess O God that sometimes we become so busy working for You and doing things in Your name when all You desire is that we just be with You. When we spend time with You we receive correct perception about what is right. When we spend time with You we receive the power of Your presence on our journey. When we spend time with You our praise is strengthened. Most of all when we spend time with You we receive You.

And when we find ourselves under attack rather than becoming as busy as our attackers, we pray for wisdom and faith to spend time with You and trust You to bring us through as more than conquerors. As our Anointer You are greater than those who attach us. As our Defender You are greater than demons that demean us. As our Lord You are greater than the lies that circulate about us. As our Redeemer You are greater than the rumors that are spread about us. As our Helper You are greater than the hindrances that come against us. As our Provider, You are greater than the persecution that rises against us. As our Protector, You are greater that the peril that threatens us. As our Savior You are greater than the spite that is done against us.

O Lord Jesus, You are greater than the jealousy that tries to belittle us. O True Vine, You are greater than the tough viciousness that is done to us. O Good Shepherd You are greater that the sticks that are used against us. For when we spend time with You Lord, the battle is removed from our hands and becomes Yours. Thank You for this time with You and in Your own name do we pray, Amen.

DAY 214

– DAY 215 –

MARK 6: 1-6

O Jesus, Christ of God, we praise You for the opportunities for growth that You send into our lives every day. Every blessing is an opportunity to grow in thanksgiving. Every challenge is an opportunity to grow in faith. Every hurt is an opportunity to grow in forgiveness. Every delay is an opportunity to grow in patience. Every trial is an opportunity to grow in strength. Every fear provides an opportunity to grow in prayer. And every discouragement and disappointment is an opportunity to grow in faith. Every moment of every day is an opportunity to grow in love.

We praise You O Jesus for visiting our homes, our jobs, our churches, our schools and our family and friendship gatherings and providing us with opportunities for growth. Forgive us O Lord when we allow our doubts, our cynicism, our fears and our short sightedness to blind us to opportunities to grow. Forgive us when we allow our preconceptions and prejudices, our arrogance and our little knowledge of You to blind us to opportunities for growth.

We know that You have great dreams and desires, great visions and great victories for us if we would just take You at Your word and trust Your track record of what You have already done in our lives as well as in the lives of others. So Lord please be patient with us. Tarry with us a little while longer. The people in Nazareth missed out on the mighty works that You could have done in their midst. We don't want to miss out on Your doing great things for us, in us and through us. O Lord heal us of the fear that prevents faith from doing great things in our lives. Heal us of the doubt that prevents deliverance from flowing into our lives. Heal us O Lord of the cynicism that prevents commitment and change from growing in our lives. Heal us of the self-pity that prevents self-confidence from growing in our lives. Deliver us from the greed that prevents Your graciousness from growing in our lives. Deliver us from the weights that prevent wholeness from developing in our lives. And deliver us from the vices that prevent Your vision of victory from developing in our lives. In Your name do we offer this prayer, Amen.

DAY 215

– DAY 216 –

LUKE 1:38

Here we are Lord, Your servants. Let it be with us according to Your word. We pray for Mary's vision. We pray that like her we will look beyond the pitfalls and see the possibilities. Help us to look beyond the problems and see potential. Help us to look beyond the gossip and see the glory. Help us to look beyond the burden and see the blessing. Help us to look beyond the obstacles and see the opportunities. Help us to look beyond self and see service. Help us to look beyond the moment and see the momentous.

Like Mary help us to look beyond where we are and see where we can end up and declare, "My soul magnifies the Lord and my spirit rejoices in God my Savior, for he has looked with favor on the lowliness of his servant. Surely, from now on all generations will call me blessed; for the Mighty One had done great things for me and holy is His name."

Even though saying yes to You can be risky business because we never know what is in store for us and because there is no negotiation regarding the terms of the relationship, when we reflect upon Your will for us, Your word to us and Your work in us, serving You is worth the risk. We may not know what or who we may leave behind as we purse Your vision for our lives but serving You is worth the risks. We may not know what sacrifices we may be called upon to make but serving You is worth the risks because You always know what is best for us. You always keep Your word to us. You always do what is best for us.

We love You O God. We live for You O Christ. We praise You Holy Spirit. We praise You God. We follow You O Christ. We celebrate You Holy Spirit. We revere in our O God. We rejoice in You O Christ. We adore You Holy Spirit. We trust You O God. We testify of You O Christ. We bless You Holy Spirit. We worship You O God. We witness for You O Christ. We work through You Holy Spirit.

O God, You have come to us in Your fullness and in Your completeness and like Your servant Mary, we say to You, "Here am I, the servant of the Lord; let it be with me according to Your word." In Your wonderful name do we offer this prayer, Amen.

– DAY 217 –

LUKE 1: 57-66

O Lord as we seek Your face and prepare to grow much fruit to Your glory, as You establish us with new names, we recognize that we may have to clash and break with some traditions. Some of them are in our family; some are on our jobs and some are even in our churches. We pray for discernment to know which traditions to maintain and which to release.

Traditions that give us the freedom to bear much fruit that You have envisioned for us in the way that You want us to bear it ought to be maintained. Traditions that serve as a foundation and not frustration ought to be maintained. Traditions that compel us and that do not confine us ought to be maintained. Traditions that push us forward rather than push us backwards to the never never land of nostalgia and how it used to be, ought to be maintained. Traditions that give us wings to fly rather than weights to keep us grounded in someone else's comfort zone ought to be maintained. Transitions that glorify You rather than satisfy somebody else's insecurities ought to be maintained. Traditions that lift our heads rather than cause us to lower our eyes ought to be maintained.

However, there are some traditions O Lord that need to be broken. Traditions of poverty and ignorance in our family and among our friends ought to be broken. Traditions of poor diet and bad health that run on in our families and among our people ought to be broken. Traditions that are satisfied with a small world and a small neighborhood and a small circle of acquaintances when a whole world waits to be conquered ought to be broken. Traditions that are in bondage to a denominational label or a small church culture rather than a kingdom vision ought to be broken. Traditions that are bound by seats rather than salvation, songs rather than stretching and dates rather than deliverance ought to be broken. Traditions that are in bondage to uniforms and their color rather than an understanding of Christ ought to be broken. Traditions that are in bondage to hairstyles rather than heart fixes ought to be broken.

O God as You establish a new identity for us, give us courage to break what needs to be broken and faith to keep what needs to be kept. In the name of the Lord Jesus Christ do we offer this prayer, Amen.

– DAY 218 –

LUKE 5: 1-6

Here we are Lord in obedience to Your word and command we have moved beyond our safety zone and have launched out into the deep and have let down our nets of expectation. We have let down our worship nets with the expectation that You will hear and You will reward. We have let down our tithing nets with expectation that You will do just what You said and open heavens windows for us.

We have let down our work nets with expectation that You will bless and reward our efforts. We have let down our nets of service with the expectation that according to Your word, if we are not weary in doing well we shall reap if we do not faint. We have let our fighting nets down with the expectation that You will give us the victory. We have let down our faith nets with the expectation that You will save and You will deliver.

We're not simply asking; we have let down our nets of expectation that according to Your will and vision for our life we will receive. We're not simply seeking; we have let down our nets of expectation that we will find. We're not simply knocking we have let down our expectation nets of assurance, that You are home O Lord and that the doors of blessing and breakthrough will be open.

Lord Jesus You went to Calvary and died for our sins so that we could become children of God and have the right of expectation. We believe that as we continue to seek Your face You will fill our nets with new direction and new clarity for our lives. When we are drained and running on empty, we believe that You are present to fill our nets with new joy. When we become tired of wrestling with the enemy and are about to give up, we believe that You are present to fill our nets with new strength and new determination.

When we are in bondage to someone or something we believe that You are present to fill our nets with salvation, another chance and deliverance. When we have sinned and fallen short of God's glory, we believe You are present to fill our nets with love and forgiveness, with grace and with mercy.

Here we are Lord. We lift our nets to You. Fill them Lord with what You know we need. We receive it! In Your name we receive it! Amen.

DAY 218

– DAY 219 –

LUKE 5: 1-11

Gracious Lord, You have called us to move beyond zones and to launch out in faith and obedience, to let down our nets with expectation and to lift them with the abundance that You put into them. Like Simon Peter we continue to be awed and even frightened by the ways that You continue to bless and enrich our lives. And when like Simon Peter we would shrink back from following You all of the way because we recognize our own sinfulness and unworthiness we pray that You would give us faith to follow You.

When we follow You we are lead from the mundane to the meaningful, from mess to the miraculous and from the petty to the powerful. When we follow You we are lead from fear to faith, from loneliness to love and from bondage to breakthroughs. When we follow You we are lead form defeat to deliverance, from sin to salvation, from earth to eternity and from hell to heaven.

After all, You have not come to condemn us but to care for us. You have not come to reject us but to recreate us. You have not come to burden us but to build us. You have not come to frighten us but to fight for us. You have not come to lessen us but to lift us.

When we follow You we receive a catch in our nets that is beyond our expectation. We remember that words of the writer of Ephesians, "Now to him who by the power at work within us is able to accomplish abundantly far more than all we can ask or imagine, to him be glory in the church and in Christ Jesus to all generations, forever and ever, Amen."

When we follow You, You put so much in our nets that this life cannot hold it all. The catch will be so great that it will spill over into eternity. We remember the words of Paul, "We know that if this earthly tent we live is destroyed, [when these earthly nets wear out and these earthly boats begin to sink], we have a building from God, a house not made with hands eternal in the heavens."

Speak Lord we your servants are listening and lead on O Lord, we Your servants will follow. We offer this prayer in Your own name, Lord Jesus, Amen.

DAY 219

– DAY 220 –

LUKE 6: 12-16

We are grateful O God for James the son of Alphaeus whose name is listed as one who was called to be with You as an apostle, a messenger, an ambassador, a witness, a servant and as a friend. We are grateful for the unstained name that he left behind. And if it is our lot O Lord to serve You in small and unnoticed ways we pray that we might do it with distinction. If it's our lot O Lord to follow rather than lead and to take a back seat to others, help us O Lord to do so without bitterness and without a spirit of jealousy.

O Lord we pray that we will be remembered first and foremost as one who belonged to You. Your grace and Your mercy have brought us through all that we have come through. Your word has never failed us and Your hands have held us back even when we resisted. You have been faithful and patient with us even when we doubted You and strayed. In thanksgiving for all that You have done and in honor of who You are and because we are seeking Your face and loving You for who You are, we pray that our names will always be linked with those who truly belong to You.

James, son of Alphaeus was his name, however we are grateful for another name to cling to. If we are in need of a friend or a Savior, we have another name to cling to. If we need forgiveness for sins and a new lease on life, there is a name to cling to. If we need to be made over into a new person or a better person or the best person that we can possibly be, there is another name to cling to. If we need deliverance from bondage and freedom from guilt and from fear, there is a name to cling to. If we desire access to the heavenly throne and power over demons there is another name to cling to. If we need healing in our body or our mind or our soul, there is another name to cling to. It is the precious and powerful, reachable and righteousness, uplifting and upstanding, holy and helping, virtuous and victorious, sacred and strengthening, name of Jesus.

Somebody said,

There is a name[we] love to hear, [We] love to sing it's worth.
It sounds like music in my ears, The sweetest name on earth

O how [we] love Jesus; O how [we] love Jesus
O how [we] love Jesus, Because he first loved [us].

(Oh How I Love Jesus, Frederick Whitfield}

In his name do we offer this prayer, Amen.

– DAY 221 –

LUKE 6: 12-17

O God, we come into Your presence to give You praise for the transforming power, presence and blood of the Lord Jesus Christ. We pray that we will know the difference between transformation and transaction.

When we say yes to what we should be saying no to, a transaction has taken place. However when we say no to what we should be saying no to and yes to what we should be saying yes to, a transformation has taken place. When we give to get in return, a transaction has taken place. However when we give from love without any expectation of return, a transformation has taken place. When we buy for today without any thought of tomorrow, a transaction has taken place. When we refuse to buy today because we are saving for tomorrow or because of certain other long-term goals, a transformation has taken place.

Transactions are for the moment but transactions are momentous. Transactions are temporary but transformations are timeless. Transactions are for the present but transactions are permanent.

We pray that we will never be content with transactions when transformation is possible. O God awaken in us a passion for transformation and forgive us we pray for those seasons and circumstances when we have been content with transactions when You desired transformation for us.

You transformed Nicodemus, the Samaritan woman and Zacchaeus even though they started out seeking only a transaction. We pray that if we seek only a transaction, You will gently lead us into transformation. You transformed the disciple known as Simon the Zealot into one of Your devoted followers. Call us away O Lord from lesser commitments and lesser things so that we will love You without restraint and serve Your kingdom without reservation.

Help us to surrender the things that we hold on to, that keep us in bondage and that prevent us from living according to the vision that You have for our lives that is greater than any vision that we could ever have for ourselves. Then help us to make a decision to follow You as You lead us from grace to glory, even as You did Simon the Zealot. In Your own name Lord Jesus do we offer this prayer, Amen.

DAY 221

– DAY 222 –

LUKE 6: 16

O Lord Jesus we pray for wisdom to walk in our privilege and live up to the many opportunities that You have poured into our lives. We pray that we will not make the error of Your disciple Judas Iscariot. When You called Judas to be in special apostolic relationship with You he could have become so much. Yet he became a traitor.

Judas could have become a leader like Simon Peter whose confession of Jesus Christ as the Son of the Living God became the foundation that the church is built upon. He could have become a leader like James who found his own path to glory. He could have become a leader like John who had to stand by himself at the cross. He could have become a leader like Andrew who was always bringing someone to Jesus. He could have become a leader like Matthew who wrote one of the Gospels. He could have become a leader like Nathaniel who was able to outgrow his narrow prejudices. He could have become a leader like Thomas who was able to overcome his doubts.

Judas could have become a leader like Philip whose desire was to see the Father. He could have become a leader like James son of Alphaeus who left us a name of unheralded faithfulness. He could have become a leader like Simon the Zealot who moved from transaction to transformation. He could have become a leader like Judas the son of James who knew Jesus not only as a teacher but also as the only true and living Lord. Judas could have even become a leader like Paul who even as a leader untimely born became a new creature in Christ even with a thorn in his flesh that would not go away.

Judas Iscariot could have become a leader with his own unique testimony but he became a traitor. He had all the opportunities to become so many other things but he became a traitor. Being a constant companion of the Lord Jesus for three years he could have become so many other things but he became a traitor.

We confess Lord that it is so easy to criticize and condemn Judas for not living up to his opportunities. Yet You have poured so much into our lives in the places where we are. Give us vision to see them, wisdom to recognize them, hearts of thanksgiving to appreciate them and then courage to live up to them so that You and You alone will get the glory from our lives. In Your name Lord Jesus do we offer this prayer, Amen.

DAY 222

– DAY 223 –

LUKE 6: 16

Gracious God, we seek Your face because we recognize that like the disciple Judas Iscariot we understand we can get sidetracked. We confess O Lord that like Judas Iscariot that there have been times when we have become sidetracked. We confess O Lord God that some of us are sidetracked even now. However we are grateful for the gospel and the witness of scripture that we can get back on the right track again.

David the man after Your own heart got sidetracked when he became involved with Bathsheba and then conspired to murder her husband. However, You put him back on the right track again when David repented of his sins. O God when our sins have gotten us off track, we pray that You will put us back on the right track again.

Elijah the prophet of fire got sidetracked when fear overtook his faith and he fled from the face of Jezebel. However he ran to You at Mt. Horeb and Your spoke to him in a still small voice and put him back on the right track again. O God when our fears get the best of us, we pray that You will put us back on the right track again.

John the Baptist our Lord's forerunner got sidetracked when he began to have doubts in prison about Jesus being the Lord's anointed. However You renewed his faith and refreshed his soul with Your mighty works. O God when our doubts sidetrack us, we pray that You will put us back on the right track again.

In Luke 15 the Prodigal Son got sidetracked when he spent his inheritance in the wrong way. However he got back on the right track again when he came to himself in a hog pen and realized how much abundance there was in his Father's house and made a decision to go back home with a repentant spirit. O God when we make the wrong decisions and adopt the wrong priorities, we pray that You will put us back on the right track again.

Peter and the other disciples got sidetracked when on the night in which Judas betrayed You, Peter denied You and the other disciples deserted You. However Lord Jesus You put them back on the right track when You appeared to them after You have been raised from the dead. O Lord when we fail You we pray that You will give us another chance and put us back on the right track again. In Your name Lord Jesus do we pray, Amen.

– DAY 224 –

LUKE 19: 29-40

Lord Jesus on that Palm Sunday, there were those who tried to shut down the praises of Your followers. However, You stood up for them and declared to Your critics and theirs, "I tell You, if these were silent, the stones would shout out (Luke 19:40)." In the same way others consider our praise to be over the top and annoying and tell us that "It don't take all that," before we allow them to stifle and shut us down, we pray for holy boldness in declaring our praise and thanksgiving for who You are and all You have done for us.

We pray we will remember that those who criticize our worship and praise were not there when You saved us and put our feet on a street called Straight. They weren't there when You set us free from guilt and shame and gave us joy and self-confidence back. They weren't there when You got us up out of that sick bed. They weren't there when You helped us raise those children. They weren't there when You helped us finish school. They weren't there when You helped us pay those bills. They weren't there when You helped us start that business. They weren't there when You helped us recover from that failure. They weren't there when You found us when we had fallen on our faces, helped us get up, dusted us off and put us back in the race.

They weren't there when we buried a loved one and didn't know how or if we could go on without them and You helped us open and live fully in a new chapter in our lives. They weren't there when we were so depressed that we wished and prayed for death and considered suicide and You gave us a reason to keep on living. They weren't there when enemies had us surrounded and had declared us finished and You said, "The end is not yet." They weren't there when our heart was so broken we didn't think we would or could ever love again and You brought someone into our lives whose love wiped our pain away. They weren't there when certain doors were closed in our faces and we didn't know what to do and unexpectedly You led us to another door we didn't even know existed.

Since they were not there and You have always been with us, we pray for continued bold and unashamed praise, even if some consider us to be nuisances. In Your name do we offer this prayer, Lord Jesus, Amen.

DAY 224

– DAY 225 –

LUKE 19: 36-40

Lord Jesus, we pray that we will not repeat the error of the Pharisees who lived while You were here on earth. They failed to recognize You because You came as God in the flesh with a different look. We pray that we will continue to seek Your face so that we will recognize You even when You come with a different look.

When others say, "Look at grief," we pray for discernment to say, "Look at God." When others say, "Look at the crisis," we pray for wisdom to say, "Look at Christ." When others say, "Look at sorrow," we pray for faith to say, "Look at the Spirit." When other say "Look at the attack," we pray for insight to say, "Look at the angels whom God sent to minister to us,: When others say, "Look at the obstacles," we pray for understanding to say, "Look at the opportunities that God has given us."

When others say, "Look at the foes," we pray we will say, "Look at the friends that God sent to us." When other say, "Look at the mountains," we pray that will we will say, "Look at the miracles God is about to bring forth." When others say, "Look at the heartache," we pray we will say, "Look at our helpers." When others say, "Look at the burdens," we pray we will say, "Look at the blessings God will bring out of those burdens.

When others say, "Look at the trouble," we pray we will say, "Look at the testimony that God will soon give to us." When others say, "Look at the valley," we pray we will say, "Look at the vision that is yet for an appointed time. But in the end, that vision will not lie because some way and somehow, God will bring it to pass." When others say, "Look at the devil," we pray we will say, "Look at deliverance," For, when we seek Your face and abide in Your presence Lord Jesus, we understand all things really do work together for good to them that love You O Lord, to those who are called according to Your purpose.

We continue to seek Your face O Lord so we will not only be able to recognize You when You come with a different look but for courage to move and to change when You come with Your life giving word and presence. We pray for faith to say, "Yes, Lord yes to Your will and to Your way." In the name of the Lord Jesus do we offer this prayer, Amen

DAY 225

– DAY 226 –

LUKE 22: 34-62

Gracious Lord, we confess that sometimes like Your disciple, Simon Peter we are inconsistent in our living for You and in our service and devotion to You. We confess that sometimes like Simon Peter our walk does not always match up with our talk. Like Peter at times we start and then we stumble. Like Peter at times we are strong and then we are stupid. Like Peter at times we are powerful and then we are pathetic. Like Peter at times we are wise and then we are weak. Like Peter at times we are faithful and then we are feeble. Like Peter at times we show great insights and then we show great ignorance. Like Peter at times we are mighty and at times we are such mess-ups.

Like Peter at times we show such great revelation and then we cause such great revulsion. Like Peter at times we are such gifts to the heart of God and then we grieve the heart of God. Like Peter there are times that I am sure that we make the heart of God so proud and then we cause such pain to the heart of God. Like Peter there are times when we are such a blessing and then we are such a burden to the Lord. Like Peter there are times when we show great love and then we just lose it.

We confess O God that sometimes in life we can mess up so much that we do not know who the real person is. Sometimes we can become so confused that we do not know who we really are. When we are at our best is that who we really are? Or is the person that we see when we are at our worst really us? Are we the person who is strong or are we the person who strays? Are we the person who is faithful or are we really the person who is full of flaws? Are we the person who is bold or are we the person who is hopelessly bound? Are we the person who prays or who is full of praise or are we the person who plays?

O God in those moments of confusion, we pray that like Simon Peter we will always remember our true identity as Your redeemed and blood bought children. Like Simon Peter help us to receive the forgiveness and the second chances that You offer us. Like Simon Peter help us to grow from guilt to grace and then from grace to glory, in spite of our inconsistencies because we know our true identities as children of God. In the name of the Lord Jesus do we offer this prayer, Amen.

– DAY 227 –

JOHN 1: 43-46

Gracious Lord, we praise You for the value and the self-worth we have in You. When Satan attacks our self-worth and others put our self-worth down, we are grateful like the disciple Philip, You think enough of us that You desire us to follow You. We are grateful You are always looking out for us.

We pray You will give us presence of mind to always remember the worth we have in You and to be able to say when our self-worth and value are under attack, "We must be worth something because of Your love for us Lord Jesus. We must be worth something because Lord Jesus, You thought enough of us to die and then rise and then prepare a place in glory for us. We must be worth something because one day Lord Jesus, You are coming back for us as well as all of those who await Your appearing. We must be something because in the meantime the Holy Spirit, God's very own presence desires to live in us. We must be worth something because Lord Jesus, You want us to follow You."

"We must be something because the Lord Jesus even now is looking for us. No matter what others say about us, no matter how our accomplishments compare to the standards or achievements of others, we must be worth something in and of ourselves because of the interest the Lord Jesus personally had in us." In Your name, we rebuke the power of Satan and the influence of any others who will try to persuade us to think less of ourselves when we have made a decision to follow You.

And like the disciple Philip, we pray we will be a blessing to others. We pray like the disciple Philip, You will get the glory from our lives even though we sometimes do not get it right. We pray like the disciple Philip, we will help lead others to Christ. Save us, O Lord, from smug and selfish self-righteousness that is content in its salvation but looks upon the unsaved conditions of others with coldness and callous disregard. Teach us, O Lord, how to be a witness for You. Give us, O Lord, a burden for lost souls. There are some Nathaniel's who need You even as we need You. Help us to reach them O God. In the name of the Lord Jesus, our friend and the friend of every sinner do we offer this prayer, Amen.

DAY 227

– DAY 228 –

JOHN 1: 43-51

Lord Jesus, You are a Savior who has a track record of exceeding all expectations. When You allowed Nathaniel the privilege of being a disciple in spite of his remark about his background, You exceeded all expectations of patience. When You told Nathaniel that he would see the angels ascending and descending upon the Son of man You exceeded all expectations of revelation. When You told Nicodemus that he had to be born again You exceeded all expectations of wisdom. When You turned down Satan's offer of the kingdoms of this world's kingdoms and accepted a cross, You exceeded all expectations of sacrifice. When You fed five thousand with a little boy's lunch You exceeded all expectations of provision. When You calmed the raging seas, You exceeded all expectations of power. When You cast out demons You exceeded all expectations of supremacy. When You were transfigured on the mountain You exceeded all expectations of glory. When You prayed in Gethsemane, not Your will but God's will be done, You exceeded all expectations of submission.

When You died on the cross You exceeded all expectations of love. When You stopped dying long enough to pray that those who crucified You be forgiven, You exceeded all expectations of forgiveness. When You stopped dying long enough to tell a dying thief that he would be with You in Paradise, You exceeded all expectations of access. When You stopped dying long enough to put Your mother into the hands of the disciple John, You exceeded all expectations of care. When You stopped dying long enough to pronounce Your work finished You exceeded all expectations of completion. When You commended, as You died Your spirit into the hands of the Heavenly Father, You exceeded all expectations of trust. When You arose from the grave You exceeded all expectations of victory. When You stepped on a cloud and went back to glory You exceeded all expectations of authority. One day when You shall return You shall exceed all expectations of blessing and reward.

When You saved some of us, when You turned some of us around, You exceeded all expectations of grace and mercy. Thank You Lord Jesus for exceeding our expectations and it is in Your all-excelling name that we offer this prayer, Amen.

– DAY 229 –

JOHN 1: 43-51B

Lord Jesus, You have not bequeathed to us a spirit of timidity but one of power and of love and of a sound mind. However, we must confess O Lord that some of our past experiences have made us battle shy. Some of us are not as close to You O Lord or active in the church today because we have been so disappointed in the past that we are afraid to become enthusiastic and involved again. We have become joy shy. Some of us have chosen to settle for some safe and secure job that is beneath our abilities or intelligence because when we stuck our neck out before or when we exerted leadership before our career ran into trouble. Jealous coworkers and an insecure boss, made life hell for us or blocked a promotion or managed to have us dismissed. We have learned our lesson about being outspoken, out front, too smart, too creative or innovative, or working too hard or doing too much. We have become courage shy.

Too often O Lord, we have allowed attacks to make us anticipation shy. We have allowed backbiting to make us breakthrough shy. We have allowed criticism to make us caring shy. We have allowed enemies to make us excellence shy. We have allowed failures to make us faith shy. We have allowed fear to make us fight shy. We have allowed greed to make us goodness shy. We have allowed ignorance to make us inspiration shy. We have allowed jealousy to make us joy shy. We have allowed meanness to make us mercy shy. We have allowed negativism to make us niceness shy? We have allowed the pettiness of others to make us praise shy? We have allowed politics to make us positive shy. We have allowed rejection to make us rejoicing shy. We have allowed sorrow to make us shout shy. We have allowed stooping to make us standing shy. We have allowed underhandedness to make us understanding shy.

O Lord will You transform us like You did Your disciple Thomas? From Thomas the doubter to Thomas the delivered. From Thomas the skeptic to Thomas the strong. From Thomas the cynic to Thomas the courageous. From Thomas the jaded to Thomas the joyful. From Thomas the lonely to Thomas the loved. From Thomas the frustrated to Thomas the fruitful. From Thomas the hesitant to Thomas the hopeful. From Thomas the bound to Thomas the brave. From Thomas who was trapped to Thomas with a testimony. In Your name, Lord Jesus, do we offer this prayer, Amen.

– DAY 230 –

JOHN 4: 23-24

Lord Christ, we are grateful for Your track record of faithfulness that assures us that You will come for us. We may not know when You will come or what You are going to say or do or how You are going to work things out. But this much we know O Lord, You will come. We do not know how long we will have to put up with evil or how long the attack will last or how long it will be before things begin to turn around for us. But this much we know, Lord You will surely come to strengthen and to save, to rescue and to redeem.

We do not know how long it will be before our prayers will be answered but this much we know, You will come with the best answer for us at the right times if we just hold on and hold out. We do not know how long it will be before our breakthroughs come but this we know O Lord You are coming to break every yoke, to bring down every stronghold, to loose every fetter and to snap every chain, to open every dungeon that the enemy has closed upon us.

We do not know how long it will be before we see the results of our labors and our efforts but this we know, O Lord You are coming to justify our faith and to let us know that our living has not been in vain and to give us the victory for His names sake and glory. We do not know how long it will be before vision becomes reality or how long the vision will tarry but this we know, You will come O Lord and that the vision will not lie but that at the end it will speak. We do not know how long it will be before we experience Your manifest presence. But this much we know, O Lord, You will come with majesty and mercy and help and healing and refreshing and renewal and move us to another dimension in our walk with the Lord.

We do not know how long it will be before You come again Lord Jesus. But this we know, You will come and every eye shall see You and every tongue shall confess that You are Lord to the glory of God the Father. Even so, come Lord Jesus. In Your name do we offer this prayer, Amen.

DAY 230

– DAY 231 –

JOHN 4: 27-30

Lord Jesus like the Samaritan woman that You met at Jacob's well over two thousand years ago, we confess that we too have carried our water pitchers for too long. Perhaps many of us can't see the results of our being in Your presence because we carry away too much of what we brought to You, O Lord. We are still holding on to our water pitchers. We come grumbling and leave grumbling. We come with a negative spirit and leave with a negative spirit. We come angry and leave angry.

We come uptight and leave uptight. We come with a grudge and leave with a grudge. We come cheap and leave cheap. We come as a liar and leave as a liar. We come with gossip and leave with more gossip. We come with bondage and we leave with bondage. We come with issues and we leave with issues.

We come asking You, O Lord to give us the strength to help us carry our water pitchers, when we ought to come asking You to help us leave those water pitchers behind once and for all. Lord Jesus we are tired of coming to this same well week after week with the same pitcher. We are tired of coming into Your presence with the same pitcher. Week after week, month after month, year after year, here we come with the same pitchers. We are ready to make a decision to leave some pitchers and get rid of some pitchers from our lives for good and forever.

Give us the desire and the strength to leave them behind once and for all and for good. In the authority of Your name and through the power of the Holy Spirit, we now declare freedom from this pitcher. From this moment on and from this day forward, we will not pick it up any more. In You name Lord Jesus, we now declare our freedom. In You name Lord Jesus, we now declare our victory. Praise You Lord Jesus.

And if O Lord, we are ever tempted to take up those pitchers again we pray that You would grant us sacred memory to remember this moment when we put them down never to pick them up again and help us by the power of the Holy Spirit to rebuke the spirit of retrogression that seeks to turn us around. In Your own name do we pray, Lord Jesus, Amen.

– DAY 232 –

JOHN 6: 5-9

O Lord, we pray that we will not let the insufficiency of what we have stopped doing keep us from doing great things for You. Instead we pray that like Andrew we will present whatever we have to work with and have been given, no matter how little it is and trust You to multiply whatever we have and whatever we are to Your glory.

Like Your disciple Andrew who brought the little boy to You with is lunch to meet a great need, we say to You, "This is all that we have and this is all we know; this strength and this experience is all we have and all we know. It seems so little in comparison to this mountain that stands before us. But we heard how You fed five thousand with two fish and five barley loaves. We heard about how You made a way out of no way and made much out of little. I heard about Your miracle working power. And so we are just asking that You do in our life what You have done before when little is put in Your hands." And some of us are witnesses that Jesus is still able to do in this time in our lives whatever he has done in days past and gone.

We know that the enemy wants us to believe that what we have to work with is insufficient for You O God to do anything with. The enemy wants us to believe that our physical strength is insufficient for us to have an effective ministry. The enemy wants us to believe that the time we have left is insufficient to still have a productive life. The enemy wants us to believe that the mistakes we have made and the time and money we have wasted is insufficient to be loved and accepted by You O God. The enemy wants us to believe that the last heartbreak and disappointment that we encountered left insufficient love to be given to another. The enemy wants us to believe that our background has made us insufficient to walk in high and lofty places.

However, we know Lord Jesus that You are still able to work wonders with what appears to be insufficient. We too can be an Andrew if we are willing to put our little into Your hands. So have Your way with whatever we have and with whatever we are and we will give You the praise. In the mighty and multiplying name of Jesus do we offer this prayer, Amen.

DAY 232

– DAY 233 –

JOHN 11: 17-27

Gracious God, we are grateful that even now You hear us. We are grateful for love that looks beyond our faults and fulfills our needs. We are grateful that You are not slack concerning Your promises and that every word that You have spoken You will fulfill. We offer You praise for who You are even now. For some of us O God our praise comes as a sacrifice because we are facing circumstances and are in situations that contradict our promise and Your promise to us. However because we know You to be faithful and true and worthy of all praise we give to You the glad "Hallelujahs" with the fruit of our lips, nevertheless.

Some of us give You praise with questions and doubts, with fears within and foes without and with the scent of fresh sin still on our lives. However because You are a merciful as well as a just God we pray that You will receive our heartfelt praise and thanksgiving anyhow. Forgive us O God and grant us Your grace and mercy to fight another day.

We praise You for the journey and for the patience and the power, Your longsuffering love and Your guiding hand that has been with us every step of the way. We thank You for our testimonies borne of tears and our wisdom gleaned from our mistakes. We thank You that when we do not know what to pray or what to say that the Holy Spirit with sighs and groans too deep for words lifts our jumbled petitions and our faltering words before the throne of grace. We praise You for the name of Jesus and the power of his cleansing blood that gives us access to the heavenlies and takes us places that we could never reach on our own.

Now Lord as we worship You fill us anew even now. We pray for fresh fire and new anointing even now. Give us new revelations and discernment even now. Work miracles and manifest Your glory even now. Bring down strongholds and grant deliverance even now. Have Your own way even now.

Drop Thy still dews of quietness, Till all our strivings cease,
Take from our souls the strain and stress, And let our ordered lives confess
The beauty of Thy peace.

(Dear Lord and Father of Mankind, John G. Whittier)

In the name of the Lord Jesus do we offer this prayer, Amen.

DAY 233

– DAY 234 –

JOHN 12: 1-3

We love You Lord Jesus and our desire is to follow You. We want to be more than a believer we want to be a follower. We can believe in You and still not follow You. Belief is a matter of the head but following is a matter of the heart. Belief is a matter of conversation but following is about commitment. Belief is a matter of debate and discussion but following is a matter of devotion and dedication. Belief is a matter of feeling but following is a matter of faithfulness.

Belief is a matter of what we say with our lips, following is what we do with our life. Belief is a matter opinion but following is a matter of obedience. Belief is a matter of how we talk and what we say but following is a matter of total surrender. Belief is a matter words but following is a matter of walk. The difference between belief and following is the difference between a part time and a full time lover. We can believe part time but we must follow full time.

That is the reason that our prayer is for love and devotion that goes beyond belief to followship and that goes beyond membership to discipleship. Like Mary of Bethany we pray for devotion that is extravagant in its giving and in its worship. We pray that we will love You so much that whatever we do is not enough in our eyesight. Give us the desire to do more for You and for the kingdom.

You have been so extravagant to us. You have been extravagant with sufficient grace that we did not ask for an abundant mercy that we did not deserve. You have been extravagant to us with Your love and Your forgiveness, Your patience and Your understanding. You have been extravagant to us with the promises of Your word and in the many ways that You continue to provide and take care of us.

You have been especially extravagant to us in the giving of Yourself O God. You came in human flesh as the Lord Jesus Christ to save us. You even abide in the indwelling presence of the Holy Spirit.

Forgive us when we hold back and fail to live up to our privilege. As Mary of Bethany poured out the contents of the alabaster flask of ointment, we pour out ourselves to You and we pray that we will be acceptable in Your sight. In the name of the Lord Jesus do we offer this prayer, Amen.

– DAY 235 –

JOHN 12: 1-8

O God, like Mary of Bethany in the scriptures our desire is to give You glory and the adoration and praise of grateful hearts. We acknowledge O God that we cannot always be concerned about our own glory and give glory to You. You will give us glory but we only receive the glory that God You give when we are prepared to give up our glory for You, O God. Forgive us O God for those times when we have been more concerned about our own glory than glorifying You.

We acknowledge O God that we cannot give true glory to You if we are always concerned about what other people will say or think. We cannot give You the glory that You deserve if we are always concerned about how others may look at us and perceive us. Forgive us O God for those times when we have been more concerned about others that we have been about glorifying You.

We acknowledge O God that we cannot give You the glory of which You are worthy if we are not willing to take some risks and challenge some of our norms, traditions and customs. We cannot give You the glory that You deserve if we are always concerned about playing it safe. Forgive us for those times O Lord that we have chosen to play it safe and choosing to maintain our traditions rather than giving You the thanksgiving of which You are worthy.

Certainly, we cannot give You the glory that You deserve O God if we are cheap and are always trying to give the least rather than the most to You who has and who will continue to give us everything. Forgive us for our cheapness and move us to extravagance in love and life, in worship and in witness.

Like Mary of ancient Bethany we recognize that once You enter, then You are Lord of the house. No matter whose name is on the deed or who pays the rent or the mortgage You are Lord of the house. When You enter our relationship You become Lord of the relationship. Once You enter our lives You are Lord of our lives. Once You enter the church You are Lord of the church.

Our politics are not Lord; You are Lord. Our traditions are not Lord; You are Lord. Our order of worship is not Lord; You are Lord. We welcome and receive You as Lord as we offer this prayer of surrender in Your name, Amen.

– DAY 236 –

JOHN 14: 8-9

O Lord Jesus, we must confess that there have been times when we like Philip have failed to recognize You as the human face of God, the very embodiment of God in human skin. We confess O Lord that even though You have been walking with us, keeping us, blessing us, making a way with all this time for us, there are times that we still don't know You. You have helped us raise our children and there are times that we still don't know You. You have helped us through school and there are times that we still don't' know You. You have been with us through seven troubles and You did not forsake us in the eighth and there are times that we still don't know You? You have saved us from dangers seen and unseen, and kept us sane when we thought we would lose our mind and there are times that we still don't know You. You have kept us from falling when one of our loved ones came home to You and we felt our whole would was crumbling in and there are times that we still don't know You.

You have delivered us from sin, from demeaning work situations and nightmarish relationships and there are times that we still don't know You. You have walked with us from the rocking of our cradle and kept us by power divine to this present moment and there are times that we still don't know You. Why are we worried because the heathens are raging? Why are we threatening to quit because people do mean things to us and say mean things to us? Why are we losing sleep because of a job, why are we becoming mean and irritable because we are under attack? O Lord You have not brought us this far to leave You? What You have for us, it is for us and no devil can snatch it out of our hand. The only way they can get it is for us to let them have it. We ought to know how faithful You are and how much You care for us by now. You O Lord are God, Almighty who works miracles and brings Your children out as more than conquerors.

Forgive us O Lord and like Philip, we pray that You will keep Your hand upon our lives as we seek Your face. We praise You for Your patience and Your faithfulness and in Your own name do we offer this prayer, Amen.

DAY 236

– DAY 237 –

JOHN 14: 20

Lord Jesus like Your disciple Judas, the son of James, we honor You and reverence Your as Lord. We obey You and trust You as Lord. We surrender to You and serve You as Lord. We follow and are faithful to You as Lord. We live for You and we will die for You as Lord. We stand upon Your word and claim Your promises because You are Lord. We defy demons in Your name and in Your name we take aback everything that the enemy has stolen from us because You are Lord. We commit all we are and everything that we have into Your care and keeping because You are Lord. We do mighty works in Your name and we expect great miracles from You because You are Lord. You are not only a great teacher, You are Lord. You are not only a mighty prophet, You are Lord. You are not only our Savior, You are our Lord.

Lord Jesus You are not just a Lord; You are King of Kings and Lord of Lords. You are Lord of love, for "greater love has no man that this, that a man lay down his life for his friends" (John 15: 13 RSV). You are Lord of life, for You said, "I came that they may have life and have it abundantly" (John 10:10, RSV). You are Lord of forgiveness. Across the ages we hear Your voice from the cross, "Father forgive them; for they know not what they do" (Luke 23: 34, RSV). You are Lord of power. You declared, "All power in heaven and on earth has been given to me" (Matthew 28: 18, RSV).

You are Lord of time. You told John on Patmos," I am Alpha and Omega, the beginning and the ending…the first and the last" (Revelation 1:8a and 11, RSV). You are Lord over death, for You said, "I was dead and see, I am alive forever and ever and I have the keys of Death and of Hades" Revelation 1:18, NRSV). You are Lord of glory. Jude wrote, "Now to him who is able to keep You from falling and to make You stand without blemish in the presence of his glory with rejoicing, to the only God our Savior, through Jesus Christ our Lord, be glory, majesty, power and authority, before all times and now and forever" (Jude 24-25, NRSV)

You are Lord! You are Lord!
You are risen from the dead and You are Lord
Every knee shall bow, every tongue and confess
That Jesus Christ is Lord.

(He Is Lord – Linda L. Johnson)

In Your name Lord Jesus do we offer this prayer, Amen.

– DAY 238 –

JOHN 15: 8

Gracious God, we are grateful for the opportunity to bear much fruit that glorifies You. When we think about how unproductive we can be on our own, when we think about our own weaknesses and failings, we are so grateful that You not only see possibilities in us but that You see much potential, much power and much productivity in us.

Now Lord teach us how to be Your disciples, Your true followers. We do not want to be like the rich young ruler whose attachment to his personal possessions, prevented him from following You all of the way. We do not want to be like Judas who allowed Satan to corrupt him to the point of betrayal. We do not want to be like Pontius Pilate whose fear of the crowd stopped him from standing up for You, as he should have. We do not want to be like Demas who followed You only for a season and then turned back to the world.

Forgive us for those times when like Simon Peter we have denied You by our thoughts and by our deeds if not in our words. Forgive us for those times when like the other disciples we have fled when we should have stood firm. Forgive us for those times when like Joseph of Arimathea we have tried to be a secret disciple or follower.

Forgive us for those times when we have allowed our own agendas, egos and issues to prevent us from following You, as we should. Forgive us for those times when we have allowed our concern about the opinions of others to prevent us from following You, as we should. Forgive us for those times when our rebellion, stubbornness and disobedience have stopped us from following You, as we should.

Teach us how to be disciples in deed. Not simply in word but in deed. Not simply in intent but in deed. Not simply around other followers or in church but in deed. We love You Lord. We truly love You, Lord. We just need Your instruction and Your patience in our efforts to live for Your glory. Grant to us faith to follow, strength to stand, excellence to endure, power to persevere, generosity to give and courage to conquer. And we will love and follow You until traveling days are done. In the name of the Lord Jesus do we offer this prayer, Amen.

– DAY 239 –

JOHN 15: 8B

O Lord Your word has promised that You will grow much fruit from our lives that will glorify You and that we will be Your disciples. Even though we may not know exactly what the fruit will look like, we pray for discernment to recognize the fruit when it does start to grow.

Help us to recognize abundance where there used to be anxiety. Help us to recognize growth where there used to be griping. Help us to recognize blessings where there used to be burdens. Help us to recognize breakthroughs where there used to be bondage. Help us to recognize prosperity where there used to be poverty. Help us to recognize deliverance where there used to be dependency. Help us to recognize delight where there used to be depression.

Help us to recognize burning where there used to be burnout. Help us to recognize fire where there used to be frozenness. You will recognize fulfillment where there used to be frustration. Help us to recognize excellence where there used to be emptiness. Help us to recognize peace where there used to be problems. Help us to recognize heaven where there used to be hell. Help us to recognize miracles where there used to be mess.

Help us to recognize God where there used to be grief. Help us to recognize Jesus where there used to be junk. Help us to recognize the Spirit where there used to be Satan. Help us to recognize clarity where there used to be confusion. Help us to recognize strength where there used to be stress. Help us to recognize hope where there used to be helplessness. Help us to recognize faith where there used to be fear. Help us to recognize transformation where there used to be trouble. Help us to recognize worship where there used to be worry.

And we will give You the praise, the glory and the honor as we bear fruit in Your name and for Your service. For, our fruitfulness and our power to grow come from You as we seek and stay in Your face and abide in Your presence. In the name of the Lord Jesus do we offer this prayer, Amen.

DAY 239

– DAY 240 –

PSALM 50: 15

O God, Your word has said to call upon You in the day of trouble and You will deliver. O God, the day is now. The time is now. The Adversary presents new challenges as we seek a closer walk with You. We need You to deliver.

We don't know if we can continue to resist the alluring voice of the tempter. We need You to deliver. We've become so frustrated in the fight against weights and sins that so easily beset. We need You to deliver.

We have painted ourselves into a corner and we don't know how we are going to get out. We need you to deliver. We don't have the courage to make the decisions and say the things we should, we need you to deliver.

Help us Lord, when we feel ourselves sinking and our commitments wavering, when we are awakened by thoughts and fears that go bump in the night or when worries and fears cause us to toss and turn at night. We need You to deliver. Great name of Jesus grant victory. Promise of God, inspire and direct. Precious Holy Spirit, strengthen right now and later when prayer time is over. Speak Lord, Your servant is listening. In Jesus name do we pray, Amen.

– DAY 241 –

PSALM 51: 10

O God, we repent of our sin and especially our betrayal of others. Create within us a clean heart, O God and put a new and a right spirit within us.

We repent of our duplicitous and contradictory actions that are so far from what we really want to be. Create within us a clean heart, O God and put a new and right spirit within us.

We repent of broken promises and the failure to call on the name of Jesus during times of temptations. Create within us a clean heart, O God and put a new and right spirit within us.

We repent for any hurt we may cause others and for pain that callousness, weakness and foolishness may bring to the lives and feeling of others. Create in us a clean heart, O God and put a new and right spirit within us.

We repent of failing to avoid the appearance of evil and for walking in paths whose outcome we know. Create in us a clean heart, O God and put a new and right spirit within us.

O God, guilt is such a heavy burden to bear. Create within us a clean heart, O God and put a new and right spirit within us. This we ask in the strong, saving, sanctifying and satisfying name of Jesus — Savior, Elder Brother, Faithful and True Friend, Word of God Incarnate, Lord of Life, Salvation, The Great Atonement, Lord, Lord, Lord, the Almighty. Amen. Save us from ourselves Lord Jesus, even now, Amen and Amen.

DAY 241

– DAY 242 –

PSALM 52: 8

O God, give us the kind of faith that trusts You when we have done what we can. We must confess O God, not wishing, desiring or even praying for the destruction of our enemies is difficult. We must confess that we feel like Your servant did in this psalm as well as others when he becomes angry and hurt at the arrogance of those who do us harm O God in our fight for right, keep us from bitterness even as we battle and help us to stay focused on justice and not simply on vengeance and personal vendettas. We pray we will not become so angry we become part of the problem rather than the solution.

We pray for faith that trusts Your faithfulness in all things. We praise you for answered prayer in small things as well as in times of crisis or in life threatening situations. We pray for presence of mind to always seek Your direction before we act or speak. We pray for patience as you work things out. Then, we pray for a thankful heart and a spirit of bold and unashamed praise as You turn things around that we have sought You for. Help us to bear fruit as abundant as the olive tree that has been planted in the rich soil of Your word, that has been attended by the redeeming caretaker, Christ Jesus our Lord and has been enriched by the anointing of Your Holy Spirit.

Give us O God, a faith that trust You at all times, in all circumstances during all seasons of life---forever and ever and ever, Amen.

DAY 242

– DAY 243 –

ACTS 1: 1-5

Lord God many years ago You told Your followers not to depart from Jerusalem but to wait for the promise of the Father. They were told that they would be baptized with the Holy Spirit. According to Your word and promise, new authority and new accomplishments, new boldness and new breakthroughs, new gifts and new glory, new power and new peace came upon them as they waited in obedience for what You, Lord Jesus, said they would receive.

As was the case with the early church, we recognize that our obedience gives You the opportunity to move. Our obedience gives You the opportunity to work miracles. Our obedience gives You the opportunity to do what You desire to do in our lives. Our obedience gives You the opportunity to bless beyond anything that we could ask or think or imagine.

We pray for obedience that produces fruit. Obedience does not produce guilt; it produces growth. Obedience does not produce shame; it produces strength. Obedience does not produce fear; it produces faith. Obedience does not produce bondage; it produces breakthroughs. Obedience does not produce weakness; it produces worth. Obedience does not produce embarrassment; it produces excellence.

You are calling us to obedience in the places and areas in our lives where we have not yielded and submitted. If we have received a word that says stop, then we must stop. If we have received a word that says go, then we must go. If we have received a word that says wait, then we must wait. If we have received a word that says tithe, then we must tithe. If we have received a word that says submit, then we must submit.

Pentecost happens when we are in obedience to the word that we have received. We submit ourselves to You O God, Father Holy Spirit in the fullness of who You are we receive again the promise of II Chronicles 7, "If my people who are called by my name would humble themselves and pray, and seek my face and turn from their wicked ways, then I will hear from heaven and forgive their sins and heal their land."

We submit ourselves to You in obedience that we too will have the Pentecost that You will for us. We offer this prayer of submission in the only name that we know, Jesus Christ, our Lord, Amen.

DAY 243

– DAY 244 –

ACTS 16: 25-34

O God, we pray that like Paul and Silas we pray for power and faith to give You the sacrifice of praise, in confining and confusing circumstances so that when others see us instead of bitterness they will see breakthroughs. Instead of cursing they will see character. Instead of defeat they will see determination. Instead of emptiness they will see excellence. Instead of frustration they will see faithfulness. Instead of grief they will see Godliness. Instead of helplessness they will see hope.

We pray that our praise will be genuine because we need You O God. No hocus pocus but You O God. No magic but You O God. No manipulation but You O God. No smart, cute or fancy phrases but You O God. No luck but You O God. Nobody else but You O God! No emotional appeals but You O God. No tricks or performances but You O God. O God we have learned from our own experiences as well as from Your word that things happen when we give to You the sacrifice of praise. Peculiar things, glorious things, wonderful things, heavenly things, miraculous things, unexplainable things, logic defying things, all happen when we give to You the sacrifice of praise.

Our hearts desire O God is to give You the sacrifice of praise. Even when our praise seems silly and fruitless, our desire is to praise You anyhow. Even when it seems as if our praise is just trailing off into the air and going nowhere, our desire is to praise You anyhow. Even when others mock our praise and consider it foolishness, our desire is to praise You anyhow. Even when life contradicts our praise, our desire is to praise You anyhow. Even when we do not feel like giving You praise, our desire is to praise You anyhow. Even when we are lonely and frustrated and the devil has us under attack, our desire is to praise You anyhow.

Even when it is midnight and we are feeling most alone and forsaken, our desire is to praise You anyhow. Even when it is midnight when others are asleep, our desire is to praise You anyhow as we meditate upon You in the watches of the night. You heard the praises of Paul and Silas at midnight and we believe that if our praise is genuine You will hear us also and Your manifest presence will show up in our circumstance. So teach us O God and help us O God to give to You the sacrifice of praise. In the name of the Lord Jesus do we offer this prayer, Amen.

DAY 244

– DAY 245 –

I CORINTHIANS 1: 3-4

Lord Jesus, we recognize that Calvary was painful for You. The embarrassment of being stripped naked, hung high and stretched wide with all of Your privates parts exposed must have been painful for You, Lord Jesus. Hearing enemies mock You and laugh at You when You have tried Your best to do the will of God must have been painful to You. Lord Jesus. Seeing Your very own handpicked disciples who had pledged undying loyalty and allegiance to You deny You, betray You and desert You must have been painful to You, Lord Jesus.

The weight of the cross that carried the sins of the world, the crown of thorns upon his head and the spear thrust in his side must have been painful to You, Lord Jesus. However You did not hold on to the pain, You released it to Your Heavenly Father. We read of Your shout of release from the cross, "Father into Your hands I commend my spirit." Because You released Your pain to Your Heavenly Father, God raised You to stoop no more and has given You a name higher than any other name, that at You name Lord Jesus every knee shall bow and every tongue shall confess that Jesus, our Savior and Master is Lord to the glory of God the Father.

Because You released the pain You were not only raised, You now minister to us because You dwell at the right hand of God, there to make intercession on our behalf and one day You will come back for us with glory and majesty and authority.

We praise You for the gospel that tells us that good news that if we are willing to release our pain to You, we to can move from pain to power. We remember the word of that old hymn,

Come ye disconsolate, where'er ye languish —
Come to the mercy seat, fervently kneel.
Here bring Your wounded hearts; here tell Your anguish,
Earth has no sorrow that heav'n cannot heal.

(Come, Ye Disconsolate, Where'er Ye Languish, Thomas Moore)

Thank You Lord for Your consolation that moves us from pain to power, from hurt to healing and from misery to ministry. In the name of the Lord Jesus, do we offer this prayer, Amen.

– DAY 246 –

I CORINTHIANS 15: 17

We praise You Lord Jesus that when You died and was buried, that You did not rest in peace. One of the greatest tragedies of the human race would have occurred if You had rested in peace. Handel's Messiah with its glorious Hallelujah Chorus and its mighty refrain, "And he shall reign forever and ever" would never have been written if the Lord Jesus had rested in peace. The former slave owner John Newton's testimony of "Amazing Grace how sweet the sound that saved a wretch like me..." would have never been written if You had rested in peace. Thomas Dorsey, the father of modern gospel would never have emerged from his anger and depression because of the death of his wife to write "Precious Lord take my hand lead me on, let me stand, if You had rested in peace.

Dr. Martin Luther King, Jr. would never have emerged as the prophet of redeeming and redemptive love if You had rested in peace. Nelson Mandela who attended worship every Sunday during his twenty-four year confinement in prison and had his soul refreshed and refilled over and over again as he heard the story of how You conquered the cross, would not have emerged as the leader of power and peace that he did if You had rested in peace. Harriet Tubman would not have become a Black Moses leading hundreds of slaves from southern bondage to northern freedom had You rested in peace. Albert Schweitzer scientist, scholar, composer and conductor would never have done the great work that he did in Africa because the Lord of Calvary inspired him, if You had rested in peace.

Some of us would still be in bondage to sin, some of us would still be lost in the darkness of confusion and depression, while still others of us would still be paralyzed by fear if You had rested in peace. Some of us have become new persons with a testimony that the Lord Jesus saves to the utmost because he did not rest in peace. All of us would be less than what we are now and none of us would be able to reach our true potential or experience our highest possible level of attainment of the Lord Jesus had rested in peace.

We are able to offer this prayer and praise and thanksgiving to You Lord Jesus in Your name because You did not rest in peace. We are able to shout, "Amen! It is so!" Lord Jesus because You did not rest in peace. Hallelujah. Amen! Amen! And Amen!

DAY 246

– DAY 247 –

II CORINTHIANS 8: 5

Gracious God, our desire is to be like the people in the churches of Macedonia were not only full of love, full of gratitude, full of praise and full of the spirit, they also gave themselves first to the Lord. First to You O Lord—not to their careers or their jobs. First to You O Lord — not to their titles or positions. First to You O Lord — not to their feelings about the pastor or certain other members.

First to You O Lord — not to their hurt feelings and wounded ego. First to You O Lord — not to a building or to a certain denomination. First to You O Lord — not to their friends and family. First to You O Lord — not to their money or their possessions. First to You O Lord — not to their will and their wants.

When we give ourselves first to the Lord, we have staying power. We serve faithfully when even though we may never be recognized when we give ourselves first to You. We can keep praying and serving when all hell is breaking loose and our others are mocking us because our living and believing seems to be in vein when we give ourselves first to You. We can give and keep on giving when we give ourselves first to You.

John the Baptist stood up to Herod when he knew Herod had the power to take his life because he had first given himself to You. Paul and Silas could offer the sacrifice of praise at midnight when they were in prison because they had first given themselves to You. Our ancestors could risk being whipped as they sneaked behind bales of cotton to pray because they had first given themselves to You.

In one of the darkest hours of his life Dr. Martin Luther King, Jr. could receive a vision of the Promised Land and the assurance that his living had not been in vain because he had first given himself to You.

The Lord Jesus could have allow himself to be hung high and stretched wide for our sins because he had first given himself completely and totally to his Father's will.

O Lord God like others who have gone before us, our prayer is for faith, love, obedience and commitment to give ourselves first to You. Help us to abide in Your presence until we make the first and primary gift of ourselves to You O Lord the center of our joy and the source of our being. In the name of the Lord Jesus do we offer this prayer, Amen.

DAY 247

– DAY 248 –

HEBREWS 13: 15

O God, we pray that we will learn to give to You the sacrifice of praise. We recognize that a sacrifice is not a sacrifice unless it truly costs us something. Therefore O God we pray that we will be able to praise You when praise is costly and when praise is difficult. We pray for faith to praise You when praise takes some effort, when we have to struggle to do it and when we do not feel like it.

When things are going well for us and we are pleased with the way You are working and moving in our lives and answering our prayers, it is appropriate and easy to give You praise. When our bodies are healthy and we are feeling fine, when our families and relationships are sailing on smooth water, when our career or job is on track and when our finances are basically in order, it is appropriate and it is easy to give You praise. When we have gotten that promotions or something else that we have prayed for, when we have received a blessing that we were not even looking for or expecting, or when You move and bless far beyond our expectation or request, it is appropriate and easy to give Your praise. Praise is easy when it is offered on the altar of thanksgiving, gratitude, favor and blessing.

However while praise is good and proper and appropriate in these situations, we pray for faith to give the sacrifice of praise. Give us faith to give You praise not when it is offered on the altar of blessings but of burdens. Give us faith to give You praise not when it is offered on the altar of bounty but of brokenness. Give us faith to give You praise not when it is offered on the altar of thanksgiving but of trouble. Give us faith to give Your praise not when it is offered on the altar of testimony but of tears. Give us faith to give You praise not when it is offered on the altar of fruitfulness but of failure. Give us faith to give You praise not when it is offered on the altar of fulfillment but of frustration.

Give us faith to give You praise not when it is offered on the altar of grace but of grief. Give us faith to give You praise not when it is offered on the altar of deliverance but defeat. Give us faith to give You praise not when it is offered on the altar of power but of pain. Give us faith to give praise not when it is offered on the altar of healing but of helplessness. In Your name Lord Jesus do we offer this prayer, Amen.

– DAY 249 –

REVELATION 1: 17-18

Gracious and forging God, we confess that even though the Lord Jesus has the keys to hell and death, we still fail to live in the freedom that he gives us. We confess that have become so accustomed to our chains that we do not realize that we are free. We confess that we have failed in the past to go beyond a certain point and have now given up trying to reach beyond where we have grown accustomed to living. We confess that we have accepted a certain place and space and have grown content to live there. We confess that we have concluded that a certain life or lifestyle is beyond us. We confess that a number of us still feel the pain from past experiences of trying to be free.

We confess that we are still living with the memory of the pain from the chains that have held us in captivity. We confess O God that the memory of pain is so vivid that we are only willing to go so far, reach so far and extend ourselves so much. The experience of living chained has made such a lasting impression on us that no one has been able to convince us that we are free. No preacher or inspirational speaker that we have heard, no song that we have sung, no book that we have read, and no conference that we have attended have so far convinced us that we are as free as we really are.

We read the Bible on a daily basis and claim the promises of God for our lives and then still live as if we are chained forgive us O God. We pray often, we come to church and feel the presence of God and still live chained, forgive us O God. We see Your blessing and Your goodness in our lives. We have testimonies of how You have given us victory and worked miracles of deliverance when defeat seems inevitable. Yet when it comes to certain things, when it comes to exercising our power, privilege and right to go to a new level and depth with the Lord we still live chained. We still live bound by a chain that has been removed. Forgive us O God.

Help us to understand and to know that any time we use the word "can't" or any time we live the word "can't" we are bound by a chain that has been removed. Help us to understand that any time we are afraid to try something because of our past failure or failures, we are bound by a chain that has been removed. Teach us O Lord how to live in the freedom that You have given to us and we shall forever give You the praise. In Your name the Lord Jesus do we offer this prayer, Amen.

DAY 249

– DAY 250 –

REVELATION 5: 1-5

Hail Lion of the Tribe of Judah. Hail Conquering King. Hail Lord Christ, You have conquered and You alone are worthy to open the Book of Life and reveal to us everything that is to take place. We obey You as Lord, follow You as King, and love You as Savior. Because we follow You O Lion of Judah and King of praise we are grateful that we can have a life of praise even in times like these.

No matter what is happening around us and to us, we can still live a life of praise. No matter what people may say about us or do to us, we can still have a life of praise. No matter the attacks the enemy has us going through; we can still have a life of praise. No matter what our past has been or the mistakes that we have made or may still make, we can still have a life of praise. Even during this time of year that is so difficult for so many because of loneliness or because they do not have what others have, we can still have a life of praise.

As children of praise, we are following the lion of Judah, the king of praise. The lion gives birth to the cubs. The lion watches over the cubs. The lion feeds, nourishes and cares for the cubs. The lion protects and defends the cubs. And if they ever stray the lion will search for the cubs. If the cubs ever become afraid all they have to do is run back to the lion. The cub's security is in the lion. And the cub's victory is in the lion. For the lion will raise that cub and teach that cub until one day that cub becomes a lion himself or herself.

We remember the words of the song as we follow You O Lord Christ, Lion of the tribe of Judah and king of praise:

I don't possess houses or land, fine clothes or jew'lry
Sorrows and cares in this old world my lot seems to be,
But I have a Christ who paid the price way back on Calv'ry
And Christ is all, all and all this world to me.

Yes Christ is all; He's everything to me.
Yes, Christ is all; He rules the land and sea.
Yes, Christ is all, without Him nothing would be.
Christ is all, all and all this world to me.

(Christ is All, Kenneth Morris)

In Your name Lord Jesus do we offer this prayer, Amen.

– DAY 251 –

LUKE 24: 12

Lord Christ, we celebrate Your resurrection and the enduring Easter message. Those of us who have made mistakes, those of us who have sinned and fallen short of the glory of God, those of us who have been under attack by the devil, those of us who have experience defeat in our lives and need to know that You are alive, Lord Christ.

You are alive to heal and help us. You are alive to love us and to lift us. You are alive to save and strengthen us. You are alive to fight with us and to fight for us. You are alive to free us and forgive us. You are alive to help us pull down the strongholds that hold our potential in captivity. You are alive to deliver us and defend us. You are alive to cleanse and care for us.

Lord Christ, in times like these, the Easter message is still needed. In times like these when the threat of terrorism hangs over our heads and gang violence stalks our streets, the Easter message is needed as much as ever. In times like these when families are disrupted as young people and others are being shipped off to war to fight in wars that were started on false pretenses, while the resources of our nation are needed for education and health care are being siphoned to keep a fight going we should have never been in, the Easter message is still as needed more than ever.

In times like these when the family structure has broken down, when parents are afraid to discipline their children and we are trying to redefine marriage in a way that the Bible, God's eternal word, does not allow, the Easter message is needed more than it ever was. In times like these Simon Peter ran to the tomb, we also need to run to the church, we also need to be reminded that human governments, human corporations, human politics, human science and human leaders do not have the last word over our lives and our destinies.

Lord Christ You have conquered death and all power is in Your hands. That means that those of us who live for You and follow You, have been given the same power to conquer and put under the authority of his name and blood every demon and power who seeks to hold us down, hold us back and keep us in captivity. During this Easter Season, we pray for resurrection power to live for You in new ways. In Your name do we offer this prayer, Amen.

DAY 251

– DAY 252 –

PSALM 27: 8

"Your face Lord do [we] seek." Like a thirsty deer looking for the brooks of water, "Your face, Lord, do [we] seek." Like a seed trying to grow up out of the place where it has been planted that is stretching for the warm nourishing rays of the sun, "Your face, Lord, do [we] seek." Like a drowning person looking for something or somebody to cling to, "Your face, Lord, do [we] seek." Like a full term pregnant woman desperately wanting to deliver the life that You have placed within her, "Your face, Lord, do [we] seek." Like a sick person looking for healing, "Your face, Lord, do [we] seek." Like a lost child in a crowd looking for their parent's face, "Your face, Lord, do [we] seek." Like a starving person looking for food, "Your face, Lord, do [we] seek." Like a person caught out side in the rain looking for shelter, "Your face Lord, do [we] seek." Like a person in pain looking for relief, "Your face, Lord, do [we] seek."

Like a person in trouble in need of salvation, "Your face, Lord, do [we] seek." Like a broken person in need of mending, "Your face, Lord, do [we] seek." Like a burning house in need of firemen, "Your face, Lord, do [we] seek." Like a flat tire in need of fixing, like a dead battery in need of a charge, like a rundown car in need of a tune up, "Your face, Lord, do [we] seek." Like someone who has made a mistake and need another chance, "Your face, Lord, do [we] seek." Like someone who has become lost and is in need of being found, "Your face, Lord, do [we] seek." Like someone who has done wrong and is in need of forgiveness, "Your face, Lord, do [we] seek." Like someone who has messed up and is in need of a miracle, "Your face, Lord, do [we] seek." Like someone who has fallen and is in need of being picked up, "Your face, Lord, do [we] seek." Like someone who has become discouraged and is in need of encouragement and renewal, "Your face, Lord, do [we] seek." Like someone who has become frustrated and is in need of hope, "Your face, Lord, do [we] seek." Even as a dying saint anticipates going home to be with You, "Your face, Lord, do [we] seek." Even as our Lord Jesus sought to do Your will, "Your face, Lord, do [we] seek." In his name do we offer this prayer, Amen.

DAY 252

– DAY 253 –

PSALM 27: 8

O God, when we are struck with major tragedies and our lives come under unsuspected and sustained attach and we become overwhelmed with fear and begin to wonder how we are going to make it, like David we will continue to seek Your face. When seeking Your face becomes difficult, we are grateful for the way that Your word has responded to our questions of just how we are going to make it.

Job gave us the answer. "After he asked his questions he declared, [God] knows the way that I take; when he has tested me, I shall come out like gold." How are we going to make it? David gave us the answer. He declared, "I had fainted unless I had believed to see the goodness of the Lord in the land of the living. Wait on the Lord; be of good courage, and he shall strengthen thin heart: wait, I say on the Lord." David gave us the answer, because after he finished asking his questions he said, "Why are You cast down O my soul, and why are You disquieted within me? Hope in God; for I shall again praise him, my help and my God."

How are we going to make it? Habakkuk gave us the answer because after he finished asking his questions he went up to his prayer tower and ended up declaring, "Though the fig tree does not blossom, and no fruit is on the vines though the produce of the olive fails and the fields yield no food; though the flock is cut off from the fold and there is no herd in the stalls, yet I will rejoice in the Lord; I will exult in the God of my salvation. God, the Lord, is my strength; he makes my feet like the feet of the deer, and makes me tread upon the heights." How are we going to make it? Jesus gave the answer. After he had finished asking his questions he looked to heaven and declared, "Father, into Your hands I commend my spirit." How are we going to make it? The Lord Jesus gave the answer, "In the world You will have tribulation but be of good cheer, I have overcome the world." How are we going to make it? The writer of I John gave the answer, "Little children, You are from God and have conquered them; for the one who is in You is greater than the one who is in the world."

In the name of the Lord Jesus, who now intercedes for us as we continue to seek Your face and gain strength to face our present crises, do we offer this prayer, Amen

DAY 253

– DAY 254 –

PSALM 27: 8C

O God, we seek Your face because our hearts desire is to know You in a much fuller and more intimate way than we can possibly know You when we only seek You in times of trouble. To seek You only when we are in trouble is to seek You in anxiety but to seek Your face is to seek You with assurance. To seek You only when we are in trouble is to seek You in our asking; to seek Your face is to know You in Your abiding. To seek You only when we are in trouble is to know You as a battler but to seek Your face is to know You as a builder. To seek You only when we are in trouble is to seek You in confusion but to seek Your face is to seek You as companion. To seek You only when we are in trouble is to cling to Your promises but to seek Your facie is to commune with Your presence.

To seek You only when we are in trouble is to seek You in desperation but to seek Your face is to seek You as delight. To seek You only when we are in trouble is to seek You in a fight but to seek Your face is to seek You as friend. To seek You only when we are in trouble is to seek You in the fire but to seek Your face is to seek You in Your fullness. To seek You only when we are in trouble is to seek You in fear but to seek Your face is to know Your faithfulness. To seek You only when we are in trouble is to seek You in grief but to seek Your face is to seek Your glory. To seek You only in trouble is to seek You in gloom but to seek Your face is to know Your gladness. To seek You only when we are in trouble only is to seek You in guilt but to seek Your face is to know Your grace.

To seek You only when we are in trouble is to seek Your help but to seek Your face is to seek Your heart. To seek You only when we are in trouble is to seek You as king but to seek Your face is to know You as kind. To seek You only when we are in trouble is to seek You as lifter but to seek Your face is to know Your laughter. To seek You only when we are in trouble is to seek You in loneliness but to seek Your face is to know Your love. To seek You only when we are in trouble is to seek You as warrior but to seek Your face is to know that You are worthy.

"'Come,' [our hearts say], 'seek [Your] face. Your face Lord, do [we] seek.'" In the name of the Lord Jesus do we pray, Amen.

DAY 254

– DAY 255 –

PSALM 41

O God, You have equated service to our Lord with service to his lambs. So on this day we pray for a heart for the poor, the homeless, the victimized and those in conditions of need, those who are less fortunate than we are. In this age and culture where there are so many homeless persons, it is so easy to develop a callous heart and a cynical spirit. It is so easy to blame the victim and resent those whose very presence reminds us of the social and economic inequities in our world. It is so easy to become self-righteous and judgmental regarding the poor. It is so easy to look past them or through them without seeing or hearing them, their voices or their children. It is so easy to become so engrossed in our pleasure that we do not see the pain of others in our midst — on our jobs, in our communities, in our churches, yes even in our families and among our friends.

O God save us from a faith that is so busy looking up to You that it does not look outward to those in need. Save us from a spirituality that has no social consciousness. Save us from a prosperity gospel that has no pity upon the poor. Save us from joy without a sense of justice. Save us from praise that has no perspective of the political sphere and how the political machinations of people can hold Your children captive. Save us from a testimony that does not touch in very concrete ways those who are troubled by economic hardship. Save us from worship with no work or singing without service.

Help us to know and recover the joy of helping others. O God whose Son was Jesus the great Shepherd of the flock who was always concerned about even the least, the last, the lost and the looked over, we pray that his spirit may possess us. In his name do we pray, Amen.

– DAY 256 –

PSALM 42: 5

O God on this day, we come against depression — that nameless dread and fear that envelopes us from seemingly out of nowhere; that hits us from out of the blue and clings so tenaciously that we can't shake it. Sometimes God in spite of Your goodness and our love and trust in Your word, we sometimes feel so lonely and that we are drifting in the air with nothing under us and that our worlds could come crashing down at any moment without notice. There are other times when we feel that any ground under our feet is shaky at best.

When we think about past mistakes and errors, wasted opportunities and painful things that have happened that we still carry with us, our souls become disquieted. When we think about present circumstances of sin and bondage, of emptiness because of a lack of companionship or because of the companion we love, of our uncertainty and tenuousness of employment that we once felt secure in — our souls become disquieted. When we reflect on the possibilities of decreasing health and the many illnesses that wait to attack us — we become disquieted. When we think about how the Adversary is constantly attempting to undermine us and our own inadequacies to handle all of his tricks and traps — our souls become disquieted. When we consider our children or other members of our families, their wellbeing and futures — our souls become disquieted.

O God in those moments when depression comes, we pray that we might immediately think of You, our Help and our Hope in times of trouble. We pray that we might remember Your word that You will keep those in perfect peace whose minds are stayed on You because they trust in You. We pray that we will remember Your word that You have not given us a spirit of cowardice but of power and love and a sound mind. We pray that we might remember the promise of Jesus that he is with us always, even unto the end of the age.

O God, we rebuke the spirit of depression. It will not be and cannot be part of our lives. In the name of Jesus we have the victory and in his name we cast it out. And if ever it rises again, we pray for remembrance of Psalm 42: 5, "Why are You cast down, O my soul, and why are You disquieted within me? Hope in God; for I shall again praise him, my help and my God." In Jesus name, Amen.

DAY 256

– DAY 257 –

PSALM 43: 3-4

O send out Your light and Your truth; let them lead [us]; let them bring [us] to Your holy hill and to Your dwelling. O God when we are surrounded by enemies and foes send out the light of Your presence and the truth of Your promise that You will neither fail us nor forsake us. When we are overwhelmed by the problems and the pressures of life, send out the light of Your never failing and all sufficient grace and the truth of Your word that You will keep us in six troubles and not forsake us in the seventh. When we are in sick beds send out the light of Your praise and the truth of Your power. When our hearts are weighed down in sorrow because we have lost a loved one, send out the light of Your comfort and the truth of Your peace. When our hearts are broken because of relationships that went sour, send out the light of Your faithfulness and the truth of Your love. When we are bound by weights and sins that so easily beset us, send out the light of Jesus Christ our Lord and Savior and the truth of the Holy Spirit our advocate. When doubts assail and fears abound send out the light of prayer and the truth that You will hear us when we call.

O God let them lead us. Not our own minds but let them lead us. Not the limited perspectives and opinions of others but let them lead us. Not the political climate or the economic conditions but let them lead us. Let Your light which shatters the darkness and Your truth which endures forever, let Your light which is unconquerable and Your truth which is infallible, let Your light which was incarnated at Bethlehem and Your truth which was poured out at Pentecost, let them lead us. Let them bring us to Your holy hill, Your sanctuary, Your church, our private prayer closets, into Your very presence. Let them lead us into worship and praise because You alone are worthy to be praised. Then we will go to the altar of God, to God our exceeding joy; and we will praise You with everything we are and everything we have because we love You and because we desire a closer walk with You and You still inhabit the praises of Your people. O God of grace and glory who has never left us and who never will, please "send out Your light and Your truth; let them lead [us]; let them bring [us] to Your holy hill and to Your dwelling." In Jesus name do we pray, Amen

DAY 257

– DAY 258 –

PSALM 44

O God, we enjoy reading Your word and being inspired by the accounts of the miracles, the deliverance and the might works You performed on behalf of Israel and Your people, the Church of the Lord Jesus Christ. O God we are lifted to new heights of faith and love when we read of how You sustained strengthened and saved our ancestors in days past and gone. We are blessed by the faith tradition that they handed down to us and our hearts are moved by their testimonies of Your mighty, way making and path finding hands in times of trouble. O God be now our God as You were God to and for them. Minister to us and comfort us as You did for them. Walk with us, talk with us, speak to us, reveal Yourself to us as You did for them. Stretch out Your mighty hand of healing, deliverance, provisions and sufficiency for us as You did for them.

We confess O God that sometimes when we are in the thick of battle and the midst of struggle we feel alone and forsaken. When enemies get the upper hand, when we are overwhelmed by what seems impossible tasks with unreasonable deadlines, when all that we can see up ahead are obstacles, roadblocks and challenges without solutions, our faith in Your faithfulness is not what it should be. We confess O God that there are times we panic when we should be in prayer and that we are moving when we should be standing still and seeking direction from You and that we are fighting our own battles when we should be trusting You to fight for us as You have promised. O God give us faith to stand firm upon Your promises when things go against us. Give us hope to hold on until our change comes. Give us the assurance of Your presence when we feel lonely.

O God of our ancestors walk with us even now. O God of the Bible speak a word to us even now. O Christ of God be incarnate in us even now. O Holy Spirit equip us with what You know that we stand in need of, even now. In the name of Jesus we pray, even now, Amen.

DAY 258

– DAY 259 –

PSALM 45

We praise You and thank You O God for the privilege of being royalty. Sons and daughters of salves though we may be, sin scarred sinners though we may be; we praise You for the royal designation that we enjoy as Your sons and daughters. We are grateful for being who we are in You. Through the blood of Your son Jesus Christ we are now a royal priesthood, a holy nation and Your own special unique and peculiar people.

O God we pray that our lives will be devoted to noble purposes and that we will never become so casual in our relationship with You that we take lightly the privilege of coming into the throne room in prayer and worship. We are humbled at Calvary our coronation event and we keep before us the cross which is our scepter. O God we pray that wherever we go we will embody kingdom principles. O God we praise You that we are part of a kingdom that cannot be shaken. We are grateful that no war or political coup can ever take away our standing in the kingdom and the redemption which seals our royalty.

We are grateful for being members of the kind of kingdom that we are. "Your throne, O God endures forever and ever. Your royal scepter is a scepter of equity; You love righteousness and hate wickedness." O God we pray that we will be instruments in helping Your will be done on earth even as it is in heaven. Now God we pray that You will grant us humility in our walk, peace in our spirit, power in our witness, perseverance in our warfare, faithfulness to our calling, joy in our service, inspiration in our presence, discernment, discretion and wisdom in judgment and victory in our temptations and trials. Help us not simply to be royalty of the kingdom in word but also in deed. In Jesus name do we pray, Amen.

DAY 259

– DAY 260 –

PSALM 46: 1-2

O God, we praise You for being our strength, our rock and our strong tower of defense. As we look at our history and past we confess that sometimes we question why some things have happened to us corporately and individually. Why did slavery happen to Africans who were the ancestors of African Americans? Why does slavery still have a lasting impact upon our lives, even after these many years? Why have Africans been colonized and African Americans been domestically colonized? Why do the wicked prosper and why do scoundrels enjoy peace?

Why suffering for so many? Why so much suffering for us individually? Why have we lost loved ones and why has sickness overtaken us? Why have the principalities and powers caused us such distress of soul and spirit? When will You arise O God and scatter Your enemies?

We anticipate understanding some things later on the banks of the land fairer that day when we will dwell forever in Your presence that we don't understand now. However we recognize that even in eternity some things may be beyond our mind to understand some issues may be too deep for us to grasp. Whatever the case, one thing we know and that is we would not have been able to make it without You. You have been and You are still our refuge, our strength, our foundation, our provider, our way maker and our friend. You have helped us bear our burdens in the heat of the day. You have given us a will and the strength to survive when others tried to crush and wipe us from the face of the earth. You have given us such an indelible thirst for You that not even slavery or our burdens can block out our worship of You.

O God no matter what happens in history and in our lives; we praise and honor You for being our refuge and strength, our very present help in trouble. Therefore we will not fear though the earth should change, though mountains shake in the heart of the sea, though its waters roar and foam, though the mountains tremble with tumult. In Jesus name do we pray, Amen.

DAY 260

– DAY 261 –

PSALM 51: 10

O God like Your servant David of old, our prayer is that You would create within us a clean heart and that You would put a new and right spirit in us. We confess that we need more than a patch up job. We need You to do more than straighten out the situation; we need You to straighten us out. Create in us a clean heart, O God. We need You to do more than deliver us from the circumstances; we need You to deliver us. Create in us a clean heart, O God. We need You to do more than rescue us; we need to be redeemed. Create in us a clean heart, O God.

We need a clean heart, one that has been washed in the blood of the Lamb. We need a clean heart whose purity will allow us to see You as our Lord has promised. Our desire is for a clean heart O God that delights itself in You and that thirsts for You like a deer panting for the water of streams. We need a clean heart O God that has been purified by the fires of life and sanctified by Your divine purpose and comes forth like gold. Our desire is for a clean heart O God even as our Lord's was when he prayed for the forgiveness of those who crucified him on the cross.

As You create compassion, commitment and conquering from Calvary and as You create miracles from mess, resurrection from rejection, power from persecution, salvation from slander, deliverance from destruction, create in us a clean heart O God and put a new and right spirit in us.

A right spirit is one that is grounded in Your word. A right spirit is one that is filled with the Holy Spirit. A right spirit is one that is free from or that is overcoming and not simply staying and stewing in anger and vengeance. A right spirit is a growing not a gnawing spirit. A right spirit is a wise spirit. A right spirit is a forgiven as well as a forgiving spirit. A right spirit is a spirit that is at peace because it has made peace with God and has the peace of Christ that passes all understanding.

A right spirit is a spirit that has been bathed in prayer. A right spirit is a spirit that is generous but not foolish. A right spirit is one that is willing to live and let live. A right spirit is one that has been broken to the point that it has reached new breakthroughs. "Create in me a clean heart and put a new and right spirit in [us]." In the name of the Lord Jesus do we offer this prayer, Amen.

– DAY 262 –

PSALM 51: 10

O God like David of old, we too pray for a clean heart and a new and right spirit. No matter how long we have had the heart we have, we believe Gracious God You will answer our prayer for a new heart. No matter how many generations in our families have had the same heart of financial bondage, O God our Father we believe You will answer our prayer for a new heart. No matter how many of our friends around us have chosen to keep the heart that they have, no matter how hurt we may be, O Christ of God we believe You will answer our prayer for a new heart.

No matter how many people tell us that we ought to keep the heart that we have and that we are too old or too far-gone to get a new heart, we believe the Lord Jesus will answer our prayer for a new heart. No matter what the odds are against our getting a new heart, we have to believe Holy Spirit that You will answer our prayer, "Create in me a clean heart, O God, and put a new and right spirit in me."

The Gospel of the Lord Jesus Christ tells us that whoever we are we can have a new heart. Our aching heart can be changed into an able heart. Our angry heart can be changed into an abundant heart. Our anxious heart can be changed into an anointed heart. Our bitter heart can be changed into a beautiful heart. Our broken heart can be changed into a bountiful heart. Our bruised heart can be changed into a believer's heart. Our cynical heart can be changed into a Christ heart. Our damaged heart can be changed into a delivered heart. Our disappointed heart can be changed into a delightful heart.

Our empty heart can be changed into an empowered heart. Our fainting heart can be changed into a fearless heart. Our greedy heart can be changed into a generous heart. Our hurting heart can be changed into a healed heart. Our insecure heart can be changed into an inspired heart. Our jealous heart can be changed into a joyful heart. Our selfish heart can be changed into a sacrificial heart. Our sinful heart can be changed into a saved heart. Our tempestuous heart can be changed into a tender heart. Our worrying heart can be changed into a worshipping heart.

No matter what kind of heart we have our prayer can be answered, "Create in me a clean heart, O God, and put a new and right spirit in me." Thank You O Triune God and in Your name do we offer this prayer, Amen.

DAY 262

– DAY 263 –

PSALM 71: 6

O God giver of life, You who have been our help in times of trouble, our fortress in times of weakness, our way-maker in times of distress, our praise is continually of You. O God our creator, sustainer and redeemer, the answer to our prayers and our guide through our way out of all trouble, our praise is continually of You.

You hear us in all things great and small, in the trivial and in the turbulent, in that which threatens life and that which is merely inconvenient. And when we think about how You bless us even in the small annoyances and requests that we bring to You, our praise is continually of You.

Our sufficiency is from You. You have brought us from the rocking of our cradles. Your own hand has created us, Your own Son has saved us and Your Holy Spirit keeps us. That's why our praise is continually of You. You are not slack concerning Your presence. Great is Your faithfulness, morning by morning new mercies we see. Your patience and Your love are wonderful beyond words and human comprehension. Your power balanced by Your pity, Your majesty balanced by Your mercy allows us to come into Your very throne room and worship and praise You. That's why our praise is continually of You.

We do not glory in ourselves or the works of our hands but to You do we offer continual praise. We do not glory in the power of others or the might of nations but to You do we offer continual praise. For Jesus Christ, for Your Holy Spirit, for the gospel, for the reality of salvation, for second, third and fourth chances, for the church and for Your word—for all of this we offer continual praise.

O God help our praise to be continual. In our frustration as well as our fulfillment, in our sickness as well as in our strength, in times of persecution as well as in times of plenty, in our dungeons as well as in our delights, in our loneliness as well as in our love, in our anxieties as well as in our accomplishments, we pray for a spirit of continual praise. Help us to wage constant war against doubt, depression and self-pity. O God grant us this day and all the days of our lives a spirit, an attitude and a lifestyle of continual praise. This we ask in Jesus name, Amen.

DAY 263

– DAY 264 –

PSALM 72

O God of grace and glory, ruler of the heavens and the earth, You who have set boundaries for mortals and nations, beyond which they cannot pass, we bring before You all that exercise authority and oversight. We bring before You bishops, pastors, prophets, teachers, administrators, counselors, elders, deacons and all others who exercise any kind of leadership or authority in Your church and in Your kingdom. These are they whose decisions and examples, whose words and whose works can impact the very souls and faith of Your people as well as the health of Your church and the wellbeing of Your kingdom. Guide them and keep them we pray. Bless them with wisdom, integrity and honor. We pray that they will always be focused on Your will and on You and that they will always love You for who You are. Give them all pastoral hearts. Keep them when they are tempted to be swayed by pride, ego, vengeance, money and the desires of the flesh. Give them humor and give them humility before the cross.

We lift before You heads of government and those who are involved in matters of state. O God rule in congresses and parliaments, in palaces and private residences of those who are presidents, prime ministers, kings and queens. Save those who rule from selfishness and taking themselves too seriously. Give them caring hearts for those over whom they have rule. May they have vision not only for themselves and their nations but also for all humanity. Most of all may they know You the true and living God, King of Kings, and Lord of Lords. May they seek Your counsel in all that they purpose to do and may they listen and follow when You speak.

Bless those who have authority in industry and in the economic community. May they always remember that a person's life does not consist in the abundance of things they possess. May they always remember that if they seek You first and Your righteousness, that if they keep people as the real bottom line, that You will praise everything else that they seek. Give them a heart for their employees and a love for their work, a passion for quality and a heart that honors You and is humble before You.

We lift before You those who have authority in education. Bless and Keep those who are training the next generation. Keep them focused on the students rather than their career. Give them fulfillment and joy in their work and give them faith compensation for all that they do. Help them to prosper as others in more lucrative professions do. Help them to stay humble before You, the source and fount of all knowledge.

Now God, we bring before You those who exercise authority in families. We bring before You parents, grandparents, foster parents, sisters, brothers, aunts, uncles, guardians and all of those who function as heads of households and heads of families. May they all feel and know the awesome responsibility of shaping lives. Keep families that are under attack. Save families in whose midst the devil has built a stronghold. Change direction in families that have produced mediocrity for generations. Give Your vision of family to those families that don't know it or have lost it. We pray that once again You will become the foundation and center of all family life.

Now God, help us to exercise proper authority over self. Give us discipline over self. Holy Spirit take charge of our thoughts. Christ of God be our elder brother and keeper. Word of God, rule over us. Peace of God, abide in us. Joy of the Lord be our strength. God our creator be forever our protector. We pray that we will always glorify You and please forgive us when we fail to do so and when we fall short of Your glory. This we ask in Jesus name, Amen.

– DAY 265 –

PSALM 73

O God, we are having trouble with bitterness again and even with jealousy. O God we must constantly battle with self-consuming anger toward those who have wronged us and those who are where we want to be and who have some of the things we would like to have. O God help us in our dealings with those whom we don't like. Help us to keep our tongue and tempers in check. Save us from the temptation to speak against them. And Lord help us to rebuke any spirit that wished anyone any misfortune because of what they have done to us or said about us. Save us from being overly sensitive to what they may or may not say or do. Give us a forgiving spirit and a loving heart even towards those that we don't care for. Help us to wish everyone well including those who are out distancing us in terms of career, possessions and money, ministry, notoriety and even personal love and happiness.

O God help us to grow the ministry and the life and the family and the relationships that You have given to us. Help us to always appreciate the blessings You have bestowed upon us — blessings that are still beyond our deserving and even our work. You do bless in abundance. Help us to stay in You, Your word, Your will, Your work and Your worship. When we are close to You we don't have time to dwell on the negative or to nurse or pet our pain. Help us in our down moments to look up to You from whom all blessings flow.

We love You Lord, help us to love Your children. Help us to move beyond our bitterness so that we can receive the bounty of Your presence and Your peace. Forgive our duplicity and our dishonesty, our gamesmanship and our selfishness and self-centeredness. Help us to overcome all of those negative feelings and passions, those resentments and jealousies that prevent us from going to a new place in You. Hear our prayer O Lord when we call to You from the depths of our hearts and grant us victory in the midst of our struggles. And please Lord help us as we struggle even with that which we cannot and dare not express. This we ask in Jesus name, Amen.

DAY 265

– DAY 266 –

PSALM 74

O God like the Psalmist of old, our hearts ache on behalf of those who suffer and who are victims of violence. We plead the cause of those whose lives are trapped in unfeeling and uncaring political and economic systems. We bring the plight of those for whom every day is a battle to just survive. We bring those whose culture and whose society makes violence against them acceptable. We bring women who are victims of violence. We bring women who are victims of domestic violence. We bring refugee women who are victims of political violence. We bring women whose cultures have imposed a ceiling on their aspirations and their being. We bring women who have been denied freedom of choice, freedom over their bodies, freedom over their destinies and freedom from fear. We bring women who are victims of educational violence and who are kept under the veil of ignorance so that generations of violence will continue. We bring women who are victims of social violence and who themselves are blamed for the violence done against them. We bring before You women who are victims of economic violence and who must work twice and three times as hard as men and who are still kept on starvation wages.

We bring before You women who are victims of sexual violence, who have been physically raped and assaulted and whose dignity and sense of self-worth has been devalued and denied. We bring women who are victims of all kinds of criminal violence and whose cries for relief and justice seem to be going nowhere. We bring women whose families and loved ones are victims of violence. See their tears O God. Hear their prayers as they cry out to You O God from pain because of what has happened to sons and daughters, to husbands and lovers, to mothers and fathers. And we bring before You women who are victims of theological violence whose oppression is justified in church, in synagogues and in mosques by a male dominated hermeneutic.

O God, You know how across denominational and faith traditions, women are among Your most loyal and devoted followers. Their faithfulness has kept faith alive in many families and in many 'hard and remote' places on the globe. We praise You for Jesus Christ and his care for and sensitivity to women. From the very beginning of the Christian faith women played a significant part in the life and ministry of Your son Jesus and were formative influences in shaping the life and character of the early church. Now God reward them for their faithfulness. Move on their behalf. Open up places in Your church that still deny them opportunities to use the gifts and to exercise the callings that You have placed as burning coals on the altars of their hearts. Equip Your daughters for the struggles that still lie ahead and bring them to the places that You would have them to be. These and all other blessings we ask in the name of Your Son Jesus who is Lord of all irrespective of gender. We pray this prayer in the name of Jesus the Lord and Savior of Mary Magdalene, the Samaritan woman, the woman with the issue of blood and the widow with two mites, Amen.

– DAY 267 –

PSALM 75

O God, You are the righteous judge of all the earth. According to Your nature and Your promise You will do right by Your children. According to Your nature and promise You will punish the wicked and defeat the devil. According to Your nature and promise You will rescue those who suffer at the hands of the violent and the ungodly. According to Your nature and promise You will establish peace with justice and justice with peace; You will exercise judgment with mercy and mercy with judgment. You will reward the faith of those whose trust in You. According to Your nature and promise Your will shall be done on earth as it is in heaven.

O God, we love You for who You are and we pray for direction until the kingdoms of this world become the kingdoms of our Lord and of his Christ. Give us patience and power as we fight the good fight of faith. Hold us close to You lest we stray. O Holy Spirit help us to pray without ceasing lest we faint in the midst of battle. We pray for faith that always keeps You in focus. Renew us even now. Speak to us afresh. When we are frustrated and overwhelmed, help us to be still so that we may hear You speak so that we may feel Your presence. Forgive us for those sins that come between us. Lead us into new ways of living that will lead to new ways of praying. Help us in the midst of life's ups and downs to remain confident in the integrity of Your word, in the sufficiency of Your power, in the certainty of Your love, in the unchanging character of Your faithfulness and in Your irrevocable commitment to justice. When praying becomes difficult, thoughts slow, words jumble and our petitions confused, again we pray that You would teach us to pray and help us to pray. This we ask in Jesus name, Amen.

DAY 267

– DAY 268 –

PSALM 76:11

O God You are worthy. O God You are awesome. Your power is awesome and so is Your love. Your wrath is awesome and so is Your forgiveness. Your glory is awesome and so is Your grace. Your righteousness is awesome and so is Your redemption. Your works are awesome and so is Your faithfulness. When we think about all that You are and all that You do for us and Your care for us we commit ourselves again to You.

We commit our hearts to love You first and foremost. We commit our souls to desire You first and foremost. We commit our spirits to cleave to You first and foremost. We commit our minds to seek Your will first and foremost. We commit our lives to follow Your word first and foremost. We commit our money to tithes and offerings first and foremost. We commit our worship to glorify You first and foremost. We commit our words to testify of You first and foremost. We commit our wills to You first and foremost. We commit our hands to Your works first and foremost. We commit our feet to walk in Your ways and precepts first and foremost.

When we think about all that You have already done, on this day we commit ourselves again to You. When we think about Your Son, Jesus and how You have acted in him to reconcile us to Yourself and to save us from the hands of the enemy, we commit ourselves to You. When we think about the Holy Spirit, our Advocate and Friend, we commit ourselves to You. When we think about the church, the gospel the promise of our Lord's second coming and the resurrection from the dead, we commit ourselves to You.

And if to the right or the left we stray, O God please forgive us. We truly love You Lord. All that we are and all that we have we give to You, for You alone are worthy. We love You Jesus. We love You Holy Spirit. In Your name O triune God do we pray, Amen.

– DAY 269 –

PSALM 77

O God, we praise You, we love You and we thank You for always being present and available in our lives. Even when we called upon You and felt that You did not hear us, You were still present and available to us. When we felt distant from You, You were still present and available to us. Even in the midnight and early morning hours when we felt lonely, You were still present and available to us. Even when our sins should have driven You away from us, You were still present and available to us. Even when we couldn't pray or didn't pray You were still present and available to us. Even when we became so engrossed or in such a hurry, that we forgot to pray, You were still present and available to us. Even when we prayed with faltering faith, wandering minds, distracted spirits or when we prayed on the run, You were still present and available to us.

When our lives were under attack and we didn't know what to do or where next to turn and what to say, You were present and available to us. When we were on sickbeds and didn't know what our future would be, You were present and available to us. When we were in bondage and so lost that we didn't think that deliverance would ever come or that we would ever find our way out of our mire, You were present and available to us. When we were about to drown in a deluge of bills and financial concerns, You were present and available to us.

Thank You God for being present and available to us. We couldn't have made it if You had not been on our side and at work within our lives giving strength, providing renewal and helping us to run on , fight on, live on, believe, on when logic and our own strength and sometimes the counsel of others said to give up. Great is Your faithfulness. Now God in the mist of this journey may we always remember that You are an ever-present help in times of trouble. And whenever we start feeling overwhelmed and start wondering how we are going to do all that we must, stir within us sacred remembrance of Your divine presence which never leaves or forsakes us. We ask these and all other mercies in the name of Jesus. We love You Lord, Amen.

DAY 269

– DAY 270 –

PSALM 78

O God help us to learn from the errors of the past generations. Help us to learn from their errors of racism. Keep us from anger and bitterness, from stereotyping and prejudice that would cause us to continue to walk in ways of ignorance and division.

Help us to learn from their errors of sexism. Both men and women are created equal in Your image. You make no distinctions in Your word between men and women regarding rights to salvation or innate intelligence. Keep us from biased interpretations of Your word, which favor male domination and chauvinism in the culture as well as in the church.

Help us to learn from their errors of homophobia. While sin is still sin, help us to love the sinner even though we condemn the sin according to our understanding of Your word. Help us never to deny persons civil or basic human rights because we disagree with their sexual preference. Save us from jokes or mockery, which brings injury to any of Your children. May we be helpful to those who are struggling with issues of their sexuality. Help us to model what it means to be both Christian and male or Christian and female.

Help us to learn from their errors of faithlessness or doubt or sin or straying. O God as we prosper may we always be prayerful. As we become more successful may we always be mindful of our souls. Keep us lest we also stray from the places our God where we met Thee. Keep our hearts lest they becoming drunk with the wine of the world we forget Thee. Shadowed beneath Your hands may we forever stand true to You our God.

Help us to learn from their failure to give tithes and offerings as well as first fruits of all that they have, according to Your word. Help us to always remember that You not only have first claim on all that we have but You have total claim on all that we have and all that we are. Help us to truly surrender all to You with a glad, generous, willing and loving spirit.

O God, we praise You for the noble examples of those who walked and lived before us. However, we realize that since they were mortal flesh like us that they erred like us. Help us to learn from the lessons of history and the mistakes of our ancestors so that our lives will be the richer, the fuller and the wiser as they glorify You in new ways. This we ask in Jesus name, Amen.

– DAY 271 –

PSALM 78: 5-8

O God, we praise You for the foundation of faith that has been handed to us by our ancestors. And we praise You for our own experiences with You which confirm and testify to the truths that have been told to us that You are good and that Your steadfast love endures forever. Now God help us to instill in the generations after us knowledge and love for You. Give us the right words and a proper knowledge of scripture. Help us to live before them the kinds of lives and set before them the kind of examples that would inspire them to walk in paths of righteousness. Help us to remember the joys and sorrows, the conflicts and the comforts, the zeal and the anxieties, the naiveté as well as the hopes of Youth. Save us from impatience and overbearing self-righteousness. Give us humility enough to apologize when we are in the wrong and sense enough to know that our Youth can also teach us.

O God, the world in which our young people are growing up in is so different from the world that we knew. Sometimes they are forced to grow up too fast and make decisions that they are not emotionally mature enough to make. Sometimes their bodies mature faster than their minds. Sometimes they are children in grown up bodies. Often they have received so many conflicting and mixed signals from the world around them and the adults who should be giving firm and loving direction to their lives. Our young people function in a fast paced technologically driven culture. Yet for them as for us sin is still sin and temptation is still temptation and while Your word is still true and eternal. Sometimes our young people are faced with issues about which there are no clear biblical mandates. Sincere Bible believing Christians fall on both sides of the moral issues with which our young people must wrestle. What about abortion? What about genetic engineering? What about invintro fertilization? What about the right to die and living wills?

O God help us to direct those young people whose lives are entrusted to our care giving guidance into the right way. We pray that our guidance will always be consistent with Your truth, our teaching will always be consistent with Your word, and our lives will always be in accordance with Your will. This we ask in Jesus name, Amen.

DAY 271

– DAY 272 –

PSALM 79

O God forgive us for our impatience that becomes weary in waiting on Your timetable. O God we know You are Sovereign and You will subdue evil and punish unrighteousness. We know that You will reward the faith of those who have put their trust in You. We know that the wicked will cease from troubling and the weary will be at rest. We know You have already drawn the boundaries of evil and determined the day, place and events which will mark their end.

However, we must confess God that when we are undergoing suffering and strife at the hands of evil people it is hard not to be impatient. When evil seems to be going unchecked it is hard not to question You about Your silence. When our faith grows weary in the struggle it is hard not to ask, "How long?" When the enemy has gotten a temporary victory and it seems as if our faith and our living are in vain, it is hard not to ask "For what?" When we see our loved ones suffer at the hands of evil or when we are in desperate straits and we cry to You for help or a sign and no answer comes it is hard not to ask, "Where are You?" When we read the promises of Your word regarding judgment upon evil and all around us things seem to be going from bad to worse, it is hard not to ask, "When?"

O God of justice whose ways are not like our ways and whose thoughts are higher than ours, we recognize that You still move in mysterious ways Your wonders to perform. Forgive us for our impatience and sometimes our impertinence. Give us strength to fight the fight of faith with confidence and a certitude that passes understanding. Renew us in times of discouragement and in our darkest hours please give us a glint of hope to keep us going. Speak to us down in the deep places of our souls that only You can touch and help us to keep our focus upon You at all times and in all circumstances. Help us never to grow weary in well doing but please give to us the assurance over and over again that we will reap if we faint not. This we ask in Jesus name, Amen.

– DAY 273 –

PSALM 80: 3

Restore us O God according to Your loving-kindness and tender mercies. Restore us O God according to Your steadfast love and omnipotent power. Restore us O God for Your purposes and Your will. Restore us O God by the name of Your Son, Jesus and by the movement of Your Holy Spirit. Restore us O God by Your word and through prayer and meditation. Restore us O God through worship and with the sacraments. Restore us O God with Your love that will not let us go. Restore us O God with sweet remembrance of what You have done in days past and gone and with the promises of what You will do in times yet to come. Restore us O God through the fellowship of the redeemed, even Your church and the blood bought saints with whom we share a common Savior and a common hope. Restore us O God with the gospel, which brings joy to any despairing heart ready to receive it. Restore us O God as You bring fourth spring after winter and daylight after midnight.

Restore us O God as only You can. Our efforts of renewal are only a chasing after the wind. When our minds and spirits are tossed and driven, restore us as only You can. When we have allowed the adversary to get the victory and are feeling disgusted with ourselves, weak and vulnerable restore us as only You can. When we have become discouraged because of the wounds that we have received in Your service, restore us as only You can. When we feel ourselves sinking and desperation and panic have overtaken faith and confidence, restore us as only You can. When the burdens we carry have weighed us down, drained our delight and sapped our strength, restore us O God as only You can. When we have reached that point at which we feel we cannot make one more step, when we are taunt and tight and are about to snap and lose it, restore us O God as only You can. When depression comes, anger builds and the negative is about to take over, when sour moods ruin sunny days and dispositions, restore us O God as only You can.

"Restore us, O God of hosts; let Your face shine, that we may be saved," in Jesus name do we pray, Amen.

DAY 273

– DAY 274 –

PSALM 81: 11-16

O God save us from ourselves. We know You have given us free will and we praise You for the gift of freedom and the responsibility that goes along with it. However, God sometimes our free will becomes the reason for our undoing. We become stubborn and rebellious and determined to do what we want and to get what we want even if what we want leads to the way of destruction. Save us from appetites and desires, from people and temptations, from attractions and flirtations that complicate our lives and cause distance from our relationship with You. Save us from a Russian roulette attitude toward life. Save us from taking foolish risks with our lives, our careers, our hearts as well as the hearts of those who love us and those whom we love. Save us from our determination to do wrong.

Save us when we become blinded by ambition and short sightedness. Save us from failure to think through our decisions and weigh the long-term effects of our actions. Save us when we feel weak and vulnerable. Save us when we want quick relief that does not satisfy in the long run. Save us when we listen more closely to the adversary and the enemy than we should. Save us from the seductive allure of whatever is the Achilles heel of our faith journey and spirituality. Save us from that which grieves Your heart and causes You pain. O God save us from flesh and fantasy. O God save us from destructive habits and from defensive haughtiness. O God save us from stubbornness and selfishness. O God save us from tantalizing temptations that lead to trouble and turmoil. O God save us from foolish thinking that tries to persuade us that we are exceptions to the rule and to Your word and that the downfalls that have happened to others who have sinned will not happen to us.

O gracious hand of God, hold us. O Jesus Christ our elder brother and Lord, walk with us. O Holy Spirit speak to us. O word of God guide us. O God our Father, gently prod us and then intervene when we don't get the message or when we refuse to hear. O Jesus Christ our elder brother, strengthen us and help us to fight against our weaknesses in Your name which gives us the victory. O Holy Spirit flow through us and lift our minds above the moment. O word of God stir within our minds Your precepts, promises and ordinances. We love You God more than life itself. Help us to walk and live in ways that reflect our love for You. In Jesus name do we pray, Amen.

– DAY 275 –

PSALM 82

O God protector of the innocent, advocate of the downtrodden, defender of all of those who turn to You, we praise You that You are still on the throne. Because You reign we know that justice will one day be done for those who are presently denied it. Because You reign we know the days of evil are numbered. Because You reign we know salvation is available for those who are in all kinds of bondage. Because You reign light is available for those who are groping in darkness. Because You reign help is available for all that are politically oppressed and economically exploited. Because You reign, truth is available for all who are victims of propaganda, lies and gossip.

Because You reign we have hope even in this present life. We praise You for hope that keeps us going when logic tells us that we have nothing to go on for. Because You reign, the nations of this world do not control the destiny of humankind. O God we pray that You will intercede even now in the political madness of these times. We pray that wars will cease, violence will be quelled, and terrorism will be no more and corrupt politics and politicians who are more concerned about self than service will be unseated.

O God Your innocent children who are victims of war need Your protection. O God vulnerable women who make up so much of the refugee population need Your protection. O God immature young men on battlefields with guns need Your protection. O God masses of people who are victims of bombings need Your protection. O God of the heavens and the earth we pray that even now that Your will, will be done on earth as it is in heaven and that the shedding of so much innocent blood will cease. We place our lives and our destinies in Your hand O God of power and compassion, and we pray that You will do right by those whose trust and whose hope is in You. This we ask in Jesus name, Amen.

DAY 275

– DAY 276 –

PSALM 83: 1

O God give us faith to handle Your silences. When we desperately need a visible sign of Your presence and affirmation and none comes, we pray for faith to handle Your silences. When our adversaries and foes are allowed to have a temporary victory over us and we reach out to You and ask why and You do not answer, give us faith to handle Your silences. When we have not been as strong as we should and the adversary has gotten the upper hand on us and we are not feeling very good about ourselves and we cry out to You for comfort and none comes, give us faith to handle Your silences. When trouble arises on every hand and we turn to You and seek answers that come naturally from the logical mind, the very kind of mind that You have given to us, and You do not answer, give us faith to handle Your silences. When Your faithful reach out for rescue and the sick reach out for healing and nothing comes give us faith to handle Your silences. When we try to pray and cannot and You know about our efforts to reach You; and all that wars against us even as we pray and we are not able to connect, give us faith to handle the silences. When the oppressed cry out for liberation and the faithful cry out for justice, give us faith to handle Your silences. When young children call to You from the depths of their being and their prayers seem to be going nowhere, O God we intercede on behalf of the immature in faith and in understanding, give us faith to handle Your silences. When tears flow and sleep flees and we seek for peace of mind and spirit and they allude us and we cannot feel Your presence, give us the faith to handle Your silences.

O God, we do not know or understand why You are silent and why it takes so long for You to move but we know You. We know that You are not slack concerning Your promises. We know that You love and care for us in ways that we cannot even begin to fathom. We know that You hear and answer prayer. We know that You are faithful to Your children. O God we pray that what we know about You will empower and enable us to stand firm when You are silent in the face of life's glaring contradictions and cruelties. Help us to be faithful Lord when the adversary attacks our thoughts and tries to get us to doubt Your existence and question Your integrity. Help us to be faithful until You move with justice and mercy and with power and perception. O God You who did not answer when even Your Son questioned You from the cross, raise us up from our Calvary moments with new power, new direction and new vision. This we ask in Jesus name, Amen

DAY 276

– DAY 277 –

PSALM 84: 1-2

O God we praise You for Your temple, Your sanctuary, Your house of worship, Your church buildings, synagogues, mosques and other worship centers. In the midst of a life full of stress and tension, we praise You for places of refreshment and renewal, inspiration and instruction, where we get a new glimpse of Your glory and Your will for our lives. We are grateful for sacred buildings in our midst that are constant reminders of another reality that reigns over us and that lives within us and among us to empower us. We pray that we will not take them for granted. Help us to have a prosper sense of stewardship and perspective in terms of the care, maintenance, construction and renovation of Your house. Help us to remember that the place where Your name rests ought to be the best, look the best and have the best. They ought to be places that are identified by a special spirit and aura present in their very stones and structure because Your Holy Spirit is present in them, around them and upon them. The place where You are worshipped ought to also be a place of outreach and service to our hurting people with their various spiritual, social, economic and educational needs. O God we pray that Your children will be blessed in many ways when they come into Your sanctuary however defined where You are worshipped and adored.

Holy Spirit flow richly and fully, be present in Your full glory in every building and place that seeks to honor our God.

We love thy church O God, Her wall before thee stand, Dear as the apple of thine eye, And grave upon they hand.

We were glad when they said unto us let us go into the house of the Lord. Our feet are standing upon holy ground and we bask in Your presence. A day in Your courts is better than a thousand. We would rather be doorkeepers in the house of our God than to dwell in the tents of the wicked. O God bless Your churches, everywhere wherever Your people assemble. Bless sacred zones and meeting places everywhere Your saints assemble to lift up hands in praise and prayer, in adoration and worship with thanksgiving. Visit us often wherever we gather that we might be instructed and guided in our living and in our works and in our witnessing for You.

Then God give us vision to look beyond where we may be worshipping so that we will always be keeping You in view. Help us never to be so caught up in the places where we worship that we lose signt of You the only true and living God of love and power and majesty who alone is deserving of all worship and devotion. We love You first and foremost O God of grace and glory. We love You first and foremost O God for who You are. Now sanctify the places wherein we seek to worship You that they may be fit fields, buildings, apartments and houses to receive the outpouring of Your Holy Spirit. This we ask in Jesus name, Amen.

– DAY 278 –

PSALM 85: 6-7

O God will You please revive us again. Sometimes God we get so caught up with church business that we lose sight of the business of the church — the business of salvation, deliverance, service and hope.

God will You please revive us again when we become cynical, self-centered in our viewpoints and self-absorbed in our own personal agendas. When we are pursuing political turf guarding aims and are involved in self-defeating, belittling personality conflicts and squabbles, will You please revive us again?

When we become weary in well doing will You please God revive us again. When our traditions become stifling and what should give us joy becomes drudgery will You please Lord revive us again? When the enemy has drained us will You please revive us again so that we may rejoice in You. Not our traditions but in You; not our accomplishments but in You; not in other people but in You.

O God when You revive us we can love those who are difficult to love. When You revive us we can see Your work where others see nothing or feel Your presence when others feel nothing. When You revive us we can work with a positive spirit, worship with a positive attitude and see the positive potential in others.

Revive us O God with a spirit of gratitude. Revive us O God with Your word. Revive us O God with Your Holy Spirit. Create within us a clean heart and renew a right spirit within us. Revive us O God through prayer and meditation. Revive us O God with the good news of salvation.

Thank You God for saving us! Thank You O God for Jesus. When we remember Your faithfulness and reflect upon our salvation we are revived. When we think that You so loved us that You gave Your only begotten Son so that whoever believes in Him would not perish but have eternal life, we are revived. When we remember that we are called to be saints and have received the adoption of redeemed children, we are revived. When we remember that Satan is defeated and in the name of Jesus we have the victory, we are revived. Help us to always think of Your goodness instead of the unkindness done by others.

DAY 278

– DAY 279 –

PSALM 86: 11-12

O God on this day, we pray for an undivided heart. We must confess that there are times when our heart is divided between our will and Your will, our flesh and faithfulness to Your commandments, our immediate desires and Your long-term goals for us. Sometimes our heart is dived among competing affections, between a higher and more resolute road and a quick fix solution for pressure and stress, between vows and commitments and between momentary pleasures. We must confess that there are times when we feel almost torn into two because of the internal war that we fight because of our divided heart. We must confess O God that at times fear takes over because of our divided heart. There are times when we feel on the verge of a mental or emotional breakdown because we feel so torn and divided in terms of loyalties, loves, commitments and desires.

O God, we desire wholeness and we desire focus. We pray for a heart that is totally devoted to You for when You are our heart's desire You arrange in proper sequence and place our other priorities. When our heart is completely given to You we can more easily rest upon Your promises and relax in Your world no matter what problems or challenges arise. When our heart is totally focused upon You, we can walk in boldness and in the full power of the anointing. When our heart is totally given to You we can more easily resist the temptations of the devil. When our heart is totally focused upon You we can have peace that flows like a river, joy that is full of glory and power to match our mountains.

O God, we pray for a heart that is undivided. For a heart that is divided against itself cannot stand. We pray for a heart that is undivided because You deserve O God an undivided heart. Your faithfulness, Your holiness and righteousness, the majesty and greatness of who You are all deserve an undivided heart. When we think of Your goodness and all that You have done for us, such love and devotion, such grace and caring, such faithfulness and love, deserve an undivided heart in worship, prayer, service, living and giving. O God even as You and Christ Jesus were one, we pray this day for an undivided heart — a heart that cleaves to You in love and faithfulness, that desires Your will first and foremost and that makes You the first object of its affection. This we ask in Jesus name, Amen.

– DAY 280 –

PSALM 87: 3

O God, we pray for Your church, Your city set upon the hill to give shelter, comfort, help and hope for a wayward and despairing humanity. God Your church and those of us who are members of it have such an awesome responsibility to point our fellow humanity to You. We pray that we will always live in such a way that it can be said of us, "Glorious things are spoken of [us]." O God we pray we will live in such a way that men and women will see our good works and give glory to You. We pray that no words that come from our mouths and no action that proceeds from our lives will bring dishonor to You or Christ who is our head. We pray that when we witness with either word or in service to those who do not know You that we will have patience and sensitivity that Your children will believe in You because of the different character of caring and living that they see in us.

Glorious is Your name O God that is above every other name. Glorious is the blood of Jesus that makes the foulest clean. Glorious is Your joy O God that is independent of the outward circumstances in which we find ourselves. Glorious is Your worship O God that lifts us beyond the cares of this present world. Glorious is Your peace O God that holds us steady in the midst of life's fluctuating circumstances. Glorious is Your grace O God that is sufficient for all of our needs. Glorious is Your Spirit O God that empowers, leads and teaches us and is Your gift to us.

O God help us to reflect Your glory so that glorious things will always be spoken of You. This we ask in Jesus' name, Amen.

DAY 280

– DAY 281 –

PSALM 88

O God, we pray for a faith that is determined to praise You even when we have questions. We recognize that it is difficult to give praise when we are assaulted by questions about the things that happen to us. However, faith means believing even when we don't understand. Faith means having assurance even when reality contradicts and denies everything that we believe in. Faith means having certitude when there is no logical reason for certitude. Faith means knowing in whom we have believed even when we don't understand for what or why or how or when. So our prayer is for faith that understands and lives out the meaning of true faith.

When we feel desolate and forsaken we pray for the uplifted look of faith. When our enemies seem to have the upper hand we pray for the uplifted look of faith. When we are confronted by challenging mountains and insurmountable odds, we pray for the uplifted look of faith. When monetary obligations go far beyond monetary resources, we pray for the uplifted look of faith. When we feel hemmed in and harried, we pray for the uplifted look of faith. When we feel as if we want to run away and hide, we pray for the uplifted look of faith. When we are tempted to lose ourselves in self-destructive and sinful forms of distractions and relief, we pray for the uplifted look of faith. When prayers are long in being answered, we pray for the uplifted look of faith. When our loved ones are under attack and in bondage and we are worried about them, when we can't communicate with them, we pray for the uplifted look of faith. When sickness comes and healing doesn't, we pray for the uplifted look of faith.

Even when death comes close, we pray for the uplifted look of faith. Wherever we are and in whatever situation we find ourselves, we pray for the uplifted look of faith that enables us to pray through even as did Jesus our Savior in Gethsemane. In his name do we pray, Amen.

– DAY 282 –

PSALM 89: 52

Blessed be Your name O God forever and ever. No matter what the devil does to disrupt our lives and cause us to question what we believe, we recognized that You are still good all the time — blessed be Your grace forever and ever. No matter how much the heathen rages and men like little boys playing with toys try to manage and manipulate our lives, we know that You hold us in the hollow of Your hand — blessed be Your personal care of us forever and ever. Even when nations act as if they are accountable to only themselves and that their survival and well-being is dependent upon their so called power politics, we know that You have set the boundaries beyond which the nations cannot pass — blessed be Your providence forever and ever.

When we would become arrogant with our technology and what we are able to accomplish, we know that You are still the divine and awesome creator—blessed be Your power forever and ever. When we sin and fall short of Your glory and are feeling disgusted with ourselves we praise You for the knowledge of Your salvation and forgiveness—blessed be Your tender mercies forever. When we would panic because of the greatness of need and the paucity of resources, You have always supplied our every need according to Your riches in glory — blessed be Your sufficient grace forever and ever. Even when we forsake our commitments and forget our vows, You are not slack concerning Your promises — blessed be Your word and eternal truths forever and ever. No matter what we do You continue to love us, even when that love must be tough — blessed be Your faithfulness forever and ever. When we can't call out to anyone else we can call upon You — blessed be the privilege of prayer forever and ever. No matter what afflicts us we are grateful for the name of Jesus that saves and delivers to the utmost — blessed be the name of Jesus forever and ever.

On this day O God, we bless Your name. We glorify, honor and praise You for who You are and what You are. We bless You not only today and tomorrow and the day after that but when travelling days are done and the curtains of death are drawn on this mortal existence then in a nobler unending day, we will bless Your name and praise You forever. In the matchless name of Jesus do we pray, Amen.

– DAY 283 –

PSALM 90: 12

O God, we praise You for life and a reasonable portion of health and strength. We praise You for a sound mind and a heart with the capacity to love. We praise You for each new day and the new opportunities for growth that each new day brings. Now O God we pray that we would be saved from arrogance and smugness that takes our life, our health, our mind and love for granted. Stir within us the urgency and desire to live every day to the fullest. Save us from the demons of procrastination when we are tempted to put off until tomorrow what can easily be done on today. Help us to be mindful that tomorrows are never promised to us and the only time we have to love, praise and serve You, the only time we have to be kind to others, the only time we have to make amends and seek forgiveness, the only time we have to do good is today. While having a consciousness of the limits of time, save us from paranoia and the tendency to be prophets of gloom. Teach us to number our days so that we may gain a wise heart.

We pray not only for a loving heart but a discerning heart. We pray not only for a generous heart but a judicious heart. We pray not only for a tender heart but a strong heart. We pray not only for a strong heart but also for a tender heart. We pray not only for an open heart but a perceptive heart. We pray not only for a just heart but also for a merciful heart. We pray not only for a sanctified heart but also for an empathetic heart. We pray not only for a holy heart but also for a sensitive heart. O God, create within us a clean heart and a renewed and right spirit within us. Help us to be sensitive to the limits as well as the broadness of life so that our hearts can be ordered to live and love to the fullest. This we ask in Jesus name, Amen.

– DAY 284 –

PSALM 91: 1

O God we praise You and thank You for being our shelter and our shadow. Shelters are often stationary to which we run. Shadows we carry with us. Our shelter and shadow, Your presence never leaves us. That's how we have made it thus. Your presence never leaves us. Whether we are stationary or mobile, whether we are fixed or moving, Your presence never leaves us. In all of our ups and downs, our foolishness and rebellion, our sinning and straying, Your presence never leaves us. We've been in enough messes and taken enough chances to have been finished, history, dead, destroyed, ruined , scandalized but Your presence has never left us.

When we needed someone to run to and somewhere to hide for renewal and rest — You were there as shelter. When the storms of life raged against us and the winds of adversity were beating upon us and we needed a fixed point of reference to hold on to lest we be blown away — You were there. In the secret places of our heart, soul, mind and spirit You ministered to us . You sheltered us when the adversary was preparing to assault us with that which we were unable to withstand in and of ourselves. We praise Your holy name.

Then when we marched forth by faith You were our ever present shadow. You went before us when we needed direction. You were beside us when we needed companionship. You were behind us when we needed to be pushed. When trouble's nighttime and problems blocked our view of You, Your blessing us in the midst of our burdens and seasons of trial, assured us that You were still there and that we were being kept by power divine.

O God we thank You for being our shelter and shadow. We pray for firmness of faith that we will live in You that when this life is over, we will abide in You and rest with You forever. In Jesus name, Amen

DAY 284

– DAY 285 –

PSALM 91: 11

Seraphim sing a new song of praise. Cherubim wing Your way throughout heaven. Archangels fight our battles. Angles do You have a fresh word from the throne of God?

O God we praise You for the heavenly host that is too awesome for us to comprehend. We praise You that we are surrounded by good spirits, helpful spirits and ministering spirits. We are grateful most of all that we have direct access to You through the blood of Jesus and the sighs and groans of the Holy Spirit. We marvel that when we needed a Savior You came Yourself in Jesus Christ, the incarnate word.

Teach us how to use all of the resources that You have placed at our disposal for victory. And God in times of discouragement would You be so kind as to pull back the curtain of heaven so we might get just a glimpse of Your glory? Thank You for Your promises to help us to look up. Thank You for Jesus who will take us up. Thank You for the Holy Spirit who keeps us up. In Jesus' name, Amen.

DAY 285

– DAY 286 –

PSALM 92: 14

Thank You God that we can always produce fruit. No matter what our age or stage, no matter how others perceive us, no matter what society says about our usefulness, no matter what the institutions we work for, make sacrifices for and give our lives to that we will always bear fruit say about our capabilities and competence — we praise You that in You and through You, we can always produce fruit.

O God help us to live day by day that we will always be able to be productive and useful. O God we pray for wisdom and sense in taking care of our bodies so that these temples will be strong and fruitful as long as life lasts. Give us discipline to exercise properly so that the tree will grow straight and strong through the years.

O God, we pray for wisdom and strength to eat and drink properly so that our bodies will be well nourished for the productivity that comes from within.

O God, we pray that You will keep our minds strong and sane. Help us not to be conformed to this world but to be transformed by the renewing of our minds so that we can live out the good, acceptable and perfect will of God. Whatever is true, whatever is honorable, whatever is just, whatever is pure, whatever is pleasing, whatever is commendable, if there is any excellence and if there is anything worthy of praise, help us to think on these things — so that we will always bear fruit.

O God keep our spirits and our souls right with You, desirous of You, abounding in You, growing in You. For we realize that a person has profited nothing if they should gain the whole world and lose their own soul. O God we pray that You would keep our souls free from bitterness, pettiness, envy, greed and an inordinate desire for the things of this world.

O God, we praise You that we have the potential of always being productive, fruit bearing and useful. Help us so to live that we will in fact and indeed always be productive, fruit bearing and useful. In Jesus' name, Amen.

DAY 286

– DAY 287 –

PSALM 93

O God, how awesome and glorious You are. When we observe the heavens, the moon and the stars that Your hands have made, we are reminded again of how awesome and glorious You are. When we observe mighty Redwoods and the tenacity of a small flower to sprout through a crack in the cement, we are reminded again of how awesome and glorious You are. When we sit quietly in fear and trembling as You move in earthquake, storm, wind and flood, we are reminded again of how awesome and glorious You are. When we observe the beauty of the rainbow after the storms which come forth in quite beauty and strength, we are reminded again of how awesome and glorious You are. When we observe the variety of birds, fish, reptiles and mammals that inhabit the earth, we are reminded again of how awesome and glorious You are. When we observe the flash of the lightning and the roar of the thunder, we are reminded again of how awesome and glorious You are. When we observed the ocean churning in its depths and moving upon its waves, we are reminded again of how awesome and glorious You are. When we observe the baptism of the sunrise with light and the glow of a sunset, we are reminded again of how awesome and glorious You are.

When we see a newborn babe that is born as a result of the bodily fluids we are reminded again of how awesome and glorious You are. When we think about how fearfully and wonderfully our human bodies are made, we are reminded again of how awesome and glorious You are. When we observe the great works that human hands can do and the great things that the human mind can conceive when they are guided by Your will and purpose, we are reminded again of how awesome and glorious You are. When we think about the greatness of Your love as manifested in Jesus Christ, the gift of Your Holy Spirit and the sufficiency of Your grace, we are reminded again of how awesome and glorious You are. When we reflect upon Your faithfulness and how morning by morning new mercies we see, in spite of ourselves, we are reminded again of how awesome and glorious You are. O God not only are Your works and not only are Your attributes and character awesome and glorious but Your very presence is more glorious and awesome than we could ever imagine. Your Holy Shekinah is more glorious and awesome that we could ever imagine. Yet You have promised that those who are pure in hearty, those You have been redeemed by the blood of Jesus, those who love your Son as they love life itself, shall see You face to face. What an awesome and blessed privilege — with mortal eyes and feeble understanding, we shall behold Your glory face to face. O God how awesome and glorious and marvelous You are to us. We praise You in the name of Jesus, Amen.

– DAY 288 –

PSALM 95: 7

O God give us ears to hear what You are saying to our lives today. We confess that sometimes our own hardness of heart and our reticence to give up what we should, our love of ourselves more than our love of You, the pull of our flesh, and our feelings towards others, prevent us from hearing Your word when You speak. We recognize that there have been times when we have prayed and You have given an answer but because Your answer is not the one that we desire to hear, we keep praying the same prayers over and over again that You have already answered. Please forgive us for being so adamant about our own way. Forgive us when our will and desires block out what Your word says and what the Spirit confirms in us over and over again. Forgive us when we allow the weights and sin that so easily beset to have their way rather than following Your word.

O God, we confess that sometimes we are so confused that we don't even know how to pray. The internal warfare is about to tear us asunder. We are torn between old loyalties and new attractions. We are torn between the voice of conscience and the voice of convenience. We are torn between the voice of salvation and the voice of sin. We are torn between the voice of fear and the voice of faith. We are torn between the voice of righteousness and the voice of relief. We are torn between the voice of commitment and the voice of curiosity. We are torn between the voice of love and the voice of lust. We are torn between the voice of excellence and the voice of the easiest. Sometimes we are so confused that we don't' even know the difference between the voice of Satan and the voice of the Spirit, the voice of the Deceiver and the voice of the Deliverer.

O God will You be so kind as to speak clearly this day and no matter how difficult the message is, help us not only to hear it and receive it but to follow it. Speak above the noise around us. Speak through the noise and confusion within us. Speak beyond the doubts and fears before us. Speak clearly Lord. Speak patiently Lord. Speak in love O Lord. Shout if You have to but speak Lord. Confound our plans if You have to but speak Lord. Help Your servants to be still long enough and to be quiet long enough so that we can hear You speak. Speak Lord Your servant is listening. This we ask in Jesus name, Amen.

– DAY 289 –

PSALM 96: 1-3

O God, we pray for a new word of witness and testimony this day. We pray for a new song of worship and adoration this day. We pray that our lives will glorify You with new commitments and new determination this day.

O God, You have been so good in the past and Your faithfulness abides in the present. You have done so much and brought us so far that we could go on and on praising You for what You have already done. There is comfort, security and joy in recounting Your great deeds, powerful acts, mighty miracles and many examples of loving kindness and tender mercies. But we pray for faith that is imaginative, insightful, creative, caring, perceptive and prayerful enough to construct a new song or word of praise for what You continue to do in our lives.

O God, we pray that we will sing to You a new song of praise this day. We are blessed with a new day, one that we have never seen before and one that we will never see again, we pray that we will have some new victories this day, receive new revelations this day and have new experiences of Your goodness this day. We pray that lessons thoroughly learned from the past will produce new fruit in our lives and that old works of our hands will be blessed in new ways.

Give us boldness with our new song. Not intrusiveness or arrogance or insensitivity or rudeness but boldness so that we will sing our new song and give a new testimony to the nations, our neighborhoods, among our family and friends and in our churches. To the end that somebody's life will be touched and transformed because we gave a new word of witness and a new song of praise to You this day. O God open our lips and life, our hearts and hands, our souls and spirit, so that our mouths will bring a new message of praise this day. In Jesus name, Amen

– DAY 290 –

PSALM 97: 11

O God let Your light of direction dawn for Your children who stumble in darkness. O God let Your light of salvation dawn for Your children who are lost in sin. O God let the light of Your promises dawn for Your children who are depressed and are about to give up hope. O God let Your light dawn for Your children who love You and who are seeking to serve You. O God let the light of Your peace dawn for Your children who feel lonely and afraid. O God let Your light of healing dawn for Your children who are afflicted both in body and in spirit. O God let Your light of grace dawn for Your children who are experiencing persecution and are wondering where You are and why You won't help and deliver even now. O God let the light of Your church dawn for Your children who need somebody to care. O God let the light of Your gospel dawn for Your children who are feeling useless, defeated and unloved. O God let the light of Your truth dawn for Your children who are misguided and confused. O God let the light of Your power dawn for Your children who feel victimized and dependent upon those who abuse, oppress and exploit them. O God let the light of Your joy dawn for Your children who have lost those things and persons in their lives who have given them joy in days past and gone.

O God of light and glory shine upon us in new and unmistakable ways this day. O Jesus Christ the light of the world shine for us in this life when so many conflicting voices call to us for allegiance. O Holy Spirit shine through us with new power and fresh anointing. O word of God shine around us for You are a lamp unto our feet and a light unto our path. And as You shine O God in Your infinitely wonderful and empowering ways, we pray for the courage and the commitment, the wisdom and the desire to walk in Your light. We pray that we might live as children of the light and that we will have the courage to leave dark thoughts, dark ways, dark attitudes and dark desires behind. We pray that not only this day but also every day of our lives that we will:

Walk in the light, beautiful light, Come where the dew drops of mercy shine bright.

Shine all around us by day and by night, Jesus the light of the world.

(Jesus, the Light of the World, J.V. Coombs)

This we ask in Jesus name, Amen.

– DAY 291 –

PSALM 98: 1

O God, You have done marvelous things. The works of Your hands are marvelous. The sun, the moon and the stars are marvelous. The balancing act that the earth does on its axis is marvelous. The high mountains that touch the sky high above the earth and the deep blue majesty of the ocean water which goes far below the surface of the earth are marvelous. The precision of the geysers and the uncertainty of the volcano are all marvelous. The variety of life that swims the sea, flies through the skies and walks upon the earth are all marvelous. The symmetry of the human body is all-marvelous.

O God, You have done marvelous things. You have done marvelous in and with our lives. You have redeemed us from sin and made us more than conquerors in circumstances and situations, which were supposed to be our undoing. You have answered prayer and made ways out of no ways. You have brought us from a mighty long ways and kept our feet from stumbling. And when we have stumbled and fallen, You have loved us with a perfect love and picked us up and given us chance after chance. You have not withheld Your tender mercies in spite of our broken promises and failed intentions. You have been better to us than we have been to ourselves. O God You have done marvelous things with and in our lives.

O God, You have done marvelous things. You have done marvelous things in the realm of salvation. You have given Jesus Christ as the author and perfecter of our faith. You have given Jesus Christ as not only the Lamb of God who takes away the sin of the world but as our personal Savior who redeems our life from the pit. You have given us an eternal word of truth that guides us in the way of salvation. You have given us the gospel, good news for the lost and despairing. You have given good news for not only the improvement but also for the transformation of all who would receive it and for the perfection of the saints. You have given us the Holy Spirit as paraclete and comforter, as guide and teacher, as power and revealer of Your will and of our gifts. You have given us the church; the fellowship of the redeemed in the midst of our battles against the principalities and powers. O God You have done marvelous things.

You have done marvelous things in creation. You have done marvelous things in and with our lives. You have done marvelous things in the realm of salvation. Therefore in this new day, one that we have never seen before and one that we will never see again, we pray that we will be able to give You a new song of praise. For You alone are worthy. In Jesus name do we pray, Amen.

– DAY 292 –

PSALM 99: 9

Holy, holy, holy! Lord God Almighty
Early in the morning our song shall rise to Thee;
Holy, holy, holy! Merciful and mighty;
God in three persons blessed Trinity!

Holy, holy, holy! All the saints adore Thee,
Casting down their golden crowns around the glassy sea;
Cherubim and seraphim falling down before Thee,
Which wert, and art, and evermore shall be.

Holy, holy, holy! Lord God Almighty!
All Thy works shall praise Thy name in earth and sky and sea;
Holy, holy, holy! Merciful and mighty;
God in three persons blessed Trinity!
(Holy, Holy, Holy! Lord God Almighty, Reginald Heber)

O Holy God, we are grateful again for the privilege of coming into Your presence. Forgive us O God when we forget what a blessed privilege and opportunity we have to come before You most Holy, most Righteous, most Majestic God and the Creator of the ends of the universe. Now God we pray that our lives would be holy, that they would be set apart for divine service. O God we pray that our speech would be holy. Take away words from our lips that are unbecoming. Take away swear and curse words. Take away gossip or other kinds of speech that is damaging to others. We pray that praise and God glorifying and edifying speech will be on our lips this day.

O God, we pray for holy service. Whatever we do help us to do it to Your glory. Whether we are feeding the hungry or caring for the sick or guiding young people or looking after the aged or taking care of our regular business, we pray that we will do it in a manner and a spirit that reflects You. We pray that our lights will so shine this day that men and women will see our good works and glorify You O God who is holy.

Now fill us with power that we might walk in ways of holiness this day and all the days of our lives. In Jesus name do we pray, Amen.

DAY 292

– DAY 293 –

PSALM 100: 3B

O God, we are Your people. You have created us and stamped us with the irreversible imprint of Your own image — we are Your people. You have loved us with an eternal love and have sent Your Son Jesus to give his life as a ransom for many — we are Your people. We have an identity beyond ethnicity, gender or national citizenship — we are Your people. Our destiny is not in the hands of other human beings because we are Your people. The devil will not get the final victory over us because we are Your people. Though our sins are as scarlet they can be as clean as snow and though they are red as crimson they can be as wool, because we are Your people.

As Your people You lead us into green pastures of provision. You protect us from dangers seen and unseen. Your all seeing eye knows plans of wolves and lions who would destroy us and You intercede on our behalf so many times and in so many ways even without our knowing it. We parse You O God and Shepherd. We pray that we will worship You, as Your people should, with praise that is biblical and unashamed. We pray that we might live as Your people and that we would let our light so shine that men and women would see our good works and give glory to You. We pray that we might give as Your people should — not only with tithes and offerings but that we would hold nothing back. We pray that we would pray, as Your people should, with boldness and persevering faith until breakthroughs come. We pray that we would pray as Your people should without ceasing. We pray that we would love as Your people should unconditionally and without limits. We pray that we would forgive as Your people should as those who have been recipients of divine forgiveness. We pray that we would work as Your people should until You call us from labor to reward. We pray that we would serve as Your people should joyfully, humbly and thankfully. We pray that we would die as Your people should with the assurance of the resurrection and eternal life with You.

O God, we are Your people and the sheep of Your pasture. That is way we enter Your courts with thanksgiving and into Your gates with praise. That is why we bless Your name. You are truly good O Lord, Your faithfulness endures forever and Your truth endures to all generations. We praise You in the name of Jesus Christ, the great Shepherd of the sheep, Amen.

– DAY 294 –

PSALM 101: 3

O God, we praise You again for the privilege of coming into Your presence and seeking from You the desires of our hearts. Today we come seeking sanctified vision. There is so much to focus on that is negative, base, offensive, vile and unholy. There is so much of Your goodness that is to be admired that the Adversary uses to tempt. There is so much that is unlike You in this life and in this world.

That's why we pray that the love of Christ will so abide in us that we will choose to see what is good in bad situations and what is best in the midst of our disappointments. We pray that Your Holy Spirit will so abide in us that we will have a discerning and wise minds and perceptive and insightful hearts that cling to that which is high and holy. We pray that Your graciousness, God our Father, will so abide in us that we will set our sights and fix our focus on whatever is true, honorable, just, pure, pleasing, commendable, as well as that which is excellent and worthy of praise.

O God, we pray not for naiveté but for a positive and helpful spirit so that we will be lifted by sanctified sight and guided by noble insight and kept by holy vision. If the eyes are windows of the soul, we pray that our windows will be clean. If the eyes are windows reflecting the soul, we pray for a pure heart and a right spirit so that what is focused on will be ordered by Your will and Your words. O God on this day sanctify our vision and order our steps so that every breath we take, every step we make every word we speak and yes every thought we think will glorify You. In Jesus name, Amen.

– DAY 295 –

PSALM 102: 27

O God, we cry out to You in the midnight hours of distress. Like the Psalmist, our days are filled with taunts from our enemies and our nights are filled with tossing and turning. Our days are filled with fighting and our nights are filled with fears. Our days are filled with problems and our nights are filled with panic. Our days are filled with burdens and our nights are filled with battles worry an anxiety. Our days wear us down and our nights do not revive. O God when sleep will not come we cry out to You. When our mind gives way to panic we cry out to You. When prayer is difficult we cry out to You. When we don't know what to pray for and what to say, we cry out to You. When we are afraid of what Your answer may be we cry out to You. When we are fearful that we might be losing our minds we cry out to You. When we feel as if we are about to crack under the pressure, we cry out to You.

Have mercy upon us O Lord even as You were merciful to Your servant David, for You are the same today as yesterday and Your years have no end.. Strengthen our arms for battle as You did Your servant David, for You are the same today as yesterday and Your years have no end. Rescue us as You rescued Your people Israel at the banks of the Red Sea, for You are the same today as yesterday and Your hears have no end. Walk with us as You walked with Shadrach, Meshach and Abednego in the fiery furnace, for You are the same today as yesterday and Your years have no end. Rescue us as You rescued Daniel in the lion's den, for You are the same today as yesterday and Your years have no end. Hear our cries as You heard Hannah, for You are the same today as yesterday and Your years have no end. Give us new joys as You gave them to Naomi, for You are the same today as yesterday and Your years have no end. Have mercy upon us in our desolation as You did with Hagar, for You are the same today as yesterday and Your years have no end. Give us new revelations in the places of our loneliness and banishment, as You did for Your servant John on Patmos — for You are the same today as yesterday and Your years have no end. Bring us back from the far country of our wandering and lift us from the hog pens of our degradation as was the case with the Prodigal Son — for You O Christ of God are the same today as yesterday and Your years have no end. Deliver us from the demons that torment and take away our lives as You did for Legion, for You O Christ of God are the same today as yesterday and Your years have no end. Rescue us from the places of our confinement and shake the prisons of our persecution as You did for Peter, Paul and Silas, for You are the same today as yesterday and Your years have no end. Grant us access to Your presence in our dying hours as You did to a thief on the cross, for You are the same today as yesterday and Your years have no end.

Breathe upon us O Holy Spirit with fresh winds of empowerment and renewal as You did to the early church that was gathered in an upper room on the Day of Pentecost, for You are the same today as yesterday and Your years have no end.

O God of our salvation give us victory over the cross and raise us imperishable, incorruptible and immortal, for You are the same today as yesterday and Your years have no end. We praise You that Your years have no end. In the name of our Savior Christ do we pray with this prayer of desperation and faith, Amen.

– DAY 296 –

PSALM 103: 7

Gracious God teach us Your way, lead and guide us in Your way, have Your way in our lives, as You did for Moses so that no matter what happens from day to day we can declare that we may not know when or where or how but "we know who." We may not know how things will turn out but "we know who." We may not know what the doctor is going to say but "we know who." We may not know how certain bills are going to get paid or where the money is coming from but "we know who."

We may not know what the bank is going to say about our application but "we know who." We may not know what the judge is going to say about our appeal but "we know who." We may not know what is going to happen on our job tomorrow morning or what will happen in our new position but "we know who." We may not know what will happen when the administration changes or if the new boss will like You are not but "We know who." I don't know what is going to happen when they put You in the fiery furnace or what will happen when they close the door to the lion's den on You but "I know who."

We may not know what life will be like now that husband or wife, mother or father, son or daughter, grandmother or grandfather, or good friend or loyal supporter have gone home to be with You O Lord but "we know who." We know your ways O God then no matter what is happening around us, we can hold our heads up and declare, "We will be all right. Things will work out somehow. We still have a future because "we know who."

When we know who, we can say yes even to Calvary. Even when disciples desert, friends deny and those we trusted betray; and even when enemies mock and the devil is have a good laugh, we can still talk about resurrection because we know Your ways O God. And God's way is not death but life, not defeat but victory and not destruction but reward. Your same almighty hand that raised Jesus from the dead to stoop no more will bring us back because that's Your way, O God. And when we fall short we can dare repent and be given another chance because Your way O God is not rejection but forgiveness and cleansing.

You made Your ways known to Moses and Your acts to the people of Israel, so teach us Your way O God because Your way is the path that leads to life and that leads to our eternal home with You. In the name of the Lord Jesus, the way, the truth and the life, do we offer this prayer, Amen.

– DAY 297 –

PSALM 103: 13

O God, we praise You not only for the fact of You forgiveness but the extent of Your forgiveness and Your deliverance. As far as the east is from the west, so far do You remove our transgressions from us. As far as the north is from the south, so far do You remove our transgressions from us. As far as the smallest ant in the pasture is from the farthest moon of Jupiter, so far do You remove sin from us. As far as ice is from fire or winter's blast is from summer's heart, so far do You remove our transgressions from us. As far as a flying fish is from a shooting star, so far do You remove our transgressions from us. As far as the rainbow is from midnight, so far do You remove our transgressions from us. As far as snails are from the seraphim, so far do You remove our transgression from us. As far as the Redwoods are from the mustard seed, so far do You remove our transgressions from us. As far as heaven is from hell so far do You remove our transgressions from us. As far as sin is from Your throne, so far do You remove our transgressions from us. As far as our Lord Jesus Christ is from the death and the grave, so far does he remove our transgressions from us. As far as the earth is from the farthest star in the universe, so far do You remove our transgressions from us. As far as Your promises are from being broken Your blessings are from running out or Your love is from being expended, so far do You remove our transgressions from us.

As far as the cross of Christ is able to reach, so far do You remove our transgressions from us. As far as the blood of Jesus is able to cleanse, so far do You remove our transgressions from us. As far as the power of the Holy Spirit is able to fall and find, love and lift, bless and bestow, so far do You remove our transgressions from us. As high as prayer is able to rise, so far do You remove our transgressions from us. As far as the promises of You word are from being broken, so far do You remove our transgressions from us. As far as You are from failure or sin, so far do You remove our transgressions from us.

Not only do You remove our transgressions from us farther than we can imagine or words can express but You drown them in the sea of forgetfulness so that they do not rise to haunt us in this life nor condemn us at Your judgment seat. As the heavens are high above the earth, so great is Your steadfast love to those who love You. As far as the east is from west, so far do You remove our transgressions from us. As a father has compassion on a child or a mother loves the fruit of her womb, so You have compassion and love on us. We praise You and love You O God, in the name of Jesus our Lord , Amen.

DAY 297

– DAY 298 –

PSALM 104: 1

O God, we praise You for the greatness of Your ministry to small things. You not only made the mountains, You also made mice. You not only created the sky, You also created the sparrows. You are not only clothed with majesty, You also created men and women in Your own spiritual image. O God of glory You hear the faintest groan from the smallest child. O God of the heavens You are not so far away or removed that You cannot help the weakest trembling, believer. O God of holiness, You look upon us with mercy when we stretch out our sin scarred hands to You. O God of infinite power You are gentle enough to hold the smallest baby in the hollow of Your hand. O God of might only You know the numbers of stars that You have placed in the heavens and yet You have numbered the hairs on our heads. Your hand has scooped out the valleys and Your hand is considerate enough to give us victories in things great and small. You see meteors that move through outer space and You also notice the tears that roll silently down our cheeks that no one else notices or sees. You direct the stars in their orbits and the planets in their courses and You guide our stumbling and fumbling feet along life's uncharted paths. You hold back the oceans swelling tides and You hold us close to Your bosom when we are afraid and lonely. You send the rain from the skies to refresh and replenish Your earth and without our asking You bless us with grace that is sufficient for all of our needs. You feed the birds and clothe the grass and bestow beauty upon the lilies of the fields. You also feed us, clothes us, and You give our lives the beauty of salvation purchased with the blood of Your only Son and our Savior, Jesus.

Your wind blows and no human can control or stop it. Your Spirit anoints and moves within our lives and nobody can stop it. No marching army, no sailing navy, no action of government, no amount of money, no ruling monarch and no demon in hell can stop Your Spirit from gifting us, filling us and blessing us. O God You are very great in things large and small. And on this day we especially praise You for ministering to small things. We praise You for Your ministry and care of us. We may be very small in the sight of others but we are big enough to be noticed and looked after by You. The world may think little of us but You thought enough of us to allow Jesus to give his life for us. You thought enough of us to bless us with the presence and ministry of the Holy Spirit who abides with us forever. For Your ministry to small things we praise You O God. In Jesus name do we offer this prayer of thanksgiving, Amen.

DAY 298

– DAY 299 –

PSALM 105: 16-17

O God, You who sent Joseph for the famine in Egypt, would You raise up men and women for such a time as this. Would You raise up preachers who rightly divide the word of Truth? Would You raise up shepherds who truly care for Your flocks? Would You raise up prophets with holy boldness? Would You raise up spokespersons who have both a word of social consciousness as well as a word of personal morality? Would You raise up saints who are merciful as well as righteous, who have a love of sinners and a passion for souls, as much as they do for their own salvation? Would You raise up saints whose talk is their walk? Would You raise up saints who are generous and gracious, who are forgiving and faithful?

O God in times like these would You raise up a generation that knows and honors You? O God we fear for this coming generation. With all of the temptations that young people face, with the openness of our society and the increasing boldness of sin, we fear for the coming generation. With the violence and sexual lewdness that confront them daily, with the abundance of drugs and the easy access to alcohol, with so many dysfunctional families, we fear for the coming generation. O God raise up parents who will teach their children that You are God and You are to be reverenced, adored, praised and served.

O God give us Josephs for such a time s this. Give us persons of vision and persons of patience. Give us persons of integrity and person of faith. Give us persons of endurance and persons of tenderness. Give us persons of strength and persons of passion. Give us persons who remember the rock from which they have been hewn. O God supplier of every need, would You raise up Josephs for such a time as this?

O God, we yield ourselves to You. If You need a Joseph in the community, in the church, in the family, in the workplace, here we are, send us. Use us O Lord to Your glory for such a time as this. Consecrate us now to Your service O Lord to be Your Josephs for this time when there is a famine of righteousness and truth in the land. This we ask in Jesus name, Amen

DAY 299

– DAY 300 –

PSALM 106: 23

O God as Moses stood in the gap in days of old when Your people angered You in the wilderness; we praise You for Jesus our intercessor and our mediator. We praise You for Jesus, the precious Lamb of glory, who takes away the sins of the world. Where would we be without Jesus? Where would we be without His blood that cleanses? Where would we be without His name that gives power over demons? Where would we be without His teachings? Where would we be without His example of prayer? Where would we be without His resurrection from the dead? Where would we be without His love and forgiveness? Where would we be without His devotion to You and to us? Where would we be without His victory over the Tempter? Where would we be without His promise of return? Where would we be without His church?

We praise You for Jesus our intercessor and mediator who though He was rich He became poor that we through His poverty might become rich. We praise You for Jesus our intercessor and mediator who came into the world to save sinners. We praise You for Jesus whose unconditional love allowed Him to give His life as a ransom for many. We praise You for Jesus who is the way out of trouble, the truth in a crooked world and the life for dying and drowning, fearful and famished souls. We praise You for Jesus who is the center of our joy.

We praise You for Jesus and His continued ministry of intercession and preparation for the saints who await His coming. O Jesus we love You more and more as the years go by. O Jesus we fall in love with You again and again and again. O Jesus we worship and adore You, Lord God Sabbath. Walk with us now and appear to us as You did to Your saints of old. May we hear Your tender voice in our moments of lostness? May we feel You touch in our moments of loneliness? May we experience Your healing in the midst of our infirmities? Our desire is to see You face to face now and to be in Your presence throughout ceaseless ages. O Jesus, friend of sinners and saints, thank You for all that You have done for us and all that You continue to do. We are privileged to pray in Your mighty, matchless and all-powerful name, Amen.

DAY 300

– DAY 301 –

PSALM 107: 20

O God heal with Your word and deliver from destruction with Your hand. God we are at a point of desperation and we need healing and we need deliverance.

Heal with Your word because we carry shackles and chains of guilt from our past. Situations of violence and abuse, sins and transgressions of days gone by, remorse over pain we have caused to others still haunt us by day and cause sleepless nights. Only Your word can heal. Not self-help books, not lectures by self-made gurus, not our degrees or relationships or possessions — only Your word can heal the scars in our hearts, the bruises in our minds, and the wounds in our souls. Heal internally we pray in the name of Jesus.

We pray for Your healing word upon all manner of physical diseases from headaches to heart diseases, from arthritis to AIDS, from common colds to cancer. We submit our high blood pressure, diabetes, prostrate problems, gout, failing sight and hearing, our psoriasis, our multiple sclerosis, our lupus to Your healing graces. We pray for You healing word over all of our mental and emotional disorders, over depression, over all kinds of nervous breakdowns, over neuroses and psychoses. We pray for Your healing word over our sins, our fears and our sorrow. O God heal us of those ways weights and sins that so easily beset us that we have difficulty in asking You to help in letting them go. Our first love is for You. Our first desire is to do Your will. Heal now as You have in days past and gone. Touch now as You have in days past and gone. Deliver by Your hand now as You have in days past and gone. Work miracles and bring down strongholds even now as You have in days past and gone — in the name of Jesus. O God we pray for Your healing word in our lives.

O God save us from self and selfishness, from stubbornness and rebellion that leads to destruction. Help us to get over the hurt that we carry that hinders Your Spirit from flowing freely in our lives. Heal us O God in whatever ways we are afflicted with the same words that created the universe, that raise Jesus and that released the Holy Spirit on the Day of Pentecost. And give us faith to receive You healing word.

When our past catches up with us—O God deliver. When we are tempted to repeat old patters of sin and straying—O God deliver. When we feel ourselves slipping down slopes that we've been down before—O God deliver. When we are inclined to break our promises to You ourselves and others — O God deliver. When we are in situations that are destructive and we don't know how to get out — O God deliver. When we are sick in body, mind and spirit — O God deliver. From financial bondage and foolish spending — O God deliver. From self-hatred, pity parties, low self-esteem and insecurity — O God deliver. From foolish attempts to keep us with the Joneses — O God deliver. In Jesus name do we pray, Amen.

From arrogance of spirit, pride and stubbornness of will — O God deliver. From sloppiness of prayer life and lack of discipline when and where we need to be strong — O God deliver. From resistance to Your word and the Spirit's leading — O God deliver. From selfishness and stinginess and cheapness and failure to give as we should according to Your word and in accordance with our blessing — O God deliver. For failure to give You the praise, glory and worship that You deserve — O God deliver.

Heal with Your word and deliver with Your almighty hand and help us to yield as You answer this prayer. In Jesus name do we ask and plead with thanksgiving. Lord we believe, help our unbelief. Deliver us from the sense of desperation that breeds doubt. We love and glorify You, Amen.

– DAY 302 –

PSALM 108: 12

O God our very present help in times of trouble, our strong tower and fortress, please help us when we are losing the fight over that which we have no control. Our best intentions notwithstanding, we must confess O God that there are some foes in life that we can't seem to beat with consistency. Some allurements are too powerful and to appealing for us to be victorious over them by relying on our own means. We appreciate those persons whom You have place in our lives for love and counsel, for direction and friendship, for support and strength. But we must also confess that there are times when even the nearest and dearest cannot help us fight the battles against some foes.

Sometimes the weights and the sins that so easily beset get the best of us. Sometimes our insecurities get the best of us. Sometimes jealousy gets the best of us. Sometimes fear gets the best of us. Sometimes our doubts get the best of us. Sometimes bad memories and hurts from the pat get the best of us. Sometimes anger gets the best of us. Sometimes guilt gets the best of us. Sometimes the devil gets the best of us. O God, we seek Your presence and Your intervention in an undeniable and unmistakable way when we find ourselves losing the battles over that which we cannot seem to handle and when we are losing the battle with our Goliaths. When the giants of life keep coming, O God, You who fought with David, please fight with us. We need power greater than the insights from self-help books or their gurus. We need more than what we receive from tele-evangelists. We sometimes need more than what we receive from worship in the congregation of the saints. We need You to speak to us directly, to hold us closely, and to fill us with new power and a new determination to live to our highest and noblest self.

O God won't You speak to us right now? Won't You draw close to us right now? Will You enfold us in Your arms right now? Can we feel new power and a fresh anointing upon our lives right now? O God will You help us? Thank You O God for hearing us as we call. You minister to our needs as we cry out from the depths of our being. We love You O God and we praise You for Jesus Christ our Savior and for the continued presence of the Holy Spirit in our lives. In Christ name do we pray with thanksgiving, Amen.

DAY 302

– DAY 303 –

PSALM 109: 22

O God please draw near to comfort and to strengthen when our hearts are heavy. We know that You never leave us but we must confess O God there are times when You seem distant. There are times when it seems as if You hide Yourself from those who seek You. O God we pray that You will not only draw near but that You will touch us in a clearly identifiable way when our hearts are heavy. May we see Your power and the evidence of our prayer, as did Paul and Silas in prison? May we see You in revelation glory, as did John on the isle of Patmos? May we hear Your voice clearly and audibly, as did Abraham? Would You visit us with angels ascending and descending to our situation as You did for Jacob? May we see You with us in the fire as did Shadrach, Meshach and Abednego? Will You show us some visible sign of Your favor as You did for Gideon? Will You speak to us through miraculous phenomenology as You did with Moses and the burning bush? Will You work a miracle of release and deliverance for us as You did for Simon Peter?

O God, we know that we walk by faith and not by sight. But there are times when we feel so overwhelmed, when we are so lonely, when we are in so much pain and confusion that we need to feel You, see You and hear You in new, faith confirming and strengthening ways. O God when we feel poor and needy and our hearts are pierced because we have been falsely accused, will You draw near and touch us? When our hearts are heavy because of loss in our lives, will You draw near and touch us? When our hearts are heavy because of persecution an even the temporary victory of enemies over us, will You draw near and touch us? When our hearts are heavy because of the loneliness of physical sickness and suffering that we can't even articulate, will You draw near and touch us?

Touch us Lord Jesus like You touched the woman with the issue of blood. Touch us Lord Jesus like You touched the man born blind. Touch us Lord Jesus like You touched the lepers. Touch us like You touched the funeral bier of the son of the widow of Nain. Touch us like You touched Legion. Touch us O God, O Lord, Jesus and we shall be cleansed, free, raised, healed and strengthened. O Lord God thank You for drawing nearer even as we call upon You and touching us with Your empowering promises, Your enabling love and the renewal of Your Holy Spirit. In Jesus name do we pray, Amen.

– DAY 304 –

PSALM 110: 4

O God, You have said that we are priests forever according to the order of Melchizedek. That means that we are redeemed forever. That means no devil can take our redemption away. That means that no sin can hold us captive as long as we plead the blood of Jesus. That means that we are able to approach You directly in Your holy of holies. That means that we can come before Your very throne. That means that when the sun ceases to shine and the stars stop twinkling and the ocean ceases to roar and the earth ceases to be and the skies are rolled up like a scroll, we will still be counted in the ranks of the redeemed. Thank You for the sufficiency of the priesthood of Jesus Christ who has redeemed us forever.

O God, You have said that we are priests forever according to the order of Melchizedek who was both priest and king. That means that we can be in the world and not necessarily of it. That means that we can serve You in whatever contexts we find ourselves. That means that the temporal is under the control of the spiritual. That means we are members of a holy nation and that we really are Your own people. That means that no matter what society says about us or how it classifies us, that we are royalty. We are Your children and Your very own seed. That means that as we have born the image of the earthly we shall bear the image of the heavenly. Thank You for the Lordship of Jesus who reigns forever. Hallelujah!

Now God, we pray that we might live up to the high calling that You have called our lives to exemplify. Wherever we are — at home, at work, in school, on our jobs, among our friends, keep us ever mindful of who we are. We are kings and priest forever after the order of Melchizedek. Thanks to You and to our Lord Jesus for the great work of salvation You have wrought in us. Now God we pray that we will so live that Your work of salvation may be done through us who are called to serve You and bless Your people as Melchizedek did to Your servant Abraham. We pray this prayer of thanksgiving and petition in the interceding name of Jesus our great mediating high priest and our king forever, Amen.

DAY 304

– DAY 305 –

PSALM 111: 1

O God, You love us wholly and completely. We are always awed and humbled when we think about the length, height, breadth and depth of Your love for us. We praise You for Jesus Christ our eternal reminder of Your love for us. We look to the cross as the supreme example of how far Your love is willing to go to redeem us. We look to the empty tomb as the reminder of the power of Your love to even conquer death. We worship Your Holy Spirit as evidence of Your continuing provision for us. We praise You for the promise of the Second Coming of the Lord Jesus Christ as the opportunity to share the eternal fellowship of Your love. We praise You for the church, which is the living embodiment of Your love in community, in fellowship, in teaching, in preaching, in caring, in service and in warfare with the principalities and powers. We praise You for the gospel, which proclaims Your love.

Such love, as Yours deserves our commitment and adoration. O God, we pray that You would save us from halfhearted devotion and service and half committed love. Like David Your servant, we pray for such a wellspring of thanksgiving for who You are and all that You have done for us that we will love You and serve You with our whole heart. We pray for Your power to lay aside whatever weights and sins in our lives to which we cling that prevent our loving You with our whole heart. We pray for detachment from the things of this world — possessions, fame and conflicting loyalties that prevent us from loving You with our whole hearts. We pray that we might overcome love of money which is the root of evil, so that we may love You with our whole heart. We pray for the overcoming of pride and ego. Which prevent us from loving You with our whole heart. Help us to keep the flesh under subjection and discipline so that we can love You with our whole heart. Help us to put family, friends and career in perspective so that we can love You with our whole heart. Help us not to make idols of our blessings so that we can love You with our whole heart.

O God, You love us so completely that You are deserving of our whole heart and on this day we give our hearts to You. In the name of Jesus do we pray this prayer of thanksgiving and love, Amen.

DAY 305

– DAY 306 –

PSALM 112: 6-9

O God, we praise You for the victory that comes to the righteous, and to those who have been redeemed by the blood of the Lord Jesus Christ. We praise You for the sure foundation upon which we stand. We stand upon Your word. We stand upon Christ our Savior. We stand upon the promises of the Comforter. We stand upon grace that is sufficient and power that knows no end.

We praise You, God, for sacred remembrance of the security we have in You. If Mt. Zion cannot be shaken by human beings neither can we. If the Alleghenies and the Rocky Mountains cannot be uprooted neither can we when we stand upon Your word and remember whose we are.

We praise You for the assurance of victory because these are times O Lord, we must confess that we feel overwhelmed and afraid because of the challenges before us O God forgive us when we forget whose we are and in whose hands we are. Forgive us when the "what ifs" get next to us and we forget whose we are and in whose hands we are. Forgive us when we lose precious sleep in worry and anxiety because we have forgotten whose we are and in whose hands we are.

Steady our hearts with Your Holy Spirit. Steady our faith with Your word. Steady our minds with Your peace. Steady our tongues with the Gospel. Steady our vision with Your sufficiency. Steady our feet with Your direction. Steady our trembling hands with the touch of Christ. Steady our resolve with Your presence. Steady our love with Your gentleness.

And please Lord, grant victory so Your kingdom will be established and Your church and Your people may go forward with hope. We pray for faith to claim victory even when we are assaulted by doubt. In Jesus name we pray, Amen.

DAY 306

– DAY 307 –

PSALM 113: 3

O Lord God, the Almighty, King of Kings, Jehovah-jireh, Jehovah-shalom, Jehovah-rophe, Jehovah-rohi, the Great I Am, You who are before the morning stars sang together or the children of God shouted for joy; we pause to praise You for who You are. We pray that this day from the rising of the sun to the going down of the same, Your name will be praised in all the earth, beginning with us. With our words we will praise You. With our thoughts we will praise You. With our lives we will praise You. Every time we are privileged to help somebody, we will not pat ourselves on the back and boast of our accomplishments. We will praise You. With every accomplishment we achieve or goal we reach, we will praise You. With every breath we take, step we make and in every beat of our hearts, we will praise You.

For when we praise You, the negative cannot enter and the devil is held at bay. When we praise You we receive power and we are drawn closer to You. When we praise You, we live in obedience to Your word which invites and commands us to praise the Lord.

O God, we praise You because all praise belongs to You. We praise You because You are worthy to be praised. Your longsuffering and sacrificial love as evidenced by Your forgiveness and the death of Jesus on Calvary, are worthy to be praised. Your provision for our warfare and welfare through the gift of the Holy Spirit, is worthy to be praised. Your all sufficient grace and strength made perfect in weakness are worthy to be praised. Your word which fades not away and Your promises that are never broken, are worthy to be praised.

Your righteousness and Your redemption, Your majesty and Your message of salvation are worthy to be praised. Your holiness and Your mercy are worthy to be praised. Your creative and sustaining life giving power are worthy to be praised. Your victory over the Evil One is worthy to be praised. Your plan of salvation for us and the hope of life eternal that we have to be with You forever, are worthy to be praised.

O God, Father, Son and Holy Spirit we praise You with everything we have and everything we are. From the rising of the sun to the going down of the same, we pray that this day our life will be a continuing testimony of song and thanksgiving to You for Your excellent greatness and exceeding loving kindnesses and tender mercies. Thank You for being our God. We dedicate our life as a praise song to You both this day and forever and ever, from the rising of the sun to the going down of the same, through Jesus Christ our Lord, Amen.

DAY 307

– DAY 308 –

PSALM 114: 7-8

O God, You are an awesome God before whom we bow and tremble and You are also a gracious and merciful God and the supplier of all our needs. We are grateful for every opportunity to come into Your presence not as trembling subjects before a tyrannical and powerful ruler, but as children before an all-wise and loving parent. In Your awesomeness the mountains tremble and through Your graciousness the rocks turn into pools of water. O God You can make the hard situations in our lives places of renewal and hope. You can make lifeless circumstances springs of life giving power. You can turn our Calvarys into places of redemption and tombs wherein we have been buried, into scenes of resurrection and victory. We thank You that in whatever circumstance we find ourselves, You can turn them around to our good and to Your glory. We praise You O God for Your watchful eye and Your continuing protection. We praise You for the victory You bring out of the hard and difficult places of life. Sometimes we confess O God that our stubbornness, our shortsightedness and our sin put us there. Sometimes the machinations of the Adversary put us there. Sometimes the viciousness of others puts us there. Sometimes our burdens, our illnesses, our addiction, habits and weaknesses appear to us as overpowering rocks. But wherever we are we praise You that You are there and You are able to make the crooked places straight, the rough places smooth and the difficult places a blessing.

We praise You O Lord for Your faithfulness that never leaves us or forsake us. We praise You O God for Your power that is able to bring forth miracles in tough situations. Spirit of the living God please flow through our lives when we are in rocky circumstances. Word of God please be fulfilled and incarnated in our lives when we climb high mountains. O Father and mother God please empower and guide us when we are weak and weary and in need of renewal, when the pressures and problems of life have worn us down and are about to wear us out.

You are able to turn rocks into pools of water and flints into springs of water. O God in Your mercy please nourish us in those places and at those times wherein we can find no word of redemption and no bright cloud on our horizon. Deliver O God for Your own namesake and glory. And we shall praise You forevermore. This we ask in Jesus name, Amen.

– DAY 309 –

PSALM 115: 3-8

O God forgive us for the latter day and contemporary idols that we make with our hands, conceive with our egos and bow down and worship and give our allegiance to. Forgive us when we make money, possessions, careers, families and relationships into idols, and give to them the kind of adoration and priority, commitment and devotion that should be reserved for only You. Forgive us when we make idols out of our bodies, our pride and ego, our schedules and our wills, and give to them the time, attention and devotion that should only be given to You.

Forgive us when like the ancients, we fail to realize that the idols we serve cannot deliver. They have no power to save or deliver. They have no power to heal or give lasting comfort or peace. The guidance of their hands, when they have hands, is faulty and limited. The vision of their eyes, when they have eyes, is shortsighted and narrow. The strength of their arms, when they have arms is weak. Their ability to hear when they have ears is skewed and prejudiced. The direction of their feet, when they have feet, is toward the grave or toward the decay that comes with time.

Only You O God are alive forevermore. Only You O God are able to supply all of our needs in this life and in the world to come. Only You O God can deliver from the pit of hell, the power of demons and the grasp of death and the hold of the grave. Only You O God can see all, hear all and only You know all, even what we really need even before we ask. Only in You can be found our sufficiency. You alone are the only true and living God worthy of all of our praise, worship, devotion and adoration. Your son Jesus is the only Savior. Your precocious Holy Spirit alone empowers and gives direction that is perfect and upright.

Our trust and our hope are in You. Kindly and gently lead us back to the path of righteousness when to the right or the left we would turn our heads away from You to the idols of our own making and our own ego. We praise You for who You are, O true and living God and we praise You for what we can become when we follow Your truth and turn from the myths and fables we create. Help us to strive to always be as faithful to You as You are to us. In the precious name of Jesus do we pray, Amen.

– DAY 310 –

PSALM 116: 10

O God strengthen our faith, the meaning of which is believing when and what we cannot see, and being able to endure difficult times not because of superior strength or goodness, but because of our trust in You. O God when our lives go through periods of affliction and times of testing, seasons of groping and grasping in the dark when we seek to discern Your will, we pray for faith that presses its ways and endures unto the breakthrough. For such is the essence of faith.

We pray for a faith that will not shrink
Tho pressed by many a foe,
That will not tremble on the brink
Of any earthly woe;
That will not murmur not complain
Beneath the chastening rod,
But in the hour of grief or pain
Will lean up its God;
A faith that shines more bright and clear
When tempests rage without,
That, when in danger, knows no fear.
In darkness feels no doubt.
Lord, give me such a faith as this,
And then, whatever may come,
I'll taste even now the hallowed bliss
Of an eternal home.

(O For a Faith that will not Shrink, William H. Bathurst)

O God in the midst of our affliction, we pray that we may keep our faith as did Daniel whose prayer life gave him power to face persecution without complaint. We pray for the faith of Ruth whose life and commitment brought blessings from adversity. We pray for the faith of Paul whose passion for You gave him strength far beyond the frailties of his health. We pray for the faith of Nehemiah who kept on building in spite of opposition. We pray for the faith of Jesus who could face the cross with the assurance of victory.

O God, we pray for faith that is so determined that we can have a testimony like the Psalmist who said, "I have kept my faith, even when I said, "I am greatly afflicted (Psalm 116:10)."" And, we pray that the keeping of our faith will give to us the henceforth of Paul when he said, "I have fought a good fight, I have finished my course, I have kept the faith. Henceforth there is laid up for me a crown of righteousness…(2 Timothy 4:7)." In Jesus name we pray, Amen.

– DAY 311 –

PSALM 117

We praise You O God for great is Your steadfast love for us. Your steadfast love is greater than our sins and greater than our fickleness. Your steadfast love is greater than our broken promises and greater than our forgotten vows. Your steadfast love is greater than Satan and greater than sickness. Your steadfast love is greater than the farthest limits of our thoughts, and it is greater than the highest reaches of our imagination. Your steadfast love is greater than any sacrifice any commitment, or any offering we could possible give to You to express our gratitude and our love. So please Lord accept our feeble and heartfelt praise that comes from the depths of our souls for Your steadfast love.

We praise You O God not only for the greatness of Your steadfast love but we praise You because You are forever God. Your faithfulness is forever. Your love is forever. Your reign is forever. Your power is forever. Your word and Your promises are forever. Your grace and mercy are forever. Your salvation through Jesus Christ is forever. Your Holy Spirit is forever. O God we can't think in forever terms. We have no real conception of forever. Everything and everyone we know but You are bound by time. But You are forever.

We praise You not only for Your immanence but also for Your transcendence. You are not only within us and within our reach; You are above us and beyond us. In times like these when there is so much happening around us that is decaying and changing we look to You O God of greatness and glory who abides forever. O Forever God we pray like Your servant of old,

Abide with me fast falls the eventide,
The darkness deepens—Lord, with me abide;
When other helpers fail and comforts flee,
Help of the helpless, O abide with me

(Abide with Me: Fast Falls the Eventide, Henry F. Lyte)

This we ask In Jesus name, Amen.

DAY 311

– DAY 312 –

PSALM 118: 5

O God once again we call unto You in our distress. Sleep will not come; we call upon You for Your peace and the assurance that everything will be made all right. We feel overwhelmed and we call upon You to establish us in a broad place. Worry is assaulting us and we can't seem to shape it. We call upon You to increase our faith so that we can truly rest in You. O God teach us how to rest in You. O God teach us how to trust You more. O God teach us how to pray in calmness and with confidence. O God sometimes the words will not come and so we call upon You with the hope that You will read what is weighing on our hearts. Sometimes O God the worries come faster than the Spirit O Lord and help us to pray through. Help us to pray when restlessness sets in and we find it hard to stay focused in our prayers and to be still.

O God forgive us of those things in our lives which make praying difficult and which make us feel that our relationship with You is compromised. O God speak to us when we don't know what to say. Bring order to our confused lives. Order our footsteps so that we might be most productive. Help us to establish the right priorities. Give us discipline to pursue what is necessary but unpleasant. Guide us when we must make difficult decisions. And when those decisions affect the lives and livelihood, the souls, the faith and the well-being of others, please help us to choose rightly.

O God, You heard Your servant David in his distress and established him in a broad place; please hear us. You are faithful; forgive us when we feel so overwhelmed that we doubt You. You are faithful; forgive us when our own insecurities and imperfections cause us to lose sight of Your faithfulness and Your love for us. O God we praise You for the journey over which You have brought us. We know that You have not brought us this far to leave us. We praise You for who You are and for all we can become when Your hand is upon our life. Help us to encourage those who are weak and who are facing difficult moments in their lives. We love You O God of David, of Jeremiah, of John the Baptist, of Esther, of Hagar and of Mary Magdalene. We love You O Jesus lover of our souls.

We shall live in the victory we have in You and we shall walk in the broad places where You lead us and show us. In the name of Jesus do we pray, Amen.

DAY 312

– DAY 313 –

PSALM 118: 22-23

O God, we praise You that You and You alone have the last word concerning our destiny. Others look at us and based upon their prejudices, their own agendas and their assessment of our gifts and abilities, form judgments about us which many times are in error. Others reject us or exclude us or unfairly categorize us. And sometimes we must confess O Lord that we accept the judgments and assessments of others concerning our self-worth and our potential.

Forgive us O Lord when we forget that You alone know us better than we know ourselves and that You and You alone have the last word about whom we are and all we become. Where others reject, You select. And when others demote, You can promote. When others discourage, You are able to deliver. When others frustrate, You fortify. When others oppose, You are able to open up opportunities for growth. When others put us down, You are able to position us in places of power and glory we would have never reached by ourselves. When other see waste You see worth. When others see trash You see treasure. When others see inferior, You see important. When others see what we are not, You see what and who we really are.

We praise You for Your redemption, Your empowering hand, and Your salvation that rescues us from the trash heaps where others have placed us and puts us as the head of the corner. We give You glory because we realize had You not been on our side then we might have forever stayed in the places where others placed us. Salvation is Your work; we praise You O God. Redemption is Your joy; we praise You O God. The second chance is Your delight; we praise You O God. Mercy is Your business; we praise You O God. Love is Your character; we praise You O God.

Now God of grace and mercy help us to live as those who have been rescued, redeemed and refined by Your hand. And we will praise You forever more and give You glory for all that we become and all that we accomplish through the blood of Your Son and the empowerment of Your Holy Spirit. In Jesus name do we pray this prayer, Amen.

DAY 313

– DAY 314 –

PSALM 119: 11

O God if Your word being placed in our hearts will prevent us from sinning against You, put it there we pray. We grow weary with repeating old patterns of sin. We grow weary with the struggle. We grow weary with the guilt and shame. We grow weary with coming to You again and again seeking forgiveness for the same things. We grow weary with our lack of resistance and lack of desire to flee temptation.

O God, we pray that as weary as we get, help us not to give up on ourselves. Help us to continue the good fight of faith and the determined fight of resistance. O God we pray for the presence of Jesus, the captain of the Lord's host, to walk so closely with us we can feel his very presence besides us fighting with us. We pray for Your Holy Spirit to direct and inspire, to strengthen and sustain us in our struggles. We confess that we have not resisted to the point of shedding of blood, as the book of Hebrews reminds us (Hebrews 12:4).

O God when we pray most earnestly, temptation seems to come most readily and most abundantly. We need Your word in our hearts so we will not continue to sin against You. We need Your word written. Your word/Word living! Your word/Word revealed! Your Word incarnate! Your word/Word active! Your word/Word victorious! Your word/Word implanted and embedded in our hearts so that as opportunities arise, we will not sin against You. Keep us this day from sin that easily besets we pray. And save us from and inspire of ourselves we pray. In Jesus' name we pray. Amen.

DAY 314

– DAY 315 –

PSALM 119: 28

O God we need You, strengthen us. Our possessions entertain but they do not strengthen. Others do the best they can, but they do not strengthen because only You can empower. Our education enlightens but it does not strengthen. What we need is not only knowledge but enduring, hoping and overcoming power. We need You to strengthen us.

We confess Lord that sometimes we grow weary. We grow weary with waiting and wanting. We grow weary of rejection and of rebuke. We grow weary even in running for You. We grow weary of our battles and of our burdens. We grow weary of people and weary with our problems. We grow weary of temptations and trial, of trouble and turmoil. We grow weary of prejudice and pain. We grow weary of racism and we grow weary of repenting again and again and again. We grow weary of hoping and weary of hindrances. O God when we grow weary and our souls begin to melt like wax and our resolve to do right as the snow, we need You to strengthen us.

Strengthen us O God according to Your word, that You will supply all of our needs. Strengthen us according to Your word that as we ask we are given, as we seek we find and as we knock doors are opened. Strengthen us according to Your word, that You will neither fail us nor forsake us. Strengthen us according to Your word, which when hidden in our hearts helps us not to sin against You. Strengthen us according to Your Word which became flesh and dwelt among us full of grace and truth. Strengthen us according to Your word, that You would send a Comforter, yea even the Holy Spirit.

O God when our souls grow weary and melt away because of sorrow, strengthen us according to Your word. For Your word is a lamp unto our feet and a light unto our path. In Jesus name, Amen.

DAY 315

– DAY 316 –

PSALM 119: 36

O God in a consumption oriented culture where the push of possessions is so great and the allure of things is so inviting, we pray that our heart will stay fixed upon Your word and our eyes will stay centered upon Your will. O God keep us away from the "got to keep up with the Jones" syndrome. Help us to be good stewards of our resources that we will not be consumed with credit card debt or carried away by spur of the moment shopping. We pray that we will be able to distinguish between wants and needs, sufficiency and greed, abundance and decadence or ostentatiousness.

We pray that we will always remember that Your word has instructed us that our lives do not consist in the abundance of things that we possess and that if we seek first the kingdom of God and his righteousness, then all things will be added to us. Your word wants us to prosper. Teach us O God the meaning of prosperity for Your children and help us to walk therein. O God we pray that our hearts desire will be for Your word which remains an eternal lamp to our feet and a light to our path. In Jesus name do we pray, Amen.

DAY 316

– DAY 317 –

PSALM 119: 105

O God, we praise You that we don't have to go through life stumbling and falling when we reach the dark places of our lives wherein we cannot see our way and do not know the way. Your written word is a lamp to our feet and Your Word incarnate is a light to our path. Your forgiveness is a lamp to our feet and Your friendship is a light to our path. Your law is a lamp to our feet and Your love is a light to our path. Your righteousness is a lamp to our feet and Your redemption is a light to our path. You compassion is a lamp to our feet and Christ is a light to our path.

Your mercy is a lamp to our feet and Your majesty is a light to our path. Your salvation is a lamp to our feet and Your sanctification is a light to our path. Your grace is a lamp to our feet and Your gospel is a light to our path. Your guidance is a lamp to our feet and growth is a light to our path. Your message is a lamp to or feet and Your might is a light to our path. Your peace is a lamp to our feet and Your presence is a light to our path. Your promise is a lamp to our feet and Your power is a light to our path. Your help is a lamp to our feet and heaven is a light to our path. Your healing is a lamp to our feet and happiness in You is a light to our path. Your way is a lamp to our feet and Your wisdom is a light to our path. Your worship is a lamp to our feet and Your work is a light to our path.

Your beauty is a lamp to our feet and Your bounty is a light to our path. Your praise is a lamp to our feet and prayer is a light to our path. Your deliverance is a lamp to our feet and discipleship is a light to our path. Your Communion is a lamp to our feet and commitment is a light to our path. Your opportunities are lamps to our feet and obedience is a light to our path. Your holiness is a lamp to our feet and hope is a light to our path. Your life is a lamp to our feet and Your lordship is a light to our path. Your comfort is a lamp to our feet and Your church is a light to our path. Your excellence is a lamp to our feet and Your endurance is a light to our path. Your faithfulness is a lamp to our feet and Your finding us is a light to our path.

Your devotion is a lamp to our feet and Your direction is a light to our path. Your affection is a lamp to our feet and Your adoration is a light to our path. The Bible is a lamp to our feet and Your blessings are lights to our path. Your faithfulness is a lamp to our feet and Your fruit is a light to our path. Your companionship is a lamp to our feet and conquests are light to

DAY 317

our paths. Your Holy Spirit is a lamp to our feet and holy service is a light to our path. Thanksgiving is a lamp to our feet and tithing is a light to our path. Your goodness is a lamp to our feet and our giving is a light to our path.

O God when we would stray, may we hear Your voice saying to us "This is the way, walk in it (Isaiah 30:21)!" We pray that we might hold our lamps close and our light high so You will be glorified in all of the ways that we shall walk and all of the paths that we shall tread. In Jesus' name do we pray. Amen.

– DAY 318 –

PSALM 20

O God, we pray for faith to trust in You when deceitful tongues and lying lips begin to do their demonic work of discouragement. O God we pray for presence of mind when we hear of ill reports spread abroad about us by others. We trust You to vindicate us. Help us to remember that deceitful tongues wag and lying lips work when we are making progress and doing that which is worthwhile. Help us to remember that deceitful tongues wag and lying lips work when the speaker is jealous and jealousy is generated because we are so blessed. Help us to remember that though deceitful tongues wag and lying lips work. No weapon formed against us will prosper.

When we would fight our own battles, O God give us faith to stand still and wait on You. When we would become angry because others mock our visions and dreams, give us faith to stand still and wait on You. When our hearts are heavy because others don't see what You have shown to us, give us faith to stand still and wait on You. When others taunt us because the vision is yet for an appointed time and is slow in becoming reality, give us faith to stand still and wait on You. When followers and supporters become discouraged because of the rumors and innuendoes, the seeds of doubt and the personal attaches of deceitful tongues and lying lips, give us faith O God to stand still and wait on You.

Give us focus so that we might work toward Your vision of growth for our lives no matter what others say or do. O God You have not brought us this far to leave us and You do not show us great and glorious things to make us appear foolish. You always come out a winner at the finishing line. We praise You for being our strong tower and defense against deceitful lips and lying tongues. In Christ Jesus we have discovered truth, life and the way incarnate in human flesh. Help us this day to walk in Your truth, to know the fullness of Your life and to find Your way in the midst of conflicting options, so that we might know the joy of victory that comes to those whose trust is in You. In the name of Jesus, the incarnated truth of Your promises of victory, we rebuke the work of deceitful lips and lying tongues and we press our way toward the prize of Your upward call of growth and grace. We love You Lord, Amen.

– DAY 319 –

PSALM 121: 7-8

O God, You who are Almighty and Omnipresent, we praise You for Your continuing and constant vigilance and for Your watchful eye, and Your abiding and eternal presence. We praise You that we cannot ever truly go to a place or find ourselves in situations, Your eye cannot see, Your presence cannot invade or Your hand cannot rescue.

O God, the terror of these times, the violence in the streets, the violence that breaks the peace and security of our homes, the violence that assaults our churches is unsettling and frightening indeed. We need You to keep our lives, to guard us from all evil and to preserve our going out and our coming in from this time forth and forevermore.

O God when we hear of news reports of how innocent people have been attacked, maimed, raped, or murdered; when we ourselves have been victimized by the threats, tenor and violence of the times, we can become paranoid and fearful. And we know You do not want us to live in fear. You do not desire Your children be intimidated, assaulted and suffer at the hands of the ungodly.

O God keep us this day. Guard us this day. Direct us this day. Protect us this day. Be our shield, our strong tower, our battle axe and our first line of defense this day. Give us power to confront sin and evildoers without fear because we know we belong to You. We pray that the day will be hastened when the violence that is so much a part of our lives will be no more. Empower Your church and Your people as we engage the battles of the struggle for freedom, peace, security and justice. Until the day of victory, keep us O God we pray from all evil. Guard our lives and bless our going out and coming in from this time on and forever more. In Jesus name, Amen.

DAY 319

– DAY 320 –

PSALM 122

O God, we pray for peace. There is so much tension in the land we feel that we continually live in a powder keg. O God we pray for peace among those who have had a history of misunderstanding and hostility. We pray for the peace of Jerusalem, Your holy city. We pray for peace with justice between Israel and Palestine and Israel and her other neighbors. We pray that the ancient land of the Bible which has been drenched in the blood of warfare for centuries will soon see the day when warring ethnic and religious groups will beat their swords into plowshares and their spears into pruning hooks, when nation shall not lift up sword against nation and neither will they study war anymore.

We pray for peace in the land where Jesus lived and we pray for peace in the land where we live. We pray that Your people who love You will grow to the largeness of Your vision so they will put egos aside and pettiness aside and work for the glory of Your kingdom and Your church. O God it is so easy for misunderstandings to arise. And sometimes we become discouraged when we must play the role of peacemaker in the midst of confusion. Give us patience for the task of reconciler. Help us to be as patient with others as You are with us. Help us to always keep Your vision of growth and maturity before us so we can help others to grow beyond their agenda and their will to Your glory.

As we pray that peace be within the walls of Jerusalem we pray that peace will abide in Your church. As Your church struggles against the principalities and powers, we pray that peace will abide within her walls. As Your church makes a bold witness for the gospel, we pray that peace will abide within her walls. As Your church attempts to do bold and imaginative things we pray that peace will abide within Your walls. As Your Church attempts to grow we pray that peace will abide within her walls.

O Christ of God give us Your peace in times like these. O Christ of God give us the peace that passes understanding that comes when we come into Your presence with prayer, lifting our supplications with thanksgiving. O Prince of Peace we seek Your peace, Your power, Your presence, Your patience and Your prayer life so that we may be equipped for our ministry of reconciliation. O Holy Spirit of peace hear us we pray. In Your divine name O Christ of peace do we pray, Amen.

– DAY 321 –

PSALM 123: 3

Have mercy upon us O Lord, have mercy upon us. When we have painted ourselves into corners and don't know what to do, have mercy upon us O Lord. When we are depressed in spirit and so distracted in mind that we have trouble praying to You, have mercy upon us O Lord. When those who are close to us don't understand, have mercy upon us O Lord. When we have hurt, betrayed or angered those whom we love and they do not want to have anything to do with us, have mercy upon us O Lord. When we are not feeling very good about ourselves, have mercy upon us O Lord. When we feel so burdened that death seems like a welcomed relief, have mercy upon us O Lord. When we feel lonely and vulnerable, have mercy upon us O Lord.

When we like sheep have gone astray, have mercy upon us O Lord. When we are tossed and driven between our love for You and desires of the flesh have mercy upon us O Lord. When we have to make hard and difficult decisions, have mercy upon us O Lord. When sleep will not come and we toss and turn at night, have mercy upon us O Lord. When we really don't know what to pray, what to say or what to do have mercy upon us O Lord. When we really don't know what we want, have mercy upon us O Lord. When we cannot share with anyone all that we really feel, have mercy upon us O Lord. When we need a pastor and cannot reach one and do not have one, have mercy upon us O Lord. When we want to get away but cannot but have to keep up appearances; when we have to keep smiling even though we feel like breaking down into tears, have mercy upon us O Lord. When we long for peace within and it flees like a shadow or escapes us like the wind, have mercy upon us O Lord. When our enemies and foes seem larger than life, have mercy upon us O Lord. When the burdens and pressures of this life are so overwhelming we have difficult offering thanksgiving and praise for Your goodness, have mercy upon us O Lord.

O God whose mercies are eternal and whose love never ceases, have mercy upon us. O God whose forgiveness and whose patience endure from one generation to another, have mercy upon us. O God whose faithfulness is new and fresh every morning, have mercy upon us. O God of David, O Christ of Simon Peter, O Holy Spirit, You renewed and refreshed the apostle Paul, have mercy upon us. We leave ourselves in Your hands and

DAY 321

we trust You for Your mercy. We love You Lord even when we are in the pit of depression. We cast our cares upon You because we know that You care for us. Forgive us of our sins, grant us Your peace in our perplexity, restore us when we have fallen and draw so close to us that we can feel Your touch upon the furrows of our foreheads. Have mercy upon us O Lord have mercy upon us we pray in Jesus name, Amen.

– DAY 322 –

PSALM 124

O Lord thank You for being on our side when demons attacked and disease would have devastated. O Lord thank You for being on our side when our own failings and flaws would have merited justice cutting off our footsteps. O Lord thank You for being on our side when others told us what we couldn't do and then tried to stop us from achieving our goals. O Lord thank You for being on our side even when we were not on our own side because of the foolish things we did and the foolish chances we took. O Lord thank You for being on our side when we didn't believe in ourselves and would have accepted our bondage as permanent. O Lord thank You for being on our side when we were too weak, too weary, to self-engrossed and too ashamed to pray.

O Lord if You had not been on our side where would we be? We would have been swept away when trials flooded in upon our lives. We would have drowned in our own sorrow and self-pity when depression descended upon us like deepening darkness. We would have been overwhelmed with doubt and worry when friends and loved ones did not understand and sickness attacked our bodies and relationships, in which we had invested so much of ourselves, fell apart. We would have been overwhelmed by loneliness when loved ones left us to join You in a land fairer that day. We would have been permanently buried by enemies when we stumbled and fell and were vulnerable to their machinations.

Thank You O God for delivering us from traps that we didn't see and from our own shortsighted pleasures which could have destroyed us. Thank You O God for delivering us from Satan, sin and the permanent strangle hold of death. Thank You O God for delivering us from guilt that is too heavy to carry and fear that paralyzes and immobilizes. For Your steadfast love, we praise You. For Your faithfulness in all generations, we adore You. For Your sufficient grace in all things and at all times, we give thanks to You. For Jesus Christ incarnate among us and now reining above us and walking with us, we love You. For the abiding presence of the Holy Spirit, we give You glory. And for the promises of Your word that are never broken, we give You honor.

And now when trials come and trouble attacks, when foes threaten and obstacle block, when loneliness descend and depression clings, when sin taints and demons appear, when we feel threatened and are tempted to worry and complain, we praise You for this testimony, "Our help is in the name of the Lord, who made heaven and earth. (Psalm 124:8)" In Your name do we pray O living God, O reigning Christ, O abiding Holy Spirit, Amen.

– DAY 323 –

PSALM 125: 1-2

O God secure us in Your word and promise so that like Mount Zion we will abide forever. O God, increase our faith, confirm our hope and perfect us in love so that like Mount Zion we will abide forever. O God we pray for focus and a mind stayed on You so that like Mount Zion we will abide forever. O God, order our footsteps in Your will and in Your word so that like Mount Zion we will abide forever. O blood of Jesus, cleanse us of our sins so that like Mount Zion we will abide forever. O Holy Spirit, empower us so that like Mount Zion we will abide forever.

O God, our fear is that we will be like chaff which the wind drives away. Our fear is that we will be tossed about with every wind and doctrine. Our fear is that we will be double minded and like the waves of the sea unstable in all of our ways. When we are unsure of our faith we stumble over every molehill and are threatened by every small cloud on the horizon. When we are unsure of who we are as Your children we fall into every trap, are susceptible to very trick and have no strength to face temptation. When we are unsure of what we believe we become easily confused and distracted. When we are unsure of our salvation we become victims all over again.

O God help us to walk in the boldness and victory of those whose trust is in You. Give us faith to stand and having done all to continue to stand. Like the mountains that surround Jerusalem so surround us, O Lord. If You surround us Satan cannot draw near. If You surround us O Lord, enemies can threaten but they cannot attack. If You surround us O Lord we have a shelter from the stormy blasts. Of You surround us O Lord we can have peace in our spirit and confidence in our stride.

O God on this day, we pray for faith that abides like Mount Zion so that You can surround us. O Lord, keep us from walking out of the shelter of Your protection. For You are our strength and our security. In Jesus name do we pray, Amen.

DAY 323

– DAY 324 –

PSALM 126

O Lord our God, we thank You for the victories of our faith. We called to You and You answered. We cried to You and You comforted. We trusted in You and You delivered. We pleaded with You and You gave the victory. We sowed and You provided the harvest. We searched and You provided the answer. We asked and You gave. You restored what was taken from us a hundredfold. You rewarded our sacrifices far beyond our efforts. You supplied our every need, and beyond that You gave us what we didn't even think to ask for. Our reality has gone far beyond our vision. You have silenced the naysayers, the doubters, the scoffers and the skeptics. And when our enemies asked us "Where now is Your God?," we praise You for the evidences and testimonies that we can point to in our lives that demonstrated that You have been blessing us all along.

And when the vision tarried and things looked bleak we praise You for the gift of faith that helped us to hold on until our breakthroughs came. We praise You for helping us to believe when we didn't have it in and of ourselves to believe under our own steam. We praise You for breathing into us Your spirit of renewal, for blessing us with a spirit of determination and for Your word, which assured us that we would reap if we did not faint. Now O God, we have seen Your goodness in the land of the living. Now O God we know that You are not slack concerning Your promises. Now O God we know that those who go out weeping, bearing the see of sowing shall come home with shouts of joy carrying their sheaves. Our fortunes and faith have been restored like the waters of the Negev. Those of us who have sown with tears have reaped with shouts of joy. Our mouths have been filled with laughter and our hearts with songs of praises.

You have done great things for us. Thank You O God for Your steadfast love and faithfulness. Thank You for making dreams come true and visions become realities. We love You O lord and we commit ourselves again to You O God of our salvation. In the name of Jesus do we pray, Amen.

DAY 324

– DAY 325 –

PSALM 127: 1-2

O Lord bless our plans and our work this day. Unless You are with us, guiding us, empowering us and overseeing us, all that we do will be a useless spinning of the wheels. We will make motions and go nowhere. We will be busy but we will accomplish nothing. We will keep schedules to no avail. We will speak words and communicate little. We will work hard and have nothing to show for our efforts. We know from past experience that "Unless the Lord builds the house, those who build it labor in vain. Unless the Lord keeps the city, the guard keeps watch in vain."

O God, we present all that we purport to do this day unto You. Guide our feet, hold our hands, guard our tongues, bless our efforts, give direction to our thoughts, give clarity to our tongues, supervise our planning and inspire our work because we don't want to run this race in vain.

And after we ask for Your guidance, give to us we pray a consciousness of Your presence. We do not want to run ahead of You. Give to us the wisdom to slow down when we should and speed up when necessary. Help us not to speak to fast or too slow. Give us an eye for opportunity and a right sense of timing. We pray for alertness of mind so we will learn every new thing You have to teach us this day for life, from Your word and from others. We pray this will glorify You and help us to do Your will in the places where You have placed us. And if to the right or the left we would stray O Lord hold us close to You in the straight and narrow, in the right and redemptive way.

And when this day's journey is ended give us sleep from our labors knowing that we have done our best. Sleep is not only a matter of tiredness of body or mind; sleep is a matter of contentment because we have done our best. Sleep is a matter of knowing that we have done Your will. Sleep is the peace that comes from knowing that Your hand has been on our life. Sleep is a matter of knowing that even while we slumber in the very likeness of death that Your eye is upon us and Your hand is rocking us. Sleep is a matter of knowing that we are Your beloved.

O God, we pray that You will give us Your blessings for our journey and a fitful night's sleep when our day is done. In Jesus name do we pray, Amen

DAY 325

– DAY 326 –

PSALM 128: 1-2

O God, we reverence You. We reverence Your word. We delight in Your presence. We reverence Your sanctuary. We reverence Your tithes and offerings. We reverence human life; we regard all human life as sacred unto You. Our delight is to reverence You. We are at our happiest when we are reverencing You. We are happiest when we know that we are living according to Your will and word and when we are doing what pleases You. We are at our happiest when we resist that which Your word forbids. We are at our happiest when we rebuke the encroachments and the discouragement of the Adversary. We are happiest when we are in communion and on one accord with You. We are happiest when we feel You living within us, when we feel Christ Jesus living within us, when we feel the presence of Your Holy Spirit upon us and we are living within Your will. In You there is truly fullness of joy and in Your presence there are pleasures forevermore. We love You Lord.

Please forgive us when we stray. Please forgive us when we take the shortsighted view of things and lean to our own understanding and to our own flesh. Please forgive us when we put our pleasure and our possessions before the vision of growth and victory You have for our lives. Please forgive us when we allow others to come between us and when because of unconfessed sin and weakness of character and the flesh we allow distance to come between us. Restore to us the joy of our salvation and save us with Your powerful and merciful hand. Do not cast us away from Your presence and blow upon us with fresh anointing and stir within us the smoldering embers of Your Holy Spirit.

We love You Lord and You know that with all of our fickleness we really do delight in doing Your will. O Lord God You who delight to hear a sinner's prayer, we confess our sins, please be merciful and forgive. You know that with all of our contradictions and inconsistencies we reverence You. We pray that every day the Holy Spirit will live within us as our senior partner. We pray that every day Your Son Jesus will walk with us as our constant companion. We pray that every day we will reverence You more and more. Savior lead us lest we stray, gently lead us all the way because we truly reverence You blessed Lord God in all of Your fullness. In Your blessed name Father, Son and Holy Spirit do we pray, Amen.

DAY 326

– DAY 327 –

PSALM 129

O God, thank You for being our protection. You thwarted the wiles of the devil. You spring the traps set by our adversaries. You turned cursing into blessings. You turned Calvary's into crowning moments. You exposed lies that were uttered against us. You prepared tables of feasting and victory for us in the presence of our enemies. You built bridges over ditches that we didn't see. You did not allow those who we thought were our friends, but who were actually our enemies to do us any harm. You have been our battle-axe when our own weapons were insufficient. Your word has been our shield and we have not had to fear the arrows of treachery that fly by day or the pestilence of fear and paralysis that stalk at night. O God we praise You for Your faithfulness.

O God we pray for sacred remembrance of what You have done in times past so that we will continue to fight the good fight of faith in the battles that are still before us. We still have high mountains to climb and we need the strength that only You can give. We still have deep valleys to tunnel through and we need the insight that only You can give. We still have wide rivers to cross and we need the hope that only You can give. We still have great foes to fight and we need the resources that only You can provide. We need financial resources to meet staggering bills and obligations. We need continued renewal of vision when the road seems long and arduous. We need Your forgiveness when we stray along the way.

O God of grace and glory, the supplier of all of our needs and the refuge of all who cry unto You, we need miracles now for what we have to face. As You have been with us in times past, will You please be present now to make ways out of no ways and to provide for what we need but do not have and know no way of getting it but You? We do not know what to do but our eyes are upon You O God of faithfulness and power; You who are an ever present help in times of trouble.

O God hear us. O Jesus help us. O Holy Spirit give us hope. O God lift us. O Jesus love us. O Holy Spirit give us life. O God strengthen us. O Jesus save us. O Holy Spirit sanctify us. O God defend us . O Jesus deliver us. O Holy Spirit direct us. And whatever You do we will be careful to give You the praise O Triune God. We pray in Your name with thanksgiving and we seek the peace of Christ that passes understanding that helps us to walk in boldness in the midst of staggering obligations and difficult challenges. According to the promise of Your word we are bold to believe and even to know the victory is ours because as we have called in faith we believe that even now the work is already done. Maranatha! Even so come Lord Jesus. Lord we believe help thou our unbelief. In Your name do we pray, Amen.

– DAY 328 –

PSALM 130: 3-4

O God if You kept a permanent record of all of our sins and all of our transgressions who would be able to stand? Who could stand Your justice and who could abide Your holiness? Who could stay in the presence of Your righteousness and Your perfection? O God we are grateful that in spite of all that we are not, we are privileged to come into the very throne room and approach You with boldness and faith that You will hear us. O God, thank You for Your love which allows us entry. Thank You for Your forgiveness that drowns our sins in the sea of forgetfulness so that they will not rise to haunt us in this life nor condemn us at Your judgment bar. Thank You for Your mercy that is extended to all generations. Thank You for the blood of Jesus, which allows us to come to You with hands that have been redeemed from sin. Thank You for Your Holy Spirit, which sanctifies us. And even when we are at our best, our righteousness is still as filthy rags in Your sight. So thank You for the One who bridges the gap so that our sins which are as scarlet have become like the fresh fallen snow and the fresh risen dew.

O God, we love You and praise You. We worship You and we adore You. There is none like You and we continue to be awed that You have made us in Your very own image. We are fearfully and wonderfully made and that we know full well. If we had ten thousand times ten thousand times ten thousand tongues, they would still prove insufficient to declare our love for You. O God please be so kind to receive the praise and adoration for the one tongue we have which recognizes the great gap between where You are and where we are. Thank You for Your love that went the distance and on Calvary reconciled us to You. Thank You for the forgiveness that has been granted once and for all to the ages of ages. We love You Lord. We love You Lord. We love You Lord. Thank You for loving us first and the forgiveness and mercy and grace You bestow upon us this and every day. Your steadfast love never leaves and Your mercies never come to an end but they are new and fresh every morning. Great is Your faithfulness. As the forgiven and redeemed work of Your hands and heart we pray this prayer in the strong name of Jesus, the one who is altogether lovely, Amen.

DAY 328

– DAY 329 –

PSALM 130: 5-6

O Lord, we wait for You. More than those who watch for the morning do we wait for You. When we come to You in prayer, when our souls reach to You for sweet communion, when deep calls unto deep, we wait for Your touch and for Your presence. O God manifest Yourself physically and visibly, as You have done in days past and gone and as You are still doing today. We wait for You. We pray for stillness of spirit and quietness of mind, we pray for closeness of hearts and integrity in life so You will honor us with Your presence. We wait for You.

As lovers wait for the call of the beloved, we wait for You. As the thirsty ground waits for refreshing raindrops, we wait for You. As those who are lost in darkness wait for the light of day, we wait for You. As expectant and excited parents wait for the birth of a child, we wait for You. As we wait for an important and expected phone call to arrive, so we wait for You. Will You show up to bless us? Will You show up and breathe peace and salvation and healing into our lives? Will You show up and just stand near to us? Will You simply show up because we love You and desire to be nearer to You. We wait for You.

We wait for You to vindicate faith and rout the devil. When evil strikes boldly and wickedness cuts deeply, we wait for You. Arise O God and let Your enemies be scattered. Let disease be decimated. Let ignorance be eliminated. Let sin be ravaged. Let death as an enemy be overcome. Let the devil be consigned to the pit of hell so that he will not trouble anymore. Let the weary know rest. Let Your children enjoy peace. Let the innocent be free from molestation and violence. Let prayers be speedily answered. Let the whole-inhabited earth praise Your name. We wait for You.

O Christ of God, we wait for You to come privately in love and publicly in majesty and power. O Holy Spirit we wait for You to bless Your people with a new Pentecost. We wait for You to bless our lives with fresh anointing. O Lord, please help us to get ourselves out of this way so that You can have full reign in our lives. Like the disciple of old who assembled themselves together in an upper room to await the promise of the Father, the Paraclete, and the Comforter, who would bring all things to remembrance and lead and direct and teach all truth — so we wait for You.

The sick who have called upon Your name, wait for You. The discouraged, who need a second and sometimes a third wind, wait for You. Those who feel overwhelmed and drained by the pressures and problems of life, wait for You. Those who are bound by all kinds of additions and who live under all kinds of yokes, wait for You. Those who have faithfully called out to You day and night and have stood in the prayer gap of intercession for loved ones and others, wait for You. Those, to whom You have given visions and dreams, wait for You. Your church waits for You. Those who love You more than life itself wait for You. Those who are still struggling with their faith and are looking for certitude, wait for You.

We wait for You. All of us, old and young, male and female, rich and poor, both agnostic and believer, wait for You. Victims of war and of ethnic cleansing and political unrest and economic turmoil, wait for You. We pray that we will not grow weary in well doing but help give us faith to know and believe that according to Your word and promise we shall reap if we faint not. We wait for You — more than those who wait for the morning. Maranantha! Even so, come Lord Jesus. In Your name do we pray, Amen.

– DAY 330 –

PSALM 131

O Lord, we confess that too often our lives are filled with the mundane and small things of life. We confess O Lord that too often we allow our minds to drift into area where they do not belong. We confess that when we would try to grow we must constantly battle with that which we are trying to grow beyond. We confess that too often we are in a constant state of warfare in which we find ourselves being pulled forward to grow or backwards to sin. We confess O Lord that too often we are consumed in issues of pride, ego, and the desire for revenge. We confess O Lord that too often we find ourselves reliving what we should or should not have done in certain situations or speculating on what we would do if certain situations should arise. We confess O Lord that we spend too much time imagining the worst possible scenarios.

O Lord please be patient with us when we forget Your steadfast love and kindness towards us. Please forgive us when we give too much liberty to the devil in our thoughts and when we fail to resist when we should. Forgive us for occupying our time with that which is not kingdom worthy or growth enhancing. Forgive us O Lord when we allow our thoughts to wander into areas where they should not be. Forgive us O Lord when we become comfortable with what does not challenge and what stunts growth. Forgive us O Lord when we fail to keep Your word in our hearts so that we will not sin against You. Forgive us O God when we fail to plead the name of Jesus for deliverance from that which we can't seem to muster the strength to fight on our own. Thank You for interceding in times when You have.

O Lord help us to slow down and rest in You. Like a child in his mother's or father's care, help us to rest and rely upon You. Help us to take the time daily to commune with You. Please speak to us in the quietness of our souls so that our lives, thoughts, hearts, and actions can be directed toward what is high and holy and toward great and marvelous things. Help us to be still and help us to focus upon You and Your will for our lives this day. We love You Lord. Thank You for loving and blessing us. Thank You for answering our prayers. Give us faith and focus so we might receive the fullness of Your blessings and Your revelation and will for us. In Jesus name do we pray, Amen.

DAY 330

– DAY 331 –

PSALM 132

O God of all generations bless the seed of Your servants. We recognize each generation must serve You for themselves; however we stand in intercession for those who will be coming after us. We pray they will know You for themselves as the only true and living God. We pray they will know Your faithfulness for themselves. We pray they will honor You with their tithes and offerings and the first fruits of all they have. We pray they will confess Jesus Christ as Savior and Lord. We pray the anointing of the Holy Spirit will rest upon them. We pray they will love You with all of their hearts and with all of their souls and with all of their minds.

O God, the coming generation will live in a world we cannot even conceive. We pray however they will have traditional values such as integrity, discipline, sound ethics, good morals and hard and honest work. We pray they will know that technology cannot deliver – only You the true and living God can bring quality and abundance of live. We pray they will know that "righteousness exalts a nation but sin is a reproach to any people (Proverbs 14:34)."

O God, we pray they will be so close to You that You will establish a new covenant with them and You would abide with them and their children forever. O God, when to the left or right they would stray, we intercede and plead for mercy on their behalf. O God as You have kept generations in times past, so keep the coming generations. More than others they will have so many means for self-destruction. Unlike others the environment will be in worse shape than it has even been before. We pray that the sins of the past will not be unduly visited upon the generations to come. O covenant keeping God, we put our seed and all generations to come in Your hand. Please bless and take care of them as You have done for us and our mothers and fathers, and their mothers and fathers, and their mothers and fathers, even to the dawn of creation. We pray this prayer in the strong and eternal name of Jesus Christ, Amen.

DAY 331

– DAY 332 –

PSALM 134

O God, we come into Your presence to praise You for all of Your servants who love You enough to find joy in doing whatever their hands find to do. We praise You for Your servants who do not clamor for the spotlights but serve in ways and in places that often go unnoticed and taken for granted. We praise You for the ushers who provide hospitality for all who enter Your sanctuary. We praise You for kitchen workers who labor to provide sustenance for the saints. We praise You for maintenance workers who labor to keep Your temple and Your house clean. We praise You for the security personnel and volunteers whose ministry is to provide for Your people to work and worship in safety. We praise You for the parking lot personnel who accommodate the vehicles of Your children who gather for worship. We praise You for office staff who answer telephones, prepare bulletins, do the filing, and who answer a variety of questions to assist Your children in various ways.

We praise You for those who work in nurseries so young parents may be able to enjoy worship. We praise You for those who look after the needs of Your pastors and preachers so they can focus on Your word. We praise You for the background choir members who never sing a lead solo but whose voices blend in with the whole so the choir can produce a pleasing sound. We praise You for those who work in the Sunday School and who provide ministries of Christian nurture and education. We praise You for those who work on the books and who attempt to keep the financial matters of Your church in order. We praise You for those who visit the sick and minister to those in need without fanfare. We praise You for those who drive vans and buses so Your children can arrive at church in safety. We praise You for those who have ministries of encouragement and who have been major blessings to more lives than anyone will ever know. We praise You for those who intercede in prayer for the well-being of the church and its pastors.

Bless all who serve You in whatever capacity with a willing spirit and a joyful attitude. We pray that their tribes will increase and that they will eat of the fat of the land. We pray they will be able to sit under their own vine and fig trees and live long, healthy and prosperous lives. In Jesus name do we pray, Amen.

– DAY 333 –

PSALM 135: 15-18

O God, we recognize that we become what we worship. Help us to worship only You O living God so we will have true life. Help us to worship only You O God of steadfast love so we will be faithful and resolute. Help us to worship only You O God of truth so we will be truthful in word and deed. Help us to worship on You O God grace and mercy so we will be gracious and merciful. Help us to worship only You O God of patience and forgives so we will be patient and forgiving of others who have wronged us. Help us to worship only You O God of power and strength so we will exercise the right kind of power. Help us to worship only You O God of glory so we will reflect the glory of Your image upon our lives. Help us to worship only You O God of holiness and righteousness so we will live holy and righteous lives. Help us to worship only You O God of live so love will be our defining and motivating and guiding principle.

Help us to worship on You O God of goodness so goodness and mercy will follow us all he days of our lives. Help us to worship only You O God of salvation and deliver so we might be instruments for saving and delivering those who are lost. Help us to worship on You O God of healing so we might be healing agents to those who are broken in body, mind and spirit. Help us to worship You O God the Father of our Lord and Savior Christ so we might live for Jesus Christ and him only. Help us to worship You Holy Spirit so that we will live by the power and under the anointing of Your Holy Spirit.

O Creator God our desire is to be like You. O Jesus Christ Our Redeemer our desire is to be like You. O Holy Spirit, our empowering comforter and guide, our desire is to be like You. Help us to follow what is highest ad noblest and best all the day of our lives. And when we would stray remind us gracious God of who we are and what our greatest desire ought to be. Give us strength to resist when we are tempted to do that which causes distance between You and us. Give us strength to resist that which slows or stunts or prevents Your vision for us from developing within us. We truly love You Lord. Now grant to us the power to live this day according to that which brings honor to You who are our first love. In Christ name do we pray, Amen.

– DAY 334 –

PSALM 136

O God, how awesome is Your presence and how mighty is Your steadfast love which endure forever.

How mighty is Your power and how awesome is Your steadfast love which endure forever.

How glorious is Your power and how marvelous is Your steadfast love which endure forever.

How marvelous is Your holiness and how glorious is Your steadfast love which endure forever.

How delightful are the thoughts of Your mind and how pleasing is Your steadfast love which endure forever.

How pleasing are the works of Your hand and how delightful is Your steadfast love which endure forever.

How great are Your promises and how mighty is Your steadfast love which endure forever.

How mighty is Your throne and how great is Your steadfast love which endure forever.

How unexplainable are Your ways and how inexhaustible is Your steadfast love which endure forever.

O God of grace and glory, O God of mercy and might, O God of fire and forgiveness, O God of conquest and comfort, O God of strength and salvation, we love You, we bless You, we magnify Your name. Thank You for loving us first, because Your steadfast love endures forever.

In the name of our ever loving, ever living, and ever saving Christ do we pray, Amen.

DAY 334

– DAY 335 –

PSALM 137

O God in the midst of life's ups and downs and in the midst of life's fluctuating and changing scenes we pray we will never lose our song. We pray we will never lose our faith. We pray we will never lose our joy of service. Amidst questions we cannot answer and trials that stretch our faith to its limits, we pray we will always be able to pray with the confidence and assurance of victory. We pray we will always be able to assert that there is light beyond the midnight no matter how deep and dark and devastating nighttime may be.

O God there are sick among us who are struggling not to hang up their harps and faith and hope. There are those who have been devastated by disappointment, heartache and pain who are considering hanging up their harp of worship. There are those who have grown weary in praying for things that have not come to pass and are considering hanging up their harps of hope. Sometimes the enemy comes close to us and whispers in our ears, "Hang up Your harps. God does not hear You and God does not care. Hang up Your harps because prayer does not work. It is only a sending forth of words into the air. It is only the vain hope of weak fools who are mired in the quicksand's of delusion."

O God when the enemy or when life come upon us with such words and we are tempted to hang up our harps or when it seems they will be torn from our hands and that our hands and our songs will dry up, we pray for a mind that turns to worship. We pray for faith to pray. We pray for peace in You and Your love and Your divine providence. We pray for a mind to remember Your promises of ultimate victory and Your unceasing love. We pray that anger and bitterness will never overtake our souls. O God when we are weeping bitter tears by the rivers of our own Babylon's please blow fresh winds of renewal and revival into our souls. And we shall praise You in temple, or field or market place or by the rivers of Babylon or wherever we may be. In Jesus name do we pray, Amen.

DAY 335

– DAY 336 –

PSALM 138: 8

O God fulfill Your purpose in us. Not our plans but Your purpose; not our wants but Your will. We confess O God that at times we are headstrong and that our desires run ahead of our prayers. We proceed full speed ahead without even asking for Your direction. And when we seek Your counsel we are often too impatient to wait for it, and too anxious to be still so we might listen to Your still small voice.

We confess O God that too often we listen to our flesh, we listen to others, we even listen to the enemy. Yet O God You know we love You and in our heart of hearts, our desire is to do You will. So O God fulfill Your purpose in us. We are grateful for Your steadfast love. Please do not forsake the works of Your hands. For without You we are like ships without rudders and sails. We go nowhere. Without You we are like fire without oxygen. Our lights soon go out. Without You we are like erupting volcanoes. We are explosive and out of control. Without You we are like bells without clangers. Our lives make no melodies. Without You we are like music without notes. We have no coordination, only confusion.

So God, we pray You will fulfill Your purpose in us. We praise You for Your steadfast love that endures forever. Please do not forsake the work of Your hands. In Jesus name do we pray, Amen.

– DAY 337 –

PSALM 139: 1-3

O God, You have searched us and known us and are acquainted with all of Your ways. You know us better than we know ourselves. You know we have a heart for You. You know that our first and primary desire is to do Your will. You also know how much we have to struggle with certain things to remain true to You and to our calling, O Lord we pray You will continue to hold us close. When we rebel against Your way of truth and Your path of righteousness, hold us close. When we work against our own growth and the vision You have for our life, hold us close. When we seem determined to persist in a trend that holds our own destruction, hold us close. When we sin and grieve Your heart, please do not withdraw Your hand from us. Keep Your face turned toward us and Your eye upon us. When we fall from grace, hold us close. When we persist in walking in our own willful ways, please Lord hold us close.

When we sacrifice long-term rewards for short-term pleasures, hold us close. When we get tired of walking the straight and narrow way, please Lord hold us close. When we want things to happen right away and are tempted to take short cuts that further delay or frustrate Your plans of good for us, please hold us close. When the devil sends temptation after temptation our way and we are inclined to forsake the riches of the kingdom for temporary relief from the stresses and strains of life, please hold us close.

Then Lord when, we reach those moments when we don't know what to do or what to say, hold us close. When we are about to make mistakes because we don't know what Your will is, hold us close. When we are about to hurt those who love us and believe in us, hold us close. When we feel harried and hemmed in, hold us close. When death begins to look attractive because we are tired of the loads we carry, hold us close to You O Lord.

We have prayed this prayer to You before; we pray it again because our souls need to cry out again unto You. O Lord You have searched us and known us. You know when we sit down and when we rise up. You discern our thoughts from far away. You are acquainted with all of our ways, so Lord hold us close.

We feel like parentless children, hold us close heavenly Father. We feel alone and weak and vulnerable hold us close O blessed Savior, Christ, our Elder Brother and Lord. We feel as if the very ground upon which we stand is shaking, unstable and about to give way beneath us, hold us close O comforting Holy Spirit. You, know us better than we know ourselves, hold us close. Lead us and we shall be led the right way, the best way, the highest way and the noblest way. Speak to us and we shall be comforted. Befriend us and we shall have a friend who sticks closer than any brother. O Spirit of comfort, please hold us close even when we come to the end of this tedious journey and face the great divide called death. We love You and will praise Your forever more, just please Lord continue to hold us close. In Your name do we pray, Amen.

DAY 337

– DAY 338 –

PSALM 139: 14

So fragile, yet so forceful; so gentle and yet so much for potential for greatness; so weak but yet so strong –God, You have fearfully and wonderfully made us and we praise You for being an example of Your handiwork. You have formed our inward parts and have knit us together in our mothers' wombs. We praise You O God for personally stamping us with Your divine hand and giving us our own identity of individuality.

You do not have a one size fits all approach to creation. You do not use a cookie cutter mold to frame and fashion us. Each of us has been custom designed. Each of us is an original, a unique representation of divine diversity. O God thank You for caring so much about us that You have made us individuals so You will recognize our voice, see our need and use our unique talent to Your glory.

God, while we celebrate our individuality, we pray we will never forget community. We are not islands living unto ourselves. We pray we will seek to serve and bless others with gifts You have given to us. Teach us and help us to live with one another. Give to us an ongoing sensitivity and consciousness of Your love for diversity in the midst of unity. Teach us the difference between unity and uniformity so that all we are as individuals will blend in with Your hopes for us as a church, a species, a community, a family, and an ethnic group.

Wonderful are Your works O God individually and collectively. Help us to let our lights so shine so others will see our good works and glorify You Creator, Sustainer, Redeemer and Friend in Jesus' name, Amen.

DAY 338

– DAY 339 –

PSALM 139: 23-24

O God, You have fearfully and wonderfully made us, You who know us better than we know ourselves. On this day we pray that You would search us and know our hearts and test us and know our thoughts. See if there is any wicked way in us and lead us in the way everlasting.

When we would become self-righteous and arrogant, search us O Lord. When we start thinking of ourselves more highly than we ought, search us O Lord. When we start being overly judgmental and critical of others, search us O God. In our moments of truth when we confront our own faults and failings we are almost too embarrassed to make this request because we know how far we fall short of the glory of God. Still for the sake of our souls, our hearts, our minds, our very lives, we pray – search us O God.

For when you search, You simply don't expose what shouldn't be, You don't simply condemn us or write us off as incorrigible, but with the skill of a surgeon, we ask You to remove what is cancerous and what is not of You. With the strength of a father we ask You to shoulder what we cannot carry ourselves. With the love of a mother we ask You to correct what is amiss. And with the wisdom of a good shepherd we ask You to lead us into the way everlasting.

If we follow the devil, we will walk in the way of death but You are the way everlasting. If we follow our own whims, we walk in the way of foolishness but You are the way everlasting. If we follow our own appetites and ravings, we walk in the way of the temporal but You are the way everlasting.

O God lead us into the way everlasting where the wicked cease from troubling and the weary are at rest. Lead us into the way everlasting because that is where Jesus is. Lead us into the way everlasting we pray, in Jesus name, Amen.

DAY 339

– DAY 340 –

PSALM 139: 23-24

Gracious God, we are grateful You love us so much that we can dare ask You to search us. We know You will see some things that offend Your holiness and grieve Your heart. We know You will see some things that should not be in our hearts and lives we may not even be aware are there ourselves. However, God You made us and You know all about us. You know the potential You have placed within us. You know the vision You have for our lives. You know our strengths and our weaknesses better than we do. And we are so grateful You know us better than the enemy.

O Lord help us to see ourselves as You see us. And then help us to live according to Your vision and Your will. We pray for deliverance from the spirit and attitude that blames others for what we should take responsibility for. Bring to our minds knowledge and remembrance of those we have wronged and then prepare us to make amends to them. We pray we will never be too big or arrogant to say, "I'm sorry." We pray we will never be too arrogant or big to say, "Forgive me." We pray we will never be too arrogant or big to say, "Thank You." We pray we will never be too arrogant or big to say, "Please."

O God as You search us and help us to see ourselves and take responsibility for our mistakes we pray we will know that all is not lost and that we can yet live to be the persons You would have us to be. Lead us to the way everlasting. As You led the children of Israel through the Red Sea, O Lord lead us. As You have led Your church in days past and gone, O Lord lead us. As You have led our ancestors from through dangers seen and unseen, O Lord lead us. And when to the right or to the left we would stray, gently lead us back into the right path.

Lead us from damnation to deliverance, from sin to salvation, from valleys low to mountains high, from rejection to redemption and from earth to eternity. Lead us in the way everlasting. And we shall give You the praise, the honor and the glory, forever and ever. In the name of the Lord Jesus do we pray, Amen.

DAY 340

– DAY 341 –

PSALM 140

Deliver us O Lord from those who would do us harm, particularly those whom we do not recognize as enemies. O Lord in this life when there are so many persons who are not what they seem, in this life when there is an abundance of wolves in sheep skins, in the life when the enemy has planted persons to bring us down, protect us from those who would do us harm whom we do not recognize as enemies.

Help us not to pray against enemies but to pray for our own discernment, regarding their enticing plans that tickle the ear and delight the mind but whose end is destruction. O God we must confess that sometimes it is so difficult to love those who are a burden to us. It is so difficult not to pray against those who betray us, who undermine us, who drain our joy, and without whom service to You would be so much more of a delight. O God we must confess that it is hard not to pray against those who cause us pain and who seem to hinder the work of Your kingdom. Sometimes we must confess we get so angry with them and with You because You allow them to be such thorns in our flesh.

O God, we must confess we cannot like them or even love them on our own. We must confess we are not even motivated to reach out to them as fellow believers. It is so much easier to keep on disliking them, talking about them, or avoiding them. Help us O Lord in our daily confrontations and interactions with those we just don't like to remember they may feel the same way about us as we feel about them. And just as You do not punish us because others do not like us or find us difficult, You are too just and kind to withdraw Your hand of mercy from others because we do not like them.

We do ask O Lord that You frustrate the plans and plots of those who would harm us. We do ask O Lord that You give us discernment to recognize truth from falsehood when we see it. We do ask O Lord that You would give us discernment so we would recognize friends from enemies and enemies from friends. We do ask O Lord that You would guard and guide our tongues and our actions so we would never give fuel to the fodder of enemies. We do ask that You would help us to search our lives to see where we may be in error.

We do ask O Lord that You would keep our souls from bitterness, our spirits from sourness and our minds focused on You O God of grace and mercy, who prepares tables before us in the presence of our enemies. We ask O Lord that in our confrontations with those who would harm us that we would always be mindful that the weapons of our warfare are not physical or carnal but spiritual. Equip us O Lord so we will live in Your strength, endure in Your patience, and receive the victory in Your way and time. In the name of Your Son who gave his life as a ransom for many, even for those who crucified him do we pray, Amen

DAY 341

– DAY 342 –

PSALM 142: 5

O God, we come into Your presence because we realize You are our only true and lasting refuge in times of turmoil and stress. Not our money-You are our only true and lasting refuge. Not our jobs or our position-You are our only true and lasting refuge. Not our age or our education or credentials-You are our only true and lasting refuge. Not our family name or our social and political connections- You are our only true and lasting refuge. Not our righteousness or our religion-You are our only true and lasting refuge.

Thanks You God for sheltering us from the stormy blast and tempest until such time we recovered to continue the good fight of faith. Thank You for being only a prayer away. Thank You for not allowing our enemies to destroy us. Thank You for Your mercy when we made our own beds hard. Thank You for being there even when we did not know You were. Thank You for rescuing us when we were vainly trying to take matters into our own hands and making a greater mess of them. Thank You for seeing what we needed even before or even when we did not have the sense to ask. O faithful and ever sufficient refuge in this the land of the living, we praise Your holy name.

Because You are our refuge we have hope that our healing will come in this the land of the living. Because You are our refuge we can believe that no matter how bleak the present or dim the forecast for the future, we can yet see dreams come true and Your will consummated for our good in this the land of the living. Because You are our refuge when others see death we see hope and help in this the land of the living. Because You are our refuge we believe our prayers long delayed in being answered will become realities in this the land of the living.

Thank You O Refuge for being a right now God. Because You are our refuge we have strength right now. Your promises for good are fulfilled right now. Your presence can be felt right now. We can have joy overwhelming and full of glory right now. We can have peace in the midst of our battles right now. We praise You O right now God. We worship You O right now Christ. We extol You O right now Holy Spirit. And we view with new vision the places where we are in this the land of the living. O refuge for the tempest tossed and strength for the weary, we bless Your name. Thank You

DAY 342

for being our Rock in a weary land and our shelter in the time of storm. Thanks You for being our strong tower and bulwark that never fails. We offer this prayer in the strong name of Jesus the tested, tried and true cornerstone through whom we become living stones, Amen.

DAY 342

– DAY 343 –

PSALM 141: 2

O God again on this day our prayer is that You will teach us to pray. We pray that our prayers will always honor and bring delight to You. We pray that the words of our mouths and the mediations of our hearts uttered and breathed in prayer will be acceptable in Your sight and a sweet savor to You.

We pray for a praying spirit that seeks Your face and favor morning, noon and night. We pray we will be saved from vain repetitions and meaningless clichés. We pray we will be delivered from wandering thoughts and requests we don't really mean.

Give us focus O God in our praying. Save us from pretension and preening self-righteousness in our prayers. We pray for a life of prayer and lifestyles that honor You. Our prayers are a delight when they emerge from hearts that are pure, eyes that are single to Your glory and lives that are holy unto You. Help us to live our prayer. Help us to pray believing and with anticipation. We love You Lord. Our delight is in You, Your word, Your will, Your Son, and Your Spirit. In Jesus name, Amen.

DAY 343

– DAY 344 –

PSALM 143: 10

O Lord teach us to do Your will and help us to lead a transformed life and forgive us when we follow our own lusts and passions. Help us to overcome lust—physical lust; lust for power; lust for things; lust for what belongs to others; lust for the spotlight. Help us to walk as children of the light as You have called us to be.

Forgive us Lord when our own weaknesses prevent us from doing Your will or grieve You or quench Your Spirit from flowing forth freely and reaching its potential in our lives. O God we pray for grace and for mercy.

You know that our greatest desire is to do Your will even when we follow our own. Teach us to do Your will and follow Your will so that our lives can be transformed thereby. Teach us Your will O Lord and lead us on level path—a levelheaded, doctrinally sound, humbly sanctified, temperate, clear thinking, right discerning, a serviceable way that is a blessing other—a level path.

Fulfill Your will in us O Lord inspite of ourselves. Forgive us of our sins and help us never to give up on ourselves. Through Jesus Christ our Lord we claim our victory and in His name do we pray, Amen.

DAY 344

– DAY 345 –

PSALM 144: 7

O Lord stretch out Your hand from on high because we are sinking fast and we need You to catch us and hold us lest we perish through our own foolishness and mistakes.

O Lord stretch out Your healing hand because from head to toe we are either sick within or sick without. We have hurts that are undiagnosed and pain that nobody know about but the two of us. We need healing internally and externally. We need healing of body, mind and spirit.

O God stretch out Your saving hand. We are in bondage Lord—financial bondage, relationship bondage, flesh bondage, habit bondage, mental and emotional bondage. O Lord God stretch out Your saving and delivering hand in Christ Jesus incarnate and intercessor.

O Lord stretch out Your blessing hand and provide for us such things we stand in need of. And when You bless God, we pray for a proper sense of stewardship as we manage our blessings.

O Lord stretch out Your merciful hand because mercy suits our case. We confess that we willfully and deliberately do those things which are displeasing in Your sight and which grieve You. O Lord please have mercy.

O Lord stretch out Your empowering hand. Equip us to do the work of ministry. Bless our mission and our missionaries. Bless our efforts and our excellence. Strengthen us for work and witness so people will see Your handiwork within us. Keep your hand upon us. We give You the glory. In Jesus name, do we pray, Amen.

– DAY 346 –

PSALM 145: 2

God, we truly love You and our desire is that our life is one continuous song of praise and service to You. We pray for a heart that will praise You every day. Not just on days set apart for worship, not just in seasons when all is well, and not just in good times – our desire is for a spirit of praise that extols You every day. In sickness and in wellness, in brokenness and in wholeness, when we can see our way clear and when we cannot, O God give us such a heart for You that we will learn to praise You every day. Our desire is to praise You on blue Mondays, on troublesome Tuesdays, on draining Wednesday, on boring Thursday, and busy Fridays, or tempting Saturdays – our desire is to praise You every day.

To praise You every day, we must have a heart of thanksgiving for blessing we sometimes take for granted. O God give us such a heart. To praise You every day we must have joy that is eternal and full of glory. O God give us such a heart. To praise You every day we must have a strong will and a determined spirit. O God give us such a will and spirit. To praise You every day we must have a love that bears all things, endures all things, hopes all things and believes all things contained in Your word. O God give us such love. To praise You every day we must have a soul that is on fire for You. O God give us such fire and such a soul. To praise You every day we must live a life of true prayer. O God help us to walk in such a life of prayer. To praise You every day we must be close to You. O God we covet such closeness. To praise You every day we must be close to You. O God we covet such closeness. To praise You every day we must live a God glorifying life. O God we strive for such a life. And if we should ever stray, we pray the Holy Spirit will direct us in finding our way back to You so we can restore the brokenness that our weaknesses have caused and the bind the rifts our sins create.

O God, You are good all of the time. We pray for faith that helps us to see Your hand of blessings, provision and care even when we experience the Middle passages and the Holocausts of life. God give us the faith to praise You every day. This we ask in Jesus name, Amen.

DAY 346

– DAY 347 –

PSALM 146

O God, we praise You for Your eternity. We extol You for Your greatness. We honor You for Your holiness. We love for Your concern for the poor. And so we bring their plight to You.

We pray for the oppressed, the victimized, the voiceless masses among Your children who suffer hunger, experience want and privation, and who are the victims of the politics and machinations of the principalities and power, the politics of greed and selfishness, the spiritual, political and economic wickedness in high places.

We bring the children of the world to You. We bring children who are victims of war, the exploitation of the sex industry, the victims of abuse, and those who suffer hunger. We bring street children to You. We bring children who are born addicted to drugs and who have a proclivity to alcohol. We bring AIDS infected children. We bring children whose potential is being snuffed out by poverty, racism and sexism. O God have mercy and alleviate suffering and minister according to Your power and mercy even now. Rescue and redeem even now.

We bring the women of the world to You. O God we come against strongholds of chauvinism, sexism, errant machismo, and exclusive spheres of male dominance and power. Search the hearts of those of us who are male. Try us and know our minds, and if there is any wicked way within us, instruct us now, purge us now, rebuke us now, cleanse us now, redeem us now, remake us now — and lead us into the way everlasting, in the name of Jesus.

Rescue we pray, mothers, daughters, sisters, wives, grandmothers, the elderly, orphans, widows, the culturally, economically, politically and personally dominated who are caste and encased in situations that have them bound.

We bring the elderly. We bring men, young adults and teenagers. We bring the hurting everywhere-in North America, South America, Africa, Asia, Australia, the Pacific Rim, the Caribbean, other islands of the seas, Europe, and other places we don't know to call. We bring those who are imprisoned unjustly. O God please have mercy. Extend Your hand of power, move within us, and liberate today so the kingdoms of this world and the strongholds of Satan become the kingdoms and strongholds of our Lord and of His Christ.

Thanks You God for hearing us. Thank You God for those who are beginning to feel relief, comfort, empowerments, salvation and liberation, even as we have called. Thank You God for the hungry who are being fed and the suffering that are being alleviated even as we have called. Thank You God for yokes that are being destroyed, for prisoners who are receiving and who will receive justice even as we have called. Thanks You God for the elderly, the lonely, the destitute, and the forgotten that are being ministered to even as we have called.

Thank You God for stirring us and touching hearts who are able to help, even as we have called. Thank You God for what You have already done, for what You are doing and for what You will yet do on behalf of the victimized and voiceless of the world, who are Your children created by Your hand, made in Your own image, saved by the blood of You Son, and now equipped by the power of Your Holy Spirit. In Jesus name we pray, Amen.

– DAY 348 –

PSALM 147: 15

O God, we praise You for Your word which reminds us of who is really in charge. Though Satan rages and sin seems to run rampart, we praise You for Your word and command which saves us from despair and surrender because we know who is really in charge. Although we become hooked on our own agenda and caught up in our own self-serving ways, we praise You for Your word and command which remind us who is really in charge.

Your word has declared that the earth is Yours and the fullness thereof, the world and they that dwell therein — we praise You O God.

Your word has declared that You have allotted the times of existence for the nations — we praise You O God.

Your word has declared that You have measured the waters in the hollow of You hand and marked off the heavens with a span; You have enclosed the dust of the earth in a measure and weighed them mountains in scales and hills in a balance — we praise You O God (Isaiah 40:12).

Your word has declared, the grass withers, the flowers fade but Your word will stand forever. Our Christ of God has declared that heaven and earth will pass away but his word will never pass away — we praise You O God.

Your word has declared that there shall be a new heaven and a new earth where wickedness and death are no more — we praise You O God.

Your word has declared You to be Creator and Your Son to be Judge, Lord and King of all the earth — we praise You O God.

Your word has declared that You send out commands to the earth and Your word runs swiftly — we praise You O God.

In Jesus name do we praise You. In Jesus name do we come before You and bow in Your presence. In Jesus name do we approach Your throne with expectancy, Amen.

DAY 348

– DAY 349 –

PSALM 149: 4

O God, we pray we will always give You pleasure O God, Creator of the heavens and the earth, You have created us in Your very own image, we pray we will always give You pleasure. O God, You who are greater than we will ever be able to conceive, we pray we will always give You pleasure. O God of our salvation we pray we will always give You pleasure. O God who has loved us enough to come personally in the life of Jesus Christ to redeem and reconcile use, we pray we will always give You pleasure.

We pray our service will give You pleasure. We pray our worship and praise will give You pleasure. We pray our prayers to You will always give You pleasure. We pray our lives will always give You pleasure. We pray our tithes and offering will always give You pleasure. We pray our efforts to be a blessing to Your children, and our brothers and sisters in humanity, will always give You pleasure. And when we sin and fall short of Your glory, please O God forgive us and know that the first desire of our heart is to give You pleasure. You are so good, and gracious and patient and kind, we delight in giving You pleasure. Your Holy Spirit is so sweet and empowering we delight in giving You pleasure. Your Son Jesus is so precious to our souls we delight in giving You pleasure. Your grace is beyond sufficient for all of our needs, we delight in giving You pleasure. We love You O God of our salvation, please accept this love song from our heart to Yours. We offer it in the name by which we receive access to the throne of grace, even Jesus Christ our Lord, Amen.

DAY 349

– DAY 350 –

PSALM 150

We praise You for who You are. We praise You for Your excellent greatness. We praise You for Your quintessential holiness. We praise You for Your righteous power. We praise You for Your ever giving life sustaining and soul saving love. We praise You for Jesus Christ, incarnate, crucified, risen, ascended, exalted, interceding, and coming back again who lives eternally. We praise You for Your Holy Spirit. We praise You for the church, battle scarred and triumphant. We praise You for oikoumene, the whole inhabited earth. We praise You for every creature upon the earth, in the air, in the sea and under the earth. We praise You for majestic mountains, turquoise skies, dancing stars, laughing daffodils, roses with thorns, and mighty oaks. We praise You for the ocean with its mighty tides, waves and mysteries.

Now we praise You for what You have done for us in Christ Jesus. We praise You for blessings we often take for granted—our families, our jobs, our health, our strength, our sound mind, our church, our friends, our admirers, our education, our possessions, our money, our salvation, our very life itself. All that we have is Yours O Lord, we make it available to You and we give it to You as a praise offering and a thank offering. We praise You for the privilege of exercising managerial stewardship over so much.

O God when we think of who You are and how much You have done for us, if we had ten thousand tongues we couldn't praise You enough. And so we praise You with the one tongue we have. We praise You in the sanctuary. We praise You in our homes. We praise You in the streets. We praise You at school. We praise You in our leisure. We praise You in laughter. We praise You with tears. We praise You in tongues. We praise You with tambourine and dance. We praise You with whatever instruments we have. With everything we have we praise You O God. Praise the Lord. Let everything and everyone who has breath praise the Lord.

Let every bear in the woods growl, Hallelujah! Let every lion in the forest roar, Hallelujah! Let every fish in the sea gulp, Hallelujah! Let every rooster that crows, cry out Hallelujah! Let every canary that chirps sing Hallelujah! Let everything that has breath, praise the Lord.

Praise the Lord! Praise the Lord, You empires! Praise the Lord, You lands! Praise the lord, You rulers, princes, presidents, and monarchs! Praise the Lord, people of every tribe in every nation, in every village and hamlet, city and state, county and province and region. Praise the Lord! For You alone O God are worthy of all praise. In Jesus name do we offer this prayer of thanksgiving and praise, Amen.

DAY 350

– DAY 351 –

GENESIS 26: 17-22

Gracious God, we praise You for Your comforting and empowering presence. We praise You for the privilege of prayer and worship. We are grateful that we can bring all of our cares and all of our hurts to You. We bring to You the hurt of rejection. Some of us are experiencing or have experienced rejection from various members of our families such as mother, father, brother, sister or those who are in our extended family network and rejection hurts O God.

Some of us are experiencing or have experienced rejection from someone we love romantically such as a spouse, a significant other, special friend or companion or someone we would like to be romantically involved with but they do not feel the same way about us. That rejection still hurts, O God.

Some of us are experiencing or have experienced rejection in our political relationships, or socials relationships, or from our peers, our colleagues or groups we would like to join or a team we would like to be part of. That rejection stills hurts, O God. Some of us are experiencing or have experienced rejection in our career, on the job, when we were turned down for a promotion or we did not land the job we wanted. That rejection still hurts, O God.

Some of us have even felt what seemed like rejection from You O God, and that rejection hurts most of all. We have earnestly prayed for something and You have sent a reject slip or a resounding no to our request. That rejection still hurts, O God. Even though we may have the experience of looking back over our lives and seeing where Your no's opened up some other doors and opportunities later on, and even though we may one day praise You for saying no to some of our prayers, the fact of the matter is that when the first no comes to us, when we become aware that You were not going to do what we have asked, and things will not turn out as we have prayed, the rejection at the moment hurts.

Gracious God we pray for the power and presence of the Lord Jesus that he may renew us and guide us to our own Rehoboth, the place of breakthrough and restoration. In Your name Lord Jesus do we offer this prayer, with praise and thanksgiving, Amen.

– DAY 352 –

DEUTERONOMY 1: 6

Gracious God we confess that like the children of Israel we have come to our own "Mt. Horebs", the places of divine visitation and worship and that like them we too have become sidetracked and distracted and we have fallen into sin. However, we have received the same word You spoke to them, "You have stayed at this mountain long enough", and for so many of us, and it really is time to move on."

We confess O God we have cried over our past long enough; it's time to move on. We have beat up on ourselves about our stupidity long enough; it's time to move on. We have talked about the money we have lost long enough; it's time to move on. We have been angry long enough; it's time to move on. We have lied and talked about how good it used to be long enough; it's time to move on. We exaggerated about how bad it was long enough; it's time to move on. We have felt sorry for ourselves long enough; it's time to move on.

Forgive us O God because we have been carrying guilt and shame long enough; it's time to move on. We have been coming up with reasons not to tithe long enough; it's time to move on. We have been living in financial bondage long enough; it's time to move on. We have been hanging around with the same negative, complaining, going nowhere, dead end crowd long enough; it's time to move on. We have been talking about what we are going to do and the changes we are going to make next week, next month, and next year long enough; it's time to move on.

Have mercy Lord because we have been talking about going back to school long enough; it's time to move on. We have been talking about opening up Your own business long enough; it's time to move on. We have been complaining about our situation long enough; it's time to move on. We have been fighting the same old battles and rehashing the same old issues long enough; it's time to move on. We have been walking around jumping at our shadow and living in fear long enough, it's time to move on.

Lord Christ You came that we might have life more abundantly. You lived, died and rose again so we might walk in newness of life. We pray for courage and faith to move from where we are to the new places You are calling us to be in You. In Your own name Lord Jesus do we offer this prayer, Amen.

DAY 352

– DAY 353 –

EXODUS 8: 8-10

O God we, confess that like Pharaoh of old, there have been times we have opted to spend one more night with the frogs, and said tomorrow when we should have said today. We confess O God there have been times when we have said, "I'll quit or I'll start doing the right thing tomorrow,. One last pack of cigarettes, one more puff of marijuana, one more snort of coke, one more vial of crack, one more injection of heroin, one night with the frogs and then I'll be ready for deliverance. Tomorrow we will be a different day. One more heavy meal, one more dessert, one more time to over eat, one more night or meal with the frogs, and tomorrow I'll start my diet. Tomorrow I'll be ready for deliverance."

"One more lie to get me out of this situation, one more night with the frogs and after that, on tomorrow I'll start telling the truth. One more night with this person, one more time of yielding to my flesh, one more night with the frogs and then after that, I'll quit. One more time to repeat this bit of gossip, I have heard and then after that, I will stop spreading the story around. One more shopping spree and after that I will put myself on a budget. One more drink, one more day of sitting around doing nothing and tomorrow I will look for a job or a new job."

"Tomorrow I will fill out the application for school. Tomorrow I will make that call to the counselor. Tomorrow I will begin putting together my plan to start my business. Tomorrow or the next paycheck I will start saving or tithing. I'll apologize tomorrow; I'll start speaking to that person I am loathing tomorrow. I'll start clearing up that misunderstanding tomorrow." Just allow me to spend one night nursing my grudge; one more night with an attitude, one more night with the frogs, tomorrow, I'll be ready to let bygones be bygones.

Forgive us God for putting off until tomorrow what we should be doing today. Forgive us for the times we have even put You off, instead of responding to Your work, will and vision today. Help us to receive the grace, love, peace and salvation the Lord Jesus Christ offers right now. Help us to begin living in new ways in him and through him, even now. Help us to remember that now is the acceptable time and now is the day of salvation. In Your name Lord Jesus do we offer this prayer, Amen.

DAY 353

– DAY 354 –

ISAIAH 58: 6-9

Gracious God, we praise You for the possibilities of breakthrough living, and we thank You for Your words of instruction to the prophet that reminds us that our breakthroughs are not just for ourselves but for others.

Lord, we praise You because You have come to destroy every yoke – not only yolks of sin and addiction but yolks of poverty, war, political oppression and corruption, yolks of ignorance, yolks of economic exploitation, yolks of violence against women, yolks of pornography and sexual abuse and misuse of children, yolks of racism and sexism, yolks of religious self-righteousness, yolks of lost self-esteem which lead to low living and self-destructive behavior.

Thank You for reminding us O Lord that fasting, the spiritual disciplines, sacrifice, obedience to the word of God lead to breakthrough living not just in our own lives but also in the lives of others who have no voice but ours. You not only look at our faithfulness to You, You also look at our forgiveness of other people who belong to You. You not only delight in our holiness, You also desire us to help others. You not only observe our speaking in tongues, You also take note to how we speak tenderly to each other.

In Your eyesight how we treat others, what we do for others, is just as important as how we bear our crosses. Help us so to live that we experience Your promised through breakthrough, "then your light shall break forth like the dawn, and your healing shall spring up quickly; Your vindicator shall go before you, the glory of the Lord shall be Your rear guard. Then You shall call, and the Lord will answer; You shall cry for help, and he will say, "Here I am." We offer this prayer in the name of our Lord Jesus, Amen.

– DAY 355 –

I CORINTHIANS 3: 5-9

O God, You are the giver of visions and You give the growth. We pray You would grow Your vision for our lives in us. Not our vision Lord but grow Your vision for us in us. Not the vision of others Lord but grow Your vision for us in us. Our vision for ourselves may be limited by our own perception of our limited power. The vision of others for us may be limited by their opinion of our capabilities. But You, O Lord, know all about us. You know us better than others and better than we know ourselves. That's why we pray that You will grow Your vision for our life in us.

Help us to see ourselves as You see us. Help us to see the potential You see. Help us to see the gifts You see. Help us to see the strength You see. Help us to see what we can do when You are with us and when Your precious anointing is upon us. Help us to see what we can do when we stand upon Your word and claim Your promises in our lives. Help us to see what we can accomplish when the very power that shaped the very ends of the universe working within us and on our behalf when the Evil One attacks. Help us to see what we can do when the very power that blossoms the rose and churns the depths of the ocean is moving upon us and within us to build us up when life has torn us down. O God help us to see us as Christ must have seen us when he died to save us because he felt we were worth saving and that we were worth his sacrifice on Calvary.

O God grow us from pettiness to power and from shame to sanctification. Grow us from caterpillars to butterflies and from sinners to saints. Grow us from where we are to where we can be when we surrender ourselves to You and Your will for us and allow You to grow Your vision for our lives in us. Forgive us for those things that stifle the growth of Your vision for us. Forgive us for the thoughts, the talk and the sins that stifle, thwart, mar and delay the growth of Your vision for us. You envision great things for us O God and we praise You for desiring the very best for us. Help us to desire the best for ourselves and to die to self daily so Your vision may grow afresh in us and so we might press on toward the upward prize of the high calling in Christ Jesus. O God of grace, God of glory and God of growth, grow Your vision in us. We yield ourselves to You through Jesus Christ our Lord, Amen.

DAY 355

– DAY 356 –

II KINGS 5: 1-14

Gracious God, we praise You for what You did for Your servant Naaman even before he was healed. Even though he was a leper, we praise You because You made him into a mighty man of valor whom You used to lead his people to victory in battle. We are grateful that what defines the worth and significance of our life is not our imperfections but our willingness to allow You to use us to do what You want to do with us.

We are grateful You see us differently than others do. Where others see disease, You see a deliverer. Where others see grief, You see a general. Where others see a leper, You see a lifter. Where others see an outcast, You see an opportunity. Where others see a reject, You see a redeemer. Where others see vileness, You see valor. Where others see worthlessness, You see a warrior.

We are grateful that when we come to church with shame written all over our faces, or with insecurity etched into our souls, or with rejection eating away at our heart, or with anger burning away at our spirit or with failure destroying our imagination, because of what people think or because of how people have made us feel about ourselves, You have a different verdict about who we are and what we can yet become.

We praise You because one-day on a hill called Calvary, Jesus Christ, the Son of God, Jesus Christ, the Prince of Glory, Jesus Christ, the Servant of the Most High God, hung on a cross and interceded for our souls when sin had made them leprous and placed them under a death sentence.

We praise You because as Naaman dipped himself in the Jordan River and was made completely clean, if we confess our sins, the Lord Jesus is faithful and just to forgive our sins and cleanse us from all unrighteousness. We are grateful that his blood prevails over any and every thing which may be in our past, or may threaten our present or that may cancel out the future You see for us. We are grateful that if anyone is in Christ Jesus, if anyone is dipped in Christ Jesus, if anyone is cleansed and washed completely in Christ Jesus, he or she is a new creation, old things are passed away and all things are made new. In Your name, Lord Jesus, do we offer this prayer with praise and thanksgiving and a new commitment to live for You, Amen.

– DAY 357 –

JOHN 1: 35-46

We praise You, Lord Jesus, because You still have a vision for our lives that is greater than any vision we can have for ourselves or that others can have for us. We pray that when You call, like Your disciple Philip, we will have faith and vision to follow even if we must say goodbye to good people like John the Baptist because You represent the highest and best for our lives.

Help us to understand that John the Baptist is our anchor but You, Lord Jesus, represent our achievement. John the Baptist is our beginning but You, Lord Jesus, represent our breakthrough. John the Baptist is our new consciousness but You, Lord Jesus, represent our new creation. John the Baptist is our caregiver but You, Lord Jesus Christ, are our conqueror. John the Baptist is our designer but You, Lord Jesus, represent our destiny. John the Baptist is our example but You, Lord Jesus, represent our excellence. John the Baptist is our foundation but You, Lord Jesus, represent our future.

John the Baptist is good but You, Lord Jesus, represent greatness. John the Baptist is our help but You, Lord Jesus, represent our hope. John the Baptist is our joy but You, Lord Jesus, are a jewel. John the Baptist is kind but You, Jesus Christ, is our King. John the Baptist is our lifter but You, Jesus, alone are Lord. John the Baptist is our minimum but You, Lord Jesus, represent our maximum. John the Baptist is nice but You, Lord Jesus Christ, have the name before which every knee shall bow.

John the Baptist is our propulsion but You, Lord Jesus, represent our promotion. John the Baptist gives revelation but You, Lord Jesus Christ, are our redeemer. John the Baptist is our seed but You Lord, Jesus are our star. John the Baptist is our start but You Lord Jesus are our Savior. John the Baptist is our signpost but You, Lord Jesus Christ, are our satisfaction.

John the Baptist is our today but You, Lord Jesus, represent our tomorrow. John the Baptist is our threshold but You, Lord Jesus, represent our testimony. John the Baptist adds value to our lives but You, Lord Jesus, have a vision for our lives that is greater than any vision we can have for ourselves or that others can have for us. John the Baptist has worth but You, Lord Jesus Christ, alone are our worship.

In Your name, Lord Jesus, do we offer this prayer, Amen.

DAY 357

– DAY 358 –

JOHN 19: 25

Gracious God we are grateful that in the scriptures both mothers as well as those who have never had children make contributions. We honor Eve as the mother of all living humans. We honor Sarah as the mother of Isaac. We honor Hagar as the mother of Ishmael. We honor Rebecca as the mother of Esau and Jacob. We honor Leah as the mother of Reuben, Simeon, Levi, Judah, Issachar, Zebulun and Dinah. We honor Rachel as the mother of Joseph and Benjamin. We honor Jochebed as the mother of Moses who refused to give up her son to Pharaoh's edict to kill the male children of her race.

We honor Bathsheba as the mother of Solomon, who was born under the correct circumstances. We honor Rizpah who fought off buzzards and animals to preserve the bodies of her four sons. We honor Elizabeth as the mother of John the Baptist. We honor Mary of Nazareth as the mother of Jesus. Each of them, with their lives, their faith, their obedience and through their seed made significant contributions to salvation history.

However, lest we forget there is no biblical record that the prophetess Deborah who led her people to victory against their oppressors ever had children. There is not biblical record that the great Queen Vashti whose name lives in history as a woman of strength, dignity and conviction, ever had children. There is no biblical record that Esther, who was willing to die to save her people, ever had children. There is no biblical record that Mary and Martha who hosted Jesus on any number of occasions had children.

There is no biblical record that the Samaritan woman at the well to whom the Lord gave living water, had children, even though she had been divorced five times. There is no biblical record that Pilate's wife, who tried to intercede for the Lord's life, ever had children. There is no biblical record that Priscilla, who partnered with the apostle Paul, along with her husband Aquila, in spreading the Gospel, ever had children.

We are grateful that in Your kingdom none of need feel excluded. You have room for Mary the mother of the Lord Jesus and Mary Magdalene a single woman who never gave birth to children. We offer this prayer of praise and thanksgiving in the precious name of our Lord Jesus Christ, Amen.

DAY 358

– DAY 359 –

JOHN 19: 25-27

Jesus, keep me near the cross; There a precious fountain,
Free to all a healing stream, Flows from Calvary's mountain.

Near the cross, a trembling soul, Love and mercy found me;
There the bright and morning star sheds its beams around me.

Near the cross I'll watch and wait, Hoping trusting ever,
Till I reach the golden strand just beyond the river.

In the cross, in the cross, Be my glory ever,
Till my raptured soul shall find rest beyond the river.
(Dec 24 – Jesus, Keep Me Near the Cross, Fanny Crosby)

Gracious Lord Jesus, You have loved us with a most tender compassion and an undying and an unyielding commitment. In spite of the attacks of the devil, You have loved us with an undying and an unyielding love. In spite of the persecution and vileness of men, You have loved us with an undying and an unyielding love. In spite of our desertions, denials, weaknesses, betrayals and flaws, You have loved us with an undying and an unyielding love.

Not even the cross of Calvary with its darkness and destruction, disgrace and death, could get You to yield Your love for us. Thank You Lord Jesus. We praise Your holy name Lord Jesus. We pray that like the disciple John we will have the courage and the commitment, the loyalty and the love, the determination and the devotion to stand near You—in pain as well as in pleasure, in the dark as well as in the light.

When we stand near Your cross we can see You in ways others who stand afar off, cannot. When we stand near Your cross we feel the cleansing and redeeming touch of Your blood. When we stand near Your cross, we receive a fresh word and a new charge for our lives. We pray for faith to stand near Your cross not simply because of what we receive but simply because we love You for who You are, even as You have loved us as we are.

And when fear and doubt assail, O Lord Christ we pray for sacred remembrance of Your undying love so we will be encouraged to stand near the cross. In Your name do we offer this prayer, Lord Jesus, Amen.

DAY 359

– DAY 360 –

RUTH 2: 8-16

Gracious God, we are grateful we have been blessed by the best. As Boaz moved Ruth from the edges of the field to the center, You have moved us from the periphery to the center. David testified that You prepared a table before him in the presence of his enemies. We praise You for the mighty moves You have made in our lives.

From the last to the first, from the tail to the head, from the bottom to the top, from renting to owning, from being an employee to being an employer, from being a borrower to being a lender, O God You have brought us from the edges of the field to the center. From addiction to the anointing, from affliction to abundance, from bondage to breakthrough, from debt to deliverance, from failure to favor, from frustration to fulfillment, from heartache to happiness, from loneliness to love, from rejection to redemption, from sinning to salvation, from strongholds to sainthood, from trouble to triumph, You have brought us from the edges to the center of the field.

Gracious God, we are grateful that You specialize in blessing with the best. That's what it means to be a Christian we have been saved by the best, blessed by the best, kept by the best, empowered by the best, promised the best and are on our way to the best place.

During the Christmas season we pray that we will always be mindful of the unspeakable gift who is Jesus Christ our Lord. "For to us a child is born. To us a Son is given and the government shall be upon his shoulders. His name shall be called Wonderful, Counselor, the Mighty God, the Everlasting Father, the Prince of Peace, and of the increase of his government and peace there shall be no end."

"God (the greatest lover) so loved (the greatest degree) the world (the greatest number) that He gave (the greatest gift) that whosoever (the greatest invitation) believeth (the greatest simplicity) in Him (the greatest person) should not perish (the greatest deliverance) but (the greatest difference) have (the greatest certainty) everlasting life (the greatest possession). Thank You God!"

Now that we have been blessed by the best, our prayer is that our lives will reflect our blessings to Your honor and glory. In the name of the Lord Jesus do we offer this prayer, Amen.

– DAY 361 –

JOHN 21: 1-8

Lord Jesus, we must confess that like the disciples of yesterday that there have been times when we have returned to former lifestyles rather than seeking Your face and abiding in Your presence until Your will has been revealed to us. We confess Lord Jesus there have been times when we have leaned to our own understanding rather than asking You to direct our paths. We confess Lord Jesus there have been times when we have listened to others rather than Your word and the Holy Spirit who always lives and abides with us and within us.

We are grateful for Your presence O resurrected, living, reigning, interceding and soon coming back Lord. We are grateful that because You live we can rise from our past. Because You live, we can rise above our present. Because You live we can rise to our future. We pray that You will develop with in us the kicking and fighting back power we need to become what You would have us to be.

When stuff happens in our life that is about to drown our relationships, our finances, our careers, and our families we pray for kicking and fighting back power. When all around us we see the drowned aspirations, dreams and hopes of those who grew tired of trying to rise above their present we pray for kicking and fighting back power. What do we do when they lie on us and our name is cast out as evil? Keep kicking. When the devil has put everything and everyone we hold dear under attack we pray for kicking and fighting back power.

When the people laugh at our dreams and throw obstacles in our way, we pray for kicking and fighting back power. When we seem to make two steps forward and three steps backwards, we pray for kicking and fighting back power. When we feel lonely, misunderstood and that nobody cares, we pray for kicking and fighting back power. When those who knew us when, throw our past up in our face, we pray for kicking and fighting back power. When our praying, our working and our living seem to be in vain, we pray for kicking and fighting back power. O triumphant and victorious Christ, we praise You for Your resurrection that strengthens us to keep kicking and fighting back against the principalities and powers that attempt to thwart our vision for our lives. In the name of the Lord Jesus do we offer this prayer, Amen.

– DAY 362 –

ACTS 1: 1-5

Lord God many years ago You told Your followers not to depart from Jerusalem but to wait for the promise of the Father. They were told they would be baptized with the Holy Spirit. According to Your word and promise, new authority and new accomplishments, new boldness and new breakthroughs, new gifts and new glory, new power and new peace came upon them as they waited in obedience for what and for who You, Lord Jesus, said they would receive.

As was the case with the early church, we recognize our obedience gives You the opportunity to move. Our obedience gives You the opportunity to work miracles. Our obedience gives You the opportunity to do what You desire to do in our lives. Our obedience gives You the opportunity to bless beyond anything we could ask or think or imagine.

We pray for obedience that produces fruit. Obedience does not produce guilt; it produces growth. Obedience does not produce shame; it produces strength. Obedience does not produce fear; it produces faith. Obedience does not produce bondage; it produces breakthroughs. Obedience does not produce weakness; it produces worth. Obedience does not produce embarrassment; it produces excellence.

You are calling us to obedience in the places and areas in our lives where we have not yielded and submitted. If we have received a word that says stop, then we must stop. If we have received a word that says go, then we must go. If we have received a word that says wait, then we must wait. If we have received a word that says tithe, then we must tithe. If we have received a word that says submit, then we must submit.

Pentecost happens when we are in obedience to the word we have received. We submit ourselves to You, O God. In the fullness of who You are we receive again the promise of II Chronicles 7, "If my people who are called by my name would humble themselves and pray, and seek my face and turn from their wicked ways, then I will hear from heaven and forgive their sins and heal their land."

We submit ourselves to You in obedience so we too will have the Pentecost You will for us. We offer this prayer of submission in the only name we know, Jesus Christ, our Lord, Amen.

DAY 362

– DAY 363 –

MATTHEW 11: 28-30

Lord Jesus, we are grateful that Your yoke fits well. Your word fits well for our worries. Your love fits well for our loneliness. Your healing fits well for our hurts whether they are internal or external. Your comfort fits well for our cares. Your strength fits well for our sorrow. Your salvation fits well for our sins. Your power fits well for our problems. Your grace fits well for our guilt. Your promises fit well for our perplexities. Your virtue fits well for our vices. Your ways fit well for our weaknesses. Your faithfulness fits well for our forlornness.

We are grateful not only for Your sufficiency but for Your partnership and companionship. You are our yoke partner. You help us carry our load and You bear what is beyond our strength to carry. On Calvary You bore our sins and transgressions. We praise You for Your hand that holds and for Your arm of power. We are grateful we can cast all of our cares upon You knowing You care for us. We are grateful You give power to the weak, and to those who have no might, You increase strength. We are grateful You are our refuge and our strength, a very present help in times of trouble.

We are grateful You are our light and our salvation and therefore we have no need to fear. We are grateful You are our shepherd and therefore all of our needs will be supplied. We are grateful You make us lie down in green pastures, You lead us beside still waters and You restore our souls. We are grateful for goodness and mercy that will follow us all the days of our lives and we shall have the privilege of dwelling in Your house forever.

Lord Jesus we are so grateful we do not have to be strong all of the time. We pray for faith to trust You enough to relax in You, in Your word and in Your arms. We pray for faith and trust to confess our sins and weaknesses, our fears and frailties, our guilt and grief, knowing You are a friend who sticks closer than any brother or sister. Hold us close Lord Jesus. Hold us tight Daddy and Mother God. Abide with us always Comforting and Empowering Holy Spirit. We need You even now. In Your own name do we pray, Amen.

DAY 363

– DAY 364 –

MATTHEW 14: 28-33

Lord Jesus, we praise You for the opportunities to defy the odds and succeed anyhow. We praise You for Your vision for us that we can go farther than others have ever gone. We praise You for lifting our vision beyond the places where we live and work and worship and see possibilities that would not have crossed our minds. We praise You for the potential You continue to see within us and pull from us.

We pray for faith to listen when You are speaking, to follow where You lead and to be obedient to the Holy Spirit. We pray for faith to stay focused on You. No matter how dark the night or how long the night we pray for faith to stay focused on You. No matter who tells us what cannot be done, when You call, when You beckon, when You invite, we pray for faith to stay focused on You. No matter how much the wind blows against us or upon us, we pray for faith to stay focused upon You. No matter how many demons rise or fears attack, we pray for faith to stay focused upon You.

And if, O Lord, we begin to lose our bearings, our perspective, our focus and our faith and begin to sin, we pray for presence of mind to call out to You for salvation. We pray we will always remember that all is not lost because we fall and all is not hopeless because we stumble. You are still in the prayer hearing and prayer answering business. You are still waiting for us to do great things. You still believe in our possibilities. You still believe in Your vision for us.

If we begin to sink, we pray we will also look up to You, our Higher Power, our Savior, our Redeemer, our Lord, our Friend, You the Master of earth and wind and skies. We pray we will refocus upon You. We pray we will be renewed through You. We pray You will lift us. You have lifted us in days past and gone, and we believe You will do it again.

We praise You for Your hand that reaches to catch us. We praise You for Your love that will not let us go or give up on us. We praise You for Your faithfulness to those who dare to walk with You. We praise You for Your wonderful miracle working power. You truly are God. In Your own name Lord Jesus do we offer this prayer, Amen.

– DAY 365 –

GENESIS 4: 3-6

Gracious God, the example of Cain in scripture is our eternal reminder that we can be in the place of worship, doing worship things, going through the motions and rituals of worship but if our hearts and minds are not focused on who worship is about, then we can still miss out on the blessing of worship and what worship ought to do and be in our lives. We pray we will always remember O God that worship is about Your adoration and praise, not our feelings or our solo or our song or our welcome address or our sermon or the order of service we are accustomed to and feel most comfortable with.

We pray we will always remember O God that worship is about Your adoration and the move of God, not our dance rendition or our announcement. Worship is about Your adoration and praise, not whether or not it is our Sunday to usher or serve or count money in the finance room. We pray we will always remember O God that worship is about Your adoration and praise not about our names being called or our contribution being recognized. We pray we will always remember O God that worship is about Your adoration and praise not about who is present or who is absent or who is preaching or who is singing.

We pray we will always remember O God that worship is about Your adoration and praise and not the business we need to take care of, the tickets we need to push or the people we need to see. We pray we will always remember O God that worship is about Your adoration and praise not about shopping around for a new companion or trying to pick up a new love interest or date. We pray we will always remember O God that worship is about Your adoration and not about our problems or what we are going through. When we focus on You, O God, then You will give us what we need to deal with everything and everyone we must.

We confess O God that many times we miss out on the message or the revelation You have for us because we are nursing hurt feelings or we are mad about something that did not go our way or we are upset because of a change of procedure or routine. We pray for focus O God so we will always give You the worship that truly honors and glorifies Your holy name. In the name of the Lord Jesus do we offer this prayer, Amen.

– DAY 366 –

EXODUS 3: 1-8

Gracious and Mighty God who called Moses to free Your people from Egyptian bondage, we worship You. We worship You because You alone are worthy of our adoration and devotion. We worship You because worship reminds us of whose side we are on and who is on our side. Pharaoh may have his army but we have You, O God. Pharaoh may have his political connections but we have You O God. Pharaoh may have more money than we can imagine but we have You, O God.

We can raise children by ourselves when we realize who is on our side and whose side we are on. We can bounce back from any setback when we realize whose side we are on. We can live down any lie and overcome the effects of any gossip when we realize whose side we are on. We can stand down any demon when we realize whose side we are on. We can hold our heads up no matter what attack we are under when we realize whose side we are on. We can find reasons to give thanks and praise no matter how difficult the situation when we realize whose side we are on. Worship helps us to understand we are not by ourselves because the presence of God is with us.

As Your presence transformed ordinary dung filled ground where Moses stood into holy ground, transform us O God. We pray we will always remember that Your presence is what makes something or someone holy. True holiness is not about dress lengths, hairstyles and make-up. Holiness is about Your presence O God. True holiness is not about a frowned up face and sour, joyless, humorless, fun-less attitude and a stern, condemning, finger pointing, self-righteous disposition. True holiness is about Your presence O God and the joy Your presence brings.

We praise You Lord Christ because You are the incarnate and living presence of divinity in messy human flesh. Because of who You are, every life You touch has become transformed into holy ground. You spoke to messed up lepers and they became clean. You spoke to a messed up storm tossed sea and it became calm. You spoke to a messed up demoniac and he became an evangelist. You spoke to a messed up divorcee and she became a fountain of living water. We praise You Lord Jesus that we too can testify to Your transforming presence and touch. In Your name do we offer this prayer, Amen.

DAY 366